ALPHABETICAL AND ANALYTICAL

CATALOGUE

OF THE

AMERICAN INSTITUTE LIBRARY.

WITH THE

RULES AND REGULATIONS, &c.

NEW YORK:
W. L. S. HARRISON, PRINTER, 2 ANN STREET.
1852.

INTRODUCTION.

The Library of the American Institute was organized in the year 1833. At a meeting of the Institute held on the fourth day of February, 1833, a resolution was offered by Robert K. Moulton, that a committee be appointed to report on the subject of a Library for the Institute, which was adopted, and Robert K. Moulton, Joseph P. Simpson, William Inglis, Clarkson Crolius, and George Bacon were appointed.

The Committee subsequently reported a plan for the organization of the Library, which was adopted on the twenty-second day of July, 1833; and the Institute then made an appropriation of five hundred dollars to the Library. On the thirteenth of February, 1834, an additional appropriation of five hundred dollars was made by the Institute.

Although the Institute made appropriations to the Library, and furnished room for its accommodation, the members of the Institute, as such, were only entitled to read the books in the Library; none except the shareholders being entitled to take books from the Library. Persons not members of the Institute were allowed to become shareholders.

The following is a copy of the heading of the original subscription paper, signed by the shareholders of the Library:

"STATISTICAL LIBRARY OF THE AMERICAN INSTITUTE.

"Subscribers to this paper agree to contribute twenty-five dollars in money or books, towards the above Library. When the contributions are completed, scrip will be issued for shares, which will entitle each contributor to one volume from the Library, 'subject to the regulations that may be adopted,' and the Reading Room will at all times be open to such contributors between certain hours of the day. The privilege may be transferred with the approbation of the Committee having charge of the Library. The most useful works, embracing modern improvements for the last fifty years, will be procured."

Thaddeus B. Wakeman, then Corresponding Secretary, and Edwin Williams, then Recording Secretary, not only signed the paper, but procured a large number of subscribers.

JAMES TALLMADGE, the President of the Institute, made a donation of Niles' Register, which had been purchased by him for one hundred dollars.

The following is a copy of the Library Scrip issued to contributors:

LIBRARY OF THE AMERICAN INSTITUTE.

This Scrip represents share for which twenty-five dollars have been paid, and entitles to the ordinary privileges of the Reading Room and Library of the American Institute, and also to take one volume from the library, subject to the terms and regulations of the Library Committee, the privilege transferable only by approbation of said Committee.

NEW YORK, 18

The first share of Library Scrip was issued on the twenty-third day of June, 1834.

The Library was first opened at the rooms of the Institute, in the year 1833, in Liberty street, near Broadway, in this city. In 1834 the Library and Institute removed to No. 41 Cortlandt street. The Institute and Library remained there until 1836, when a lease was taken by the Institute of the 2d floor of No. 187 Broadway, at a rent of $1000 a year, where they remained for three years. In 1839 the Institute and Library were removed to rooms in the new City Hall in the Park, rented from the corporation for four years, at a rent of $400. In 1843 the corporation granted a free lease to the Institute for 10 years, subject to the right of the corporation to terminate the same when wanted for public purposes. In 1848 the corporation terminated the lease, additional rooms being wanted for court rooms.

In November, 1848, the Institute hired the second floor of the building corner of Broadway and Anthony street, at the rent of $1000 per year. There being no accommodation for the Library in those rooms, the books were carefully packed up and stored.

After the close of the Annual Fair in the fall of the year 1848, there appeared to be a general desire among the members to obtain a permanent location for the Institute.

The Institute having accumulated about $17,000, being the surplus proceeds of their Fairs, in the spring of 1849 purchased the building now occupied by them, No. 351 Broadway, for $45,000, on which there is now a mortgage for $25,000, payable on May 1st,

1854, to meet which the Institute have now invested, on bond and mortgage, $10,000.

The Institute removed to their new building in June, 1849, and the Library was then unpacked and re-opened, for the use of the shareholders and members of the Institute.

The Library Room is 80 feet long, by 25 feet wide, and has been handsomely fitted up by the Institute with glass cases, gas fixtures, &c., at an expense of $702 19.

Connected with the Library is a Reading Room furnished with the newspapers published in the city of New York, and one newspaper from each of the principal cities in the United States, and also with the principal periodicals and scientific magazines published in the United States and Great Britain.

As the Institute had at various times voted appropriations of money to the Library, increasing its value, questions arose as to the relative right of the shareholders and the Institute in the Library. The members of the Institute were not entitled to take a volume from the Library until the first day of May, 1850, when that privilege was given to them by the new By-Laws.

For the purpose of settling the questions as to the rights of the shareholders, a paper was drawn up and signed by fifteen of them, releasing their rights as such, to the Institute, and which was presented at a meeting held on 11th of April, 1850; whereupon a resolution was passed that shareholders who should release their rights in the Library, should be life-members of the Institute, and a special vote of thanks to those shareholders who had so released their rights was passed.* Since that time nearly all the shareholders have released their rights and become members of the Institute for life.

Up to that time, April 11, 1850, the Institute had contributed to the Library for the purchase of books	$2,478 25
Contributed by shareholders, in money and books	2,494 29
Donations made by members and others, valued at	1,270 00
Since 1st May, 1850, the Institute has expended for books	948 03
Total amount contributed and expended for books for the Library	$7,190 57

* Sinclair Tousey, Livingston Livingston, James Van Norden, James J. Mapes, Martin E. Thompson, Israel Foote, John S. Bowron, Adoniram Chandler, William Hagar, Edward T. Backhouse, John Disturnell, David Banks, John J. Cowenhoven, J. W. Benedict, R. R. Boyd.

Since May, 1850, when the present committee was elected, there have been added to the Library 1280 volumes, and its gradual increase has been provided for by an annual appropriation, passed by the Institute on the sixth day of March, 1851, of $500 a year for five years. The Library is now composed of 5860 volumes.

We add, for the information of the members, the By-Laws of the Institute relating to the Library, and the Rules and Regulations of the Library now in force, which were adopted May 23, 1850.

LIV. LIVINGSTON,
RALPH LOCKWOOD,
JACOB C. PARSONS,
H. P. BLACKMAN,
GORDON L. FORD, } Library Committee.

NEW YORK, *January* 1st, 1852.

BY-LAWS RELATIVE TO THE LIBRARY.

SEC. 49. It shall be the duty of the Library Committee to make selections for the Library, and adopt rules and regulations in accordance with which books may be taken therefrom, and exercise a general superintendence over all affairs connected with the Library, which rules and regulations must be submitted to the Institute for confirmation at its next regular meeting, after their adoption by said committee.

SEC. 50. All members who shall have paid regularly and punctually their annual dues, and the Shareholders of the Library, shall be entitled to take books from the Library, at such times and subject to such rules and regulations as may be established, in the manner prescribed in the foregoing section.

SEC. 51. Any member availing himself of the privilege named in the preceding section, who shall not strictly comply with, and observe the rules and regulations prescribed as aforesaid, shall, upon being reported to the Institute, be suspended from his rights as a member, until restored thereto by a vote of two thirds of the members present at any stated meeting of the Institute; and if he shall refuse or neglect a compliance with such rules and regulations for the term of six months, he may be expelled by a vote of the Institute, and his name be stricken from the roll of members.

SEC. 81. Whenever any member of the Institute shall make a donation to the Library of Books, none of which shall then be duplicates of books in the Library, and which shall, in the opinion of the Library Committee, be suitable for the Library, and worth in their opinion the sum of one hundred dollars, he shall, upon such committee making a report of the same to the Institute, and upon such report being adopted, become a Life member of the Institute.

RULES AND REGULATIONS

OF THE

AMERICAN INSTITUTE LIBRARY.

ADOPTED MAY 23, 1850.

SECTION 1. The Library and Reading Room shall be open daily, (except Sundays, New Year's Day, Fourth of July, Annual Thanksgiving, and Christmas,) to wit: from 8 o'clock, A. M., until 7½ o'clock, P. M., on Mondays, Wednesdays, Fridays, and Saturdays, and until 10 o'clock, P. M., on Tuesdays, and Thursdays, during the months of April, May, June, July, August, September and October; and from 8½ o'clock, A. M., until 6 o'clock, P. M., on Mondays, Wednesdays, Fridays and Saturdays, and until 10 o'clock, P. M., on Tuesdays and Thursdays, during the months of January, February, March, November and December.

SECTION 2. The Librarian shall make a full and accurate catalogue of all the books, pamphlets, maps, charts, newspapers, &c., belonging to the Library of the Institute, and arrange and number them in proper order, which shall at all times be open to the inspection of the members; he shall make a record of all books presented to the Institute, in a book provided for that purpose, with the names of the donors.

SECTION 3. He shall enter, in a book to be kept for that purpose, the number of every volume delivered by him, the name of the person to whom delivered, the time of taking and returning the same, together with the forfeitures arising from every default.

SECTION 4. He shall collect all Library dues and forfeitures incurred by the members, and account for the same to the Treasurer of the Library Committee at the close of each month, or oftener, if required by the said Committee.

SECTION 5. He shall report monthly to the Library Committee the names of such members as may refuse to pay their forfeitures, or lose or damage any book belonging to the Library, and the names of all delinquents, with the amount of dues remaining unpaid.

SECTION 6. He shall replace the books in proper order upon the shelves as soon as may be after they are returned, having first examined them with care and ascertained whether they have been injured or defaced.

SECTION 7. He shall see that the books, Library and Reading Room, are kept in good order, shall duly observe the instructions which may be given him by the Library Committee, and take care that the regulations relative to the loaning of books be strictly adhered to.

SECTION 8. He shall ascertain during the first week in each month, by examination of the account of each member, the book or books not then returned to the Library in due season, and he shall cause the same to be procured of the members in default.

SECTION 9. He shall deliver to any member applying personally, or to his written order, one volume, if it be a folio or quarto, and one book or set, (not exceeding three volumes) if an octavo or volume of less size.

SECTION 10. Every member may detain each book or set delivered as aforesaid, if it be a folio or quarto, three weeks, an octavo two weeks, or a book or set of less size one week, except new publications, which until they shall have been in the Library two months, shall not be detained, an octavo, or book of less size, longer than one week, and which shall not be renewed.

SECTION 11. Any member who shall detain a book or set longer than the time above limited respectively, shall forfeit and pay to the Librarian, for every day a volume is so detained, if it be a folio four cents, a quarto three cents, an octavo two cents, if it be a duodecimo or smaller volume, or a pamphlet, one cent, provided always a whole set be taken out and part of it be detained longer than the time above limited, the fine shall be exacted for each book not returned; and if such a book be detained one week beyond the time above limited, the forfeiture shall be doubled. The Library Committee shall have power to remit fines upon a proper excuse being given.

SECTION 12. If any member lose or injure a book, periodical or newspaper, he shall pay to the Librarian the value of the book lost, or a sum equal to the injury done to such book, periodical or newspaper, which amount shall be fixed by the Librarian, and if the book lost or injured be one of a set, he shall pay the Librarian, for the use of the Institute, the full value of said set, and may thereupon receive the remaining volumes as his property.

SECTION 13. No member shall be permitted to receive a book from the Library or be entitled to the privileges of the Reading Room, until he shall have paid all sums due from him to the Institute for annual dues, fines, &c., and made good all damages and losses which he may have occasioned.

SECTION 14. The books marked in the Catalogue as books of reference, thus (*) and such others as may from time to time be specially designated by the Library Committee, shall not be taken from the Library, except by special permission of a member of the Library Committee.

SECTION 15. None but members shall be allowed the privilege of the Reading Room, unless introduced by a member of the Institute.

SECTION 16. Any member may have the privilege of introducing a friend not a resident of the city; whose name shall be registered by the Librarian in a book provided for that purpose, and who will receive a ticket of admission to the Reading Room for the term of two weeks.

SECTION 17. No periodical work shall be taken from the Room until two months shall have elapsed from the time of its being received.

ALPHABETICAL CATALOGUE.

The Asterisk (*) prefixed to a Title indicates that the Book is reserved for reference, and prohibited from Circulation.

ABBOTT, A. Cuba and the Cubans. 8vo. New York, 1850.

ABERCROMBIE, JOHN. Inquiries concerning the Intellectual Powers and the Investigation of Truth. 18mo. New York, 1833.

ABERCROMBIE, JOHN. The Philosophy of the Moral Feelings. 18mo. New York, 1833.

ABSTRACT of Infantry Tactics. 12mo. Boston, 1830.

ABSTRACT of the Most Important Alterations of General Interest, introduced by the Revised Statutes. 8vo. Canandaigua, 1830.

*ACADEMIE der Kaufleute oder encyclopædisches Kaufmanns lexicon vormals herausgegeben von Prof. C. G. Ludovici, und nun umgearbeitet von Johan C. Schedel. 6 vols. 8vo. Leipzig, 1797.

*ACCOMPANIMENT to Tanner's Universal Atlas. 12mo. Philadelphia, 1843.

ACHERLEY, ROGER. The British Constitution, or the Fundamental Form of Government in Britain. Fol. London, 1727.

*ACTS. (See Congress.)

ADALBERT, PRINCE. Travels, translated by Sir Robert H. Schromburgh, and John E. Taylor. 2 vols. 8vo. London, 1849.

ADAM, ALEXANDER. Roman Antiquities; or, an Account of the Manners and Customs of the Romans. 8vo. Edinburgh, 1792.

ADAMS' ANECDOTES. 12mo. London.

ADAMS, GEORGE. An Essay on Electricity. 8vo. London, 1792.

ADAMS, HANNAH. An Abridgment of the History of New England. 12mo. Boston, 1807.

ADAMS, JOHN QUINCY. Report upon Weights and Measures. 8vo. Washington, 1821. *Presented by Dr. Samuel Akerly.*

ADAMS, JOHN QUINCY. The Lives of James Madison and James Monroe, with Historical Notices of their Administration. 12mo. Buffalo, 1850.

ADAMS, JOHN QUINCY. The Duplicate Letters. The Fisheries, and the Mississippi. Documents relating to the Negotiation of Ghent. 8vo. Washington, 1822.

ADAMS, MRS., Wife of John. Letters, with a Memoir by C. F. Adams, and John Q. Adams' Letters to his Son. 12mo. Boston, 1848.

ADAMS, NATHANIEL. Annals of Portsmouth. 8vo. Portsmouth, 1825.

ADDISON, JOSEPH. The Works of. 3 vols. 8vo. New York, 1850.

ADDISON, JOSEPH. Evidences of the Christian Religion. 24mo. Chiswick, 1819.

ADDRESSES of the Philadelphia Society for the Promotion of National Industry. 8vo. Philadelphia, 1819. *Presented by Dr. Samuel Akerly.*

ADLINGTON, JOHN H. The Cyclopædia of Law, or the Correct British Lawyer. 8vo. London, 1820.

AGAPIDA, FRAY ANTONIO. A Chronicle of the Conquest of Granada. Vol. 1. 8vo. Philadelphia, 1829. (See Irving, Washington.)

AGRICULTURE FRANCAISE par M. M. Les Inspecteurs de Agriculture. 3 vols. 8vo. Paris, 1843.

AIKEN, JOHN. Select Works of the British Poets, with Prefaces. 3 vols. 8vo. Philadelphia, 1850.

VOL. I.

Ben Jonson,	Prior,	A. Phillips,	Lyttleton,
Cowley,	Gay,	Collins,	Goldsmith,
Milton,	Green,	Dyer,	Johnson,
Waller,	Tickell,	Shenstone,	Armstrong,
Dryden,	Hammond,	Churchill,	J. Warton,
J. Phillips,	Somerville,	Young,	T. Warton,
Parnell,	Pope,	Akenside,	Mason,
Rowe,	Swift,	Gray,	Cowper,
Addison,	Thompson,	Smollett,	Beattie.

VOL. II.

Falconer,	Chatterton,	Grahame,	Bowles,
Barbauld,	Gifford,	Joanna Baillie,	Coleridge,
Sir Wm. Jones,	Burns,	Bloomfield,	Montgomery,
Crabbe,	Rogers,	Wordsworth,	Sir Walter Scott.

VOL. III.

Southey,	Kirke White,	Milman,	Hood,
Lamb,	Byron,	Shelley,	Hemans,
Hogg,	Elliott,	Keats,	Norton,
Moore,	Wilson,	Hunt,	Pollok,
Landor,	Proctor,	Cunningham,	Croly.
Campbell,	Barry Cornwall,	Clare,	

AIKEN, LUCY. Memoirs of the Court of Charles I. 2 vols. 8vo. Philadelphia, 1833.

*AINSWORTH'S DICTIONARY. English and Latin, abridged by Thomas Morell. 8vo. Philadelphia.

AKERLY, SAMUEL. Elementary Exercises for the Deaf and Dumb. 8vo. New York, 1821. *Presented by the Author.*

*ALBANY ARGUS. A Daily Newspaper. 2 vols. fol. 1827–1828.

ALBERONI, CARDINAL JULIUS. Political Testament. 8vo. London, 1753.

ALBERTI, FRANCOIS. Grand Dictionnaire François-Italien, et Italien-François. 2 vols. 4to. A. Bassano.

*ALBION. A Journal of News, Politics and Literature. 8 vols. fol. New York, 1839 to 1846.

ALDEN, TIMOTHY. Account of Sundry Missions among the Senecas and Munsees. 18mo. New York, 1827.

ALDEN, TIMOTHY. A Collection of American Epitaphs and Inscriptions, with occasional Notes. 5 vols. 18mo. New York, 1814.

ALEXANDER, A. A History of Colonization on the Western Coast of Africa. 8vo. Philadelphia, 1846.

ALEXANDER, J. E. Transatlantic Sketches. 8vo. Philadelphia, 1833.

ALGAROTTI, COUNT. Essay on Painting. 12mo. New York, 1833.

ALI BEY. Travels in Morocco, Tripoli, Cyprus, Egypt, Arabia, Syria, and Turkey. 2 vols. 8vo. Plates 4to. Philadelphia, 1816.

ALISON, ARCHIBALD. History of Europe from the Commencement of the French Revolution in 1789 to 1815. 4 vols. 8vo. New York, 1850.

ALISON, ARCHIBALD. Essays. (See Modern British Essayists.)

ALLEN, CAPT. W. H. and T. R. H. Thompson. A Narrative of the Expedition to the River Niger, in 1841. 2 vols. 8vo. London, 1848.

ALLEN, PAUL. A History of the American Revolution. 2 vols. 8vo. Baltimore, 1822.

Allen, R. L. Domestic Animals; History and Description of the Horse, Mule, Cattle, Sheep, Swine, Poultry, and Farm Dogs. 12mo. New York, 1848. *Presented by C. M. Saxton, Esq.*

Allen, William. American Biographical and Historical Dictionary. 8vo. Boston, 1832.

Allen, Zachariah. Sketches of the State of the Useful Arts and of Society, Scenery, &c., in Great Britain, France, and Holland: or the Practical Tourist. 2 vols. 12mo. Hartford, 1835.

America and the Americans, by a Citizen of the World. 8vo. London, 1833.

America; or a General Survey of the Political Situation of the Several Powers of the Western Continent. By a Citizen of the United States. 8vo. Philadelphia, 1827.

*American Advertising Directory. 12mo. New York, 1832.

American Agriculturalist. Designed to Improve the Planter, the Farmer, the Stockholder, and the Horticulturist. A. B. & R. L. Allen, Editors. 8 vols. 8vo. New York, 1843–1849. *Presented by Messrs. Saxton & Miles.*

*American Almanac, and Repository of Useful Knowledge. 21 vols. 12mo. Boston, 1830–1850.

American Annual Register. Edited by Jos. Blunt. 8 vols. 8vo. New York, 1827–1833.

*American and Commercial Daily Advertiser. Fol. Baltimore, 1803.

American Common Place Book of Prose. 12mo. Boston, 1832.

*American Encyclopædia, or Universal Dictionary of Arts and Sciences. 7 vols. 4to. New York, 1805. *Presented by Philip Van Rensselaer, Esq.*

American's Guide. 12mo. Philadelphia, 1832. *Presented by John P. Veeder, Esq.*

American Husbandry. Containing an Account of the Soil, Climate, Production and Agriculture of the British Colonies in North America and the West Indies. 2 vols. 8vo. London, 1775.

American in England. By the Author of "A Year in Spain." 2 vols. 12mo. New York, 1835.

American Institute. Journal. 4 vols. 8vo. New York, 1836–1839.

American Institute. Reports. 5 vols. 8vo. Albany, 1843, 1846–1850.

AMERICAN INSTITUTE OF INSTRUCTION. Introductory Discourse and Lectures. 3 vols. 8vo. Boston, 1831, 1832, 1833.

AMERICAN JOURNAL OF MEDICAL SCIENCE. 4 vols. 8vo. Boston, 1826–1828.

AMERICAN LANCET. 8vo. New York, 1830, 1831.

AMERICAN MAGAZINE. By Noah Webster. 8vo. New York, 1787.

AMERICAN MAGAZINE of Useful and Entertaining Knowledge. 8vo. Boston, 1835.

AMERICAN MEDICAL and Philosophical Register. Conducted by David Hosack and J. W. Francis. 4 vols. 8vo. New York, 1814.

AMERICAN MEDICAL RECORDER. Conducted by an Association of Physicians. 3 vols. 8vo. Philadelphia, 1822–1824.

AMERICAN MONTHLY MAGAZINE, and Critical Review. 8vo. New York, 1817. *Presented by Dr. Samuel Akerly.*

AMERICAN MUSEUM, or Repository of Fugitive Pieces. Edited by Matthew Carey. 14 vols. 8vo. Philadelphia, 1787–1792.

AMERICAN QUARTERLY REVIEW. 5 vols. 8vo. Philadelphia, 1827.

AMERICAN RAILROAD JOURNAL, and Mechanic's Magazine. Edited by D. K. Minor. 11 vols. 8vo. New York, 1838–1844.

AMERICAN REGISTER, or Summary Review of History, Politics and Literature. 2 vols. 8vo. Philadelphia, 1817.

AMERICAN REMEMBRANCER; or an impartial collection of Essays, Resolves, Speeches, &c., relative to the Treaty with Great Britain. 2 vols. 8vo. Philadelphia, 1795.

AMERICAN REPERTORY of Arts, Sciences, and useful Literature. 12mo. 1831.

AMERICAN REVIEW; a Whig Journal of Politics, Literature, Art, and Science. 7 vols. 8vo. New York, 1845–1848.

AMERICAN REVIEW; or, History of Politics and General Repository of Literature and State Papers. 3 vols. 8vo. Philadelphia, 1811, 1812.

AMERIQUE HISTOIRE PITTORESQUE. 4 vols. 8vo. Paris, 1839–1843.

Vol. 1. Brésil, par M. Ferdinand Denis; et Columbie et Guyanes par M. C. Famin.

2. Etats-Unis d'Amerique par M. Rond de Rochille.

3. Chili, &c., par M. César Famin; Patagonie, &c., par M. Frederick Lacroix; et Iles Diverses, &c., par M. Le Commandeur Bory de St. Vincent, et par M. Frederic Lacroix.

Amerique Histoire Pittoresque. Continued.

Vol. 4. Mexique et Guatemala par M. de Larenaudière; et Perou par M. Lacroix.

Ames, Fisher. Works, with notices of his Life and Character. 8vo. Boston, 1809.

Amos, A. & J. Ferard. A Treatise on the Law of Fixtures. 8vo. New York, 1830.

Amos, Andrew. The Great Oyer of Poisoning: the Trial of the Earl of Somerset for the Poisoning of Sir Thos. Overbury, in the Tower of London. 8vo. London, 1846.

Analectic Magazine. 14 vols. 8vo. Philadelphia, 1813–1819.

Analogies and Contrasts; or, Comparative Sketches of France and England. 2 vols. 8vo. London, 1848.

Anastasius, or Memoirs of a Greek. 2 vols. 12mo. New York, 1831.

Anderson, Adam. Historical and Chronological Deductions of the Origin of Commerce. 2 vols. fol. London, 1764.

Anderson, Æneas. Narrative of the British Embassy to China in 1792, 1793, 1794. 8vo. London, 1796.

Anderson, William. System of Anatomy. 4to. New York, 1822.

Andrews, John. History of the War with America, France, Spain, and Holland. 4 vols. 8vo. London, 1785.

Andrews, William W. The Correspondence and Miscellanies of John Cotton Smith, LL.D., with an Eulogy. 8vo. New York, 1847.

Angeloni, Baptista. Letters on the English Nation. 12mo. London, 1756.

Annales des Haras et de l'Agriculture. 3 vols. 8vo. Paris, 1845–1847.

Annales de la Société Royale d'Horticulture de Paris. 6 vols. 8vo. Paris, 1841–1846.

Annals of Horticulture, and Year Book of Information on Practical Gardening. 8vo. London, 1846.

Anniversary, The, or Poetry and Prose for 1829. Edited by Allan Cunningham. 12mo. London, 1829.

Annual Register. 43 vols. 8vo. London, 1758 to 1800.

Annual Register, or a View of History, Policy, and Literature for the Year 1768. 8vo. London, 1768.

ANONYMIANA, or Ten Centuries of Observations on various Authors and Subjects. Compiled by a very learned and Reverend Divine. 8vo. London, 1818.

ANSELL, CHARLES. Treatise on Friendly Societies. 8vo. London, 1835.

ANSLEY, E. A. Elements of Literature, or an Introduction to the Study of Rhetoric and Belles Lettres. 12mo. Philadelphia, 1849.

ANSTED, D. T. The Ancient World, or Picturesque Sketches of Creation. 8vo. Philadelphia, 1847.

ANSWER to "the Olive Branch, or Faults on Both Sides." By a Federalist. 12mo.

ANTHING FREDERICK. History of the Campaigns of Count Alexander Suworow Rymnikski, with a Preliminary Sketch of his Private Life and Character, from the German. 2 vols. 8vo. London, 1799.

ANTHON, CHARLES. A Pilgrimage to Treves. 12mo. New York, 1845.

ANTHON, CHARLES. (See Smith, William.)

*APPLETON'S DICTIONARY of Machines, Mechanics, Engine Works, and Engineering. A to HEL. Vol. 1. 8vo. New York, 1851.

APPLETON'S LIBRARY MANUAL, containing a Catalogue Raisonée of upwards of 12,000 of the most important Works in every department of knowledge in all the modern languages. 8vo. New York, 1849.

APPRENTICE, THE. A Weekly Journal of Art, Science, and Literature. 2 vols. 4to. London, 1844–1845.

ARABIAN NIGHTS' ENTERTAINMENTS. 2 vols. 24mo. Exeter, 1827.
Do. do. 8vo. Philadelphia, 1835.
Do. do. 8vo. Philadelphia, 1848.
Do. do. (See Lane, E. W.)

ARBLAY, MADAME D'. Diary and Letters. Edited by her Niece. 7 vols. 8vo. London, 1843.

ARCANA OF SCIENCE AND ART. 5 vols. 12mo. London, 1828–1837.

ARISTOTLE. Treatise on Poetry, with Notes on the Translation and on the Original, and two Dissertations on Poetical and Musical Imitations. By Thomas and Daniel Twinning. 2 vols. 8vo. London, 1812.

ARMSTRONG, JOHN. A Treatise on Agriculture, with Notes by J. Buel. 12mo. New York, 1845.

ARNOTT, NEIL. Elements of Physics, or Natural Philosophy. 2 vols. 8vo. Philadelphia, 1831. *Presented by Samuel Pierce, Esq.*

Arrian on Coursing. The Cynegeticus of the Younger Xenophon, from the Greek, with Annotations and a Memoir, and some Account of the Canes Venatici of Ancients. By a Graduate of Medicine. 8vo. London, 1831.

Arrian's Voyage round the Euxine Sea. 4to. Oxford, 1805.

*Art-Journal, The. 5 vols. 4to. London, 1847–1851.

Artisan, The. A Monthly Journal of the Operative Arts. 8 vols. 4to. London, 1844–1851.

Ashburnham, John. A Narrative of his Attendance on Charles I., with a Vindication of his Character and Conduct, &c. 2 vols. 8vo. London, 1830.

Ashly, John. Memoirs and Considerations concerning the Trade and Revenues of the British Colonies in America.

Ashmead, Elias. History of the Order of the Garter. 12mo. London, 1715.

Asiatic Researches, or Transactions of the Society instituted in Bengal for Inquiring into the Arts, Sciences, and Literature of Asia. 8vo. London, 1798.

Aspen, J. The Naval and Military Exploits in the reign of George III. 18mo. London, 1820.

Athenæum, The. 6 vols. 4to. London, 1844–1846.

Atkinson, William. Principles of Political Economy, or the Laws of the Formation of National Wealth. 8vo. London, 1840. *Presented by Hon. James Tallmadge.*

*Atlas, The. A General Newspaper. Fol. London, 1827–1829.

Attempt to Rectify the Public Affairs of the United Kingdom and Empire. 3 vols. 8vo. London, 1804.

Aubigne, J. H. Merle d'. Germany, England and Scotland; or Recollections of a Swiss Minister. 12mo. New York, 1849.

Aubigne, J. H. Merle d'. The History of the Reformation in the 16th Century. A new Translation by H. Beveridge. 4 vols. 8vo. Glasgow, 1845.

Aubigne, J. H. Merle d'. The Protector, a Vindication. 12mo. New York, 1847.

*Audubon, J. J., and Rev. John Bachman. The Quadrupeds of America. 8vo. New York, 1851.

AUSTIN, JAMES T. Life of Elbridge Gerry. 2 vols. 8vo. Boston, 1828.

AUSTRALIA, Picture of. 12mo. London, 1829.

AUSTRIA AND THE AUSTRIANS. 2 vols. 8vo. London, 1837.

AUTOBIOGRAPHY of a Country Curate; or, Passages of a Life without a Living. 2 vols. 8vo. London, 1836.

AUTOBIOGRAPHY of a Workingman. By one who Whistled at the Plough. 8vo. London, 1848.

AYSCOUGH, GEO. E. The Works of George Lord Lyttleton. 12mo. Dublin, 1775.

BABBAGE, CHARLES. Economy of Machinery and Manufactures. 12mo. Philadelphia, 1832.

BACON, FRANCIS, LORD. The Works of. 4 vols. 4to. London, 1765.

BACON, FRANCIS, LORD. Essays, Moral, Economical and Political. 12mo. Boston, 1833.

BAILEY, ALEXANDER M. One Hundred and Six Copper Plates of Mechanical Machines, and Implements of Husbandry. Fol. London, 1782.

BAILEY, NATHAN. Dictionarium Britannicum, or a Complete Universal Etymological English Dictionary. Fol. London, 1736.

BAILEY, NATHAN. Universal Etymological English Dictionary. 8vo. London, 1775.

BAILEY, PHILIP JAMES. Festus. A Poem. 12mo. Boston, 1845.

BAIN, WILLIAM. Essay on the Variation of the Compass. 8vo. Edinburgh, 1817. *Presented by Dr. Samuel Akerly.*

BAINES, EDWARD. History of the Cotton Manufactures in Great Britain. 8vo. London, 1835.

BAINES, EDWARD. History, Directory, and Gazetteer of the County Palatine of Lancaster. 2 vols. 8vo. Liverpool, 1824.

BAIRD, ROBERT. Impressions and Experiences in the West Indies and North America in 1849. 8vo. Philadelphia, 1850.

BAKEWELL, FREDERIC C. Natural Evidences of a Future Life. 8vo. London, 1835.

BAKEWELL, ROBERT. An Introduction to Geology, edited, with an appendix, by Professor B. Silliman. 8vo. New Haven, 1839.

BALDWIN, EBENEZER. Annals of Yale College. 8vo. New Haven, 1838.

BALDWIN, SAMUEL. A Survey of British Customs. 4to. London, 1770.

BANCKS, JOHN. The History of Germany. 12mo. London, 1763.

BANCROFF, AARON. Life of George Washington. 2 vols. 24mo. Boston, 1826.

BANCROFT, GEORGE. History of the United States, from the Discovery of the American Continent. 3 vols. 8vo. Boston, 1850.

BANKER'S MAGAZINE. (See Homans, J. Smith.)

BANKS, T. C. Genealogical and Heraldic Gleanings, illustrative of the history and descent of the English Nobility. 4to. London, 1737.

BARBARITIES of the Enemy Exposed, in a Report of the Committee of the House of Representatives, and the Documents accompanying said Report. 12mo. Worcester, 1814.

BARBER, J. W. AND HENRY HOWE. Historical Collections of the State of New York. 8vo. New York, 1844.

BARCLAY, HERBERT. A Volume from the Life of. 12mo. Baltimore, 1833.

BARCLAY, ROBERT. An Apology for the True Christian Divinity; being an Explanation and Vindication of the Principles and Doctrines of the Quakers. 8vo. New York, 1826. *Presented by the Society of Friends.*

BARETTI, JOSEPH. An Account of the Manners and Customs of Italy. 2 vols. 8vo. London, 1768.

BARHAM, FRANCIS. The Political Works of Cicero. 2 vols. 8vo. London, 1842.

BARLOW, JOEL. The Hasty Pudding; a Poem, with a Memoir on Maize or Indian Corn, compiled by D. J. Browne. 12mo. New York, 1847.

BARLOW, PETER. Essay on the Strength and Stress of Timber. 8vo. London, 1826.

BARNARD, D. D. Speeches and Reports. 12mo. Albany, 1838.

BARNARD, HENRY. School Architecture. 8vo. New York, 1848.

BARNARD, LIEUTENANT. A Three Years' Cruize in the Mozambique Channel, for the Suppression of the Slave Trade. 12mo. London, 1848.

BARRINGTON, ARCHIBALD. A Familiar Introduction to Heraldry, explaining the Principles of the Science, and showing its Application to the Study of History and Architecture. 12mo. London, 1848.

BARRINGTON, D. The Possibility of Approaching the North Pole asserted. With an Appendix by Colonel Beaufoy. 8vo. New York, 1818.

BARRINGTON, D. Miscellanies. 4to. London, 1781.

BARROW, JOHN. A Description of Pitcairn's Island, and its Inhabitants, &c. 18mo. New York, 1832.

BARROW, JOHN. Some Account of the Public Life, and a Selection from the Unpublished Writings of the Earl of Macartney. 2 vols. 4to. London, 1807.

BARROW, JOHN. The Life and Correspondence of Admiral Sir William Sidney Smith. 2 vols. 8vo. London, 1848.

BARROW, JR., JOHN. Excursions in the North of Europe, through parts of Russia, Finland, Sweden, Denmark and Norway. 12mo. London, 1835.

BARROW, SIR JOHN. Voyages of Discovery and Research within the Arctic Regions, from 1818 to the Present Time. 12mo. New York, 1846.

BARRY, P. The Fruit Garden: a Treatise. 12mo. New York, 1851.

BARTHELEMI, ABBÉ. Travels of Anacharsis the Younger, in Greece, from the French. 4 vols. 8vo. Philadelphia, 1804.

BARTRAM, WILLIAM. Travels through North and South Carolina, Georgia, and the East and West Floridas. 8vo. Philadelphia, 1791.

BAYARD, JAMES. A Brief Exposition of the Constitution of the United States. 12mo. Philadelphia, 1834.

BEACH, W. The American Practice of Medicine. 3 vols. 8vo. New York, 1836.

BEATTIE, JAMES. Poetical Works. (See Milton.)

BEATTIE, JAMES. Life and Writings. (See Forbes, Sir William.)

BEATTIE, JAMES. Elements of Moral Science. 2 vols. 12mo. Baltimore, 1813.

BEAUMONT, GUSTAVE DE, ET ALEXIS DE TOCQUEVILLE. Système Pénitentaire aux Etats-Unis et de son Application en France. 8vo. Paris, 1833.

BEAUTIES of the most Eminent Periodical British Classics. 12mo. Boston, 1802.

BECK, LEWIS C. Gazetteer of the States of Illinois and Missouri. 8vo. Albany, 1823.

BECK, LEWIS C. Botany of the Northern and Middle States. 12mo. Albany, 1833.

Beckford, Peter. Thoughts on Hunting, in a Series of Familiar Letters to a Friend, with a Chapter on Coursing. 8vo. London, 1847.

Beckford, William. Italy, and Sketches of Spain and Portugal. 2 vols. 8vo. London, 1834.

Beekman, Professor. A Concise History of Ancient Institutions, Inventions, and Discoveries in Science and Mechanic Arts. 2 vols. 12mo. London, 1823.

Belisarius. Life of. (See Mahon, Lord.)

Belknap, Jeremy. The History of New Hampshire. 3 vols. 8vo. 1812.

Bell, James. A System of Geography. 6 vols. 8vo. Glasgow, 1832.

Bell, Robert. Wayside Pictures through France, Belgium, and Holland. 8vo. London, 1849.

Bell, Robert. The Life of the Right Honorable George Canning. 12mo. New York, 1846.

Beltrami, J. C. La Découverte des Sources du Mississippi. 8vo. New Orleans, 1824.

Beltrami, J. C. A Pilgrimage in Europe and America. 2 vols. 8vo. London, 1828.

Beman, David. Mysteries of Trade. 8vo. Boston, 1825.

Bennett, John. The Arcanum, comprising a concise Theory of Practicable Elementary and Definitive Geometry. 8vo. London, 1838.

Bennett, Rev. Moses P. Lectures on Theology. 12mo. Kitaming, 1826.

Bennett, Thomas. A Confutation of Quakerism. 12mo. Cambridge, 1709.

Benson, Egbert. Memoir read before the Historical Society of the State of New York. 12mo. Jamaica, 1825.

Benson, Robert. Memoirs of the Life and Writings of the Reverend Arthur Collier. 8vo. London, 1838.

Bentham, Jeremy. Principles of Legislation, from the French of Dumont, with additions by John Neal. 8vo. Boston, 1830.

Bentley, Richard. The Works of, Collected and Edited by Alexander Dyce. 3 vols. 8vo. London, 1836.

Bentley's Miscellany. 10 vols. 8vo. New York, 1838–1842.

Bericht uberdie erste allegemeine oesterreichische Gewerbsprodukten-Ausstrellung im Jahre 1835. 8vo. Wien.

BERNEAUD, THIEBAUT DE. The Vine Dressers' Manual. 8vo. New York, 1829. *Presented by Dr. Samuel Akerly.*

BERRIAN, WILLIAM. Travels in France and Italy, in 1817, 1818. 8vo. New York, 1821.

BERTHOLLET, C. L. and A. B. Elements of the Arts of Dyeing, with Notes by Andrew Ure. 2 vols. London, 1824.

BERTHOLLET, C. L. Essay on the New Method of Bleaching, with Notes by Robert Kerr. 12mo. Edinburgh, 1790.

BERTRAND, ANT. F. Private Memoirs relative to the Last Year of the Reign of Louis XVI., King of France. 3 vols. 8vo. London, 1797.

BERWICK, JAMES FITZ-JAMES, Duke of. Life. 8vo. London, 1738.

BIBLIA SAGRADA, LA. Traducidos de la Vulgata Latina en Español, por de S. Miquel. 8vo. New York, 1824. *Presented by Gen. A. Chandler.*

BIBLIOTHEQUE du Magnetisme Animal, par Membre de la Societé du Magnetisme. 7 vols. 8vo. Paris, 1817–1819.

BIGELOW, ANDREW. Travels in Malta and Sicily, with Sketches of Gibraltar, in 1827. 8vo. Boston, 1831.

BIGLAND, JOHN. Natural History of Birds, Fishes, Reptiles, and Insects. 12mo. Philadelphia, 1828.

BIGLAND, JOHN. A Geographical and Historical View of the World, with Notes, &c., by Jedediah Morse. 5 vols. 8vo. Boston, 1811.

BIGLY, C. A. Aurifodina, or Adventures in the Gold Regions. 12mo. New York, 1849.

BINGHAM, JOSEPH. The Antiquities of the Christian Church. 2 vols. 8vo. London, 1850.

BIOGRAPHIE MODERNE. Lives of Remarkable Characters, from the Commencement of the French Revolution to the Present Time. From the French. 3 vols. 8vo. London, 1811.

BION, M. The Construction and Principal Uses of Mathematical Instruments, with additions by Edward Stone. London, 1758.

BISCHOFF, JAMES. A Comprehensive History of the Woolen and Worsted Manufactures, and the Natural and Commercial History of the Sheep. 2 vols. 8vo. London, 1842.

BLACK HAWK. Life of. Dictated by Himself. 12mo. Boston, 1834.

BLACKLOCK, AMBROSE. A Treatise on Sheep. 18mo. New York, 1841.

Blackstone, Sir William. Commentaries on the Laws of England. 2 vols. 8vo. New York, 1836.

Blackstone, Sir William. Commentaries on the Laws of England, with Notes and Additions by Edward Christian, and John Frederick Archibald. 4 vols. 8vo. Philadelphia, 1825.

Blackwood's Edinburgh Magazine. 16 vols. 8vo. New York. 1841–1847, and 1851.

Blackwood's Edinburgh Magazine. 8vo. Boston, 1833.

Blair, Hugh. Lectures on Rhetoric and Belles Lettres. 2 vols. 8vo. Philadelphia, 1802.

Blake, Rev. John L. The Farmer's Every-Day Book. 8vo. Auburn, 1850. *Presented by the Publishers, Messrs. Derby, Miller & Co.*

Blake, Rev. John L. Conversations on Political Economy. 12mo. Boston, 1828.

*Blake, Rev. John L. A General Biographical Dictionary. 8vo. New York, 1845.

Blanc, Louis. The History of Ten Years, 1830–1840: or France under Louis Philippe. Translated by W. R. Kelly. 2 vols. 8vo. Philadelphia, 1848.

Blanc, Louis. History of the French Revolution of 1789, from the French. 8vo. Philadelphia, 1848.

Blanc, Gilbert. Observations on the Diseases of Seamen. 8vo. London, 1789.

Blessington, Countess of. Idler in Italy. 3 vols. 8vo. London, 1839.

Blessington, Countess of. Idler in France. A Sequel to the Idler in Italy. 2 vols. 8vo. London, 1842.

Bloodgood, S. Dewitt. A Treatise on Roads, their Historical Character, and Utility. 12mo. Albany, 1838.

Blue Book. Register of all the Officers and Agents, Civil, Military and Naval, in the Service of the United States. 8vo. Washington, 1841.

Blue Laws of Connecticut, or the Code of 1650. 12mo. Hartford, 1822.

Blunt, Edward M. American Coast Pilot and Shipmaster's Assistant, by John Blunt. 8vo. New York, 1826.

Blunt, Edward M. The American Coast Pilot, Improved by E. & G. W. Blunt. 8vo. New York, 1832.

BLUNT, EDMUND M. The American Coast Pilot, Improved by E. & G. W. Blunt. 8vo. New York, 1842. *Presented by George W. Blunt.*

BLUNT, JOSEPH. American Annual Register. 8 vols. 8vo. New York, 1827–1833.

BOADEN, JAMES. Memoir of Mrs. Inchbald. 2 vols. 8vo. London, 1833.

BOCCACCIO, GIOVANE. The Decameron, or Ten Days' Entertainment. From the Italian, with Remarks on the Life and Writing of Boccaccio, &c. 8vo. London, 1845.

BOECKEN des Nieuwen Testaments und Psalmen des Davids. 18mo. 1746.

Ditto. 18mo. t'Amsterdam, 1723.

BOHN, H. C. General Catalogue of Books. 8vo. London, 1847.

BOITARD, M. Manuel Complet de l'Amateur des Roses. 18mo. Paris, 1836.

BOITARD, M. Nouveau Manuel Complet des Instruments d'Agriculture et de Jardinage les plus Modernes. 8vo. Paris, 1844.

BOLINGBROKE, HENRY ST. JOHN, LORD. Life and Works. 4 vols. 8vo. Philadelphia, 1841.

BOLTON, JR., ROBERT. A History of the County of Westchester. 2 vols. 8vo. New York, 1848. *Presented by the Author.*

BOMBET, L. A. C. The Life of Haydn and Mozart, with Observations on Metastasio, and on the Present State of Music in France and Italy, with Notes by William Gardiner. 12mo. Boston, 1839.

BONAPARTE, JOSEPH NAPOLEON. Biographical Sketch of. 8vo. London, 1833.

BONAPARTE, NAPOLEON. Memoirs. (See Bourrienne.)

BONAPARTE, NAPOLEON. Life of. (See Scott, Sir Walter.)

BONAPARTE, NAPOLEON. Life. (See Van Ess, W. L.)

BONAPARTE, NAPOLEON. (See Buonaparte.)

BONJEAN, JOSEPH. Monographie de la Pomme de Terre. 8vo. Paris, 1846.

BONNER, EDMUND. The Life and Defence of the Conduct and Principles of the Venerable and Calumniated Bishop of London, by a Tractarian British Critic. 8vo. London, 1842.

BONNYCASTLE, SIR R. H. Spanish America, or an Account of the Dominions of Spain in the Western Hemisphere. 8vo. Philadelphia, 1819.

BONNYCASTLE, SIR R. H. Newfoundland in 1842. A Sequel to the Canadas in 1841. 2 vols. 8vo. London, 1842.

*BOOTH, JAMES C. and C. MORFIT. The Encyclopædia of Chemistry. 8vo. Philadelphia, 1850.

BOSSU, CAPT. Travels through Louisiana, from the French by J. R. Forster. 2 vols. 8vo. London, 1775.

BOSTON MEDICAL INTELLIGENCER. 8vo. Boston, 1826–1828.

BOSTON MEDICAL AND SURGICAL JOURNAL. 8vo. Boston, 1829.

BOSTON TEA PARTY, Retrospect of,—with a Memoir of George R. T. Hewes. By a Citizen of New York. 8vo. New York, 1834.

BOSWELL, JAS. Life of Samuel Johnson. Additions and Notes by John W. Croker. 2 vols. 8vo. Baltimore, 1832.

BOTANY. Principles of. 8vo.

BOTTA, CHARLES. History of the War of Independence of the United States of America. From the Italian by George A. Otis. 2 vols. 8vo. New Haven, 1834.

BOUCHARLAT, M. An Elementary Treatise on Mechanics, from the French by E. H. Courtenay. 8vo. New York, 1850.

BOUCHER, JONATHAN. A View of the Causes and Consequences of the American Revolution. 8vo. London, 1797.

BOUCHETTE, JOSEPH A. Topographical Description of the Province of Lower Canada, with Remarks upon Upper Canada, and on the relative Connection of both Provinces with the United States of America. 8vo. London, 1815.

BOUDINOT, ELIAS. A Star in the West, or an attempt to Discover the long lost Ten Tribes of Israel. 8vo. Trenton, 1816.

BOURNE, OLIVER. A Treatise on the Steam Engine in its Application to Mines, Mills, Steam Navigation and Railroads. By the Artisan Club. 4to. New York, 1851.

BOURRIENNE, M. Life of Napoleon Bonaparte. 8vo. Philadelphia, 1832.

BOUSSINGAULT, J. B. Rural Economy in its Relations with Chemistry, Physics and Meteorology; or Chemistry applied to Agriculture. Translated, with an Introduction and Notes, by Geo. Law. 12mo. New York, 1850.

BOUTERWEK, FREDERICK. History of Spanish Literature, from the Original German by T. Ross, with additional Notes by the Translator. 12mo. London, 1847.

BOWEN, HENRY L. Memoir of Tristam Burges, with Selections from his Speeches and Occasional Writings. 8vo. Philadelphia, 1835.

BOYD, HUGH. Works. (See Campbell, L. D.)

*BOYER, ABEL. French and English Dictionary. 8vo. Boston, 1835.

BOYLE, ROBERT. Works. Epitomized by Richard Boulton. 3 vols. 8vo. London, 1699.

BOYS, EDWARD. Narrative of a Captivity, and Adventures in France and Flanders. 12mo. London, 1831.

BRACKENRIDGE, H. M. Recollections of Persons and Places in the West. 12mo. Philadelphia.

BRACKENRIDGE, H. M. Voyage to South America. 2 vols. 8vo. London, 1820.

BRADFORD, ALDEN. History of Massachusetts from 1764 to 1775. 3 vols. 8vo. Boston, 1822.

BRADFORD, DUNCAN. The Wonders of the Heavens; being a Popular View of Astronomy. 4to. Boston, 1845.

BRADHURST, LORD. Speech. (See Observations.)

BRADLEY, THOMAS. Practical Geometry, Linear, Perspective and Projection. 8vo. London.

BRADY, J. H. Law of Debtor and Creditor. 12mo. London, 1832.

BRADY, WILLIAM. The Kedge Anchor, or Young Sailor's Assistant. 8vo. New York, 1847.

BRAINARD, REV. DAVID. Memoirs of. (See Edwards, Jonathan.)

*BRANDE, WILLIAM T. A Dictionary of Science, Literature, and Art. 8vo. New York, 1843.

BRANDE, WILLIAM T. Manual of Chemistry. 2 vols. 8vo. London, 1833.

BRANT, JOSEPH. (THAYENDANGEA.) Life. (See Stone, William L.)

BREREWOOD, EDWARD. Enquiries touching the Diversity of Languages and Religions. 12mo. London, 1654.

BRESCIANO, G. Z. Lezioni di Storia delle Leggi e dé Custumi dé Popoli sino alla Republica di Roma. Vol. 1. 8vo. Milano, 1809.

*Brewster, David. The Edinburgh Encyclopædia. 20 vols. 4to. Philadelphia, 1832.

Brewster, David. The Life of Sir Isaac Newton. 18mo. New York, 1832.

Brewster, David. Treatise on Optics, with additions by A. D. Bache. 12mo. Philadelphia, 1833.

Brewster, David. Letters on Natural Magic. 18mo. New York, 1832.

Bridgeman, Thomas. The Young Gardener's Assistant. 8vo. New York, 1845. *Presented by the Author.*

Brisbane, Albert. Social Destiny of Man ; or Association and Reorganization of Industry. 12mo. Philadelphia, 1840.

Brissot, J. P. and Etienne Claviene. The Commerce of America with Europe. 12mo. New York, 1795.

Bristed, John. Resources of the United States. 8vo. New Haven, 1835.

British Almanac of the Society for the Diffusion of Useful Knowledge, for 1841, 1842, and 1845. 3 vols. 12mo. London.

British Chronologist, The. 3 vols. 8vo. London, 1775.

British Empire. The History of, from 1765 to 1783, containing a History of the Origin, Progress, and Termination of the American Revolution. 2 vols. 8vo. Philadelphia, 1803.

British Essayists. The Spectator, Rambler, Idler, Adventurer, Connoisseur, Tatler, and Guardian. 3 vols. 8vo. London, 1825–1829.

British India. Historical and Descriptive Account of, from the Most Remote Period to the Present Time. 3 vols. 18mo. New York, 1832.

Brockedon, William. Journals of Excursions in the Alps, the Pennine, Graian, Cottian, Rhetian, Lepontian, and Bernese. 8vo. London, 1845.

Broderip, W. J. Zoological Recreations. 8vo. Philadelphia, 1849.

Brodie, George. A History of the British Empire, from the Accession of Charles I., to the Restoration. 4 vols. 8vo. Edinburgh, 1822.

Brook, Benjamin. The History of Religious Liberty. 2 vols. 8vo. London.

*Brookes, R. and Joseph Collyer. A Dictionary of the World ; Geographical, Historical, and Biographical. Fol. London, 1772.

Brougham, Henry, Lord. Historical Sketches of Statesmen who flourished in the Time of George III., with Remarks on the French Revolution. 8vo. London, 1843.

Brougham, Henry, Lord. Lives of Men of Letters and Science, who flourished in the Time of George III. 12mo. Philadelphia, 1846.

Brougham, Henry, Lord. Political Philosophy. 3 vols. 8vo. London, 1849.

Brown, J. Thoughts on Civil Liberty, Licentiousness, and Faction. 12mo. Dublin, 1765.

Brown, Thomas. Lectures on the Philosophy of the Human Mind. 2 vols. 8vo. Hallowell, 1829.

Brown, Thomas. The Book of Butterflies, Sphinges, and Moths. 3 vols. 18mo. London, 1834.

Brown, Thomas. The Etherial Physician; or Medical Powers of Electricity. Revised, with a brief Account of its Medical Practice, by Jesse Everitt. 8vo. Albany, 1827.

Brown, Thomas. The Timber Measurer's, Merchant's, and Shipmaster's Assistant. 8vo. New York, 1822.

Brown, Thomas, and Jesse Everitt. The Etherial Physician; or the Medical Powers of Electricity Demonstrated. 8vo. Albany, 1823.

Brown, William. Antiquities of the Jews. 2 vols. 8vo. London, 1820.

Browne, Arthur. Miscellaneous Sketches or Hints for Essays. 2 vols. London, 1798.

Browne, D. J. The Trees of America, Native and Foreign. 8vo. New York, 1846. *Presented by the Author.*

Browne, D. J. The American Poultry Yard, with an Appendix by Samuel Allen. 12mo. New York, 1850.

Browne, J. Ross. Etchings of a Whaling Cruize, with Notes of a Sojourn on the Island of Zanzibar, and a Brief History of the Whale Fishery in its past and present condition. 8vo. New York, 1846.

Browning, Robert. Poems. 2 vols. 12mo. Boston, 1850.

Browning, W. S. A History of the Huguenots; a new Edition, continued to the Present Time. 8vo. Philadelphia, 1845.

Bruce, John. First Principles of Philosophy. 12mo. Edinburgh, 1785.

Bryant, Edwin. What I Saw in California; being a Journal of a Tour in 1847–1848. 8vo. New York, 1849.

Brydone, P. A Tour through Sicily and Malta. 12mo. New York, 1813.

Buchanan, Claudius. Christian Researches in Asia. 12mo. New York, 1812.

Buck, Charles. Anecdotes; Moral, Religious, and Entertaining. 12mo. Boston, 1843.

Buckingham, Joseph S. America, Historical, Statistical, and Descriptive. 3 vols. 8vo. London.

Buckingham, Joseph S. The Eastern and Western States of America. 3 vols. 8vo. London.

Buckingham, Joseph S. Slave States of America. 2 vols. 8vo. London.

Buckingham, Joseph T. Specimens of Newspaper Literature, with Personal Memoirs, Anecdotes, and Reminiscences. 2 vols. 8vo. Boston, 1850.

Budge, John. The Practical Miner's Guide. 8vo. London, 1845.

Budgell, Eustace. Memoirs of the Life and Character of the Earl of Orrery, and of the Family of the Boyles. 8vo. London, 1732.

Buel, Jesse. The Farmer's Companion; or Essays on the Principles and Practice of American Husbandry. 12mo. Boston, 1840. *Presented by A. B. Allen.*

Buist, Robert. The American Flower Garden Directory. 8vo. Philadelphia, 1839.

Bulkeley, John, and John Cummins. A Voyage to the Southern Seas. 12mo. London, 1753.

Bull, Marcus. Experiments on Fuel. 8vo. Philadelphia, 1827.

Bulletin de la Societé d'Encouragement pour l'Industrie Naturale. 4 vols. 4to. Paris, 1844.

Bulwer, Henry Lytton. The Monarchy of the Middle Classes—France, Social, Literary, Political. 2d Series. 2 vols. 12mo. London, 1836.

Bulwer. (See Lytton.)

Buonaparte, Napoleon. Life. (See Hazlitt, William.)

Buonaparte, Napoleon. History of. (See Lockhart, J. G.)

Buonaparte, Napoleon. (See Bonaparte.)

Burgess, George. Martyrdom of the Saint Peter and Saint Paul. A Poem. 12mo. Providence, 1834.

*Burke, John, and John B. Encyclopædia of Heraldry; or General Armory of England, Scotland, and Ireland. 3d Edition, with Supplement. 8vo. London, 1849.

BURKE, WILLIAM. The Mineral Springs of Virginia, with remarks on their Use, and the Diseases to which they are Applicable. 12mo. New York, 1846.

BURNET, JACOB. Notes on the Early Settlement of the North Western Territory. 8vo. New York, 1847.

BURNS, ROBERT. The Works of, with his Life, by Allan Cunningham. 8vo. London, 1845.

BURNS, ROBERT. Poetical Works. 2d vol. 24mo. New York, 1825.

BURR, AARON. Private Journal. (See Davis, Matthew L.)

BURR, AARON. Examination of the Charges against, and also Letters on his Political Defection. 8vo. 1804–1808.

*BURR, DAVID H. Atlas of the State of New York. Fol. New York, 1829.

BURRISH, ONSLOW. Batavia Illustrata; or, A View of the Policy and Commerce of the United Provinces. 8vo. London, 1742.

BURTON, RICHARD. Historical Remarks on the Ancient and Present State of London and Westminster. 4to. Westminster, 1810.

BURTON, ROBERT. The Anatomy of Melancholy, by Democritus Junior. A New Edition, enlarged by Democritus Minor. 8vo. New York, 1850.

BUSH, REV. GEORGE. The Life of Mohammed. 18mo. New York, 1831.

BUSHBY, JAMES. Journal of a Recent Visit to the Principal Vineyards of Spain and France. 8vo. Philadelphia, 1838.

BUTLER, CHARLES. Reminiscences of, with a Letter to a Lady on Ancient and Modern Music. 12mo. New York, 1825.

BUTLER, FREDERICK. The Farmer's Manual. 12mo. Weathersfield, 1821.

BUTLER, SAMUEL. Poetical Remains. (See Thyer, Robert.)

*BUTTERWORTH, REV. J. New Concordance to the Holy Scriptures. 8vo. Boston, 1821.

*BUYS, EGBERT. A Dictionary of Terms of Arts. 4to. Amsterdam, 1768.

BYRNE, J. C. Twelve Years' Wanderings in the British Colonies, from 1835 to 1847. 2 vols. 8vo. London, 1848.

BYRON, GEORGE GORDON, LORD. Works in Verse and Prose, including his Letters, Journals, etc., with a Sketch of his Life. 8vo. Hartford, 1849.

BYRON, GEORGE GORDON, LORD. Marino Faliero, Doge of Venice. A Tragedy. 18mo. Philadelphia, 1821.

BYRON, GEORGE GORDON, LORD. Life. (See Galt, John.)

CAFFARO, FATHER. Defence of the Drama. 12mo. New York, 1826.

CALDWELL, CHARLES. Discourse on the Genius and Character of the Rev. Horace Holley. 8vo. Boston, 1828.

CALMET, AUGUSTINE. The Phantom World, or the Philosophy of Spirits, Apparitions, &c. Edited, with an Introduction and Notes, by the Rev. H. Christmas. 2 vols. 8vo. London, 1850.

*CALMET'S Dictionary of the Bible, with the Fragments Incorporated by Charles Taylor. 8vo. London, 1849.

CAMDEN, THEOPHILUS. History of the War in Spain and Portugal, with a Memoir of the Duke of Wellington. 8vo. London, 1813.

CAMDEN, WILLIAM. Camden's Britannia. Fol. London, 1695.

CAMERON, MRS. Englishwomen in Past and Present Times. 18mo. London, 1841.

CAMPBELL, E. S. N. Dictionary of the Military Science. 12mo. London, 1844.

CAMPBELL, GEORGE. Philosophy of Rhetoric. 8vo. New York, 1834.

CAMPBELL, JOHN. A Political Survey of Britain. 2 vols. 4to. London, 1774.

CAMPBELL, JOHN, LORD. The Lives of the Lord Chancellors and Keepers of the Great Seal of England. 7 vols. 8vo. Philadelphia, 1847–1848.

CAMPBELL, JOHN, LORD. The Lives of the Chief Justices of England, from the Norman Conquest till the Death of Lord Mansfield. 2 vols. 8vo. London, 1849.

CAMPBELL, JOHN, LORD. Lives of the British Admirals. Vols. 6 and 8. 8vo. London, 1814.

CAMPBELL, JOHN D. and STEPHEN CAMBRELLING. The American Chancery Digest. 8vo. New York, 1828.

CAMPBELL, JOHN W. Biographical Sketches, with other Literary Remains. Compiled by his Widow. 8vo. Columbus, 1838.

CAMPBELL, LAURENCE DUNDAS. The Miscellaneous Works of Hugh Boyd, the Author of the Letters of Junius. 2 vols. 8vo. London, 1800.

CAMPBELL, MRS. MARIA. Revolutionary Services and Civil Life of General William Hull, prepared from his manuscripts: with the History of the Campaigns of 1812, and Surrender of the Post of Detroit. By his Grandson James F. Clarke. 8vo. New York, 1848.

CAMPBELL, THOMAS. Frederick the Great: His Court and Times. 2 vols. 8vo. London, 1845.

CAMPBELL, THOMAS. Life of Petrarch. 2 vols. 8vo. London, 1841.

CAMPBELL, THOMAS. Life of Mrs. Siddons. 12mo. London, 1839.

CAMPBELL, W. W. Annals of Tryon County, or the Border Warfare of New York during the Revolution. 8vo. New York, 1831.

CANFIELD, HENRY J. The Breeds, Management, Structure and Diseases of the Sheep. 12mo. Salem, Ohio, 1848.

CANNING, GEORGE. Memoirs of the Life of. 2 vols. 12mo. New York, 1830.

CANNING, GEORGE. Life. (See Bell, Robert.)

CANNING, GEORGE. Political Life of. (See Stappleton, A. E.)

CANTILLON, PHILIP. The Analysis of Trade, Commerce, Coin, Bullion, Banks and Foreign Exchanges. 8vo. London, 1759.

CAPPER, JAMES. Observations on the Winds and Monsoons. 4to. London, 1801.

CARDING AND SPINNING MASTER'S ASSISTANT. 8vo. Glasgow, 1832.

CARDONNE, M. A. Miscellany of Eastern Learning. 2 vols. 12mo. London, 1772.

CAREY, H. C. Essays on the Rate of Wages. 12mo. Philadelphia, 1835.

CAREY, MATTHEW. Essays on Political Economy. 8vo. Philadelphia, 1822.

CAREY, MATTHEW. Essay on Banking. 12mo. Philadelphia, 1816.

CAREY, MATTHEW. The Olive Branch, or Faults on Both Sides. 8vo. Philadelphia, 1815.

CAREY, MATTHEW. Vindiciæ Hibernicæ, or Ireland Vindicated. 8vo. Philadelphia, 1823.

CAREY, MATTHEW. American Pocket Atlas. 12mo. Philadelphia, 1813.

CAREY, MATTHEW. Miscellaneous Essays. 8vo. Philadelphia, 1830.

CARLYLE, THOMAS. The Life of Frederic Schiller, comprehending an Examination of his Works. 12mo. New York, 1846.

CARLYLE, THOMAS. Oliver Cromwell's Letters and Speeches. 2 vols. 12mo. New York, 1848.

CARLYLE, THOMAS. Essays. (See Modern British Essayists.)

Caroline, Queen. Trial of. 2 vols. 8vo. London, 1820.

Carpenter, S. C. Select American Speeches, Forensic and Parliamentary, with Prefatory Remarks. 2 vols. 8vo. Philadelphia, 1815.

Carr, Sir John. A Tour through Holland in 1806. 8vo. Philadelphia, 1807.

Carr, Thomas L. A Manual of Roman Antiquities. 8vo. London, 1836.

Carrel, Armand. History of the Counter Revolution in England for the Re-establishment of Popery under Charles II. and James II., with the History of the Reign of James II. By the Rev. Hon. C. J. Fox. 12mo. London, 1846.

Carter, N. H. Letters from Europe in 1825, 1826, 1827. 2 vols. 12mo. New York, 1829.

Carver, Jonathan. Travels through the Interior Parts of North America. 8vo. Philadelphia, 1796.

Carver, Jonathan. Travels through the Interior Parts of North America. 8vo. London, 1781.

Cary, Henry. A Lexicon to Herodotus, Greek and English. Adapted to the Text of Gaisford and Baehr. 8vo. Oxford, 1843.

Cary, Henry. Memorials of the Great Civil War in England, from 1646 to 1652. 2 vols. 8vo. London, 1842.

Cary, Henry F. Lives of the English Poets from Jonson to Kirke White. 12mo. London, 1846.

Cary, Henry F. The Early French Poets; with a Sketch of the History of French Poetry, by Henry Cary. 12mo. London, 1846.

Cass, Lewis. France, its King, Court and Government. 8vo. New York, 1840.

Castillo, Dias Del. Memoirs, containing an Account of the Discovery and Conquest of Mexico and New Spain, translated by J. I. Lockhart. 2 vols. 8vo. London, 1844.

Catalogue of the Apprentice's Library. 12mo. New York, 1833.

Catalogue of Engravings, by the Most Esteemed Artists. 8vo. New York, 1830.

Catalogue of Fruits and Ornamental Trees, Shrubs, Vines, Plants, &c. 8vo. Flushing, 1844, 1845.

Catalogue of the Great Exhibition of the Works of all Nations. 8vo. London, 1851.

CATALOGUE of the Library of the Corporation of London. 8vo. London, 1828.

CATALOGUE of the New York Mercantile Library. 8vo. New York, 1830.

CATALOGUE of the New York Mercantile Library. 8vo. New York, 1844. *Presented by the Directors.*

CATALOGUE of the New York Mercantile Library. 8vo. New York, 1850. *Presented by the Directors.*

CATALOGUE of the Library of the New York Historical Society. 8vo. New York, 1813. *Presented by Dr. Samuel Akerly.*

CATALOGUE of the New York Society Library. 8vo. New York, 1813.

CATALOGUE of the New York Society Library. 8vo. New York, 1850. *Presented by Philip N. Forbes, Esq.*

CATBUSH, JAMES. A System of Pyrotechny. 8vo. Philadelphia, 1825.

CATLIN, GEORGE. Illustrations of the Manners, Customs, and Condition of the North American Indians. Seventh edition. 2 vols. 8vo. London, 1848.

CATTON, JR., CHARLES. Thirty-six Animals, Drawn from Nature, with a Description of each Animal. 4to. New Haven, 1825.

CAUSSIDIERE, CITIZEN. Memoirs of, or Secret History of the French Revolutions of 1848. 2 vols. 8vo. London, 1848.

CAVALLO, TIBERIUS. The Elements of Natural and Experimental Philosophy, with additional Notes, by F. X. Brosius. 2 vols. 8vo. Philadelphia, 1813.

CAVALLO, TIBERIUS. Treatise on Electricity. 2 vols. 8vo. London, 1786.

*CENSUS of the State of New York, for 1835. Fol. Albany, 1836.

*CENSUS of the State of New York, for 1845. Fol. Albany, 1846.

CENTRAL Society of Education. Papers on Education. 2 vols. 12mo. London, 1837.

CERVANTES, MIGUEL DE. History and Adventures of the renowned Don Quixote. Translated by T. Smollett. 4 vols. 24mo. New York, 1814.

CERVANTES, MIGUEL DE. Don Quixote de la Mancha. From the Spanish. 8vo. London, 1847.

CERVANTES, MIGUEL DE. El Buscapié, with the Illustrative Notes of Don Adolfo de Castro. From the Spanish, with a Life of the Author, and some Account of his Works, by Thomasina Ross. 8vo. London, 1849.

CHALMERS, GEORGE. The Poetic Remains of some of the Scottish Kings. 8vo. London, 1842.

CHALMERS, GEORGE. Estimate of the Comparative Strength of Great Britain. 12mo. London, 1786.

Ditto. ditto. 12mo. London, 1794.

CHALMERS, GEORGE. An Introduction to the History of the Revolt of the American Colonies. 8vo. Boston, 1845.

CHALMERS, THOMAS. Discourses on the Application of Christianity to the Affairs of Life. 8vo. New York, 1821.

CHALMERS, THOMAS. Memoirs of his Life and Writings. (See Hanna, Rev. W.)

CHALMERS, THOMAS. Political Economy in Connection with the Moral State and Moral Prospects of Society. 12mo. New York, 1832.

CHAMBERLAYNE, JOHN. The Present State of Great Britain, with Remarks upon its Ancient State. 8vo. London, 1755.

CHAMBERS, ROBERT. Cyclopædia of English Literature. 2 vols. 8vo. Boston, 1850.

CHAMBERS, ROBERT. The History of Scotland. 12mo. London, 1849.

CHAMBERS, WILLIAM, AND ROBERT. Information for the People. 8vo. Edinburgh, 1842.

CHANDLER, T. B. The Life of Samuel Johnson, D. D. 12mo. New York, 1805.

CHANNING, WILLIAM E. Discourses, Reviews, and Miscellanies. 8vo. Boston, 1833.

CHAPIN, LORIN D. The Vegetable Kingdom, or Hand Book of Plants and Fruits. 12mo. New York, 1843.

CHAPMAN, J. G. The American Drawing Book. 4to. New York, 1847.

CHAPONE, MRS. Letters on the Improvement of the Mind. 24mo. New York, 1818.

CHAPPELL, EDWARD. Narrative of a Voyage to Hudson's Bay. 8vo. London, 1817.

CHAPTAL, JOHN ANTHONY. Chemistry applied to Agriculture. 12mo. Boston, 1835.

CHASE, SAMUEL. Trial. Reported by Samuel H. Smith and Thomas Lloyd. 2 vols. 8vo. Washington, 1805.

CHASTELLUX, MARQUIS DE. Travels in North America in 1780, 1781, 1782. 8vo. New York, 1827.

CHATEAUBRIAND, F. A. DE. Portrait of Bonaparte; being a View of his Administration, together with an Ode to Napoleon. 18mo. New York, 1814.

CHATEAUBRIAND, F. A. DE. The Congress of Verona, comprising a portion of Memoirs of his Own Time. 2 vols. 8vo. London, 1838.

CHATHAM, WILLIAM PITT, EARL OF. Speeches of Chatham, Burke, and Erskine. Selected by a Member of the Philadelphia Bar. 8vo. Philadelphia, 1834.

CHATHAM, WILLIAM PITT, EARL OF. Correspondence. Edited by William Stanhope Taylor and J. H. Pringle. 4 vols. 8vo. London, 1840.

CHATHAM, WILLIAM PITT, EARL OF. Letters. 12mo. New York, 1804.

CHATHAM, WILLIAM PITT, EARL OF. Anecdotes of the Life of, and of the Principal Events of his Time, with his Speeches in Parliament, from 1736 to 1778. 2 vols. 8vo. Dublin, 1790.

CHATTERTON, LADY. Rambles in the South of Ireland during 1838. 2 vols. 8vo. London, 1839.

CHAVANNES, D. A. Exposé de la Methode Elementaire de H. Pestalozzi. 12mo. A Vevey, 1805.

CHEEVER, HENRY T. The Island World of the Pacific. 12mo. New York, 1851.

CHEMIST, THE. 8vo. London, 1834.

CHEMISTRY. Institutes of Experimental Chemistry. 2 vols. 8vo. London, 1759.

CHESTERFIELD. The American Chesterfield, or Way to Wealth, Honor, and Distinction. 24mo. Philadelphia, 1828.

CHESTERFIELD, LORD. Miscellaneous Works. (See Maty, M.)

CHILD, DAVID LEE. Culture of the Beet, and Manufacture of Beet Sugar. 12mo. Boston, 1840.

CHIPMAN, NATHANIEL. Principles of Government. A Treatise on Free Institutions. 8vo. Burlington, 1833.

CHITTY, JOSEPH. A Practical Treatise on Bills of Exchange, &c. With Notes, by a Gentleman of the Philadelphia Bar. 8vo. Philadelphia, 1826.

CHRISTELYKE BEDENCKINGEN voor een Glovige Ziele Item Den Leder Jacobs of rechten wegh ra den Hemel. 18mo. Amsterdam, 1676.

CHRISTIAN LIBRARY. Comprising a Series of Standard Works in Religious Literature. Vol. 1. 4to. Philadelphia, 1833.

CHRISTMAS, REV. HENRY. Canada in 1849. Pictures of Canadian Life; or the Emigrant Churchman. By a Pioneer of the Wilderness. 2 vols. 8vo. London, 1850.

CHRISTMAS, REV. HENRY. The Cradle of the Twin Giants, Science and History. 2 vols. 8vo. London, 1849.

*CHRONICLE EXPRESS. A Semiweekly Newspaper. 2 vols. fol. New York, 1802–1804.

CHRONICLES of London Bridge, by an Antiquary. 12mo. London, 1827.

CHRONICLES of the Seasons, or the Progress of the Year; being a course of Daily Instruction and Amusement. 2 vols. 12mo. London, 1844.

CHRONOLOGY, or an Introduction and Index to Universal Biography and Knowledge. 12mo. New York, 1833.

CHURCH, R. S. A Digested Index to the Report of the Superior Court, and the Court for the Correction of Errors. 2 vols. 8vo. New York, 1812.

CHURCHILL, C. Poems. 2 vols. 8vo. 1768.

CIBBER, COLLEY. An Apology for his Life, forming a History of the Stage for Forty Years. A new edition, with Explanatory Notices, by Edmond Bellchambers. 8vo. London, 1822.

CICERO, M. T. Life and Letters. By Middleton, Melmouth and Heberdeen. 8vo. London, 1848.

CICERO, M. T. The Letters of, to several of his Friends, with Remarks by Wm. Melmouth. 3 vols. 8vo. London, 1833.

CICERO, M. T. Select Orations. (See Duncan, Wm.)

CICERO, M. T. Life. (See Middleton, Conyers.)

CICERO, M. T. Works. (See Barnham, Francis.)

CIST, CHARLES. Cincinnati in 1841, its Early Annals and Future Prospects. 12mo. Cincinnati, 1841.

*CITY GAZETTE and Daily Advertiser. 4 vols. fol. Charleston, 1795–96–97, and 1800.

CIVIL ENGINEER and Architect's Journal. 2 vols. 8vo. London, 1837–38.

CLARENDON, EDWARD, EARL OF. History of the Rebellion and Civil Wars of England. 6 vols. 8vo. Boston, 1827.

CLARK, AARON. Manual of Parliamentary Practice. 12mo. New York. 1826.

CLARK, W. G. The Literary Remains of, including the Ollapodiana Papers, the Spirit of Life, &c. 8vo. New York, 1844.

CLARKE, ANDREW. Tour in France, Italy and Switzerland, during 1840–1841. 8vo. London, 1843.

CLARKE, EDWARD DANIEL. Travels in Europe, Asia and Africa. 2 vols. 12mo. New York, 1813.

CLARKE, EDWARD DANIEL. Travels in Various Countries of Europe, Asia and America. 2 vols. 12mo. New York, 1813.

CLARKE, EDWARD DANIEL. Travels in Various Countries of Europe, Asia and Africa. 11 vols. 8vo. London, 1817–24.

CLARKE, EDWARD DANIEL. Life and Remains. (See Otter, William.)

CLARKE, W. The Young Scholar's History of England, from the First Invasion of the Romans to the Accession of Queen Victoria. 12mo. London, 1849.

CLARKSON, THOMAS. Portraiture of Quakerism. 2 vols. 8vo. New York, 1806.

CLARKSON, THOMAS. History of the Abolition of the African Slave Trade by the British Parliament, abridged by Evan Lewis. 12mo. Washington, 1816.

CLAY, HENRY. Life and Speeches. (See Mallory, Daniel.)

CLAY, HENRY. Biography of. 12mo. 1830.

CLINTON, DEWITT. Tribute to the Memory of, a Comprehensive Sketch of his Life. By a Citizen of Albany. 12mo. Albany, 1828.

CLINTON, DEWITT. Memoirs of. (See Hosack, David.)

CLINTON, DEWITT. Introductory Discourse before the Literary and Philosophical Society. 8vo. New York, 1815.

COBB, J. H. Manual of the Mulberry Tree. 12mo. Boston, 1833.

COBBETT, JAMES P. A Ride of 800 miles in France. 12mo. London, 1824.

COBBETT'S Monthly Sermons. 12mo. London, 1821.

Cobbett, William. Paper against Gold, or History and Mystery of the Bank of England. 12mo. New York, 1834.

Colden, Cadwallader. The History of the Five Indian Nations of Canada. 12mo. London, 1755.

Colden, Cadwallader D. Life of Robert Fulton. 8vo. New York, 1817.

Coleridge, Samuel T. Biographia Literaria; or Biographical Sketches of my Literary Life and Opinions. Prepared for Publication in part by H. N. Coleridge, and Compiled and Published by his Widow. 2 vols. 12mo. New York, 1848.

Coleridge, Samuel T. Letters, Conversations, and Recollections. 2 vols. 12mo. London, 1836.

Coleridge, Samuel T. The Friend; a Series of Essays. 8vo. Burlington, 1831.

Collection of all the Protests made in the House of Lords. 12mo. London, 1747.

Collection of Testimonies concerning Several Ministers of the Gospel. 12mo. London, 1760.

Collections of the New York Historical Society. 8vo. New York, 1821.

Collingwood, G. L. Newnham. Selections from the Correspondence of Lord Collingwood. 8vo. New York, 1829.

Collins, William. Poetical Works. (See Milton.)

Collyer, John. Practical Treatise on the Laws of Partnership. With Notes and American Cases, by Willard Phillin and Edward Pickering. 8vo. Springfield, 1834.

Collyer, W. B. Lectures on Scripture Facts. 8vo. Boston, 1813.

Colman, George. Prose and Poetical Works. 3 vols. 12mo. London, 1787.

Colman, Henry. European Agriculture, and Rural Economy, from Personal Observation. 2 vols. 8vo. Boston, 1846–1848.

Colman, Henry. European Life and Manners, in Familiar Letters to Friends. 2 vols. 8vo. Boston, 1849.

Colman, Henry. Fourth Report of the Agriculture of Massachusetts, Counties of Franklin and Middlesex. 8vo. Boston, 1841.

Colton, C. C. Lacon; or Many Things in a Few Words. 12mo. New York, 1832.

Colton, Rev. Walter. Deck and Port; or Incidents of a Cruize to California, &c. 12mo. New York, 1850.

Colton, Rev. Walter. Ship and Shore, in Madeira, Lisbon, and the Mediterranean. Revised by the Rev. Henry T. Cheever. 12mo. New York, 1850.

Colton, Rev. Walter. Three Years in California. 12mo. New York, 1850.

Columbus, Christopher. Personal Narrative of the First Voyage to America. From a Manuscript discovered in Spain. 8vo. Boston, 1827.

Combe, George. The Constitution of Man, with Additions by Joseph A. Warne. 12mo. Boston, 1847.

Combe, George. The Life and Correspondence of Andrew Combe, M. D. 8vo. Philadelphia, 1850.

Commentarii de Rebus in Scientia Naturali et Medicina Gestis. Vols. 35. 8vo. Leipzig, 1793.

Commercial Journal. Fol. 1814–16. New Haven.

Commercial Regulations of Foreign Countries. 8vo. Washington, 1819.

Commercial Relations of the United States, with Foreign Nations. 8vo. Washington, 1842.

Communications to the Board of Agriculture, on Subjects relative to Husbandry and Internal Improvements of the Country. 7 vols. 4to. London, 1804–11.

Companion to the Newspaper, and Journal of Facts in Politics, Statistics and Public Economy, 1834. 8vo. London, 1835.

*Compendium of the Enumeration of the Inhabitants and Statistics of the United States. Fol. Washington, 1841.

Comstock, John L. Introduction to the Study of Botany. 12mo. Hartford, 1833. *Presented by G. S. West, Esq.*

Comstock, John L. History of the Greek Revolution. 12mo. New York, 1828.

Comte et Dunoyer, M. M. Le Censeur ou Examen des Actes et des Ouvrages qui tendent a detruire ou a Consolider la Constitution de l'Etat. Vols. 2 and 3. 8vo. Paris, 1814–15.

Comyn, Samuel. A Treatise on the Law relative to Contracts and Agreements. 2 vols. 8vo. New York, 1823.

Condorcet, Marquis de. The Life of Voltaire, with Memories of Himself. From the French. 2 vols. 12mo. London, 1790.

Confessional, The, or an Inquiry into the Right, Utility, &c., of establishing Systematical Confessions of Faith and Doctrine in Protestant Churches. 8vo. London, 1760.

Congress of the United States.

Acts of, 1st Session, 6th Congress, 1800. 8vo. Philadelphia. (See Laws of the United States.)

Compendium of the Sixth Census of the United States. Fol. Washington, 1841.

Documents relating to the Defalcation of Samuel Swartwout and others. 8vo. Washington, 1838–39.

History of Congress. Vol. 1. 8vo. Philadelphia, 1834.

History, Rise, &c., of the Indian Tribes of the United States. (See Schoolcraft, Henry R.)

Index to Documents and Reports of the House of Representatives, from 1789 to 1839. 8vo. Washington.

Journal of Congress from 1774 to 1786. 10 vols. 8vo. Philadelphia, 1800. *Presented by Dr. Samuel Akerly.*

Journal of the Senate of the United States. 13 vols. 8vo. viz.,

2d	Session,	6th	Congress,	1800.
1st and 2d	"	8th	"	1803–5.
1st and 2d	"	9th	"	1805–7.
1st	"	10th	"	1807–9.
2d	"	13th	"	1813–14.
1st and 2d	"	14th	"	1815–17.
2d	"	15th	"	1818–19.
1st and 2d	"	16th	"	1819–21.

Journal of the House of Representatives. 6 vols. 8vo. viz.,

2d and 3d	Sessions,	13th	Congress,	1813–15.
1st and 2d	"	14th	"	1815–17.
2d	"	15th	"	1818–19.
1st and 2d	"	16th	"	1819–21.

Messages of the Presidents of the United States. 6 vols. 8vo. Washington, 1840, 1841, 1844 and 1847.

Congress of the United States—Continued.

Reports of the Commissioners of Patents. 7 vols. 8vo. Washington, 1843–1850.

Report of the Secretary of State on the Commercial Regulations of Foreign Nations. 8vo. Washington, 1842.

Report of the Secretary of the Treasury on the Condition of the State Banks. 8vo. Washington, 1841.

Ditto. Ditto. On the State of the Finances. 2 vols. 8vo. Washington, 1845, 1849–1850.

Speeches, Addresses and Messages of the Presidents of the United States, from Washington to John Quincy Adams. 8vo. Philadelphia, 1825.

Ditto. From Washington to Jackson. 8vo. New York, 1839.

Ditto. From Washington to Polk. (See Williams, Edwin.)

State Papers and Public Documents of the United States. 81 vols. 8vo. Washington, 1800–1821.

State Papers and Public Documents of the United States, from 1787 to 1818, including Confidential Documents. 12 vols. 8vo. Boston, 1817–1819.

Testimony in the New Jersey Contested Election. 8vo. Washington, 1840.

Connecticut. History of. By a Gentleman of the Province. 12mo. New Haven, 1829.

*Connecticut Courant, &c. Fol. Hartford, 1800–1802.

*Connecticut Herald. Fol. New Haven, 1811 and 1812.

*Connecticut Journal. A Weekly Newspaper. Fol. New Haven, 1814–1816.

Conseils Généraux de l'Agriculture des Manufactures et du Commerce 1841, 1842, 1845, 1846. 2 vols. 4to. Paris, 1845–1846.

Convention of 1821. Reports of its Proceedings and Debates, by N. H. Carter and William L. Stone, Reporters, and M. T. C. Gould, Stenographer. 8vo. Albany, 1821.

Conversations on Vegetable Physiology. By the Author of "Observations on Chemistry, Natural Philosophy," &c. 12mo. New York, 1830.

Conway, Derwent. Switzerland, the South of France, and the Pyrenees in 1830. 2 vols. 18mo. Edinburgh, 1831.

Cook, Aurelian. An Essay on History Royal, in the Life and Reign of Charles I. 12mo. London, 1685.

Cook, James. Narrative of Voyages round the World. 2 vols. 24mo. New York, 1824.

Cooke, George W. The History of Party. 3 vols. 8vo. London, 1836.

Cooper, J. Fennimore. The History of the Navy of the United States of America. 2 vols. 8vo. London, 1839.

Cooper, J. Fennimore. The American Democrat. 12mo. Cooperstown, 1838.

Cooper, Thomas. Treatise on the Law of Libel and the Liberty of the Press. 8vo. New York, 1830.

Cooper, Thomas. Treatise on Dyeing and Calico Printing. 8vo. Philadelphia, 1815.

Copley, Esther. A History of Slavery, and its Abolition. 18mo. London, 1844.

Coppinger, Joseph. American Practical Brewer and Tanner. 8vo. New York, 1815. *Presented by Dr. Samuel Akerly.*

Coreal, Francois. Voyages aux Indes Occidentales. 2 vols. 12mo. Paris, 1722.

Corkran, J. F. History of the National Constituent Assembly of France. 2 vols. 8vo. London, 1849.

Correspondence between the Countess of Hartford, and the Countess of Pomfret. 3 vols. 12mo. London, 1806.

Corry, John. Detector of Quackery. 12mo. London, 1802. *Presented by Dr. Samuel Akerly.*

Corsair, The. A Gazette of Literature, Art, Dramatic Criticism, Fashion and Novelty. 4to. New York, 1839. *Presented by Gen. A. Chandler.*

Cortes, Ferdinand. Histoire de la Conquete du Mexique. 2 vols. 18mo. A la Haye, 1692.

Corticelli, Salvadore. Regole ed Osservazioni della Lingua Toscana. 8vo. Bassano, 1823.

Cossigny, J. F. C. Supplément aux Recherches Physiques et Chimiques sur la Fabrication de la Poudre a Canon. 8vo. Paris, 1808.

Costello, Louisa Stuart. Memoirs of Eminent English Women. 4 vols. 8vo. London, 1844.

Costello, Louisa Stuart. Jacques Cœur. The French Argonaut and his Times. 8vo. London, 1847.

Cotton Spinner's Manual. 12mo. Glasgow, 1835.

Courtenay, Edward. An Elementary Treatise on Mechanics. 8vo. New York, 1833.

Courtenay, Thomas P. Commentaries on the Historical Plays of Shakspeare. 2 vols. 8vo. London, 1840.

Cousin, Victor. Report on the State of Public Instruction in Prussia. Translated by Sarah Austin. 18mo. New York, 1835.

Cowper, William. The Works of, comprising his Poems, Correspondence and Translations, with a Life of the Author. By the editor, Robert Southey. 15 vols. 12mo. London, 1836–37.

Cowper, William. Poems. 24mo.

Cox, Ross. Adventures on the Columbia River. 8vo. New York, 1832.

Cox, Samuel H. Quakerism not Christianity. 8vo. Boston, 1833.

Coxe, Margaret. The Life of John Wycliffe, D. D. 12mo. Columbus, 1840.

Coxe, William. Travels into Poland, Russia, Sweden and Denmark. 5 vols. 8vo. London, 1792.

Cozzens, Jr., I. A Geological History of Manhattan, or New York Island. 8vo. New York, 1843.

Crabbe, George. Poems, Tales, &c. 2 vols. 12mo. London, 1847.

Crabbe, George. English Synonymes. 8vo. Boston, 1819.

Craigie, David. Elements of General and Pathological Anatomy. 8vo. Edinburgh, 1848.

Cramer, Carl G. Rasereien der Liebe. 12mo. Arnstadt and Rudolstadt, 1801.

Craufurd, John. Journal of an Embassy to the Court of Ava in 1827. 2 vols. 8vo. London, 1834.

CRAUFURD, JOHN. Journal of an Embassy to the Courts of Siam and Cochin China, exhibiting a View of the Actual State of their Kingdoms. 2 vols. 8vo. London, 1830.

CRELL, D. LORENZ. Chemisches Journal. 3 vols. 12mo. Lemgo, 1778–1798.

CRELL, D. LORENZ. Chemisches Annalen. 4 vols. 12mo. Helmstadt, 1796–1798.

CRESSÉ, A. J. B. BOUVET DE. Histoire de la Catastrophie de Saint Domingue. 8vo. Paris, 1824.

CRITICAL REVIEW, or Annals of Literature. 69 vols. 8vo. London, 1762–1795.

CROKER, T. C. The Popular Songs of Ireland, collected and edited, with Introductions and Notes. 8vo. London, 1839.

CROMWELL, OLIVER. Letters and Speeches. (See Carlyle, Thomas.)

CROSLEY, M. A. Tour to London, or New Observations on England and its inhabitants. From the French. By Thomas Nugent. 2 vols. 8vo. London, 1772.

CROUCH, HENRY. Complete View of the British Customs. 8vo. London, 1731.

CROWE, E. E. The History of France. Vols. 2 and 3. 12mo. Philadelphia, 1831.

CRUMP, W. H. The World in a Pocket Book. 18mo. Philadelphia, 1842.

CRUNDUN, JOHN. Convenient and Ornamental Architecture. 8vo. London, 1805.

CULTIVATOR, THE. A Monthly Publication, designed to Improve the Soil and the Mind. Conducted by Jesse Buel and Luther Tucker. 5 vols. 4to. Albany, 1834–1842.

CULTIVATOR, THE. A Monthly Journal, devoted to Agriculture, Horticulture, Floriculture, &c., &c. New Series. Luther Tucker, editor, &c. 7 vols. 8vo. Albany, 1844–1850.

CUMBERLAND, RICHARD. The Observer. A new edition in 3 vols. 12mo. London, 1822.

CUMBERLAND, WILLIAM AUGUSTUS, DUKE OF. Historical Memoirs of, including the Military and Political History of Great Britain during that Period. 8vo. London, 1747.

Cunningham, Allan. The Lives of the most eminent British Painters and Sculptors. 3 vols. 18mo. New York, 1833.

Currie, W. W. Memoir of the Life, Writings and Correspondence of James Currie. 2 vols. 8vo. London, 1831.

Curwen, Samuel. Journal and Letters. (See Ward, George A.)

Cushing, Caleb. Review of the Late Revolution in France. 2 vols. 12mo. Boston, 1833.

Cuvier, Baron. The Animal Kingdom. (The Crustacea, &c., by P. A. Latreille.) From the French, with Notes, by H. McMurtrie. 4 vols. 8vo. New York, 1831.

Dagley, Richard. Death's Doings. 2 vols. 8vo. Boston, 1828.

Dales, Major Samuel. An Essay on the Study of the History of England. 8vo. London, 1809.

Dallaway, James. A Series of Discourses upon Architecture in England, and an Historical Account of Master and Free Masons. 8vo. London, 1833.

Dalrymple, William. Travels through Spain and Portugal in 1774, with a short Account of the Spanish Expedition against Algiers in 1775. 4to. London, 1777.

Damer, Mrs. G. L. Dawson. Diary of a Tour in Greece, Turkey, Egypt and the Holy Land. 2 vols. 8vo. London, 1842.

Dana, James D. A System of Mineralogy, comprising the most recent Discoveries. 8vo. New York and London, 1850.

Dante, Alighieri. The Vision: or Hell, Purgatory and Paradise. Translated by the Rev. H. F. Cary. 8vo. London, 1850.

D'Arblay, Madame. (See Arblay, Madame D'.)

Darby, William. A Tour from New York to Detroit in 1818. 8vo. New York, 1819. *Presented by Dr. Samuel Akerly.*

Darby, William. Universal Gazetteer, or a New Geographical Dictionary. 8vo. Philadelphia, 1827.

Darwin, Charles. Journal of Researches into the Natural History and Geology of the Countries visited during a Voyage round the World. 12mo. London, 1845.

Darwin, Erasmus. A Plan for the Conduct of Female Education. 12mo. Philadelphia, 1798.

Darwin, Erasmus. Botanic Garden. 2 vols. 8vo. London, 1799.

Darwin, Erasmus. Memoir of his Life. (See Seward, Anna.)

Darwin, Erasmus. Phytologia: or the Philosophy of Agriculture and Gardening. 8vo. Dublin, 1800.

Daunt, William J. O'Neil. Personal Recollections of Daniel O'Connell. 2 vols. 8vo. London, 1848.

Davalos, J. E. Limina, apud Peruvianos. 12mo. Monspellii, 1787.

Davenant, Sir William. Works. 8vo. London, 1673.

Davies, David. The Case of Laborers in Husbandry, stated and considered. 8vo. Dublin, 1796.

Davies, Thomas. Memoirs of the Life of David Garrick. 2 vols. 12mo. London, 1784.

Davis, A. J. The Principles of Nature, Her Divine Revelations, and a Voice to Mankind. 8vo. New York, 1850.

Davis, J. B. More Subjects than One. 12mo. London, 1807.

Davis, Matthew L. The Private Journal of Aaron Burr. 2 vols. 8vo. New York, 1838.

Davis, N. S. A Text Book on Agriculture. 12mo. New York, 1848.

Davy, Sir Humphrey. Elements of Agricultural Chemistry. A New Edition, with Instructions for the Analysis of Soils, and Copious Notes, embracing the Recent Discourses in Agricultural Chemistry. By John Shier. 8vo. Glasgow, 1844.

Davy, Sir Humphrey. Elements of Experimental Philosophy. 8vo. Philadelphia, 1812.

Dawes, Rufus. Athenia of Damascus. A Tragedy. 12mo. New York, 1839.

Dawson, Thomas. Memoirs of St. George, the English Patron, and of the Order of the Garter. 12mo. London, 1714.

Debate on the Seminole War. 12mo. Washington, 1819.

Debtor's Prison. A Tale of a Revolutionary Soldier. 18mo. New York, 1834.

Defoe, Daniel. The Life and Adventures of Robinson Crusoe, with a Memoir of the Author, and an Essay on his Writings. 8vo. New York.

De la Beche, H. T. A Selection of Geological Memoirs, contained in the Annales des Mines, written by Brongniart, Humboldt, Von Buch and others. 8vo. London, 1836.

De la Beche, H. T. Geological Manual. 8vo. Philadelphia, 1832.

De la Fond, M. Segand. Traité de l'Electricité. 12mo. Paris, 1776.

Delafond, O. Traité sur la Maladie de Poitrine du Gros Betail. 8vo. Paris, 1844.

Delano, Amasa. A Narrative of Voyages and Travels, comprising Three Voyages round the World. 8vo. Boston, 1817.

Dellon, M. An Account of the Inquisition at Goa, in India. 18mo.

De Lolme. (See Lolme.)

Del Rio, Antonio. Description of the Ruins of an Ancient City in Guatemala; and also a Critical Investigation and Research into the History of the Americans, by P. F. Cabrera. 4to. London, 1822.

De Morgan, Augustus. The Differential and Integral Calculus. 8vo. London, 1842.

Dendy, Walter Cooper. The Philosophy of Mystery. 12mo. New York, 1845.

Dennis, Jr., Jonathan. Silk Manual. 18mo. New York, 1839.

Dennis, Mr. Remarks on Prince Arthur, an Heroic Poem; with some Critical Observations upon Virgil. 12mo. London, 1696.

De Pambour. (See Pambour.)

De Pratt. (See Pratt.)

De Quincey, Thomas. The Logic of Political Economy. 8vo. Edinburgh, 1844.

De Ronde. (See Ronde.)

D'Haussez. (See Haussez.)

D'Homergue, John, and P. S. Dupinceau. Essays on American Silk. 12mo. Philadelphia, 1830.

DIBDIN, THOMAS F. Introduction to the Greek and Latin Classics. 2 vols. 8vo. London, 1827.

DICK, THOMAS. The Improvement of Society by the Diffusion of Knowledge. 18mo. New York, 1833.

DICK, THOMAS. The Practical Astronomer. 12mo. New York, 1846.

DICK, THOMAS. The Works of. 5 vols. 12mo. Philadelphia, 1847.

DICKENS, CHARLES. Works. Cricket on the Hearth. The Chimes. Christmas Carol.

DICKINSON, JOHN. The Poetical Writings of. 2 vols. 8vo. Wilmington, 1801.

DICKINSON, SAMUEL N. Help to Printers and Publishers. 12mo. Boston, 1835.

DICKSON, ADAM. The Husbandry of the Ancients. 2 vols. 8vo. Edinburgh, 1788.

DICKSON, W. S. A Narrative of his Confinement and Exile. 8vo. Dublin, 1812.

DICKSON & Co. A Catalogue of Plants. 8vo. Edinburgh, 1792.

*DICTIONARY of Arts and Sciences, by a Society of Gentlemen. 4 vols. 8vo. London, 1763–1764.

DICTIONARY of Chemistry, with Additions and Notes, by Mrs. A. H. Lincoln. 12mo. New York, 1830.

*DICTIONNAIRE de l'Academie Françoise. 2 vols. 4to. Vismes, 1778.

DIPLOMACY of the United States. 8vo. Boston, 1826.

DIPLOMATIC CORRESPONDENCE of the American Revolution, edited by Jared Sparks. 12 vols. 8vo. Boston, 1829.

DIPLOMATIC CORRESPONDENCE of the United States of America, from 1783 to 1789. 7 vols. 8vo. Washington, 1833.

DISCOURSE on the Advantages of Science. 12mo. Boston, 1831.

DISCOURSES on Davila, or a Series of Papers on Political History, by an American Citizen. 8vo. Boston, 1805.

DISCOVERY and Adventure in Africa. 18mo. New York, 1832.

DISCOVERY and Adventure in the Polar Seas and Regions. 18mo. New York, 1833.

D'ISRAELI, I. Curiosities of Literature. 5 vols. 12mo. London, 1823.

D'ISRAELI, I. Curiosities of Literature. Illustrated by Bolton Corney. 8vo. London, 1838.

D'ISRAELI, I. Miscellanies of Literature. 3 vols. 12mo. New York, 1841.

DITSON, GEORGE L. Circassia, or a Tour to the Caucasus. 8vo. New York, 1850.

DIXON, GEORGE. Voyage Autour du Monde. 2 vols. 8vo. Paris, 1789.

DOBSON, Mrs. The Life of Petrarch. 2 vols. 18mo. Philadelphia, 1809.

DOCUMENTS relatifs aux Canaux. 4to. Paris, 1840.

DODD, CHARLES R. A Manual of Dignities, Privileges and Precedence. 12mo. London, 1844.

DODD, GEORGE. British Manufactures. 3 vols. 18mo. London, 1845.

DOGGETT, JOHN. New York Directory, from 1842–1843 to 1851–1852. 10 vols. 8vo.

DOLBEAR'S Science of Penmanship. 2 vols. 12mo. New York, 1836.

DON QUIXOTE. (See Cervantes.)

DONALDSON, PETER. Review of the Present Systems of Medicine and Chirurgery of Europe and America. 8vo. New York, 1821. *Presented by Dr. Samuel Akerly.*

DOW, ALEXANDER. The History of Hindostan. From the Persian. 3 vols. 8vo. London, 1803.

DOWNING, A. J. A Treatise on the Theory and Practice of Landscape Gardening, adapted to North America. 8vo. New York, 1841.

DOWNING, A. J. Cottage Residences; or a Series of Designs for Rural Cottages, &c. 8vo. New York, 1842.

DOWNING, A. J. The Fruits and Fruit Trees of America. 8vo. New York, 1847.

DOYLE, JOHN. Catalogue of a Collection of Ancient and Modern Books. 8vo. New York, 1848.

DOYLE, MARTIN. A Cyclopædia of Practical Husbandry, and Rural Affairs in General. A new edition, enlarged and revised by the Rev. W. Rhane. 8vo. London, 1844.

DOYLE, MARTIN. The Flower Garden. With Notes and Observations by L. D. Gale. 12mo. New York, 1835.

DRAKE, B. AND E. D. MANSFIELD. Cincinnati in 1826. Cincinnati, 1827.

Drake, Daniel. Natural and Statistical View, or Picture of Cincinnati and the Miami Country. 12mo. Cincinnati, 1815.

Drake, Samuel G. Biography and History of the Indians of North America. 8vo. Boston, 1835.

Drake, Samuel G. Indian Captivities, or Life in a Wigwam. 8vo. Auburn, 1850.

Drelincourt, Charles. Vertroostingen der Geloovige Ziele Tegen de verschrickingen des Doodts. 18mo. t'Amsterdam, 1719.

Dreury, Charles Stewart. A Memoir on Suspension Bridges. 8vo. London, 1832.

Drummond, Henry. The Condition of the Agricultural Classes of Great Britain and Ireland. 2 vols. 8vo. London, 1842.

Drummond, William H. Autobiography of Archibald Hamilton Rowan, with additions and illustrations. 8vo. Dublin, 1840.

Duane, William. A Visit to Columbia in 1822–1823. 8vo. Philadelphia, 1836.

Duer, William A. Outlines of the Constitutional Jurisprudence of the United States. 12mo. New York, 1833.

Duer, William A. The Life of William Alexander, Earl of Sterling, with Selections from his Correspondence. 8vo. New York, 1847.

Duffie, Rev. Cornelius R. Sermons, with a Memoir of the Author. 2 vols. 8vo. New York, 1829.

Dufour, John J. The American Vine Dresser's Guide. 12mo. Cincinnati, 1826.

Duhamel, M. A Practical Treatise of Husbandry. 4to. London, 1762.

Dumas, Alexandre. Impressions of Travel in Egypt and Arabia Petræa. Translated by a Lady. 12mo. New York, 1839.

Dumas, Alexandre. The Progress of Democracy. Translated by an American. 12mo. New York, 1841.

Dumas, M. Traité de Chimie appliquee aux Arts. 4 vols. 8vo. Paris, 1828–1835.

Duncan, Henry. Sacred Philosophy of the Seasons. 4 vols. 12mo. New York, 1846.

DUNCAN, JONATHAN. The Dukes of Normandy, from the Time of Rollo to the Expulsion of King John by Philip Augustus of France. 12mo. London, 1839.

DUNCAN, JONATHAN. The Religious Wars of France. 12mo. London, 1840.

DUNCAN, WILLIAM. Cicero's Select Orations. 8vo. New York, 1802.

DUNN, HENRY. Guatemala, or the United Provinces of Central America. 8vo. New York, 1828.

DUPAN, MALLET. History of the Destruction of the Helvetic Union and Liberty. 12mo. Dublin, 1765.

DUPIN, BARON. Commercial Power of Great Britain. 2 vols. 8vo. London, 1825.

DUPIN, BARON. Mathematics applied to Useful and Fine Arts. Adapted to the State of the Arts in England, by George Birkbeck. 8vo. London, 1827.

DURAND, THOMAS. Memoirs and Select Remains of an Only Son. 12mo. Andover, 1823.

DWIGHT, HENRY E. Travels in the North of Germany in 1825–1826. 8vo. New York, 1829.

DWIGHT, N. Sketches of the Lives of the Signers of the Declaration of Independence. 12mo. New York, 1830.

DWIGHT, THEODORE. History of the Hartford Convention. 8vo. New York, 1833.

DWIGHT, THEODORE. The Roman Republic of 1849. 12mo. New York, 1851.

DWIGHT, JR., THEODORE. The American Penny Magazine and Family Newspaper. 3 vols. 8vo. New York, 1845–1847.

DWIGHT, TIMOTHY. The Conquest of Canaan. A Poem. 12mo. Hartford, 1785.

DWIGHT, TIMOTHY. Theology explained and defended. In a series of Sermons. 4 vols. 8vo. New Haven, 1823.

DWIGHT, TIMOTHY. Travels in New England and New York. 4 vols. 8vo. New Haven, 1821.

DYCKMAN, J. G. American Militia Officer's Manual. 12mo. New York, 1825.

DYMOND, JONATHAN. Essays on the Principles of Morality. 12mo. New York, 1844. *Presented by the Society of Friends.*

EARTHQUAKE at Lima and the Port of Callao, 1746, Relation of. 8vo. London, 1748.

EAST INDIA SKETCH-BOOK. Comprising an Account of the Present State of Society in Calcutta, Bombay, &c. 2 vols. 12mo. London, 1832.

EATON, JOHN H. Life of Andrew Jackson. 8vo. Philadelphia, 1824.

EATON, WILLIAM. The Life of. 8vo. Brookfield, 1813.

EBELINGS, C. D. Erdbeschreibring und Geschichte von Amerika. Die vereinten Staaten von Nordamerika. 8vo. Hamburg, 1816.

ECHARD, LAWRENCE. The History of the Revolution and the Establishment of England, in 1688. 12mo. London, 1725.

ECHARD, LAWRENCE. A General Ecclesiastical History. 2 vols. 12mo. London, 1712.

ECLECTIC REPOSITORY and Analytical Review. Edited by a Society of Physicians. 10 vols. 8vo. Philadelphia, 1811–1820.

ECONOMIA POLITICA. Scrittori Classici Italiani di. 50 vols. 8vo. Milano, 1803–1816.

Part Antica.

Vol. 1. Serra, della Moneta, Turbolo, sulle Monete.
2. Davanzati, Lezioni, sui Cambj., Scaruffi, su le Monete.
3. Montanini, dello Moneta.
4, 5. Broggia, die Tributi, della Monete.
6, 7. Neri, Observazioni, Documenti.

Part Moderna.

Vol. 1. Bandini, Discorso Economico, 1737. Algarotti, sul Commercio.
2. Belloni, ditto. Pagnini Pregio delle Cose.
3, 4. Galiani, della Moneta.
5. Galiani, Dialogues, sur le Commerce des Blés.
6. Galiani, Discorso sulla Conservazione del Grano.

Economia Politica—Continued.

7–10. Genovesi, Ant., Lezioni di Economia Civile e Opusculi Economici.

11, 12. Beccaria, Ces., Elementi di Economia Pubblica e Relazione sul Misure, 1780.

13, 14. Carli, Gian-Rin. Delle Monete, 1766.
Carli, Gian-Rin. Censimento de Milano.
Carli, Gian-Rin. Bilanci Economici, e del libero Commercio de Grani.

15. Verri, Pietro, Sull' Economia Politica.

16. Verri, Pietro, dull'Annona, sulle Monete Tariffa di Milano, 1774.

17. Verri, Pietro, Memorie sulla Economia delle Milano; della Tortura, 1777; Opuscoli.

18. Zanon, Ant., Lettere sull'Agricoltura, &c.

19. Zanon, Ant., Apologia delle Mercatura; dell'Utilita delle Academie di Agricoltura, &c.

20. Paoletti, Ferd., Pensieri sopra l'Agricoltura, 1769, I verri mezzi di render felici la Societa, 1772.

21, 22, 23. Ortes, Giam., Economia Nazionale, 1774.

24. Ortes, Giam., Sulla Popolazione; Scienze Utili; delle Opinioni; Letters al Algarotti, &c.

25, 26. Ortes, Giam., Errori Popolari; Religione e Governe.

27. Ortes, Giam., dei Fidecommessi.

28, 29. Briganti, Filippo, Esame Economico, 1780.

30. D'Arco, Giam. G., Sulla Popolazione; dell'Annona.

31. D'Arco, Giam. G., del Commercio; dei Transiti; Scottoni dell' Estrazione.

32. Filangieri, Gaetano, delle Leggi Politiche ed Economiche, 1780.

33. Vasco, Giam., della Moneta; de Corpi d'Arti; de la Mendicite, 1770–1780.

34. Vasco, Giam., Felicita Pubblica, 1767; Usura Libera.

35. Vasco, Giam., del Setificio; Elstratti di Economia Politica.

36. Mengotti, Fran., Commercio de Romani; il Colbertismo, 1787–1791.

37. Palmieri, Giusep., Pubblica Felicita.

38. Palmieri, Giusep., Sulle Tariffe; Ricchezza Nazionale.

39. Delfico, Melf., Liberta del Commercio.

ECONOMIA POLITICA—Continued.

Corniano, Giam., Sulle Monete ; dell'Agricoltura.
Solera, M., Sur les Valeurs.
40. Cantalupo, Dom. di Gen. dell'Annona.
Carracioli, Ditto.
Scrofani, S. Ditto.
41. Ricci, Lodov., Riforma degl' Instituti Pii della Modena, 1787.
49. Neri, Pompeo., della Materia Frumentaria.
Palmieri, Sull Lusso, Ortes, sulla Popolazione, &c.
50. Indici.

EDDY, THOMAS. Life. (See Knapp, Samuel L.)

EDGAR, PATRICK N. American Race, Turf Register, Sportsman's Herald and General Stud Book. Vol. 1. 8vo. New York, 1833.

EDGAR, SAMUEL. The Variations of Popery. Edited by the Rev. C. Sparry. 8vo. New York, 1849.

EDGEWORTH, MARIA. Popular Tales. 2 vols. 12mo. Philadelphia, 1819.

EDGEWORTH, RICHARD L. Memoirs, begun by Himself and concluded by his Daughter, Maria Edgeworth. 8vo. London, 1844.

EDINBURGH Annual Register. 13 vols. 8vo. Edinburgh, 1808–1815.

EDINBURGH New Philosophical Journal. Conducted by Robert Jameson. 8 vols. 8vo. Edinburgh, 1843–1847.

EDINBURGH REVIEW. 7 vols. 8vo. New York, 1835–1851.

EDUCATOR, THE. Prize Essays, by John Lalor, J. A. Heraud, E. Higginson, J. Simpson, and Mrs. G. R. Porter. 12mo. London, 1839.

EDWARDS, JONATHAN. Memoirs of the Rev. David Brainerd, Missionary to the Indians. With additions by S. E. Dwight. 8vo. New Haven, 1822.

EDWARDS, WILLIAM H. A Voyage up the River Amazon, including a Residence at Para. 8vo. New York, 1847.

ELDON, LORD CHANCELLOR. Life. (See Twiss, Horace.)

*ELLIOT, JONATHAN. The Debates in the several State Conventions on the Adoption of the Federal Constitution. 4 vols. 8vo. Washington, 1836.

ELLIOT, JONATHAN. Historical Sketches of the Ten Mile Square, forming the District of Columbia. 18mo. Washington, 1830.

ELLIOT, WILLIAM. Patentee's Manual. 8vo. Washington, 1830.

ELLIS, HENRY. Journal of the Proceedings of the late Embassy to China. 8vo. Philadelphia, 1818.

ELLIS, ROBERT. British Tariff. 12mo. London, 1836.

Ditto Ditto. 12mo. London, 1843.

ELLIS, WILLIAM. Polynesian Researches. 4 vols. 12mo. New York, 1833.

ELLSWORTH, H. L. Digest of Patents, 1790–1841. 2 vols. 8vo. Washington, 1842.

ELLSWORTH, H. W. Valley of the Upper Wabash, Indiana, with Hints on its Agricultural Advantages. 12mo. New York, 1838.

ELMWOOD, E. Yankee among the Nullifiers. An Autobiography. 12mo. New York, 1833.

ELPHINSTONE, MOUNTSTUART. An Account of the Kingdom of Caubul and its Dependencies. 2 vols. 8vo. London, 1842.

EMERSON, JAMES. Letters from the Ægean. 8vo. New York, 1829.

EMERSON, RALPH WALDO. Poems. 12mo. Boston, 1847.

EMMET, THOMAS ADDIS. Memoirs of. (See Haines, Charles G.)

EMMONS, RICHARD. The Battle of Bunker Hill, or the Temple of Liberty. An Historic Poem. 12mo. New York, 1839. *Presented by Gen. A. Chandler.*

EMPORIUM of Arts and Sciences. Conducted by John R. Coxe. 5 vols. 8vo. Philadelphia, 1812–1814.

*ENCYCLOPÆDIA AMERICANA. A Popular Dictionary of Arts, Sciences, Literature, History, Politics and Biography. Edited by Francis Lieber and E. Wigglesworth. 13 vols. 8vo. Philadelphia, 1829–1833.

*ENCYCLOPÆDIA PERTHENSIS, or Universal Dictionary of Knowledge. 24 vols. 8vo. Edinburgh, 1816.

ENGLAND. Critical History of. 2 vols. 8vo. London. 1728.

ENGLAND AND AMERICA. A Comparison of the Social and Political State of both Nations. 8vo. New York, 1834.

ENGLAND AND THE ENGLISH. By the Author of "Pelham," &c. 2 vols. 12mo. New York, 1833.

ENGLAND AND FRANCE. A Comparative View of the Social Condition of both Countries, from the Restoration of Charles II. to the present time. With Remarks on Lord Orford's Letters—the Life of the Marquise du Deffand—the Life of Racheal Lady Russell—Fashionable Friends, a Comedy. By the Editor of Madame du Deffand's Letters. 2 vols. 8vo. London, 1844.

England Illustrated, or a Compendium of the Natural History, Geography, Topography, and Antiquities of England and Wales. 2 vols. 4to. London, 1764.

English, George B. A Narrative of the Expedition to Dongola and Sennaar. 8vo. Boston, 1823.

Entertaining and Marvellous Repository. Vol. 1. Boston, 1827.

Entick, John. A Historical Survey of London, Westminster, Southwark and Places Adjacent. 4 vols. 8vo. London, 1766.

Erman, Adolph. Travels in Siberia; including Excursions Northwards down the Obi to the Polar Circle, and Southward to the Chinese Frontier. From the German by W. D. Cooley. 2 vols. 8vo. Philadelphia, 1850.

Espy, James P. The Philosophy of Storms. 8vo. Boston, 1841.

Etudes de Gites Minéraux. 4to. Paris, 1836.

Euclid. Elements of. (See Lardner, Dionysius.)

Euler, Leonard. Letters on Natural Philosophy. Edited by David Brewster. With Notes by John Griscom. 2 vols. 18mo. New York, 1833.

Europe. Secret History of. 3 vols. 12mo. London, 1715.

Europe. Secret History of. 12mo. London, 1712.

European Magazine and London Review. 8vo. London, 1788.

Eustace, John Chetwold. A Classical Tour through Italy. 2 vols. 8vo. Paris, 1837.

Evans, John. Shakspeare's Seven Ages, or the Progress of Human Life. 12mo. New York, 1831.

Evans, John. Sketch of the Denominations of the Christian World. 12mo. Amherst, 1832.

Everett, Alexander H. New Ideas on Population, with Remarks on the Theories of Malthus and Godwin. 8vo. Boston, 1823.

Ewbank, Thomas. A Descriptive and Historical Account of Hydraulic and other Machines for Raising Water. 8vo. New York, 1842.

EWING, THOMAS. Geography for Schools and Private Students, revised by William Darby. 12mo. New York, 1820.

EXAMINER, THE. Barent Gardenier, Editor. 4 vols. 8vo. New York, 1813–1815.

EXPOSITION des Produits de l'Industrie Francaise en 1844. Rapport du Jury Central. 3 vols. 8vo. Paris, 1844.

FABER, FREDERICK W. The Styrian Lake, and other Poems. 12mo. London, 1842.

FAIN, BARON. Memoir of the Invasion of France by the Allied Armies, and of the last six months of the Reign of Napoleon. 8vo. London, 1834.

FAIRFAX, LORD. The Correspondence of, comprising Memoirs of the Reign of Charles I., edited by George W. Johnson; and Memorials of the Civil War, edited by Robert Bell. 4 vols. 8vo. London, 1848–1849.

FAIRFIELD, SUMNER L. Abaddon, the Spirit of Destruction; and other Poems. 8vo. New York, 1830.

FAIRFIELD, SUMNER L. Last Nights of Pompeii, a Poem; and Lays and Legends. 8vo. New York, 1832.

FAIRFIELD, SUMNER L. Poems and Prose Writings. 8vo. Philadelphia, 1841.

FAIRMAN, WILLIAM. The Stocks Examined and Compared, or a Guide to Purchasers in the Public Funds. 8vo. London, 1798.

FAME AND GLORY of England Vindicated; being an Answer to "The Glory and Shame of England." By Libertas. 12mo. New York, 1842.

FANSHAWE, LADY. Memoirs of Herself, with Extracts from the Correspondence of Sir Richard Fanshawe. 12mo. London, 1830.

FARINGTON, JOSEPH. Memoirs of the Life of Sir Joshua Reynolds, with some Observations on his Talents and Character. 8vo. London, 1819.

FARLEY, EDWARD. Imprisonment for Debt Unconstitutional, &c. 8vo. London, 1787.

FARMER'S CABINET. 4 vols. 8vo. Philadelphia, 1836–1840.

Farmer's Library. Animal Economy. 2 vols. 8vo. London.

Farmer's Magazine. 10 vols. 8vo. London, 1844–1851.

Featherstonhaugh, G. W. A Canal Voyage up the Minnay Sotor. 2 vols. 8vo. London, 1847.

Federal Convention of the United States. Secret Proceedings and Debates of 1787. 8vo. Albany, 1821.

Federalist, The. A Collection of Essays on the New Constitution. 12mo. New York, 1788.

Federalist, The. (See Hamilton, Alexander.)

Fellows, John. An Exposition of the Mysteries, or Religious Dogmas and Customs of the Ancient Egyptians, Pythagoreans and Druids; also an Inquiry into the Origin, History and Purport of Freemasonry. 8vo. New York, 1835.

Fellows, John. Posthumous Works of Junius; with an Inquiry respecting the Author, and a Sketch of the Life of John Horne Tooke. 8vo. New York, 1829.

Fellows, John. The Veil Removed, or Reflections on Humphrey's Essay on the Life of Israel Putnam. 12mo. New York, 1843. *Presented by the Author.*

Felton, S. The Portraits of English Authors on Gardening, with Biographical Notices. 8vo. London, 1830.

Fenn, John. Paston Letters. Original Letters written during the Reigns of Henry VI., Edward IV., and Richard III., by various Persons of Rank or Consequence. With additional Notes, &c., by A. Ramsay. 8vo. London, 1849.

Ferary, P. Senenis e Societate ieso de Florum Cultura. 4to. Rome, 1633.

Ferguson, Adam. History of the Roman Republic. 8vo. Philadelphia, 1845.

Fessenden, Thomas G. Essay on the Law of Patents. 8vo. Boston, 1810.

Fessenden, Thomas G. Ladies' Monitor: a Poem. 12mo. Bellows Falls, 1818.

Fessenden, Thomas G. Register of Arts. 8vo. Philadelphia, 1808.

Fessenden, Thomas G. The Complete Farmer and Rural Economist. 12mo. New York, 1851. *Presented by C. M. Saxton, Esq.*

Fielding, Henry. History of Tom Jones, the Foundling. 4 vols. 24mo. Philadelphia, 1828.

Fielding, Henry. The Interesting History of Amelia. 2 vols. 12mo. New York, 1826.

Fischer, E. S. Elements of Natural Philosophy. With Notes and Additions, by M. Biot. Edited by John Farrar. 8vo. Boston, 1827.

Fisher, Daniel. System of Military Tactics. 8vo. New York, 1805. *Presented by Dr. Samuel Akerly.*

Fish, Wilbur. Travels in Europe. 8vo. New York, 1838.

Fitz-Adam, Adam. The World. 3 vols. 18mo. London, 1796.

Fleet, Samuel. The Rural Library. A publication of Standard Works on Agriculture, Gardening and Domestic Economy. 8vo. New York, 1838. *Presented by the Editor.*

Fleming, John. Molluscuous Animals, including Shell Fish. 8vo. Edinburgh, 1838.

Fletcher, James. The History of Poland, from the earliest period to the present time. 18mo. New York, 1833.

Fletcher, Rev. J. P. Notes from Nineveh, and Travels in Mesopotamia, Assyria and Syria. 8vo. Philadelphia, 1850.

Flint, Abel. Geometry and Trigonometry, with a Treatise on Surveying. Enlarged by George Gillet. With a Treatise on Logarithms, by F. A. T. Barnard. 8vo. Hartford, 1833.

Flint, Timothy. A Condensed Geography and History of the Western States and the Mississippi Valley. 2 vols. 8vo. Cincinnati, 1828.

Flint, Timothy. The History and Geography of the Mississippi Valley. 8vo. Cincinnati, 1832.

Ditto. Ditto. 8vo. London, 1832.

Flint, Timothy. Lectures on Natural History. 12mo. Boston, 1833.

Florian, M. Consalvo of Cordova, or the Conquest of Grenada, with a Sketch of the History of the Moors in Spain. Translated by Mrs. Heron. 3 vols. 12mo. Perth, 1792.

Fontenelle, Bernard. Conversations on the Plurality of Worlds. With additions, &c., by a Gentleman of the Inner Temple. 8vo. London, 1760.

FORBES, FRANCIS. The Improvement of Waste Lands. 8vo. London, 1728.

FORBES, F. E. Five Years in China, from 1842 to 1847, with an Account of the Occupation of the Islands of Labnan and Borneo by the English. 8vo. London, 1848.

FORBES, MAJOR. Eleven Years in Ceylon, comprising Sketches of the Field Sports and Natural History of that Colony, and an Account of its History and Antiquities. 2 vols. 8vo. London, 1841.

FORBES, SIR WILLIAM. An Account of the Life and Writings of James Beattie. 8vo. New York, 1807.

FORCE, PETER. The National Calendar and Annals of the United States. 9 vols. 12mo. 1822–1823--1828--1830--1835.

FORD, RICHARD. The Spaniards and their Country. 12mo. New York, 1848.

FOREIGN QUARTERLY REVIEW. 7 vols. 8vo. New York, 1834–1842.

FORM BOOK. By a Member of the Philadelphia Bar. 12mo. Philadelphia, 1830.

FORTUNE'S EPITOME of the Stocks and Public Funds. 12mo. London, 1824.

FOSCOLO, UGO. Essays on Petrarch. 8vo. London, 1823.

FOSTER, JOHN. An Essay on the Evils of Popular Ignorance. 12mo. New York, 1850.

FOSTER, MRS. M. E. A Hand Book of Modern European Literature. 12mo. Philadelphia, 1850.

FOUQUÉ, F. DE LA MOTTE. Undine and Sintram and his Companions. From the German. 12mo. New York, 1845.

FOWLER, JOHN. Journal of a Tour in the State of New York, in 1830. 12mo. London, 1831.

FOWLER, W. The Eastern Mirror: an Illustration of the Sacred Scriptures. 8vo. Exeter, 1814.

FOWLER, WILLIAM C. English Grammar. The English Language in its Elements and Forms. 8vo. New York, 1850.

FOX, GEORGE. Journal or Historical Account of his Life, Travels, &c. 8vo. Philadelphia. *Presented by the Society of Friends.*

FOX, GEORGE. Memoirs of his Life. (See Tuke, Henry.)

FOX, MARIA. Memoirs of. Consisting chiefly of Extracts from her Journal and Correspondence. 8vo. London, 1846.

FRANCE ARCANA GALLICA. The Secret History of France for the last Century. By the Author of the Secret History of Europe. 8vo. London, 1714.

FRANCIS, G. H. Orators of the Age, comprising Portraits, Critical, Biographical, and Descriptive. 8vo. London, 1847.

FRANKLIN, BENJAMIN. Life and Writings. (See Sparks, Jared.)

FRANKLIN, BENJAMIN. Memoirs of his Life and Writings, by Himself. 8vo. Philadelphia, 1818.

FRANKLIN, BENJAMIN. Works, with his Life, written by Himself. 18mo. Baltimore, 1835.

FRANKLIN, BENJAMIN. Works, with a Life, written by Himself. 24mo. New York, 1825.

*FRANKLIN INSTITUTE, Journal of the. Edited by Thomas P. Jones. 8vo. Philadelphia, 1828. (Continued.)

FREART, ROLAND. A Parallel of the Ancient Architecture with the Modern. Fourth Edition, with additions. 8vo. London, 1723.

FREDERICIAN CODE, The. 2 vols. 8vo. Edinburgh, 1761.

FREDERICK II. OF PRUSSIA. His Court and Times. (See Campbell, Thomas.)

FREDERICK II. OF PRUSSIA. Life, with Observations, Authentic Documents, and a Variety of Anecdotes. From the French. 2 vols. 8vo. London.

FREDERICK II. OF PRUSSIA. Posthumous Works, from the French, by Thomas Holcroft. 13 vols. 8vo. London, 1789.

Vol. 1. History of his own Times.
2, 3. History of the Seven Years' War.
4. Bavarian War, &c.
5. Political, Philosophical, and Satirical Miscellanies.
6–13. Correspondence.

FREEMAN, JAMES. Sermons and Charges. 8vo. Boston, 1832. *Presented by Gen. A. Chandler.*

FREMONT, J. C. Report of the Exploring Expedition to the Rocky Mountains in 1842, and to Oregon and California in 1843–1844. 8vo. Washington, 1845. *Presented by Hon. James F. Simmons.*

FRENCH IN ALGIERS.

1. The Soldier of the Foreign Legion.
2. The Prisoners of Abd-el-Kader.

From the German and French, by Lady Duff Gordon. 12mo. New York, 1845.

FRENEAU, PHILIP. A Collection of Poems. 2 vols. 24mo. New York, 1815.

FROISSART, SIR JOHN. Chronicles of England, France and Spain, and the Adjoining Countries, from the Reign of Edward II. to the Coronation of Henry IV. From the French, by Thomas Johnes. With a Life of the Author, &c., &c., by Rev. John Lord. 4to. New York.

FROST, J. Art of Swimming. 8vo. New York, 1818. *Presented by Dr. Samuel Akerly.*

FUGITIVE PIECES on Various Subjects, by Several Authors. 2 vols. 12mo. London, 1771.

FULTON, ROBERT. Life. (See Colden, C. D.)

FULTON, ROBERT. A Treatise on the Improvement of Canal Navigation. 4to. London, 1796.

FUME, JOSEPH. A Paper of Tobacco. Treating of the Rise, Progress, Pleasures and Advantages of Smoking, with Anecdotes of Distinguished Smokers and a Critical Essay on Snuff. 12mo. London, 1839.

FURLONG, LAWRENCE. The American Coast Pilot. 8vo. Newburyport, 1804.

FURNISS, WILLIAM. The Old World, or Scenes and Cities in Foreign Lands. 8vo. New York, 1850.

FURNISS, WILLIAM. Waraga, or the Charms of the Nile. 12mo. New York, 1850.

GAILLARD, THOMAS. The History of the Reformation in the Church of Christ, continued from the Close of the 15th Century. 8vo. New York, 1847.

GALL, F. J. The Origin of the Moral Qualities and Intellectual Faculties of Man, and the Condition of their Manifestations. 6 vols. 12mo. Boston, 1835.

GALLATIN, ALBERT. The Right of the United States of America to the North Eastern Boundary claimed by them. 8vo. New York, 1840.

GALLIER, JAMES. American Builder's General Price Book and Estimator. 8vo. New York, 1833.

GALLOWAY, ELIJAH. History of the Steam Engine. 8vo. London, 1828.

GALLOWAY, ELIJAH. History and Progress of the Steam Engine, with an Appendix by Luke Hebert. 8vo. London, 1832.

GALT, JOHN. The Life of Lord Byron. 18mo. New York, 1832.

GALT, JOHN. Life and Studies of Benjamin West. 8vo. Philadelphia, 1816.

GALT, JOHN. Life of Cardinal Wolsey. 12mo. London, 1846.

GANILH, CHARLES. An Enquiry into the Various Systems of Political Economy. From the French, by D. Borleau. 8vo. New York, 1812.

GARDENER and Practical Florist. 3 vols. 8vo. London, 1843–1844.

GARDNER, D. P. The Farmer's Dictionary. 8vo. New York, 1846.

GARLAND, HUGH A. The Life of John Randolph of Roanoke. 2 vols. 8vo. New York, 1850.

GARRICK, DAVID. Life. (See Davies, Thomas.)

GASPARIN, CTE. DE. Cours d'Agriculture. 4 vols. 8vo. Paris, 1846--1848.

GASS, PATRICK. A Journal of Voyages and Travels through the Interior Parts of North America. 8vo. Pittsburg, 1800.

*GAZETTE OF THE UNITED STATES, and Philadelphia Daily Advertiser. 4 vols. fol. 1798--1800--1801.

GAZETTEER of the State of New York. 8vo. Albany, 1842.

GENERAL Delusion of Christians. 8vo. London, 1714.

GENLIS, MADAME LA COMTESSE DE. Memoirs of Herself. 2 vols. 8vo. New York, 1825.

GENTLEMAN'S MAGAZINE and Historical Chronicle. By Sylvanus Urban. 11 vols. 8vo. London, 1826--1831.

GEOGRAPHY for Youth. 12mo. London, 1790.

GEOLOGICAL SURVEY of the State of New York. 2 vols. 8vo. Albany, 1839--1840--1841.

George, Anita. Annals of the Queens of Spain, from the Period of the Conquest of the Goths down to the Reign of Isabel II. 12mo. New York, 1850.

George IV. Diary illustrative of the Times of, interspersed with Original Letters from Queen Caroline, and from Various other Distinguished Persons. 4 vols. 8vo. London, 1838.

Gera, Le Dr. Fo. De La Fabrication du Fromage, Traduit de l'Italien par Vor. Rendu. 8vo. Paris, 1843.

Gibbings, Richard. An Exact Reprint of the Roman Index Expurgatorius. 12mo. Dublin, 1837.

Gibbon, Edward. History of the Decline and Fall of the Roman Empire. 8vo. Philadelphia, 1830.

Ditto. Ditto. With an Introductory Memoir of the Author, by William Youngman. 8vo. London, 1834.

Ditto. Ditto. Abridged. 2 vols. 8vo. Dublin, 1790.

Gibbs, George. Memoirs of the Administrations of Washington and John Adams. 2 vols. 8vo. New York, 1846.

Gibson, H. S. Miscellaneous Poems. 12mo. Philadelphia, 1834.

Gilbart, James W. A Practical Treatise on Banking. 8vo. New York, 1851.

Gilbert, J. E. Le Médecin Naturaliste, ou Observations de Médecure et d'Histoire Naturelle. 12mo. Lyons and Paris, 1809.

Gill, Thomas. The Technical Repository. 9 vols. 8vo. London, 1822–1826.

Gillies, John. History of Ancient Greece, its Colonies and Conquests, Literature, Philosophy and the Fine Arts. 8vo. Philadelphia, 1831.

Gilroy, Clinton G. A Practical Treatise on Dyeing, and Calico Printing. 8vo. New York, 1846.

Gilroy, Clinton G. The Art of Weaving, by Hand and by Power. 8vo. New York, 1845. *Presented by the Author.*

Gilroy, Clinton G. The History of Silk, Cotton, Linen, Wool, and other Fibrous Substances. 8vo. New York, 1845. *Presented by the Author.*

Giraud, Jr., J. P. The Birds of Long Island. 8vo. New York, 1844.

Gleig, G. R. Memoirs of the Life of Warren Hastings. 3 vols. 8vo. London, 1841.

Gleig, G. R. The History of the Bible. 2 vols. 18mo. New York, 1833.

Gliddon, George R. Ancient Egypt, revised and corrected, with an Appendix. 4to. Philadelphia, 1848.

Godwin, William. An Inquiry concerning Political Justice and its Influence on General Virtue and Happiness. 2 vols. 4to. London, 1793.

Goldsmith, J. General View of the Manners, Customs and Curiosities of Nations. 2 vols. 12mo. Philadelphia, 1817.

Goldsmith, J. Geographical View of the World. Revised and improved by James G. Percival. 12mo. New York, 1826.

Goldsmith, Oliver. History of the Earth, and Animated Nature. 4 vols. 8vo. Philadelphia, 1830.

Goldsmith, Oliver. History of England. 3 vols. 8vo. London, 1790.

Goldsmith, Oliver. Miscellaneous Works, with an Account of his Life and Writings. 4 vols. 8vo. London, 1801.

Goldsmith, Oliver. Life. (See Prior, James.)

Golovine, Ivan. The Russian Sketch Book. 2 vols. 8vo. London, 1848.

Good, John M. Book of Nature. 8vo. New York, 1830.

Good, John M. Dissertation on the Best Means of Maintaining and Employing the Poor. 12mo. London, 1798. *Presented by Dr. Samuel Akerly.*

Goodman, Dr. Godfrey. The Court of King James I. From the Original Manuscripts, by John S. Brewer. 2 vols. 8vo. London, 1839.

Goodman, John D. American Natural History. 3 vols. 8vo. Philadelphia, 1826.

Goodman, John D. Rambles of a Naturalist. With Reminiscences of a Voyage to India, by R. Coates. 12mo. Philadelphia, 1833.

Gordon, Patrick. Geography Anatomatized, or the Geographical Grammar. 8vo. London, 1735.

Gordon, Thomas. History of the Greek Revolution, and of the Wars and Campaigns arising from the Struggles of the Greek Patriots in Emancipating their Country from the Turkish Yoke. 2 vols. 8vo. Edinburgh, 1844.

Gordon, Thomas F. Digest of the Treaties and Statutes of the United States, relating to Commerce, Navigation and Revenue. 8vo. Philadelphia, 1830.

GORDON, THOMAS F. Gazetteer of the State of New York. 8vo. Philadelphia, 1836.

GORDON, THOMAS F. Gazetteer and History of New Jersey. 8vo. Trenton, 1834.

GORDON, THOMAS F. Gazetteer of the State of Pennsylvania. 8vo. Philadelphia, 1832.

GRAHAM, J. A. A Descriptive Sketch of the Present State of Vermont. 8vo. London, 1797.

GRAHAME, JAMES. The History of the United States of North America. 4 vols. 8vo. London, 1836.

GRAND MAGAZINE, The. 8vo. London, 1758.

GRANVILLE, A. B. The Spas of England and Principal Sea Bathing Places. 2 vols. 8vo. London, 1841.

GRANVILLE, A. B. The Spas of Germany. 8vo. London, 1839.

GRATTAN, THOMAS C. The History of the Netherlands. 12mo. Philadelphia, 1831.

GRAY, ANDREW. A Treatise on Spinning Machinery. 8vo. Edinburgh, 1819.

GRAY, ASA. The Botanical Text Book. 12mo. New York, 1842.

GRAY, THOMAS. Poetical Works. (See Milton.)

GRAY, THOMAS. Observations on a General Iron Railway, or Land Steam Conveyance. 8vo. London, 1825.

GRAYDON, ALEXANDER. Memoirs of his Own Time, with Reminiscences of Men and Events of the Revolution. Edited by J. S. Littell. 8vo. Philadelphia, 1846.

GREAT BRITAIN. Colonial Policy of. By a British Traveller. 12mo. Philadelphia, 1816.

GREAT METROPOLIS. 12mo. New York, 1837.

Ditto. By the Author of Random Recollections of the Lords and Commons. 12mo. Philadelphia, 1838.

GREECE. Sketches of Modern Greece. By a Young English Volunteer. 2 vols. 8vo. London, 1828.

GREEN, JACOB. Text Book of Chemical Philosophy. 8vo. Philadelphia, 1829.

Greenbank's Periodical Library. A Reprint of New and Standard Works. 3 vols. 8vo. Philadelphia, 1833.

Green, Gen. Nathaniel. Sketches of his Life, &c. (See Johnson, Wm.)

Greene, George W. Historical Studies. 12mo. New York, 1850.

Gregg, Josiah. Commerce of the Prairies, or the Journal of a Santa Fé Trader. 2 vols. 12mo. New York, 1844. *Presented by the Author.*

Gregoire, H. An Inquiry concerning the Intellectual and Moral Faculties, and Literature of Negroes. Translated by D. B. Warden. 8vo. Brooklyn, 1810.

Gregory, Jacob. Dissertatio Inauguralis de Mortis Cælimutatione Medenis. 18mo. Edinburgh, 1776.

*Gregory, G. Dictionary of Arts and Sciences. 3 vols. 4to. New York, 1821.

Griffith, William. Historical Notes of the American Colonies, and Revolution, from 1754 to 1775. 8vo. Burlington, New Jersey.

Griffiths, John W. Treatise on Marine and Naval Architecture. 4to. New York, 1850.

Grim, Charles F. An Essay toward an Improved Register of Deeds. 8vo. Washington, 1838–1839.

Grimm, Baron de. Historical and Literary Memoirs and Anecdotes, selected from the Correspondence of, and Diderot, with the Duke of Saxe-Gotha, and many other Distinguished Persons, between 1753 and 1790. From the French. 4 vols. 8vo. London, 1815.

Grimshaw, William. History of England. 12mo. Philadelphia, 1820.

Ditto. Ditto. 12mo. Philadelphia, 1823.

Griscom, John. A Year in Europe. 2 vols. 8vo. New York, 1823.

Griswold, Rufus W. The Poets and Poetry of America. 8vo. Philadelphia, 1850.

Griswold, Rufus W. The Prose Writers of America. 8vo. Philadelphia, 1847.

Grund, Francis J. The Americans in their Moral, Social and Political Relations. 2 vols. 8vo. London, 1837.

Grund, Francis J. Aristocracy in America, from the Sketch Book of a German Nobleman. 2 vols. 12mo. London, 1839.

GRUND, F. J. The Merchant's Assistant, or Mercantile Instructor. 8vo. Boston, 1834. *Presented by J. P. Veeder, Esq.*

GUILLET, PETER. Timber Merchant's Guide. 8vo. Baltimore, 1823.

GUINEA. An Historical Account of, and the Slave Trade. 12mo. London.

GUIZOT, F. General History of Civilization in Europe, from the Fall of the Roman Empire to the French Revolution. With occasional Notes by C. S. Henry. 4 vols. 12mo. New York, 1846.

GUIZOT, F. History of the English Revolution of 1640, from the Accession of Charles I. to his Death. Translated by William Hazlitt. 12mo. London, 1846.

GULDEN-SPIEGEL, ofte Opweckinge tot Christelycke Deughden, &c. 18mo. Amsterdam, 1670.

GURNEY, JOSEPH J. Observations on the Distinguishing Views and Practices of the Society of Friends. 8vo. New York, 1840. *Presented by the Society of Friends.*

GURNEY, JOSEPH J. A Winter in the West Indies. 8vo. London, 1841.

GUTHRIE, WILLIAM. Cicero de Oratore, or his Three Dialogues upon the Character and Qualifications of an Orator. 12mo. Oxford, 1808.

GUTHRIE, WILLIAM. General History of England. 3 vols. fol. London, 1744.

GUTHRIE, WILLIAM. New System of Modern Geography. 4to. London, 1795.

GUTHRIE, WILLIAM. New System of Geography and Universal History; and also Astronomical Geography, by James Ferguson. Improved by the Rev. I. Evans, and the Rev. Archibald Forbes. 2 vols. 8vo. London.

HACKLEY, CHARLES W. A Treatise on Algebra, containing the latest Improvements. 8vo. New York, 1849.

HACKLEY, CHARLES W. Elements of Trigonometry, Plane and Spherical. 8vo. New York, 1838.

HADLEY, W. HOBART. The American Citizen's Manual of Reference. 8vo. New York, 1840.

HAGEDORN, FRIEDRICH VON. Samtliche Poetische Werke. 3 vols. 12mo. Carlsruhe, 1777.

HAGEMERSTER, JULIUS DE. Report on the Commerce of the Ports of New Prussia, Moldavia and Wallachia. Translated by T. F. Friebuer. 8vo. London.

HAINES, CHARLES G. Memoir of Thomas Addis Emmet. 12mo. New York, 1829.

HALE, DAVID. Memoir of. (See Thompson, Joseph P.)

HALIBURTON, THOMAS C. The Attaché, or Sam Slick in England. 4 vols. 8vo. London, 1843.

HALIBURTON, THOMAS C. An Account of Nova Scotia. 2 vols. 8vo. Halifax, 1829.

HALL, BASIL. Account of a Voyage of Discovery. 8vo. Philadelphia, 1818.

HALL, BASIL. Extracts from a Journal written on the Coast of Chili, Peru and Mexico, in 1820–1821–1822. 2 vols. 12mo. Philadelphia, 1824.

HALL, BASIL. Travels in America in 1827–1828. 2 vols. 12mo. Philadelphia, 1829.

HALL, FRANCIS. Travels in Canada and the United States. 8vo. Boston, 1818.

HALL, JOHN CHARLES. Interesting Facts connected with the Animal Kingdom, with some Remarks on the Unity of our Species. 8vo. London, 1841.

HALL, J. SPARKER. The Book of the Feet, a History of Boots and Shoes. 12mo. New York, 1847.

HALLAM, HENRY. The Constitutional History of England, from the Accession of Henry VII. to the Death of George II. 8vo. New York, 1849.

HALLAM, HENRY. View of the State of Europe during the Middle Ages. 2 vols. 8vo. Philadelphia, 1824.

HALLIDAY, SIR ANDREW. Annals of the House of Hanover. 2 vols. 8vo. London, 1826.

HALLIWELL, JAMES O. The Autobiography and Correspondence of Sir Simonds d'Ewes, Bart. 2 vols. 8vo. London, 1845.

HALSTED, CAROLINE A. Richard III. as Duke of Gloucester and King of England. 8vo. Philadelphia, 1844.

HAMILTON, ALEXANDER. Collection of Facts and Documents relative to the Death of. By the Editor of the Evening Post. 8vo. New York, 1804.

HAMILTON, ALEXANDER. The Works of, comprising his Writings and Correspondence. Edited by John C. Hamilton. 5 vols. 8vo. New York, 1851.

HAMILTON, ALEXANDER, and James Madison, and John Jay. Federalist, or a Collection of Essays on the New Constitution of the United States. 8vo. Hallowell, 1831.

HAMILTON, ROBERT. An Inquiry concerning the National Debt of Great Britain. 8vo. Philadelphia, 1816.

HAMILTON, WILLIAM. Remarks on Several Parts of Turkey. 4to. London, 1809.

HANBURY, WILLIAM. A Complete Body of Planting and Gardening. 2 vols. fol. London, 1770.

HANDMAID to the Arts. 2 vols. 8vo. London, 1764.

HANNA, REV. WILLIAM. Memoirs of the Life and Writings of Thomas Chalmers. 3 vols. 12mo. New York, 1850.

HANSARD, T. C. Treatises on Printing and Type Founding. 8vo. Edinburgh, 1841.

HARDIE, JAMES. Description of the City of New York. 12mo. New York, 1827.

HARDIE, JAMES. The New Biographical Dictionary and American Remembrancer of Departed Merit. 4 vols. 8vo. New York, 1805.

HARPER, ROBERT G. Select Works. 8vo. Baltimore, 1814.

HARPER'S FAMILY LIBRARY. 50 vols. 18mo. New York, 1832–1833.

Abercrombie, John. Inquiries concerning the Intellectual Powers.
Abercrombie, John. The Philosophy of Moral Feelings.
Barrow, John. Description of Pitcairn's Island.
Brewster, David. Life of Sir Isaac Newton.
Brewster, David. Letters on Natural Magic.
British India. Historical and Descriptive Account of.
Bush, Prof. George. The Life of Mohammed.
Cunningham, Allan. Lives of the British Painters and Sculptors.
Dick, Thomas. The Improvement of Society.
Discovery and Adventure in Africa.
Discovery and Adventure in the Polar Regions.
Euler, Leonard. Letters on Natural Philosophy.

HARPER'S FAMILY LIBRARY—Continued.

Fletcher, James. The History of Poland.
Galt, John. The Life of Lord Byron.
Gleig, Rev. G. R. The History of the Bible.
Humboldt, A. von. Travels, &c.
James, G. P. R. The History of Charlemagne.
James, G. P. R. The History of Chivalry.
Lander, R. and J. Expeditions to the Niger.
Lives and Voyages of Drake, Cavendish and Dampier.
Lockhart, J. G. The History of Buonaparte.
Macgillivray, William. The Travels, &c., of Humboldt.
Milman, H. H. The History of the Jews.
Mudie, R. Guide to the Observation of Nature.
Natural History of Insects.
Paulding, James K. Life of Washington.
Russel, Rev. M. View of Ancient and Modern Egypt.
Scott, Sir Walter. Letters on Demonology and Witchcraft.
Sketches of Venitian History.
Southey, Robert. Life of Nelson.
St. John, J. A. Lives of Celebrated Travellers.
Taylor, W. C. History of Ireland.
Thatcher, B. B. Indian Biography.
Turner, Sharon. The Sacred History of the World.
Williams, Rev. J. Life of Alexander the Great.

HARPER'S New Monthly Magazine. 3 vols. 8vo. New York, 1850–1851.

*HARRIS, JOHN. Lexicon Technicum, or Universal English Dictionary of Arts and Sciences. 2 vols. fol. London, 1716.

HARROP. History of the Irish Rebellion in 1798. 8vo. Philadelphia, 1833.

HART, N. C. Documents relative to the House of Refuge. 8vo. New York, 1832.

HASKELL, DANIEL, and J. Calvin Smith. A Complete Descriptive and Statistical Gazetteer of the United States of America. 8vo. New York, 1843.

HASTINGS, WARREN. Memoirs of the Life of. (See Gleig, G. R.)

HATFIELD, MISS. She Lives in Hopes; or, Caroline. 2 vols. Hingham, 1832.

HATTON, SIR CHRISTOPHER. Memoirs of the Life of. (See Nicholas, Sir Harris.)

HAUPT, HERMAN. General Theory of Bridge Construction. 8vo. New York, 1851.

HAUSSEZ, BARON. Great Britain in 1833. 2 vols. 12mo. Philadelphia, 1833.

HAWKINS, SIR JOHN. The Life of Samuel Johnson, L.L. D. 8vo. London, 1787.

HAWKS, REV. F. L. The Monuments of Egypt an Eye-witness for the Bible. 8vo. New York, 1850.

HAWTHORNE, NATHANIEL. Journal of an African Cruiser, comprising Sketches of the Canaries, the Cape De Verds, Liberia, Sierra Leone and other places on the West Coast of Africa. 12mo. New York, 1845.

HAWTHORNE, NATHANIEL. Mosses from an Old Mance. 12mo. New York, 1846.

HAWTHORNE, NATHANIEL. The Scarlet Letter, a Romance. 12mo. Boston, 1850.

HAY, D. R. A Nomenclature of Colors, Hues, Tints and Shades, applied to the Arts and Natural Sciences, to Manufactures, and other Purposes of General Utility. 8vo. Edinburgh, 1845.

HAYDN. Life. (See Bombet, L. A. C.)

HAZLITT, WILLIAM. Lectures on the English Comic Writers, together with Lectures on the English Poets. Edited by his Son. 12mo. New York, 1845.

HAZLITT, WILLIAM. Lectures on the Dramatic Literature of the Age of Elizabeth. 12mo. New York, 1849.

HAZLITT, WILLIAM. Lectures on the Dramatic Literature of the Age of Elizabeth, and also; the characters of Shakspeare's Plays. 12mo. New York, 1849.

HAZLITT, WILLIAM. Select British Poets. 8vo. London, 1824.

Chaucer,	Roscomon,	Shenstone,	Coleridge,
Spencer,	Pomfret,	Mallet,	Wordsworth,
Sidney,	Dorcet,	Akenside,	Southey,
Drayton,	Phillips,	Young,	Scott,
Daniel,	Halifax,	Gray,	Lamb,
Suckling,	Parnell,	Churchill,	Montgomery,
Wither,	Prior,	Goldsmith,	Byron,
Waller,	Pope,	Armstrong,	Moore,

HAZLITT, WILLIAM. Select British Poets—Continued.

Milton,	Gay,	Warton,	Thurlow,
Cowley,	Blair,	Cowper,	Keats,
Marvell,	Swift,	Rogers,	Milman,
Butler,	Thomson,	Campbell,	Bowles,
Denham,	A. Philips,	Bloomfield,	Proctor.
Dryden,	Collins,	Crabbe,	
Rochester,	Dyer,	Hunt,	
Burns,	Chatterton,	Shelley,	

HAZLITT, WILLIAM. Table Talk: Opinions on Books, Men, and Things. 12mo. New York, 1845.

HAZLITT, WILLIAM. The Life of Napoleon Buonaparte. 3 vols. 12mo. New York, 1847.

HEAD, SIR F. B. A Narrative. 8vo. London, 1839.

HEAD, SIR GEORGE. A Home Tour through the Manufacturing Districts of England in the Summer of 1835. 12mo. New York, 1836.

HEADLEY, J. T. Letters from Italy. 12mo. New York, 1845.

HEADLEY, P. C. The Life of the Empress Josephine, first wife of Napoleon. 12mo. Auburn, 1850.

HEBBE, DR. GUSTAVUS C. Universal History. (Ancient). 2 vols. 8vo. New York, 1848. *Presented by the Author.*

HEBER, REGINALD. Life of, by his Widow. 2 vols. 8vo. New York, 1830.

HEBER, REGINALD. Poetical Works. (See Hemans.)

*HEBERT, LUKE. Engineer's and Mechanic's Encyclopædia. 2 vols. 8vo. London, 1838.

HEDGE, FREDERIC H. Prose Writers of Germany. 8vo. Philadelphia, 1849.

HEEREN, ARNOLD H. L. Ancient Greece. Translated by George Bancroft. 8vo. Boston, 1842.

HEISS, SIEN'R. The History of the Empire. 2 vols. 12mo. London, 1729.

HEMANS, HEBER, AND POLLOK. Poetical Works. 8vo. Philadelphia, 1831.

HENCKEL, J. F. Pyritologia, or a History of the Pyrites. 8vo. London, 1757.

HENDERSON, ANDREW. The Practical Grazier, or a Treatise on the Proper Selection and Management of Live Stock. 8vo. Edinburgh, 1826. *Presented by Dr. Henderson.*

HENDERSON, JAMES. A History of the Brazil. 4to. London, 1821.

Henry, Patrick. Life. (See Wirt, William.)

Henry V. Memoirs of his Life and Character. (See Tyler, J. E.)

*Herald, The. A Gazette for the Country. 2 vols. fol. New York, 1795–1797.

Herbert, Charles. Italy and Italian Literature. 8vo. London, 1835.

Hermit, The, or the Sufferings and Adventures of Philips Quarll. 12mo. London, 1807.

Hermit in London, or Sketches of English Manners. 12mo. New York, 1820.

Heron, A. M. Des Metaux en France, Rapport de l'Exposition des Produits de l'Industrie Francaise en 1827 sur les Objects relatifs a la Metallurgie. 8vo. Paris, 1827.

Heron, Robert. The Letters of Junius, with Notes and Illustrations, Historical, Political, Biographical and Critical. 2 vols. 8vo. Philadelphia, 1804.

Heron, Robert. Universal Geography. 2 vols. 8vo. Edinburgh, 1796.

Herschel, Sir John F. W. A Treatise on Astronomy. 12mo. Philadelphia, 1834.

Herschel, Sir John F. W. Outlines of Astronomy. 8vo. Philadelphia, 1849.

Herty, Thomas. A Digest of the Laws of the United States of America. 8vo. Baltimore, 1800.

Heylin, Peter. Cosmographie—containing the Chorographie and History of the World. Fol. London, 1657.

Hickey, W. The Constitution of the United States of America, with an Alphabetical Analysis; the Declaration of Independence; the Prominent Political Acts of George Washington, &c., &c. 8vo. Philadelphia, 1847.

Hieover, Harry. Stable Talk and Table Talk, or Spectacles for Young Sportsmen. 2 vols. 8vo. London, 1845.

Higgins, W. M. The Entertaining Philosopher, a Familiar Explanation of the most Interesting Phenomena of Natural and Experimental Philosophy. 12mo. London, 1844.

Hildreth, Richard. The History of the United States of America, from the Discovery of the Continent to 1787. 3 vols. 8vo. New York, 1849, and vol. 1, second series, 8vo. New York, 1851.

Hill, Frederick. National Education: its Present State and Prospects. 2 vols. 12mo. London, 1836.

HILL, ISAAC. The Farmer's Monthly Visitor. Vol. 3. fol. Concord, 1841. *Presented by Caleb Stark, Esq.*

HILL, RICHARD. Life. (See Sidney, Edwin.)

HILLHOUSE, JAMES A. Hadad, a Dramatic Poem. 8vo. New York, 1825.

HINMAN, R. R. Letters from the English Kings and Queens to the Governors of the Colony of Connecticut. 12mo. Hartford, 1836.

HINTS AND SKETCHES. By an American Mother. 12mo. New York, 1839.

HIPPISLEY, SIR JOHN COX. Correspondence and Communications concerning the Introduction of Treadmills into Prisons. 8vo. London, 1823.

HISTORICAL REGISTER of the United States. Edited by T. H. Palmer. 3 vols. 8vo. Philadelphia, 1814.

HISTORY of Passive Obedience, &c. 4to. London, 1689.

HISTORY of Wonderful Inventions. 12mo. New York, 1845.

HITCHCOCK, EDWARD. Elementary Geology, with an Introductory Notice by John P. Smith. 12mo. New York, 1844.

HITCHCOCK, EDWARD. Report on the Geology, Mineralogy, Botany and Zoology of Massachusetts. 8vo. Amherst, 1833.

HODGSON, ADAM. Remarks during a Journey through North America in 1819–1820–1821. 8vo. New York, 1823.

HOEFER, FERDINAND. Histoire de la Chimie. 2 vols. 12mo. Paris, 1842.

HOFFY, A. (Ed'r.) The Orchardist's Companion, a Quarterly Journal, devoted to the Cultivation of Fruits of the United States. 4to. Philadelphia, 1841. *Presented by the Editor.*

HOLCROFT, THOMAS. Caroline of Lichtfield. 2 vols. 24mo. New York, 1815.

HOLCROFT, THOMAS. Travels from Hamburg through Westphalia, Holland and the Netherlands to Paris. 2 vols. 4to. London, 1804.

HOLDEN'S TRIENNIAL DIRECTORY, for 1805–1806–1807. 8vo. London, 1805.

HOLLAND, W. M. The Life and Political Opinions of Martin Van Buren. 12mo. Hartford, 1835.

HOLLEY, MRS. MARY A. Observations on Texas; Historical, Geographical and Descriptive. 12mo. Baltimore, 1833.

HOLLEY, O. L. The New York State Register. 8vo. New York, 1845.

Holley, Rev. Horace. Genius and Character of. (See Caldwell, Charles.)

Holmes, Abiel. American Annals, or a Chronological History of America. 8vo. Cambridge, 1805. *Presented by Dr. Samuel Akerly.*

Holmes, William R. Sketches on the Shores of the Caspian, Descriptive and Pictorial. 8vo. London, 1845.

Holstein, H. D. Memoirs of Gilbert Moteer La Fayette. 12mo. New York, 1824.

Holtzapffel, Charles. A New System of Scales of Equal Parts, applicable to Various Purposes of Engineering, Architectural and General Science. 8vo. London, 1838.

Holtzapffel, Charles. Turning and Mechanical Manipulations. Vol. 2. 8vo. London, 1846.

*Holy Bible, with Arguments, &c., composed by Mr. Ostervald. 8vo. London, 1799.

Homans, J. Smith. The Banker's Magazine and Statistical Register. 5 vols. 8vo. Boston, 1849–1851.

Home, Henry, Lord Kames. Elements of Criticism, edited by Abraham Mills. 8vo. New York, 1833.

Hopkins, Ezekiel. The Whole Works of, with a Memoir of the Author. 8vo. London, 1846.

Hoppus, E. The Gentleman's and Builder's Repository, or Architecture Displayed. 4to. London.

Horatius, Q. Flaccus. Carminum, etc. 24mo.

Horatius, Q. Flaccus. Opera. 8vo. Philadelphia, 1823.

Hordynski, Joseph. History of the Polish Revolution, and the Events of the Campaign. 8vo. Boston, 1833.

Hosack, David. Essays on Various Subjects of Medical Science. 3 vols. 8vo. New York, 1824–1830.

Hosack, David. Inaugural Discourses delivered at the opening of Rutger's Medical College. 8vo. New York, 1826.

Hosack, David. Memoir of Dewitt Clinton. 4to. New York, 1829.

Houel, Ephrem. Traité Complet de l'Elève du Cheval en Bretagne. 8vo. Avranches, 1842.

HOUSTON, GEORGE. The Farmer's, Mechanic's, Manufacturer's and Sportsman's Magazine. 8vo. New York, 1827.

HOWARD, FRANK. Color as a Means of Art, being an Adaption of the Experience of Professors to the Practice of Amateurs. 8vo. London, 1849.

HOWARD, JOHN. The State of the Prisons in England and Wales. 2 vols. 4to. Warrington.

HOWE, HENRY. Memoirs of the Most Eminent American Mechanics. 12mo. New York, 1840.

HOWITT, WILLIAM. German Experiences; addressed to the English, both Stayers at Home and Goers Abroad. 12mo. London, 1844.

HOWITT, WILLIAM. Homes and Haunts of the Most Eminent of the British Poets. 2 vols. 8vo. New York, 1847.

HOYLE'S RULES for Playing Fashionable Games. 24mo. New York, 1830.

HUGHES, THOMAS. The Practice of Making and Repairing Roads, of Constructing Foot-paths, Fences, and Drains. 8vo. London, 1838.

HULL, GEN. WILLIAM. Life, &c. (See Campbell, Mrs. M.)

HUMBOLDT, ALEX. VON. Aspects of Nature, in Different Lands and Different Climates. Translated by Mrs. Sabine. 8vo. Philadelphia, 1849.

HUMBOLDT, ALEX. VON. Cosmos; a Sketch of a Physical Description of the Universe. From the German by E. C. Otté. 2 vols. 12mo. New York, 1850.

HUMBOLDT, ALEX. VON. Political Essays on the Kingdom of New Spain. From the original French, by John Black. 2 vols. 8vo. New York, 1811.

HUMBOLDT, ALEXANDER VON. Travels, &c. (See Macgillivray, W.)

HUME, DAVID. Essays and Treatises on Several Subjects. 2 vols. 8vo. Edinburgh, 1793.

HUME, DAVID. History of England, continued to George IV. by Tobias Smollett and J R. Miller. 4 vols. 8vo. Philadelphia, 1832.

HUME, DAVID. The History of England. 7 vols. 8vo. London, 1789.

HUME, DAVID. Private Correspondence, with several Distinguished Persons, between the years 1761 and 1776. 4to. London, 1820.

HUME, DAVID, and T. Smollett. The History of England. 8vo. London, 1835.

HUMPHREYS, DAVID. Miscellaneous Works. 8vo. New York, 1804.

HUNT, LEIGH. Imagination and Fancy; or Selections from the English Poets, illustrative of those First Requisites of their Art, with maskings of the best passages, Critical Notices of the Writers, and an Essay in answer to the Question, "What is Poetry?" 12mo. New York, 1845.

HUNTER, H. Sacred Biography, or the History of the Patriarchs. 4 vols. 8vo. Burlington, 1806.

HUNTER, JAMES. The Improved Scotch Swing Plough, with Practical Illustrations on Plough Making and Ploughing. 8vo. Edinburgh, 1843.

HUNTER, JOHN D. Manners and Customs of several Indian Tribes located west of the Mississippi. 8vo. Philadelphia, 1823.

HUNTER, W. P. Narrative of the Expedition to Syria, under the Command of Admiral Sir Robert Stopford. 2 vols. 8vo. London, 1842.

HUNTINGTON, COUNTESS OF. The Life of Selina, by a Member of the Houses of Shirley and Hastings. 2 vols. 8vo. London, 1844.

HUTCHINSON, THOMAS. The History of the Province of Massachusetts Bay. 8vo. London, 1828.

HUTTON, CHARLES. Course of Mathematics, corrected and improved by Olinthus Gregory, with the Additions of Robert Adrian. 2 vols. 8vo. New York, 1831.

HUTTON, CHARLES. Treatise on Mensuration. 8vo. London, 1812.

IFFLAND, A. W. Dramatische Werke. Vols. 8 and 12. 12mo. Leipzig, 1799–1800.

IMISON, JOHN. School of Arts. 8vo. London, 1787.

IMPERIAL AND COUNTRY Annual Register for 1810, containing a History of Great Britain, &c. 8vo. London, 1811.

IMPERIAL MAGAZINE. 16 vols. 8vo. Liverpool and London, 1819–1834.

INCHBALD, MRS. Memoir of. (See Boaden, James.)

INCHIQUIN, the Jesuit's Letters, by some Unknown Foreigner. 8vo. New York, 1810.

INDERWICK, JAMES. Journal of Surgical and Medical Practice on board the United States Brig "Argus." 2 vols. 4to. 1813.

INDIA. Picture of; Geographical, Historical, and Descriptive. 2 vols. 12mo. London, 1830.

INFANT EDUCATION, or Remarks on the Importance of Educating the Infant Poor. 12mo. New York, 1827.

INFANTRY TACTICS. Abstract of. 12mo. Boston, 1830. *Presented by Gen. A. Chandler.*

INFANTRY TACTICS; or Rules for the Exercises and Manœuvres of the Infantry of the United States Army. 2 vols. 8vo. Washington, 1825. *Presented by Gen. A. Chandler.*

INGLIS, HENRY D. A Journey throughout Ireland in 1834. 8vo. London, 1838.

INLAY, GILBERT. Topographical Description of the Western Territory of North America. 8vo. London, 1797.

INTRODUCTORY DISCOURSE and Lectures delivered before the American Institute of Instruction. 3 vols. 8vo. Boston, 1831–1832–1833.

INVENTOR'S ADVOCATE and Patentee's Recorder. 5 vols. 4to. London, 1839–1841. *Presented by J. W. Cochran, Esq.*

IRELAND. The Annals of. Translated from the Original Irish of the Four Masters, by Owen Connellan, with Annotations by Philip MacDermott and the Translator. 4to. Dublin, 1846.

IRELAND. The Irish Tourist; or the People and the Provinces of. 12mo. London.

IRELAND and its Rulers since 1829. 8vo. London, 1843.

IRVING, THEODORE. The Conquest of Florida, by Hernando de Soto. 12mo. New York, 1851.

IRVING, WASHINGTON. The Rocky Mountains, or Scenes, Incidents and Adventures in the Far West. 2 vols. 12mo. Philadelphia, 1843.

IRVING, WASHINGTON. Biography and Poetical Remains of Margaret M. Davidson. 12mo. Philadelphia, 1841.

IRVING, WASHINGTON. The Works of. 14 vols. 8vo. New York, 1849.

Vol. 1. The History of New York, from the beginning of the World to the End of the Dutch Dynasty.
2. The Sketch Book.
3, 4, 5. Columbus and his Companions.

IRVING, WASHINGTON. Works of—Continued.

6. Bracebridge Hall.
7. Tales of a Traveller.
8. Astoria.
9. The Crayon Miscellany.
10. Captain Bonnyville's Adventures.
11. Oliver Goldsmith, a Biography.
12, 13. Mahomet and his Successors.
14. The Conquest of Granada.

ISAACS, HYAM. Ceremonies, Customs, Rites and Traditions of the Jews. 8vo. London, 1836.

JACKSON, ANDREW. Life. (See Eaton, John H.)

JACKSON, CHARLES T. Second and Third Reports on the Geology of the State of Maine. 3 vols. 8vo. Augusta, 1838–1839.

JACKSON, CHARLES T. Third Annual Report on the Geology of the State of Maine. 8vo. Augusta, 1839.

JACKSON, JR., DANIEL. Alonzo and Melissa, or the Unfeeling Father. An American Tale. 24mo. Exeter, 1823.

JACKSON, JAMES. Memoir of his Son, James Jackson, Jr. 8vo. Boston, 1835.

JACKSON, WILLIAM. The Constitution of the several Indian States of America, &c. 8vo. London, 1783.

JACOB, WILLIAM. An Historical Inquiry into the Production and Consumption of the Precious Metals. 8vo. Philadelphia, 1832.

JACQUEMIN, EMILE. L'Allemagne, Agricole Industrielle et Politique Voyages faits en 1840–1842. 8vo. Paris, 1842.

JAMES, G. P. R. Dark Scenes of History. 12mo. New York, 1850.

JAMES, G. P. R. The History of Charlemagne. 18mo. New York, 1833.

JAMES, G. P. R. The History of Chivalry. 18mo. New York, 1833.

JAMES, G. P. R. The Life of Henry IV. King of France and Navarre. 2 vols. 12mo. New York, 1850.

James, William. Naval Occurrences of the Late War between Great Britain and the United States of America. 8vo. London, 1817.

*Jamieson, Alexander. A Dictionary of Mechanical Science, Arts, Manufactures and Miscellaneous Knowledge. 4to. London, 1829.

Janes, John. Sketches of Travels in Sicily, Italy and France. 12mo. Albany, 1820.

Jardine, Sir William. Natural History. (See Naturalist's Library.)

Jarvis, W. C. The Republican, or Essays on the Principles and Policy of the Free States. 12mo. Pittsfield, 1820.

Jay, William. A Review of the Causes of the Mexican War. 12mo. Boston, 1849.

Jay, William. The Life of John Jay. 2 vols. 8vo. New York, 1833.

Jefferson, Thomas. Life. (See Linn, William.)

Jefferson, Thomas. Life. (See Tucker, George.)

Jefferson, Thomas. Memoir, Correspondence and Miscellanies. Edited by Thomas Jefferson Randolph. 4 vols. 8vo. Boston, 1830.

Jefferson, Thomas. Notes on the State of Virginia. 12mo. Boston, 1832.

Jefferson's Manual. The Constitution of the United States and the Rules of the Senate and House of Representatives. 12mo. Washington, 1828.

Jeffrey, Francis, Lord. Contributions to the Edinburgh Review. (See Modern British Essayists.)

Jeffreys, Thomas. The Natural and Civil History of the French Dominions in North and South America. Fol. London, 1760.

Jenkins, John. The Art of Writing. 8vo. Cambridge, 1816.

Jenner, Edward. The Life of, with Illustrations of his Doctrines, and Selections from his Correspondence, by John Baron. 2 vols. 8vo. London, 1838.

Jennings, Isaac. Medical Reform, a Treatise on Man's Physical Being and Disorders, embracing an Outline of a Theory of Human Life, and a Theory of Disease, its Nature, Cause and Remedy. 12mo. Oberlin, 1847.

Jesse, John H. George Selwyn and his Contemporaries, with Memoirs and Notes. 4 vols. 8vo. London, 1843.

JESSE, JOHN H. Literary and Historical Memorials of London. 2 vols. 8vo. London, 1847.

JESSE, JOHN H. Memoirs of the Court of England, from the Revolution in 1688 to the Death of George III. 3 vols. 8vo. London, 1843.

JESSE, JOHN H. Memoirs of the Court of England, during the Reign of the Stuarts, including the Protectorate. 4 vols. 8vo. London, 1840.

JESSE, JOHN H. Memoirs of the Pretenders and their Adherents. 2 vols. 8vo. London, 1845.

JOHNSON, G. W. A Dictionary of Modern Gardening. 12mo. London, 1846.

JOHNSON, G. W. The Gardener. 3 vols. 18mo. London, 1849.

JOHNSON, J. F. Proceedings of the General Anti-Slavery Convention, held in London, 1843. 8vo. London, 1844.

JOHNSON, SAMUEL. Life. (See Boswell, James.)

JOHNSON, SAMUEL. Life. (See Hawkins, Sir John.)

JOHNSON, SAMUEL. The Works of. Edited by Arthur Murphy. 2 vols. 8vo. New York, 1832.

JOHNSON, SAMUEL, D. D. Life. (See Chandler, T. B.)

JOHNSON, S. W. Rural Economy, containing a Treatise on Prize Building, &c., &c. 8vo. New Brunswick, 1806.

JOHNSON, THEODORE T. Sights in the Gold Regions, and Scenes by the Way. 12mo. New York, 1849.

JOHNSON, WALTER R. A Report on American Coal. 8vo. Washington, 1844.

JOHNSON, WILLIAM. Sketches of the Life and Correspondence of General Nathaniel Greene. 2 vols. 4to. Charleston, 1822.

*JOHNSON, WILLIAM M. AND THOMAS EXLEY. The Imperial Encyclopædia. 4 vols. 4to. London.

JOHNSTON, CHARLES. Travels in Southern Abyssinia, through the Country of Adal to the Kingdom of Shoa. 2 vols. 8vo. London, 1844.

*JOHNSTON, CUTHBERT W. The Farmer's Encyclopædia: a Dictionary of Rural Affairs, adapted to the United States, by Gouverneur Emerson. 8vo. Philadelphia, 1844.

Johnston, James F. W. Contributions to Scientific Agriculture. 8vo. Edinburgh and London, 1849. *Presented by the Author.*

Johnston, James F. W. Lectures on Agricultural Chemistry and Geology. 12mo. New York, 1842. *Presented by James P. Wright, Esq.*

Johnston, James F. W. Lectures on Agricultural Chemistry and Geology. 8vo. Edinburgh and London, 1847. *Presented by Joseph Cowdin, Esq.*

Johnston, James F. W. Lectures on the General Relations which Science bears to Practical Agriculture, with Notes and Additions. 8vo. New York, 1850.

Johnston, James F. W. Notes on North America, Agricultural, Economical and Social. 2 vols. 8vo. Boston, 1851.

Jones, J. Seawell. A Defense of the Revolutionary History of the State of North Carolina. 8vo. Boston, 1834.

Jones, Sir William. Memoir of the Life and Writings. (See Teignmouth, Lord.)

Jones, William. The History of the Life of Nader Shah, King of Persia. 8vo. London, 1773.

Jones, W. A. Literary Studies; a Collection of Miscellaneous Essays. 12mo. New York, 1847.

Josephine, (Wife of Napoleon.) Life of. (See Headley, P. C.)

Josephus, Flavius. The Works of, translated by William Whiston. Revised and Illustrated, with Notes, by Rev. Samuel Burder. 2 vols. 4to. Boston, 1823.

Josephus, Flavius. Works, translated by William Whiston. 2 vols. 8vo. Boston, 1829.

Josephus, Flavius. Works. 4 vols. 8vo. New York, 1809.

Josephus, Flavius. Works. Revised and Illustrated, with Notes, by Samuel Burder. 4 vols. 8vo. New York, 1823.

Journal of the American Institute. 4 vols. 8vo. New York, 1836–1839.

*Journal of the Franklin Institute. Edited by Thomas P. Jones. 42 vols. 8vo. Philadelphia, 1828–1851. (Continued.)

Journal of Civilization, published under the Superintendence of the Society for the Advancement of Civilization. 8vo. London, 1842.

JOURNAL of the Convention of the State of New York. 8vo. Albany, 1821.

JOURNAL of the Debates and Proceedings in the Convention of Delegates chosen to Revise the Constitution of Massachusetts. 8vo. Boston, 1821.

JOURNAL of Health, conducted by an Association of Physicians. 8vo. Philadelphia, 1830.

JOURNAL of the Royal Agricultural Society of England. 5 vols. 8vo. London, 1840–1845.

JOURNAL of Science and the Arts, edited at the Royal Institution of Great Britain. 5 vols. 8vo. New York, 1817–1818.

JOURNAL of the Votes and Proceedings of the General Assembly of the Colony of New York, from 1691 to 1765. 2 vols. fol. New York, 1764–1766.

JOYCE, J. Scientific Dialogues. 3 vols. 18mo. Philadelphia, 1815.

JUAN, GEORGE, AND ANTONIO DE ULLOA. A Voyage to South America. 2 vols. 12mo. Dublin, 1758.

Ditto. Ditto. 2 vols. 12mo. London, 1758.

JUKES, J. D. Excursions in and about Newfoundland during 1839–40. London, 1842.

JULIEN, STANISLAS. Résume des Principaux Traités Chinois sur la Culture des Muriers et l'Education des Vers a Soil. 8vo. Paris, 1837.

JUNIUS. Letters. (See Heron, Robert.)

JUNIUS. Posthumous Works. (See Fellows, John.)

JUNIUS Identified with a Distinguished Living Character. 8vo. New York, 1818.

JUSTICE'S GUIDE, The, or Digest for Justices of the Peace. 8vo. New York, 1825.

KALM, PETER. Travels into North America, translated by J. R. Forster. Vol. 2. 8vo. London, 1772.

KAMES. (See HOME.)

KATER, HENRY, AND DION. LARDNER. A Treatise on Mechanics. 12mo. Philadelphia, 1832.

KAVANAGH, JULIA. Woman in France during the 18th Century. 12mo. Philadelphia, 1850.

KEATING, W. H. Narrative of Long's Expedition to the Source of St. Peter's River, Lake Winneypeck, Lake of the Woods, &c. 2 vols. Philadelphia, 1824.

KEIGHTLEY, THOMAS. The History of Rome, with a Chronological Table of Contemporary History, by J. T. Smith. 8vo. Boston, 1839.

KELLY, CHRISTOPHER. History of the French Revolution, &c. 2 vols. 4to. London, 1817.

KELLY, CHRISTOPHER. New and Complete System of Universal Geography, or a History of the World and its Inhabitants. 2 vols. 4to. London, 1817.

KELTY, MARY ANN. Memoirs of the Lives and Persecutions of the Primitive Quakers. 12mo. London, 1844.

KEMBLE, J. M. The Saxons in England. A History of the English Commonwealth till the Period of the Norman Conquest. 2 vols. 8vo. London, 1849.

KENDALL, EDWARD AUGUSTUS. Travels through the Northern Part of the United States in 1807–1808. 3 vols. 12mo. New York, 1809.

KENDALL, GEORGE W. Narrative of the Santé Fé Expedition. 2 vols. 12mo. New York, 1846.

*KENDALL, GEORGE W. The War between the United States and Mexico Illustrated. Fol. New York and Philadelphia, 1851.

KENNEDY, JOHN P. Memoirs of the Life of William Wirt. 2 vols. 8vo. Philadelphia, 1850.

*KENRICK, WILLIAM. A New Dictionary of the English Language. 4to. London, 1773.

KENT, EDWARD, DUKE OF. Life. (See Neale, Erskine.)

KENT, JAMES. Commentaries on American Law. 4 vols. 8vo. New York, 1826.

KENT, NATHANIEL. Hints to Gentlemen of Landed Property. 8vo. London, 1776.

KEPPELL, HENRY. The Expedition to Borneo for the Suppression of Piracy, with Extracts from the Journal of James Brooke. 12mo. New York, 1816.

KERR, HENRY. Travels through the Western Interior of the United States. 8vo. Elizabethtown, 1816. *Presented by Dr. Samuel Akerly.*

KERR, ROBERT. Memorial relative to the Invention of a New Method of Bleaching. 12mo. Edinburgh, 1792. *Presented by Dr. Samuel Akerly.*

KESSEY, JESSE. Treatise on Fundamental Doctrines of the Christian Religion. 12mo. Philadelphia, 1815.

KEYSLER, JOHN GEORGE. Travels through Germany, Bohemia, Hungary, Switzerland, Italy and Lorrain. 4 vols. 8vo. London, 1756.

KILBOURN, JOHN. Ohio Gazetteer, or Topographical Dictionary. 12mo. Columbus, 1821.

KIMBALL AND JAMES' Business Directory for the Mississippi Valley, 1844. 8vo. Cincinnati.

KING, CHARLES. A Memoir of the Construction, Cost and Capacity of the Croton Aqueduct, compiled from Official Documents. 4to. New York, 1843.

KING, ROBERT. The Covenanters in the North. 12mo. Aberdeen, 1846.

*KINGSLEY, J. L. AND J. P. PIRSSON. Laws and Practices of all Nations and Governments relating to Patents for Inventions, with Tables of Dues and Forms. 8vo. New York, 1848.

KIPPS, DR. A. Narrative of the Voyages undertaken by the Order of Prince Henry, with the Life of Captain Cook, with particulars of his Death. 4to. London, 1790.

KIRWAN, RICHARD. Anfangsqrunde der Mineralogie, eus dem Englischen von D. Lorens von Crell. 12mo. Berlin and Stetten, 1799.

KITTO, JOHN. Palestine; the Bible History of the Holy Land. 2 vols. 8vo. London, 1841.

KNAPP, SAMUEL L. Biographical Sketches of Eminent Lawyers, Statesmen, and Men of Letters. 8vo. Boston, 1821.

KNAPP, SAMUEL L. Female Biography, containing Notices of Distinguished Women of Different Nations and Ages. 12mo. Philadelphia, 1843.

KNAPP, SAMUEL L. Lectures on American Literature, with Remarks on some Passages of American History. 8vo. New York, 1829.

KNAPP, SAMUEL L. Library of American History, or Reprint of Standard Works. 4to. New York, 1835.

KNAPP, SAMUEL L. Life of Thomas Eddy. 8vo. New York, 1834.

KNAPP, SAMUEL L. The Bachelor, and other Tales. 12mo. New York, 1836.

KNEELAND, ABNER. Review of the Evidences of Christianity. 12mo. New York, 1829.

KNIBBE, DAVID. Katechisatie over her Kort Begrogp. 18mo. Leyden, 1697.

KNICKERBOCKER MAGAZINE. 37 vols. 8vo. New York, 1833–1851.

KNIGHT, CHARLES. Half Hours with the Best Authors, Selected and Arranged, with Short Biographical and Critical Notices. 4 vols. 12mo. New York, 1849.

KNIGHT, CHARLES. London. 6 vols. 4to. London, 1841–1844.

KNIGHT, FRANKLIN. Fac Similes of Letters from George Washington to Sir John Sinclair, on Agriculture, and other topics. 4to. Washington, 1844.

KNIGHT, FRANKLIN. Letters on Agriculture, from George Washington to Arthur Young and Sir John Sinclair; with Statistical Tables and Remarks, by Thomas Jefferson, Richard Peters, and other gentlemen, on the Economy and Management of Farms in the United States. 4to. Washington, 1847. *Presented by the Editor.*

KNIGHTON, LADY. Memoir of Sir William Knighton. 8vo. Philadelphia, 1838.

KNOX, VICESIMUS. Elegant Extracts. A New Edition, by James G. Percival. 6 vols. 8vo. Boston.

KNOX, VICESIMUS. The Spirit of Despotism. 8vo. London, 1822.

KNOWLES, JOHN. The Elements and Practice of Naval Architecture, or a Treatise on Ship Building. 4to. London, 1822.

KOHLRAUSCH, FREDERICK. A History of Germany, from the Earliest Period to the Present Time. From the last German Edition by James D. Hoas. 8vo. New York, 1805.

KORNER, CARL T. Correspondence. (See Simpson, Leonard.)

KORNER, CARL T. The Life of Carl Theodor Korner, written by his Father, with Selections from his Poems, Tales, and Dramas. From the German by G. F. Richardson. 2 vols. 8vo. London, 1845.

KOTZEBUE, MORITZ VON. Narrative of a Journey into Persia. 8vo. Philadelphia, 1820.

KUGLER, FRANCIS. The Pictorial History of Germany, during the Reign of Frederick the Great, illustrated by Adolph Menzel. 8vo. London, 1845.

LACROIX, S. F. Elements of Algebra, from the French by John Tarrar. 8vo. Cambridge, 1825.

LADY'S MAGAZINE. 8vo. London, 1774.

LA FAYETTE, GILBERT MOTEER. Memoirs of. (See Holstein, H. D.)

LAIGN, SAMUEL. Notes of a Traveller on the Social and Political State of France, Prussia, Switzerland, Italy and other parts of Europe. 8vo. Philadelphia, 1846.

LAMARTINE, ALPHONSE DE. History of the Girondists. 3 vols. 12mo. New York, 1850.

LAMBERT, ELI. A Treatise on Dower. 8vo. New York, 1834.

LANCASTER, JOSEPH. Improvements in Education, with a Sketch of the New York Free Schools. 12mo. New York, 1807. *Presented by Dr. Samuel Akerly.*

LANDER, RICHARD AND JOHN. Journal of an Expedition to the Niger. 2 vols. 18mo. New York, 1833.

LANE, EDWARD W. Selections from Kur-an, with an Interwoven Commentary. 8vo. London, 1843.

*LANE, EDWARD W. The Thousand and One Nights, or the Arabian Nights' Entertainments. A new translation from the Arabic, with Copious Notes. 3 vols. 8vo. London, 1839.

LANGALLERIE, MARQUIS DE. Memoirs of. 12mo. London, 1710.

LANGHORNE, JOHN AND WILLIAM. Plutarch's Lives. 8vo. London, 1829.

LANGLEY, B. AND T. Gothic Architecture. 4to. London, 1747.

L'ARDECHE, LAURENT. History of Napoleon, from the French, with 500 Illustrations after Designs by Horace Vernet, and 20 Original Portraits. 8vo. New York, 1848.

Lardner, Dionysius. First Six Books of the Elements of Euclid. 8vo. London, 1848.

Lardner, Dion. History of Maritime and Inland Discovery. 2 vols. 12mo. Boston, 1833.

Lardner, Dion. Popular Lectures on Science and Art. 2 vols. 8vo. New York, 1846.

Lardner, Dion. Popular Lectures on the Steam Engine, with additions by James Renwick. 12mo. New York, 1828.

Lardner, Dion. The Steam Engine, familiarly explained and illustrated, with an Historical Sketch of its Invention and Progressive Improvement. With Additions and Notes by James Renwick. 8vo. Philadelphia, 1849.

Lardner, Dion. Treatise on Hydrostatics and Pneumatics. With Notes by R. F. Joslin. 12mo. Philadelphia, 1832.

Las Cases. Journal of the Private Life and Conversation of the Emperor Napoleon, at St. Helena. 3 vols. 8vo. New York, 1823.

Last of the Plantagenets; an Historical Romance, illustrating some of the Public Events and Domestic and Ecclesiastical Manners of the 15th and 16th Centuries. 12mo. London, 1839.

Lasteyrie, C. P. Abhandlung über des Spanische Schafvieh ausdem Franzoesischen ubersezt aus Herrn Lecbarzt Thaer's englischer Landwirthchaft. 12mo. Hamburg, 1800.

Lasteryrie, C. P. A Treatise on Pastel or Woad, translated by H. A. S. Dearborn. 12mo. Boston, 1816.

Latham, John. A General History of Birds. 5 vols. 4to. Winchester.

Lathbury, Thomas. Guy Fawkes, or a Complete History of the Gunpowder Treason, 1605. 12mo. London, 1839.

Lathrop, Joseph. Sermons on the Mode and Subjects of Christian Baptism. 12mo. New York, 1808.

Lathrop, Leonard E. The Farmer's Library, or Essays on the Science of Agriculture. 12mo. Rochester, 1828.

Latrobe, Charles J. The Rambler in Mexico. 8vo. London, 1846.

Lavater. The Pocket Lavater, or the Science of Physiognomy. 18mo. New York, 1813.

LAWSON, J. Episcopal Church of Scotland, from the Reformation to the Revolution. 8vo. Edinburgh, 1844.

LAYARD, AUSTIN H. Nineveh and its Remains. 2 vols. 8vo. New York, 1850.

LEAKE, STEPHEN M. An Historical Account of English Money. 8vo. London, 1793.

LEAKE, WILLIAM M. Travels in the Morea, with a Map and Plans. 3 vols. 8vo. London, 1830.

LE BLOND, M. L'Arithmetique et la Géométrie de l'Officier. 8vo. Paris, 1767.

LECOUNT, PETER A. Practical Treatise on Railways. 8vo. Edinburgh, 1839.

LECTURES on Agricultural Chemistry and Geology. 12mo. New York, 1842.

LECTURES on the Application of Chemistry and Geology to Agriculture. 12mo. New York, 1844.

LEDYARD, JOHN. Life. (See Sparks, Jared.)

LEE, GEN. CHARLES. The Life and Memoirs of. 12mo. New York, 1813.

LEE, HENRY. Memoirs of the War in the Southern Department of the United States. 8vo. Washington, 1827.

LEE, HENRY. The Campaigns in the Carolinas in 1781. 8vo. Philadelphia, 1824.

LEE, MRS. R. Memoir of Baron Cuvier. 12mo. New York, 1833.

LEE, RICHARD HENRY. Life of Arthur Lee. 2 vols. 8vo. Boston, 1829.

LEFEORE, SIR GEORGE. The Nerves; their Influence and Importance in Health and Disease. 8vo. London, 1844.

LEGARÉ, HUGH S. Writings of, edited by his Sister. 2 vols. 8vo. Charleston, 1846.

LEGENDS of the Library at Lilies, by the Lord and Lady There. 2 vols. 12mo. Philadelphia, 1833.

LEGGET, WILLIAM. A Collection of the Political Writings of. Selected and Arranged, with a Preface, by Theodore Sedgewick, Jr. 2 vols. 12mo. New York, 1840.

Legitimate Consequences of Reform, and an Exposure of the Abuses in Church and State, with a Detailed Account of the Chief Acts of the Grey Administration. 8vo. Edinburgh, 1834.

Le Gros, W. B. Fables and Tales, suggested by the Frescoes of Pompeii and Herculaneum. 4to. London, 1835.

Leland, Thomas. The History of the Life and Reign of Philip, King of Macedon. 4to. London, 1761.

Lemaire, M. Memoire sur l'Administration de la Police, in MS., written in 1776. Fol. Paris.

Lempriere, I. Universal Biography. Selections and Additions by Eleazer Lord. 2 vols. New York, 1825.

Lempriere, William. Popular Lectures on the Study of Natural History, &c. 8vo. London, 1830.

Leoni, James. Designs for Public and Private Buildings. Fol. London, 1726.

Le Sage, Alain René. Adventures of Gil Blas of Santillane, translated by Tobias Smollett. 3 vols. 12mo. New York, 1824.

Le Sage, Alain René. The Devil upon Two Sticks. 12mo. London, 1758.

Lescallier, C. Vocabulaire des Termes de Marinè, Anglois-François et François-Anglois. 8vo. Paris, 1800.

Lessons on Shells, by the Author of "Lessons on Objects." 18mo. New York, 1842.

Lester, C. Edwards, and Andrew Foster. The Life and Voyages of Americus Vespucius. 8vo. New York, 1846.

Letters and Essays in favor of Public Liberty. 3 vols. 12mo. London, 1774.

Letters between John Locke and Several of his Friends. 12mo. London, 1708.

Letters from Buenos Ayres and Chili, with an Original History of Chili, by the Author of "Letters from Paraguay." 8vo. London, 1819.

Letters from Virginia, from the French. 12mo. Baltimore, 1816.

Letters from the Danube, by the Author of "Gisella," "Second Love," &c. 2 vols. 8vo. London, 1847.

LETTERS from the Old World, by a Lady of New York. 2 vols. 12mo. New York, 1840.

LETTERS of a Mother to her Daughter. 12mo.

LETTERS of the British Spy. 18mo. Baltimore.

LETTERS on the Eastern States. 12mo. New York, 1820.

LETTERS on the Natural History and Internal Resources of the State of New York. By Hibernias. 12mo. New York, 1822.

LETTERS on the Writings of the Fathers of the First Two Centuries, with Reflections on the Oxford Tracts, and Strictures on the Records of the Church. By Misopapisticus. 8vo. London, 1844.

LEWALD, FANNY. The Italians at Home. From the German by the Countess d'Avigdor. 2 vols. 12mo. London, 1848.

LEWIS, G. H. The Life of Robespierre, with Extracts from his Unpublished Correspondence. 12mo. Philadelphia, 1849.

LEWIS, M. G. Life and Correspondence. 2 vols. 8vo. London, 1839.

LEWIS, AND CLARK, CAPTAINS. The Navigator. 12mo. Pittsburgh, 1818.

LIBERIA, or the Early History, &c., of the American Colony of Free Negroes on the Coast of Africa. 18mo. Edinburgh, 1831.

LIEBIG, JUSTUS. Chemistry in its Applications to Agriculture and Physiology, edited from the Manuscript of the Author by Lyon Playfair. 8vo. London, 1843.

Ditto. Ditto. 12mo. Cambridge, 1843.

LIFE'S LESSONS. A Narrative by the Author of "Tales that might be true." 12mo. New York, 1839.

LINCOLN, WILLIAM. History of Worcester. 8vo. Worcester, 1837.

LINDLEY, GEORGE AND JOHN. Guide to the Orchard and Fruit Gardens. Notes and Additions by Michael Floy. 12mo. New York, 1833.

*LINDLEY, JOHN. The Vegetable Kingdom, or the Structure, Classification, and Uses of Plants. 8vo. London, 1846.

LINDMARK, JOHN. The Vigilant Farmer, a Western Tale; and the Magic Stone, an Eastern Tale. 18mo. New York, 1832.

LINGARD, JOHN. A History of England, from the Invasion of the Romans. 5th Edition. 4 vols. 8vo. Paris, 1840.

LINN, WILLIAM. Life of Thomas Jefferson. 12mo. Ithica, 1834.

LINN, WILLIAM. Sermons, Historical and Characteristical. 12mo. New York, 1791.

LINQUET, M. Memoirs sur la Bastille. 8vo. Londres, 1783.

LIST OF THE LORDS Spiritual and Temporal. 12mo. London, 1741.

LITURGIE FRANÇAISE. 18mo.

LIVERPOOL, STRANGERS IN, or a History and Descriptive View of the Town of Liverpool and its Environ. 12mo. Liverpool, 1825.

LIVES and Voyages of Drake, Cavendish, and Dampier. 18mo. New York, 1832.

LIVES of Eminent Scotsmen. By the Society of Ancient Scots. 2 vols. 18mo. London, 1821.

LIVES of John Leland, Thomas Hearne, and Anthony A. Wood, and an Account of their Writings and Publications, from Original Papers. 2 vols. 8vo. Oxford, 1762.

LIVINGSTON, ROBERT R. Essay on Sheep. 8vo. New York, 1809.

Ditto. Ditto. 8vo. New York and Boston, 1809–1811.

LIVIUS, TITUS. History of Rome. Translated, with Notes and Illustrations, by George Baker. 6 vols. 8vo. Baltimore, 1823.

LIVIUS, TITUS. The Roman History, from the Foundation of Rome to the Middle of the Reign of Augustus, with the Supplement of the learned John Freinshomins. 8vo. London, 1840.

LOCKE, JOHN. An Essay concerning the Human Understanding, with a Life of the Author. 2 vols. 8vo.

LOCKHART, J. G. The History of Buonaparte. 2 vols. 18mo. New York, 1833.

LOLME, J. L. DE. The Constitution of England. 8vo. London, 1821.

Ditto. Ditto. 12mo. London, 1796.

LONDON. (See Knight, Charles.)

*LONDON ENCYCLOPÆDIA. 22 vols. 8vo. London.

LONDON JOURNAL of Arts and Sciences. Vol. 1. 8vo. London, 1820.

*LONDON JOURNAL of Arts and Sciences, and Register of Patent Inventions. Conducted by William Newton. Conjoined series. — vols. 8vo. London, 1832–1851. *Presented by the Editor, in part.*

London Quarterly Review. 9 vols. 8vo. New York, 1834–1842.

London and Westminster Review. 4 vols. 8vo. New York, 1836–1840.

Long, George. The Geography of America and the West Indies. 8vo. London, 1841.

Longworth, David. American Almanac, New York Register, and City Directory, 1796, 1797, 1803 to 1817–1818. 15 vols. 12mo.

Longworth, Thomas. New York Register and City Directory, 1818–1819 to 1842–1843. 22 vols. 12mo.

Loomis, Elias. The Recent Progress of Astronomy, especially in the United States. 8vo. New York, 1850.

*Loosey, Charles F. Collection of Laws of Patent Privileges for all the Countries of Europe, the United States and West Indies. 8vo. Vienna, 1849.

Lord, E. Principles of Currency and Banking. 12mo. New York, 1829.

Lossing, Benson J. Seventeen Hundred and Seventy Six, or the War of Independence. 8vo. New York, 1849.

Lossing, Benson J. The Pictorial Field Book of the Revolution. 2 vols. 8vo. New York, 1851.

Louis XIV. Memoirs of Himself, and addressed to his Son. From the French. 2 vols. 8vo. London, 1806.

Low, David. Elements of Practical Agriculture. Adapted to the United States, by S. Fleet. 8vo. New York, 1839. *Presented by Samuel Fleet, Esq.*

Low, Hugh. Sarawak; its Inhabitants and Productions. 8vo. London, 1848.

Lowe, Joseph. Present State of England in Regard to Agriculture, Trade and Finance. 8vo. New York, 1824.

Lowndes, T. The Duties, Drawbacks and Bounties of Customs and Excise, payable in Great Britain on Merchandise. 8vo. Liverpool, 1803.

Lowrie, W. F. Toxicologie, or a Treatise on Internal Poisons. 8vo. New York, 1832.

Lyell, Sir Charles. A Second Visit to the United States of America. 2 vols. 8vo. New York, 1849.

LYNCH, W. F. Narrative of the United States Expedition to the River Jordan, and the Dead Sea. 8vo. Philadelphia, 1850.

Ditto. Ditto. 12mo. New York, 1850.

LYTTON, SIR E. BULWER. Harold, the Last of Saxon Kings. 3 vols. 8vo. London, 1849.

MAANDELYKE wittreksels of Boekzaal der Geleerde Waerelt. 12mo. Amsterdam, 1739.

MABLY, ABBE DE. Remarks on the Government and Laws of the United States. 8vo. London, 1784.

MACALLESTER, OLIVER. A Series of Letters discovering the Scheme projected by France in 1759. 4to. London, 1767.

MACAULAY, THOMAS B. Essays, Critical and Miscellaneous. 8vo. Philadelphia, 1850.

MACAULAY, THOMAS B. The History of England from the Accession of James II. 2 vols. 8vo. New York, 1849.

MACAULEY, JAMES. History of the State of New York. 3 vols. 8vo. New York, 1829.

MACBEAN, ALEXANDER. Dictionary of the Bible. 8vo. London, 1779.

MACFARLANE, CHARLES. Lives and Exploits of Banditti and Robbers. 2 vols. 8vo. New York, 1833.

MACFARLANE, CHARLES. Turkey and its Destiny. 2 vols. 8vo. Philadelphia, 1850.

MACGILLIVRAY, W. The Travels and Researches of Alexander Von Humboldt. 18mo. New York, 1833.

MACGOWAN, REV. JOHN. Looking Glass for Professors of Religion, consisting of Tracts and Tract Subjects. 12mo. New York, 1810.

*MACGREGOR, JOHN. Commercial Statistics, a Digest of the Productive Resources, Commercial Legislation, Customs, Tariffs, &c., &c., of all Nations. 3 vols. 8vo. London, 1844–1847.

MACHIAVELLI, NIC. Works, translated by Ellis Farneworth. 4 vols. 8vo. London, 1775.

MACHINES. Book of Plates of. Fol.

MACKINTOSH, SIR JAMES. The History of England. 3 vols. 12mo. Philadelphia, 1830.

MACKINTOSH, SIR JAMES. General View of the Progress of Ethical Philosophy. 8vo. Philadelphia, 1832.

MACKINTOSH, SIR JAMES. Miscellaneous Works. (See Modern British Essayists.)

MACKRAY, WILLIAM. Effects of the Reformation upon Civil Society. 12mo. New York, 1830.

MACNEVIN, WILLIAM J. Ramble through Switzerland. 8vo. Dublin, 1803. *Presented by Dr. Samuel Akerly.*

MAFFITT, JOHN N. Cabinet of Religion, Education, &c. Vol. 5. 8vo. New York, 1831.

MAGAZINE of Domestic Economy. 7 vols. 8vo. London, 1831–1842.

MAGAZINE of Domestic Economy. New Series. 2 vols. 8vo. London, 1831 and 1842.

MAGAZINE of Horticulture. Conducted by C. M. and P. B. Hovey. 17 vols. 8vo. Boston, 1835–1851.

MAGAZINE of Science, and School of Arts. 6 vols. 8vo. London, 1840–1845.

MAGNETISME ANIMAL. Memoirs pour servir a l'Histoire et a l'Etablissement du. 8vo. Paris, 1809.

MAHAN, D. H. Elementary Course of Civil Engineering. 8vo. New York, 1838.

MAHON, LORD. The Life of Belisarius. 12mo. Philadelphia, 1832.

MAIN, THOMAS J., AND THOMAS BROWN. The Marine Steam Engine. 8vo. London, 1849.

MAINTENON, MADAME DE. Secret Correspondence with the Princess des Ursins, from the French. 3 vols. 8vo. London, 1827.

MAISON Rustique du XIX[e] Siecle. 5 vols. 8vo. Paris, 1844–1845.

MALHAN, REV. JOHN. Naval Gazetteer, or Seaman's Complete Guide. 2 vols. 8vo. Boston, 1797.

MALLORY, DANIEL. The Life and Speeches of Henry Clay. 2 vols. 8vo. New York, 1843. *Presented by the Author.*

*MALTE BRUN, M. A System of Universal Geography. With Additions and Corrections by James G. Percival. 3 vols. 4to. Boston, 1834.

MALTE BRUN, M. Tableau de la Pologue Ancienne et Moderne. Nouvelle Edition par a L. Chodzko. 2 vols. 8vo. Paris, 1830.

MALTE BRUN, M. Universal Geography, or a Description of all parts of the World on a New Plan. 8 vols. 8vo. Boston, 1824.

MALTHUS, T. R. An Essay on the Principles of Population. 3 vols. 8vo. London.

MANNING, ROBERT. Book of Fruits. 12mo. Salem, 1838.

MANTELL, GIDEON A. Geological Excursions round the Isle of Wight, and along the Adjacent Coast of Dorcetshire. 12mo. London, 1847.

MANUAL for the Use of the Convention to Revise the Constitution of the State of New York. 12mo. New York, 1846.

MANUAL for the Use of the Legislature of the State of New York for 1845. 18mo. Albany, 1845.

MAPES, JAMES J. American Repertory of Arts, Sciences and Manufactures. 4 vols. 8vo. New York, 1840–1842. *Presented by the Editor.*

MARBOIS, BARBE. History of Louisiana. 8vo. Philadelphia, 1830.

MARMONTEL, J. F. Memoirs of. 2 vols. 12mo. Philadelphia, 1807.

MARMONTEL, J. F. Moral Tales, from the French. 2 vols. 24mo. London.

MARSEILLE. Tableau Historique, et Politique, Ancienne et Moderne. 12mo. Marseille, 1810.

MARSHALL, H. History of Kentucky. 2 vols. 8vo. Frankfort, 1824.

MARSHALL, JOHN. Life of George Washington. 5 vols. 8vo. Philadelphia, 1804.

MARSHALL, JOHN. Writings on the Federal Constitution. 8vo. Boston, 1839.

MARSHALL, MR. The Rural Economy of the Midland Counties. 2 vols. 8vo. London, 1796.

MARSHALL, MR. The Rural Economy of Norfolk, comprising the Management of Landed Estates and the Present Practice of Husbandry in that County. 2 vols. 8vo. London, 1795.

MARSHALL, MR. The Rural Economy of the Southern Counties. 2 vols. 8vo. London, 1798.

MARSHALL, MR. The Rural Economy of Yorkshire. 2 vols. 8vo. London, 1796.

MARSHALL, MR. Treatise on Planting and Rural Ornament. 2 vols. 8vo. London, 1803.

MARTIN, BENJAMIN. Bibliotheca Technologica; or a Philological Library of Literature, Arts and Sciences. 8vo. London, 1787.

MARTIN, J. Dictionaire de Poche. 12mo. Leipzig.

MARTIN, JOHN. French Homonyms, or a Collection of Words, Similar in Sound but Different in Meaning and Spelling. 12mo. New York, 1807. *Presented by Dr. Samuel Akerly.*

MARTIN, JOSEPH. History and Gazetteer of Virginia. 8vo. Charlottesville. 1836.

MARTIN, R. MONTGOMERY. British Colonial Library. 8 vols. 12mo. London, 1836–1838.

Vol. 3. Southern Africa.
4, 5. West Indies, &c.
6. Nova Scotia, &c.
7. British Possessions in the Mediterranean.
8, 9. History of the Possessions of the East India Company.
10. British Possessions of the Indian and Atlantic Oceans.

MARTIN, R. MONTGOMERY. China, Political, Commercial and Social. 2 vols. 8vo. London, 1847.

MARTIN, REV. HENRY. Memoir of. (See Sargent, Jr., John.)

MARTINEAU, HARRIET. How to Observe. Morals and Manners. 12mo. New York, 1838.

MARTINELLI, JULES. Manuel d'Agriculture. 12mo. Bordeaux, 1846.

MARTYN, THOMAS. The Language of Botany, being a Dictionary of Botanical Terms. 8vo. London, 1807.

MAS, POCCO. Scenes and Adventures in Spain from 1835 to 1840. 2 vols. 8vo. London, 1845.

MASON, JOHN M. Sermons, Essays and Miscellanies. 4 vols. 8vo. New York, 1832.

MASSACHUSETTS Agricultural Repository and Journal. Conducted by the Trustees of the Massachusetts Agricultural Society. 9 vols. 8vo. Boston, 1801–1826. *Presented by the Society.*

*MASSACHUSETTS Mercury. Fol. Boston, 1800.

MASSILLON, J. B. Sermons, Selected and Translated by William Dickson. 2 vols. 8vo. Philadelphia, 1818.

MASSY, W. Essays on the Origin and Progress of Letters. 12mo. London, 1763.

MATHER, WILLIAM W. Elements of Geology, for the Use of Schools and Academies. 18mo. New York, 1838.

MATTHISSON, F. Letters, written from Various Parts of the Continent, translated by Anne Plumptree. 8vo. London, 1799.

MATY, M. Miscellaneous Works of Lord Chesterfield. 2 vols. 4to. London, 1777.

MAUNDER, SAMUEL. Treasury of History. 12mo. London, 1850.

MAUNDER, SAMUEL. Treasury of Natural History. 12mo. London, 1849.

MAVOR, WILLIAM. An Historical Account of the most Celebrated Voyages, Travels and Discoveries, from the Time of Columbus to the Present Period. 12 vols. 4, 5–9–13–16, 17, 18, 19, 20, 21, 22, 23. 18mo. Philadelphia, 1802–1803.

MAVOR, WILLIAM. The British Tourists. 5 vols. 18mo. London, 1798.

MAXWELL, JOHN S. The Czar, his Court and People, including a Tour in Norway and Sweden. 8vo. New York, 1848.

MAXWELL, W. H. Legends of Cheviots and the Lammemuir; a Companion to "the Wild Sports of the West." 8vo. London, 1849.

MAXWELL, W. H. Rambling Recollections of a Soldier of Fortune. 8vo. Dublin, 1842.

MAXWELL, W. H. Wild Sports of the West. 12mo. London, 1850.

McCARTNEY, WASHINGTON. The Origin and Progress of the United States. 12mo. Philadelphia, 1847.

*McCULLOCH, J. R. A Dictionary, Practical, Theoretical and Historical, of Commerce and Commercial Navigation. 8vo. London, 1835.

McCULLOCH, J. R. Principles of Political Economy. 8vo. London, 1830.

McCulloch, J. R. Statistical Account of the British Empire. 2 vols. 8vo. London, 1837.

McCulloch, J. R. The Literature of Political Economy. 8vo. London, 1845.

*McCulloch, J. R. Universal Gazetteer, a Dictionary, Geographical, Statistical and Historical, of the World, adapted to the United States by Daniel Haskel. 2 vols. 8vo. New York, 1845.

McCulloch, W. Torrens. The Use and Study of History. 8vo. Dublin, 1842.

McKenney, Thomas. Sketches of a Tour to the Lakes. 8vo. Baltimore, 1827.

McLean, John. Notes of a Twenty-Five Years' Service in the Hudson's Bay Territory. 2 vols. 8vo. London, 1849.

Mease, James and Thomas Porter. Picture of Philadelphia. 12mo. Philadelphia, 1831.

Mechanics' Magazine. Edited by J. C. Robertson. 4 vols. 8vo. London, 1844–1845.

Mechanics' Magazine, and Register of Inventions and Improvements. Edited by D. K. Minor. 9 vols. 8vo. New York, 1833–1837.

Mechanics' Magazine, Museum, Register, Journal, and Gazette. 9 vols. 8vo. London, 1823–1829.

Mechel, J. F. Manual of Anatomy. From the French, with Notes by A. Sidney Doane. 3 vols. 8vo. New York, 1831.

Medical and Surgical Register. 8vo. New York, 1818.

Medical Intelligencer, Conducted by Jerome V. C. Smith. 4to. Boston, 1823–1824.

Medical Repository, The. Conducted by Samuel L. Mitchell, and Elihu H. Smith. 15 vols. 8vo. New York, 1804–1812.

Melish, John. Travels through the United States of America. 8vo. London, 1818.

Memoires d'Agriculture, d'Economie, Rurale et Domestiqua. Publics par la Society Royal et Centrale d'Agriculture. 40 vols. 8vo. Paris, 1814–1846.

Memoirs, Historical and Military, with a Military Dictionary. 12mo.

MEMOIRS of the American Academy of the Arts and Sciences. 4to. Boston, 1785.

MEMOIRS of the Board of Agriculture of the State of New York. 2 vols. 8vo. Albany, 1821–1826.

Ditto. Ditto. Vol. 3. 8vo. Albany, 1826.

Ditto. Ditto. 4to. New York, 1792.

MEMOIRS of the House of Bradenburg, by the Hand of a Master. 12mo. London, 1751.

MEMOIRS of a Nullifier, written by Himself. By a Native of the South. 12mo. Columbia, 1832.

MEMOIRS of the Philadelphia Society for Promoting Agriculture. 5 vols. 8vo. Philadelphia, 1815–1826.

MEMOIRS, Secret, of the Royal Family of France, during the Revolution. By a Lady of Rank. 8vo. Philadelphia, 1826.

MEMOIRS of what has passed in Christendom from 1672–1679. 12mo. London.

MENDAM, REV. JOSEPH. An Index of Prohibited Books, by command of Gregory 16th in 1835. 12mo. London, 1840.

MERCANTILE CALCULATION. A New System of, with a Description of Universal Trade, by an old Merchant. 4to. London, 1795.

MERCHANTS' MAGAZINE. Edited by Freeman Hunt. 25 vols. 8vo. New York, 1839–1851. (Continued.)

MERIMEE, PROSPER. The History of Peter the Cruel, King of Castile and Leon. 2 vols. 12mo. London, 1849.

MERRILL, ELIPHALET. Gazetteer of New Hampshire. 8vo.

MESSAGES delivered to the Common Council during the Mayoralty of Gideon Lee. 8vo. New York, 1833–1834.

MESSAGE from the President of the United States. 8vo. Washington, 1842.

METAL, A Treatise on the Progressive Improvement and Present State of Manufactures in. 3 vols. 12mo. London, 1842.

METCALF, SAMUEL L. New Theory of Terrestrial Magnetism. 8vo. New York, 1833.

METROPOLITAN MAGAZINE. 3 vols. 8vo. New York, 1841–1842.

MICHELET, M. History of France, translated by G. H. Smith. 2 vols. 8vo. New York, 1847.

MICHELET, M. History of the Roman Republic, translated by William Hazlitt. 12mo. London, 1847.

MICHELET, M. The Life of Luther, translated by William Hazlitt. 12mo. London, 1846.

MIDDLETON, CONYERS. The Life of M. T. Cicero. 8vo. London, 1839.

MEGNET, F. A. History of the French Revolution, from 1789 to 1814. 12mo. London, 1846.

MILDMAY, WILLIAM. Political Treatises. 4to. London, 1766.

MILES, PLINY. Mnemotechny, or the Art of Memory, Theoretical and Practical, with a Mnemotechnic Dictionary. 12mo. New York, 1849.

MILITARY MEMOIRS of Four Brothers. By the Survivor. 8vo. London, 1829.

MILL, JOHN STUART. Principles of Political Economy. 2 vols. 8vo. Boston, 1848.

MILLER, EBENEZER. A Companion to the Atlas, or a Series of Geographical Fables, on a New Plan. 8vo. London, 1838.

MILLER, JOHN. Memoirs of the Life of General Miller in the Service of the Republic of Peru. 2 vols. 8vo. London, 1828.

MILLER, JONATHAN P. The Condition of Greece in 1827 and 1828. 12mo. New York, 1828.

MILLINGEN, J. G. The History of Duelling, including Narratives of the Most Remarkable Personal Encounters, from the Earliest Period to the Present Time. 2 vols. 8vo. London, 1841.

MILLS, CHARLES. The History of the Crusades. 8vo. Philadelphia, 1844.

MILMAN, H. H. The History of the Jews, from the Earliest Period to the Present Time. 3 vols. 18mo. New York, 1833.

MILTON, JOHN. Prose and Poetical Works. 8vo. London, 1834.

MILTON, Young, Gray, Beattie and Collins. Poetical Works. 8vo. Philadelphia, 1836.

MINERVA, THE, or Literary, Entertaining, and Scientific Journal. Edited by George Houston and James G. Brooks. 2 vols. 8vo. New York, 1824–1825.

MINOT, GEORGE R. The History of the Insurrections in Massachusetts. 8vo. Boston, 1810.

MINSTREL, THE, or a Selection of Admired Songs. 18mo. Albany, 1822.

MINUTES and Proceedings of the Institution of Civil Engineers. 2 vols. 8vo. London, 1844. *Presented by the Society.*

MIRABEAU, a Life History. 12mo. Philadelphia, 1848.

*MISCELLANEOUS Newspapers. Fol. 1802–1803.

*MISCELLANEOUS Newspapers. Fol. 1823–1824.

MISCELLANIES, first published under the name of the "Talisman," by G. C. Verplanck, W. C. Bryant and R. C. Sands. Vol. 2. 18mo. New York, 1833.

MISSIONARY HERALD for 1821. 8vo. Boston.

MITCHEL, O. M. The Planetary and Stellar Worlds. 12mo. New York, 1851.

MITCHEL'S Map of the World. An Accompaniment to. 8vo. Philadelphia, 1837.

MITFORD, MARY RUSSELL. Our Village, or Sketches of Rural Character and Scenery. 2 vols. 8vo. London, 1848.

MITFORD, WILLIAM. The History of Greece, with a Brief Memoir of the Author, by Lord Redesdale. 8 vols. 8vo. London, 1838.

MODERN BRITISH ESSAYISTS. 8 vols. 8vo. Philadelphia, 1848–1850.

Vol. 1. Critical and Miscellaneous Essays. By T. B. Macaulay.
2. Miscellaneous Essays. By Archibald Alison.
3. Works of the Rev. J. Sidney Smith.
4. Recreations of Christopher North. By John Wilson.
5. Critical and Miscellaneous Essays. By Thomas Carlyle.
6. Contributions to the Edinburgh Review. By Francis, Lord Jeffrey.
7. Critical and Miscellaneous Writings and Essays. By T. N. Talfourd, and James Stephens.
8. Miscellaneous Works of Sir James Mackintosh.

MODERN GAZETTEER, or Geographical Dictionary of the World. 2 vols. 8vo. Edinburgh, 1810.

MODERN TRAVELLER, THE. 4 vols. 18mo. London, 1826–1827.

MODERN TRAVELLER, THE. 10 vols. 18mo. Boston, 1830–1831.

Molina, J. Ignatius. The Geography, Natural and Civil History of Chili. Translated by Richard Alsop. 2 vols. 8vo. Middletown, 1808.

Moll, L. Colonization et Agriculture de l'Algérie. 2 vols. 8vo. Paris, 1845.

Monroe, James. Narrative of a Tour of Observation through the Northeastern and Northwestern parts of the United States. 12mo. Philadelphia, 1818.

Monroe, James. View of the Foreign Affairs of the United States. 8vo. Philadelphia, 1797.

Monstrelet Euguerraud, The Chronicles of. Translated by Thomas Johnes. 2 vols. 4to. London, 1849.

Montagu, Edward W. Reflections on the Rise and Fall of the Ancient Republics. 8vo. London, 1769.

Montagu, Mary W. Letters and Works. Edited by Lord Wharncliffe. 2 vols. 8vo. Philadelphia, 1837.

Montaigne, Michel de. The Works of, comprising his Essays, Letters, and Journey through Germany and Italy, with Notes from all the Commentators, &c., &c. Translated by William Hazlitt. 8vo. Philadelphia, 1849.

Montefiore, J. American Trader's Companion. 8vo. Philadelphia, 1811.

Montefiore, Joshua. Commercial Dictionary. 3 vols. 8vo. Philadelphia, 1804.

Montesquieu, Charles de Secondat, (Baron de). Spirit of Laws, from the French, by Thomas Nugent. 2 vols. 8vo. London, 1823.

Montgaillard, M. Mir. Situation of England in 1811. 8vo. New York, 1812.

Montgomery, James. Journal of Voyages and Travels in the South Sea Islands, China, India, &c. 3 vols. Boston, 1832.

Montgomery, James. Practical Detail of the Cotton Manufacture in the United States of America. 8vo. Glasgow, 1840.

Monthly Magazine, The, or British Register. 8 vols. 8vo. London, 1815–1819.

Monthly Review, or Literary Journal. 4 vols. 8vo. London, 1756–1766–1767, and 1788.

Monthly Review, or Literary Journal, from 1749 to 1816. 187 vols. 8vo. London.

Moore, John. View of the Causes and Progress of the French Revolution. 2 vols. 8vo. London, 1795.

Moore, John. View of Society and Manners in France, Switzerland, Germany, and Italy. 2 vols. 12mo. Philadelphia, 1783.

Moore, John H. The Practical Navigator. 8vo. London, 1796.

Moore, John H. The Practical Navigator and Seaman's Assistant. 8vo. London, 1782.

Moore, N. F. Ancient Mineralogy. 12mo. New York, 1834.

Moore, Oliver. The Staff Officer, or, the Soldier of Fortune. 2 vols. 12mo. Philadelphia, 1833.

Moore, S. S. and T. W. Jones. The Traveller's Dictionary, or, a Pocket Companion. 8vo. Philadelphia, 1802.

Moore, Thomas. Lalla Rookh, an Oriental Romance. 8vo. London, 1820.

Moore, Thomas. Memoirs of the Life of Richard B. Sheridan. 8vo. Philadelphia, 1825.

Moore, Thomas. Poetical Works. 8vo. Philadelphia, 1831.

More, Hannah. Life, &c. (See Thompson, Henry.)

More, Hannah. Sacred Dramas, chiefly intended for Young Persons. 12mo. Newark, 1806.

More, Hannah. The Works of. 2 vols. 8vo. New York, 1848.

Morell, Thomas. Studies in History, containing the History of England from James I. to the Death of George III. 2 vols. 12mo. London, 1822.

Morgan, Lady. Florence Macarthy, an Irish Tale. 2 vols. 12mo. Philadelphia, 1819.

Morgan, Lady. France in 1829–1830. 2 vols. 12mo. New York, 1830.

Morgan, Lady. Woman and her Master. 2 vols. 8vo. London, 1840.

Morgan, Mr. Moral Philosopher. 3 vols. 8vo London, 1737.

Morin, Arthur. Expériences sur les Roues Hydrauliques. 4to. Paris, 1836. *Presented through M. Alexandre Vattemare.*

Morin, Arthur. Expériences sur le Tirage des Voitures, Faites en 1837 et 1838. 4to. Paris, 1839. *Presented through M. Alexandre Vattemare.*

MORRIS, GEORGE P. The Deserted Bride, and other Poems. 8vo. New York, 1838.

MORRIS, GOUVERNEUR. Life. (See Sparks, Jared.)

MORSE, JEDEDIAH. American Universal Geography. 2 vols. 8vo. Boston, 1805.

MORSE, JEDEDIAH. Annals of the American Revolution. 8vo. Hartford, 1824.

MORSE, JEDEDIAH. Report on Indian Affairs. 8vo. New Haven, 1822.

MORSE, JEDEDIAH. The American Gazetteer. 2 vols. 8vo. Boston, 1810.

MORSE, JEDEDIAH, and Elijah Parrish. A Compendious History of New England. 8vo. London, 1808.

MOISE, MISS PENINA. Fancy's Sketch Book. 12mo. Charleston, 1833.

MORTIMER, JOHN. Report of the Trial of the Reading Mail Robbers. 12mo. Philadelphia, 1830.

MOULTON, R. K. The Constitutional Guide. 18mo. New York, 1834.

MOZART. Life. (See Bombet, L. A. C.)

MUCH INSTRUCTION from Little Reading, or Extracts from some of the most Approved Authors. 5 vols. 12mo. New York, 1827.

MUDIE, ROBERT. A Popular Guide to the Observation of Nature. 18mo. New York, 1833.

MÜGGE, THEODORE. Switzerland in 1847, and its Condition, Political, Social, Moral and Physical, before the War. Edited by Mrs. Percy Sinnett. 2 vols. 8vo. London, 1848.

MUHLENBURG, H. A. The Life of Major General Peter Muhlenburg of the Revolutionary Army. 12mo. Philadelphia, 1849.

MULLER, JOHN VON. Universal History. From the German. 4 vols. 12mo. Boston, 1834.

MULTHUS, T. R. Additions to an Essay on the Principle of Population. 8vo. Georgetown, 1831.

MURAT, ACHILLES. The United States of North America, with a Note on Negro Slavery, by Junius Redivivus. 12mo. London, 1833.

MURPHY, JOHN. Treatise on the Art of Weaving. 8vo. Glasgow, 1831.

MURRAY, HUGH. The Encyclopædia of Geography. Revised, with Additions, by Thomas G. Bradford. 3 vols. 8vo. Philadelphia, 1838.

MURRAY, JOHN F. The World of London. A New Series. 2 vols. 8vo. London, 1845.

MURRAY, LINDLEY. English Grammar. 8vo. New York, 1814.

MURRAY, LINDLEY. The Power of Religion on the Mind in Retirement, Affliction, and at the Approach of Death. 12mo. New York, 1838. *Presented by the Society of Friends.*

MURRAY, W. R. The Cyclopædia of Useful and Entertaining Knowledge. 8vo. Boston, 1850.

MUSEUM OF HISTORY, or Narrations of the Most Wonderful Adventures, Remarkable Trials, Judicial Murders, Prison Escapes, Heroic Actions and Astonishing Occurrences in Ancient and Modern Times. 8vo. New Haven.

MUSGRAVE, G. M. Excursions to Paris, Tours, and Rouen, with a Few Memoranda on French Farming. A New Edition of the "Parson, Pen, and Pencil." 8vo. London, 1849.

MUSGRAVE, G. M. The Parson, Pen, and Pencil; or Reminiscences and Illustrations of an Excursion to Paris, Tours, and Rouen, with a Few Memoranda on French Farming. 3 vols. 8vo. London, 1848.

NAPOLEON. History of. (See l'Ardeche, L.)

NAPOLEON. (See Bonaparte or Buonaparte.)

NARRATIVE of the Transactions relative to the Capture of the American Ship "Olive Branch." 8vo.

*NATIONAL INTELLIGENCER. 20 vols. fol. Washington, 1819–1826–1831–1851. *Presented by G. W. Murray, Esq., in part.*

NATIONAL MAGAZINE and Industrial Record, edited by Redwood Fisher. 3 vols. 8vo. New York, 1845–1846.

NATIONAL TALES. 2 vols. 12mo. New York, 1825.

NATURAL HISTORY of Insects. 18mo. New York, 1833.

NATURAL PHILOSOPHY, with an Explanation of Scientific Terms, &c. Published under the Superintendence of the Society for the Diffusion of Useful Knowledge. 4 vols. 8vo. London.

NATURALIST'S LIBRARY. Edited by Sir William Jardine. 40 vols. 12mo. Edinburgh, 1834–1844.

MAMMALIA.

Vol.	Author	Subject	Part	Memoir
Vol. 1.	Jardine, Sir W.	Monkeys;		with Memoir of Buffon.
2.	"	Lions, Tigers, &c.		" Cuvier.
3.	"	Ruminating Animals.	Part 1.	" Camper.
4.	"	" "	" 2.	" Hunter.
5.	"	Pachyderms.		" Sloane.
6.	Hamilton, R.	Whales.		" Lacepede.
7.	Macgillivray, W.	British Mammas.		" Aldrovandi.
8.	Hamilton, R.	Amphibious Carnivora.		" Peron.
9.	Smith, C. H.	Dogs.	Part 1.	" Pallas.
10.	"	"	" 2.	" D'Azara.
11.	Waterhouse, G. R.	Marsupialia.		" Barclay.
12.	Smith, C. H.	Horses, Asses, Zebras, &c.		" Gesner.
13.	"	Introduction to Mammalia.		" Drury.

ORNITHOLOGY.

Vol.	Author	Subject	Part	Memoir
Vol. 1.	Jardine, Sir W.	Humming Birds.	Pt. 1.	with Memoir of Linnæus.
2.	"	"	" 2.	" Pennant.
3.	"	Gallinaceous Birds.		" Aristotle.
4.	"	Game Birds.		" Raffles.
5.	Selby, P. J.	Pigeons.		" Pliny.
6.	"	Parrots.		" Bewick.
7.	Swainson, W.	Birds of Western Africa.	Part 1.	" Bruce.
8.	"	"	" 2.	" Le Vaillant.
9.	Jardine, Sir W.	British Birds.	" 1.	" Sibbald.
10.	Swainson, W.	Fly Catchers.		" Haller.
11.	Jardine, Sir W.	British Birds.	" 2.	" Smellie.
12.	"	"	" 3.	" Walker.
13.	"	Sun Birds.		" Willughby.
14.	"	British Birds.	" 4.	" Wilson.

ICTHYOLOGY.

Vol. 1. Jardine, Sir. W. Fishes of the Perch Family, with Memoir of Banks.
2. Bushnan, J. S. Fishes, their Structure and Uses. " Salviani.
3. Schomburgk, R. H. Fishes of Guiana, Part 1; with an Account of the Author.
4. Hamilton, R. British Fishes, Part 1; with Memoir of Rondelet.
5. Schomburgk, R. H. Fishes of Guiana, Part 2. " Burckhardt.
6. Hamilton, R. British Fishes. Part 2. " Humboldt.

NATURALIST'S LIBRARY. (Continued.)

ENTOMOLOGY.

Vol. 1.	Duncan, J.	Introduction to Entomology. With Memoir of Swammerdam and De Geer.		
2.	Duncan, J.	Beetles.	With Memoir of	Ray.
3.	"	British Butterflies.	"	Werner.
4.	"	British Moths, Sphinxes, &c.	"	Madame Merian.
5.	"	Foreign Butterflies,	"	Lamarck.
6.	Dunbar.	Bees.	"	Huber.
7.	Duncan, J.	Exotic Moths.	"	Latreille.

NAVIGATION. Connected View of the whole Internal Navigation of the United States. 8vo. Philadelphia, 1826.

NEAL, JOHN. Rachel Dyer, a North American Story. 12mo Portland, 1828.

NEAL, JOHN. The Down Easters, &c., &c. 2 vols. 12mo. New York, 1833.

NEALE, ERSKINE. The Life Book of a Laborer, or the Curate, with his Trials, Sorrows, Checks and Triumphs. 12mo. London, 1842.

NEALE, ERSKINE. The Life of Edwark, Duke of Kent. 8vo. London, 1850.

NEALE, W. H. The Mohammedan System of Theology. 8vo. London, 1828.

NEANDER, AUGUSTUS. The Life of St. Chrysostrom, from the German, by the Rev. J. C. Stapleton. 8vo. London, 1845.

NELSON, HORATIO, LORD. Letters to Lady Hamilton, with a Supplement of Interesting Letters by Distinguished Characters. 2 vols. 8vo. London, 1814.

NELSON, HORATIO, LORD. Life. (See Southey, Robert.)

*NEUMAN AND BARETTI'S Dictionary of the Spanish and English Languages. 2 vols. 8vo. Boston, 1837.

NEVEN, E. J. A. Commentaire sur les Lois Rurales Tranearsis. 8vo. Paris, 1845.

NEWCASTLE MAGAZINE. 8vo. Newcastle, 1823.

NEW ENGLAND JOURNAL of Medicine and Surgery. 8vo. Boston, 1811–1817–1824.

*NEW ENGLAND PALLADIUM and Russell's Gazette. Fol. 1799–1802, Boston.

NEWMAN, SAMUEL P. Elements of Political Economy. 12mo. Andover, 1835.

NEW MONTHLY MAGAZINE and Literary Journal. 3 vols. 8vo. Boston, 1833–1834.

NEWTON, JOHN. Letters. 12mo. Philadelphia, 1795.

NEWTON, SIR ISAAC. Life. (See Brewster, David.)

NEWTON, SIR ISAAC. Principia: the Mathematical Principles of Natural Philosophy. Translated by Andrew Motte. To which is added Newton's System of the World. Revised and Corrected, with a Life of the Author, by N. W. Chittenden. 8vo. New York, 1848.

NEW WHIG GUIDE. 16mo. London, 1819.

*NEW YORK American. 4 vols. fol. 1827–1828–1829.

*NEW YORK Business Directory for 1841–1842. 12mo. New York.

*NEW YORK Chronicle Express. 2 vols. fol. 1802–1804.

NEW YORK CITY.

Longworth's American Almanac, Register, and Directory, 1796 to 1818–1819. By David Longworth. 18 vols. 12mo.

Longworth's Register and Directory, 1818–1819 to 1842–1843. By Thomas Longworth. 22 vols. 12mo.

Doggett's Directory, 1842–1843 to 1851–1852. By John Doggett. 10 vols. 8vo.

Report of the Committee of Arrangements of the Common Council for the Funeral Obsequies of William Henry Harrison. 8vo. New York, 1841.

Report of the Committee of Arrangements of the Common Council for the Funeral Ceremonies of Andrew Jackson. 8vo. New York, 1845.

*NEW YORK Evening Post. 2 vols. fol. 1802–1803.

NEW YORK Farmer and American Gardener's Magazine. New Series. Edited by D. K. Minor. 4to. New York, 1833.

NEW YORK Farmer and Horticultural Repository. Samuel Fleet, Editor. 4 vols. 4to. New York, 1828–1831.

NEW YORK Farmer and Mechanic, devoted to Agriculture, Mechanics, Manufactures and the Arts. Samuel Fleet, Editor. 4 vols. 8vo. New York, 1844–1846. *Presented by W. H. Starr, Esq.*

Ditto. Ditto. New Series. W. H. Starr and J. M. Stearns, Editors. 4to. New York, 1847.

*NEW YORK Gazette and General Advertiser. 2 vols. fol. 1799–1801.

*NEW YORK Herald and Weekly Register. Fol. 1803–1805.

*NEW YORK Journal and State Gazette. Fol. 1784–1785–1786–1790.

NEW YORK Military Magazine. Vol. 1. 8vo. New York, 1841. *Presented by Gen. A. Chandler.*

NEW YORK REVIEW. 6 vols. 8vo. New York, 1839–1841.

NEW YORK Review and Athenæum Magazine. 2 vols. 8vo. New York, 1825–1826.

NEW YORK STATE.

Census of 1845. Fol. Albany. *Presented by Hon. Uzziah Wenman.*

Documentary History of, arranged under the direction of Christopher Morgan, by E. B. O'Callaghan. 2 vols. 8vo. Albany, 1849. *Presented by Col. E. T. Backhouse.*

Journals and Documents of the Senate and Assembly. 7 vols. 8vo. 1831–1833–1838–1839–1840–1841–1850.

Journals of the Senate. 2 vols. fol. 1824–1826. *Presented by R. M. Meigs, Esq., and Gen. A. Chandler.*

Journal of the Assembly. 5 vols. fol. 1820–1826. *Presented by R. M. Meigs, Esq., and Gen. A. Chandler.*

Journals of the Votes and Proceedings of the General Assembly of the Colony of New York, from 1691 to 1765. 2 vols. fol. New York, 1766.

Natural History of. 15 vols. 4to. Albany, 1842.

Part 1. Zoology, by James E. De Kay. 5 vols.
2. Botany, by John Torrey. 2 vols.
3. Mineralogy, by Lewis C. Beck. 1 vol.
4. Geology, by James Hall, E. Emmons, William M. Mather, and Lardner Vanuxem. 4 vols.
5. Agriculture, by E. Emmons. 2 vols.
6. Paleontology, by James Hall. 1 vol.

Report of the Canal Commissioners and Acts of the Legislature respecting Canals. 8vo. New York, 1827.

*New York Tribune. 2 vols. fol. 1841–1843.

New York Weekly Museum, or Polite Repository of Amusement and Instruction. 2 vols. 8vo. New York, 1815–1818.

Ney, Marshal. Memoirs of. Published by his Family. 8vo. Philadelphia, 1834.

Nichol, J. P. Views of the Heavens. 12mo. New York, 1840.

Nicholas, Sir Harris. A History of the Royal Navy, from the Earliest Times to the Wars of the French Revolution. 2 vols. 8vo. London, 1847.

Nicholas, Sir Harris. Memoirs of the Life and Times of Sir Christopher Hatton. 8vo. London, 1847.

Nichols, John. Recollections and Reflections, Personal and Political, as Connected with Public Affairs during the Reign of George III. 2 vols. 8vo. London, 1822.

Nichols, John. The Epistolary Correspondence of Sir Richard Steele, including Familiar Letters to his Wife and Daughters. 2 vols. 8vo. London, 1809.

*Nicholson, Peter. An Architectural and Engineering Dictionary. 2 vols. 4to. London, 1835.

Nicholson, Peter. Principles of Architecture. Sixth edition. Revised and Corrected by Joseph Gwilt. 8vo. London, 1848.

Nicholson, Peter. The Mechanic's Companion. 8vo. Philadelphia, 1832.

*Nicholson, William. British Encyclopædia, or Dictionary of Arts and Sciences. 6 vols. 8vo. London, 1809.

Nicholson, William. Dictionary of Practical and Theoretical Chemistry. 8vo. London, 1808.

Nickelsburger, Jacob. Koul Jacob in Defence of the Jewish Religion. 8vo. New York, 1816.

Niebuhr, B. G. History of Rome, epitomized from the larger work by Travers Twiss. 8vo. London and Oxford, 1845.

Niebuhr, Carsten. Travels through Arabia and Other Countries in the East. Translated by Robert Heron. 2 vols. 8vo. Edinburgh, 1792.

Niles, Hezekiah. Journal of the Proceedings of the Friends of Domestic Industry. 8vo. Baltimore, 1831.

*NILES, HEZEKIAH. Weekly Register. 70 vols. 8vo. Baltimore, 1811.

NOAH, M. M. Travels in England and Spain, and the Barbary States, in 1813–1814–1815. 8vo. New York, 1819.

NO FICTION, a Narrative founded on Recent and Interesting Facts. 2 vols. 18mo. Boston, 1821.

NORMANDIE AGRICOLE, LA. Journal d'Agriculture Pratique, d'Economie Rurale et d'Horticulture. 4 vols. 8vo. Caen, 1843–1847. *Presented through M. Alexandre Vattemare.*

NORTH AMERICAN Medical and Surgical Journal. Conducted by H. L. Hodge, Franklyn Bache, &c. 4 vols. 8vo Philadelphia, 1826–1827.

NORTH AMERICAN REVIEW. 1825 to 1832. 17 vols. 8vo. Boston.

NUEVO TESTAMENTO, El, de Nuestro Señor Jesus Cristo. 12mo. Nueva York, 1819.

NUTTALL, P. AUSTIN. A Classical and Archæological Dictionary of the Manners, Customs, Laws, Institutions, Arts, &c., of the celebrated Nations of Antiquity, and of the Middle Ages. 8vo. London, 1850.

NUTTALL, THOMAS. Manual of the Ornithology of the United States, and of Canada. 12mo. Cambridge, 1832.

OBSERVATIONS on Modern Gardening. 8vo. London, 1770.

OBSERVATIONS on the Speech of Lord Bradhurst in the House of Peers. 12mo. New York, 1818.

O'CALLAGHAN, J. Usury or Interest proved to be Repugnant to the Divine and Ecclesiastical Laws, and Destructive to Civil Society. 12mo. New York, 1824.

OCEAN AND THE DESERT. By a Madras Officer. 2 vols. 8vo. London, 1846.

O'CONNELL, DANIEL. Personal Recollections. (See Daunt, W. I. O'Neil.)

O'CONNELL, JOHN. Recollections and Experiences, during a Parliamentary Career, from 1833 to 1848. 2 vols. 8vo. London, 1849.

ODART, COMTE. Ampélographie ou Traité des Cépages. 8vo. Paris, 1845. *Presented through M. Alexandre Vattemare.*

OGDEN, JOHN C. Tour through Canada. 12mo. Wilmington, 1800.

OLIVE BRANCH, SIMON. The Looker-on. A Periodical Paper. 2 vols. 12mo. Philadelphia, 1796.

OLIVER, BENJAMIN L. Rights of an American Citizen, with a Commentary on State Rights, and on the Constitution and Policy of the United States. 8vo. Boston, 1832.

OLNEY, SARAH H. Extracts from Blair's Lectures on Rhetoric, &c., &c. 4to.

ONDERDONK, JR., HENRY. Documents and Letters relating to the Revolutionary Incidents of Queens County. 12mo. New York, 1846. *Presented by the Author.*

OPDIKE, GEORGE. A Treatise on Political Economy. 12mo. New York, 1851.

OPIE, AMELIA. Illustrations of Lying in all its branches. 24mo. Exeter, 1829.

ORDERS and Resolutions of the House of Commons. 12mo. London, 1747.

O'RIELLY, B. Greenland, the Adjacent Seas, and the North West Passage. 8vo. New York, 1818.

ORMONDF, JAMES, DUKE OF. The Life of. 8vo. London, 1797.

OSBORN, FRANCIS. Miscellaneous Works. 2 vols. 18mo. London, 1722.

OSGOOD, REV. DAVID. Sermons. 8vo. Boston, 1824.

OSSIAN. Poems, translated by James Macpherson. 2 vols. 12mo. Berwick, 1795.

Ditto. Ditto. 2 vols. 24mo. New York, 1827.

O'SULLIVAN, MORTIMER. A Guide to an Irish Gentleman in Search for a Religion. 12mo. Philadelphia, 1833.

OTTER, WILLIAM. Life and Remains of Edward Daniel Clarke. 8vo. New York, 1827.

OUDIN, CÆSAR. Tresor des Deux Langues Françoise et Espagnole. 8vo. Lyons, 1775.

OUR NEIGHBORHOOD, or Letters on Horticulture and Natural Phenomena. Interspersed with Opinions on Domestic and Moral Economy. 8vo. New York, 1831.

Ouseley, William G. Remarks on the Statistics and Political Institutions of the United States. 8vo. Philadelphia, 1832.

Outlines of History from the Earliest Period to the Present Time. 12mo. Philadelphia, 1831.

Ouviere, Felix Pascalis. An Account of the Contagious Epidemic, Yellow Fever, which prevailed in Philadelphia in 1797. 8vo. Philadelphia, 1798.

Overnan, Frederick. Practical Mineralogy, Assaying and Mining. 12mo. Philadelphia, 1851.

Overman, Frederick. The Manufacture of Iron, with an Essay on the Manufacture of Steel. 8vo. Philadelphia, 1850.

Oxberry, W. The Actor's Budget of Wit and Merriment. 8vo. London.

Page, M. Le. The History of Louisiana, or the Western Parts of Virginia and Carolina. 18mo. London, 1763.

Page, Richard. A Critical Examination of 12 Resolutions of Mr. Joseph Hume, respecting the Loan of 15,000,000 for Slave Compensation. 8vo. London, 1839. *Presented by Joseph Hume, Esq.*

Pain, William. The Builder's Companion and Workman's General Assistant. Fol. London, 1762.

Pain, William. The Carpenter's and Joiner's Repository. Fol. London, 1787.

Pain, William and James. British Palladio, or the Builder's General Assistant. Fol. London, 1797.

Paine, Jr., Elijah. Report of Cases in the Circuit Court of the United States. 8vo. New York, 1827.

Paine, Martyn. Letters on the Cholera Asphyxia. 8vo. New York, 1832.

Paine, Jr., Robert Treat. Works in Prose and Verse, with Notes, and a Sketch of his Life, Character, and Writings. 8vo. Boston, 1812.

Paine, Thomas. Age of Reason. 18mo. New York, 1794.

PAINE, THOMAS. Political Writings. 2 vols. 8vo. New York, 1830.

PALEY, WILLIAM. Complete Works. 8vo. London, 1849.

PALEY, WILLIAM. The Principles of Moral and Political Philosophy. 8vo. Canandaigua, 1822.

PAMBOUR, CHEV. F. M. G. DE. Treatise on Locomotive Engines upon Railways. 8vo. London, 1836.

PAMPHLETS, viz: An Argument in Defence of the Colonies; Thomas Paine's Common Sense; and Plain Truths, by Candius. 8vo. London and Philadelphia, 1774–1776.

PAMPHLETS. (See the List.)

PARDOE, MISS. The City of the Magyar, or Hungary and her Institutions in 1839–1840. 3 vols. 8vo. London, 1840.

PARDOE, MISS. The Court and Reign of Francis I., King of France. 2 vols. 8vo. Philadelphia, 1849.

PARIS, JOHN A. The Elements of Medical Chemistry. 8vo. London, 1825.

PARK, MUNGO. The Journal of a Mission to the Interior of Africa in 1805. 4to. London, 1815.

PARK, MUNGO. Travels in the Interior Districts of Africa. 8vo. London, 1800.

PARKE, SAMUEL. Chemical Catechism, with Notes, Illustrations and Experiments. 8vo. London, 1814.

PARKE, SAMUEL. Thoughts on the Laws relating to Salt. 8vo. London, 1817. *Presented by Dr. Samuel Akerly.*

PARKER, JOHN A. The Quadrature of the Circle. 8vo. New York, 1851. *Presented by Hon. Henry Meigs.*

PARKER, RICHARD G. Aids to English Composition. 12mo. New York, 1845.

PARKINSON, RICHARD. A Tour in America in 1798–1799 and 1800. 2 vols. 8vo. London, 1805.

PARKMAN, JR., FRANCIS. The California and Oregon Trail; being Sketches of Prairie and Rocky Mountain Life. 12mo. New York, 1849.

PARLIAMENTARY REGISTER; or History of the Proceedings and Debates of the House of Commons. 7 vols. 8vo. London, 1782, 1783, 1784, 1787 and 1788.

PARMLY, L. S. Lectures on the Natural History and Management of the Teeth. 8vo. New York, 1820. *Presented by Dr. Samuel Akerly.*

PARROT, FREDERICK. Journey to Ararat, translated by W. D. Cooley. 12mo. New York, 1846.

PARRY, WILLIAM E. Journal of a Second Voyage for the Discovery of a North West Passage. 8vo. New York, 1824.

PARRY, WILLIAM E. Voyages for the Discovery of the North West Passage. 12mo. New York, 1827.

PARTRIDGE, WILLIAM. Practical Treatise on Dyeing, &c. 12mo. New York, 1823. *Presented by Dr. Samuel Akerly.*

PASCALIS, FELIX A. Exposition of the Dangers of Interments in Cities. 8vo. New York, 1823.

PATENT Right Oppression Exposed, or Knavery Detected. 12mo. Philadelphia, 1814.

*PATENTS. A List of, granted by the United States from 1790 to 1829, together with the Patent Laws. 8vo. Washington, 1831.

*PATENTS. Commissioners' Reports of, 1843–1848. 6 vols. 8vo. Washington. *Presented by the Commissioners.*

*PATRON of Industry. Fol. New York, 1820.

PATTIE, JAMES O. The Personal Narrative of, edited by Timothy Flint. 12mo. Cincinnati, 1833.

PAULDING, JAMES K. A Life of Washington. 2 vols. 18mo. New York, 1835.

PAULDING, JAMES K. The Dutchman's Fireside. Vol. 1. 12mo. New York, 1831.

PAYNE, JOHN. Universal Geography. 4 vols. 8vo. New York, 1800.

PAZOS, VICENTE. Letters on the United Provinces of South America, from the Spanish, by Platt H. Crosby. 8vo. New York, 1819.

PEACE-REPUBLICAN'S MANUAL, or the French Constitution of 1793 and the Declaration of the Rights of Man and of Citizens. 8vo. New York, 1817. *Presented by Dr. Samuel Akerly.*

PEARCE, JOHN C. and John H. Niles. Gazetteer of the States of Connecticut and Rhode Island. 8vo. Hartford, 1819.

PEARCE, ROBERT R. History of the Inns of Court and Chancery. 8vo. London, 1848.

PEARCE, ROBERT R. Memoirs and Correspondence of Richard Marquis Wellesley. 3 vols. 8vo. London, 1846.

PEBRER, PABLO. Taxation, Revenue, Expenditures, Power, Statistics and Debt of the whole British Empire. 8vo. London, 1833.

PEERAGE of England. 2 vols. 12mo. London, 1795.

PENSCELLWOOD PAPERS. Comprising Essays on the Souls and Future Life of Animals, Capital Punishment, &c., &c. By the Author of "Dr. Hookwell," "the Primitive Church," &c. 2 vols. 8vo. London, 1846.

PENN, GRANVILLE. A Comparative Estimate of the Mineral and Mosaical Geologies. 2 vols. 8vo. London, 1820.

PENN, GRANVILLE. Memorials of the Professional Life and Times of Sir William Penn. 2 vols. 8vo. London, 1833.

PENNANT, THOMAS. A Journey from London to the Isle of Wight. 4to. London, 1841.

*PENNY CYCLOPÆDIA and Supplement. 16 vols. large 8vo. London, 1833–1846.

PENNY MAGAZINE. 5 vols. 8vo. London, 1832–1836.

PEPÉ, GENERAL. Memoirs, comprising the Principal Military and Political Events of Modern Italy, written by Himself. 3 vols. 8vo. London, 1846.

PEPYS, SAMUEL. Life, Journals and Correspondence, including a Narrative of a Voyage to the Tangier. 2 vols. 8vo. London, 1841.

PERCIVAL, C. G. An Abridged Account of the Misfortunes of the Dauphin. 8vo. London, 1838.

PERCY ANECDOTES. The Revised Edition, with a Valuable Collection of American Anecdotes. 8vo. New York, 1845.

PERDICARIS, G. A. The Greece of the Greeks. 2 vols. 12mo. New York, 1846.

PERKINS, NATHAN. Discourses. 8vo. Hartford, 1795.

PERKINS, SAMUEL. Historical Sketches of the United States. 12mo. New York, 1830.

PERRINE, DR. HENRY. Tropical Plants. 8vo. Washington, 1838. *Presented by the Author.*

PETRARCH. Essays on. (See Foscolo, Ugo.)

PETRARCH. Life of. (See Campbell, Thomas.)

PETRARCH. Life of. (See Dobson, Mrs.)

PETTY, WILLIAM. Several Essays in Political Arithmetic. 12mo. London, 1699.

PETZHOLDT, ALEXANDER. Lectures to Farmers on Agricultural Chemistry. 12mo. London, 1844.

PETZHOLDT, ALEXANDER. Lectures to Farmers on Agricultural Chemistry. 8vo. New York, 1846.

PHARMACOPŒIA of the United States of America. 8vo. Boston, 1820. *Presented by Dr. Samuel Akerly.*

PHILADELPHIA Medical Museum. Conducted by John Rodman Coxe. 2 vols. 8vo. Philadelphia, 1805–1809.

PHILADELPHIA Society for the Promotion of National Industry. Addresses of. 8vo. Philadelphia, 1819.

PHILIP, A. P. W. A Treatise on the Means of Preserving Health, and particularly the prevention of Organic Diseases. 8vo. London, 1830.

PHILIPS, Curran, and Grattan. Speeches of. 8vo. Philadelphia, 1831.

PHILLIPS, J. A General History of Inland Navigation, Foreign and Domestic. 8vo. London, 1809.

PHILLIPS, SIR RICHARD. A Familiar Cyclopædia and Dictionary of the Arts of Life and Civilization. 8vo. London.

PHILLIPS, SIR RICHARD. Four Dialogues between an Oxford Tutor and a Disciple of the Common Sense Philosophy. 8vo. London, 1824. *Presented by Dr. Samuel Akerly.*

PHILLIPS, SIR RICHARD. Golden Rules of Social Philosophy, or a System of Practical Ethics. 8vo. London, 1826. *Presented by Dr. Samuel Akerly.*

PHILLIPS, SIR RICHARD. Twelve Essays on the Proximate Causes of the Material Phenomena of the Universe. 8vo. London, 1821.

PHILLIPS, WILLARD. Manual of Political Economy. 8vo. Boston, 1828.

PHILLIPS, WILLARD. The Inventor's Guide. 12mo. Boston, 1837.

PHILLIPS, WILLIAM. An Outline of Mineralogy and Geology. 12mo. New York, 1816.

PHILO JUDÆUS. Opera exegetica in Libros Mosis. Fol. Col., 1613. *Presented by James Darrack, Esq.*

PHILOSOPHICAL Dictionary for the Pocket. 8vo. London, 1765.

PHILOSOPHICAL Transactions and Collections, Abridged. By John Lowthrop and Henry Jones. 13 vols. 4to. London, 1732–1756.

PHILOSOPHICAL Transactions of the Royal Society of London. 5 vols. London, 1781–1785.

PHILOSOPHIE. Les Crimes de la. 8vo. Paris, 1804.

PICARD, L'ABBÉ. L'Agriculture Raisonnée ou Manuel Complet et Spécial du Cultivateur. 12mo. Niort, 1844. *Presented through M. Alexandre Vattemare.*

PICQUOT, A. General Gazetteer, or Geographical Dictionary. Abridged from Brookes. 12mo. London, 1823.

PICTURE OF AUSTRALIA. 12mo. London, 1829.

PIGOT & SONS. General Directory of Manchester, Salford, &c., for 1830. Manchester, 1830.

PIKE, JR., BENJAMIN. Illustrated Descriptive Catalogue of Optical, Mathematical, and Philosophical Instruments. 2 vols. 12mo. New York, 1848. *Presented by the Author.*

PIKE, NICHOLAS. A New and Complete System of Arithmetic. Revised by Chester Dewey. 8vo. Troy, 1822.

PILKINGTON, JAMES. The Artist's and Mechanic's Repository, and Workingman's Informant. 12mo. Philadelphia, 1840.

PINKERTON, JOHN. A General Collection of Voyages and Travels in various parts of America. 3 vols. 4to. London, 1819.

PINKNEY, WILLIAM. Life, Writings and Speeches. (See Wheaton, Henry.)

PINNOCK, W. The Guide to Knowledge. 4to. London, 1833.

PITKINS, TIMOTHY. Statistical View of the Commerce of the United States. 8vo. New York, 1817.

PITKINS, TIMOTHY. History of the United States, from 1763–1797. 2 vols. 8vo. New Haven, 1828.

PITKINS, TIMOTHY. Statistical View of the Commerce of the United States. 8vo. New York, 1818.

Pitman, Isaac. A Manual of Phonography, or Writing by Sound. 8vo. London, 1842. *Presented by E. A. Harris.*

Pitt, William. (See Chatham.)

Playfair, William. History of Jacobinism. With an Appendix by William Porcupine. 2 vols. 8vo. Philadelphia, 1796.

Plough Boy, The. 3 vols. 4to. Albany, 1819–1822.

Plowden, Francis. The History of Ireland, from its Union with Great Britain. 3 vols. 8vo. Dublin, 1811.

Plutarch's Lives. (See Langhorne, J. and W.)

Poe, Edgar A. The Works of. With Notices of his Life and Genius, by N. P. Willis, J. R. Lowell, and R. W. Griswold. 3 vols. 12mo. New York, 1850.

Poems, by a Collegian. 12mo. Charlotteville, 1833.

Poems, by a Proser. 12mo. New York, 1831.

Political Economy. Tracts on Sundry Topics on. 8vo. Boston, 1834.

Political Magazine, 1785–1786. 4 vols. 8vo. London.

Politician's Creed, or Political Extracts. By a Lover of Social Order. 3 vols. 8vo. London, 1799.

Pollok, Robert. Life and Remains. (See Scott, James.)

Pollok, Robert. Political Works. (See Hemans.)

*Polyglot Lexicon. A New Dictionary in Four Languages, the French, Dutch, German, and English. By a Society of Learned Men. 2 vols. 8vo. London, 1848.

Poole, John. Sketches and Recollections. Vol. 2. 8vo. Philadelphia, 1835.

Poor Laws. Extracts from the Report of the Poor Law Commissioners. 8vo. London, 1833.

Poor Laws. Report of the Commissioners of. 4 vols. 8vo. London, 1834.

Poor Laws. Reports Addressed to the Poor Law Commissioners. 12mo. London, 1834.

Poore, Benjamin P. The Rise and Fall of Louis Philippe, ex-King of the French, giving a History of the French Revolution, from its Commencement in 1789. 12mo. Boston, 1848.

Pope, Alexander. The Works of. Vols. 2 and 6. 12mo. New York, 1809.

Pope, Alexander. The Works of. 4 vols. 4to. London, 1769.

Pope, Charles. Practical Abridgment of the Laws of Customs and Excise relative to the Import, Export, and Coasting Trade. 8vo. London, 1819.

Pope, Thomas. Treatise on Bridge Architecture. 8vo. New York, 1811.

Poppe, D. Joh. H. M. Technologisches Lexicon. 8vo. Stuttgardt und Tuebingen, 1816.

Porny, Mark A. Elements of Heraldry. 8vo. Eton, 1765.

Porny, Mark A. Models of Letters in French and English. 12mo. London, 1798.

Port Folio. A Monthly Magazine. Conducted by Oliver Oldschool. 5 vols. 8vo. Philadelphia and New York, 1809–1811.

Porter, David. Journal of a Cruise made to the Pacific Ocean in 1811–1813–1814. 2 vols. Philadelphia, 1815.

Porter, George R. The Nature and Properties of the Sugar Cane. 8vo. Philadelphia, 1831.

Porter, George R. The Progress of the Nation. 3 vols. 12mo. London, 1838.

Portlock and Dixon's Voyage round the World. Abridged. 8vo. London, 1789.

Portugal, Civil War in, and the Siege of Oporto. By an Officer of Hussars. 12mo. London, 1836.

Potalis, M. Speech. 12mo. New York, 1802.

Powell, Thomas. The Living Authors of England. 12mo. New York, 1849.

Poyntz, Albany. A World of Wonders, with Anecdotes and Opinions concerning Popular Superstitions. 8vo. London, 1845.

Pozzo, A. Rules and Examples of Perspective proper for Painters and Architects. Fol. London, 1707.

Practical Mechanic's and Engineer's Magazine. 3 vols. 8vo. Glasgow, 1841–1847.

Practical Mechanic's Journal. 4 vols. 4to. London, 1848–1851.

Pradt, M. de. Europe after the Congress of Aix-la-Chapelle. Translated, with Notes, by George A. Otis. 8vo. Philadelphia, 1820.

PRECEPTOR, THE. Containing a General Course of Education. 2 vols. 8vo. London, 1769.

PRESCOTT, WILLIAM H. Biographical and Critical Miscellanies. 8vo. New York, 1845.

PRESCOTT, WILLIAM H. History of the Conquest of Mexico. 3 vols. 8vo. New York, 1851.

PRESCOTT, WILLIAM H. History of the Conquest of Peru. 2 vols. 8vo. New York, 1851.

PRESCOTT, WILLIAM H. History of the Reign of Ferdinand and Isabella, the Catholic. 3 vols. 8vo. Boston, 1840.

PRESTWICH'S RESPUBLICA; or a Display of the Honors, Ceremonies and Ensigns of the Commonwealth, &c., &c. 4to. London, 1787.

PREVOST, ABBÉ. The History of Margaret of Anjou, Queen of England. From the French. 2 vols. 12mo. London, 1775.

PRICE, RICHARD. Observations on Reversionary Payments. With Additions by William Morgan. 2 vols. 8vo. London, 1792.

PRIDEAUX, MATHIAS. An Introduction for the Reading of all sorts of Histories, with a Synopsis of Councils, by John Predeaux. 12mo. Oxford, 1655.

PRIEST, JOSIAH. American Antiquities, and Discoveries in the West. 8vo. Albany, 1834.

PRIESTLEY, JOSEPH. General History of the Christian Church. 6 vols. 8vo. Northumberland, 1802.

PRIESTLEY, JOSEPH. Memoirs of his own Life, with a Continuation by his Son. 2 vols. 8vo. Northumberland, 1806.

PRIESTLEY, JOSEPH. The Rudiments of English Grammar. 8vo. London, 1825.

PRINCE, WILLIAM R. AND WILLIAM. A Treatise on the Vine, embracing its History from the Earliest Ages to the Present Day. 8vo. New York, 1830. *Presented by the Authors.*

PRINCE, WILLIAM R. AND WILLIAM. The Pomological Manual, or a Treatise on Fruits. 8vo. New York, 1832. *Presented by the Authors.*

PRINGLE, JOHN. Observations on the Diseases of the Army. 8vo. London, 1753.

Prior, James. The Life of Oliver Goldsmith. 8vo. Philadelphia, 1837.

Prison Labor, Thoughts on. By a Student of the Inner Temple. 8vo. London, 1824.

Proceedings of the Church Missionary Society for Africa and the East. 8vo. London, 1825.

Proceedings of the New York Historical Society, 1844. 8vo. New York, 1845.

Proud, Robert. The History of Pennsylvania. 2 vols. 8vo. Philadelphia, 1798.

Psalms of David, in the Nestorian Language, printed at Ooroomiah, Persia, about 1840. *Presented by Homan Hallock, Esq.*

Pulpit Cyclopædia and Christian Minister's Companion. 4 vols. 8vo. London, 1844.

Pulzsky, Theresa. Memoirs of a Hungarian Lady, with an Historical Introduction, by Francis Pulzsky. 12mo. Philadelphia, 1850.

Purdy, John. New Sailing Directory for the Ethiopic or Southern Atlantic Ocean to the Rio de la Plata and the Cape of Good Hope, &c. 8vo. London, 1829.

Pursh, Frederick. A Systematic Arrangement and Description of the Plants of North America. 2 vols. 8vo. London, 1814.

Putnam, George P. American Facts. 12mo. London, 1845.

Putt, Charles. Essays on Civil Policy or the Science of Legislation. 8vo. London, 1830.

Pye, John. Patronage of British Art, an Historical Sketch, comprising an Account of the Rise and Progress of Arts and Artists in London. 8vo. London, 1845.

Quarterly Journal of the Geological Society of London. 8vo. London, 1845.

Quarterly Review. 1827–1830. 6 vols. 8vo. Boston.

Quill, Charles. The American Mechanic. 18mo. Philadelphia, 1838.

Quin, Michael J. Steam Voyages on the Seine, the Moselle, and the Rhine, with Railroad Visits to the Principal Cities of Belgium, &c., &c. 2 vols. 8vo. London, 1843.

QUINCY, JOSIAH. The History of Harvard University. 2 vols. 8vo. Cambridge, 1840.

RAFFLES, SIR THOMAS S. The History of Java. 2 vols. 8vo. London, 1830.

RAFFLES, SIR THOMAS S. Memoir of his Life and Public Services. 2 vols. 8vo. London, 1835.

RAFINESQUE, C. S. Analyse de la Nature ou Tableau de l'Universe et des Corps Organises. 12mo. Palerme, 1815.

RAINSFORD, MARCUS. An Historical Account of the Black Empire of Hayti. 4to. London, 1805.

RALEIGH, SIR WALTER. Memoirs of his Life. (See Thompson, Mrs. A. T.)

RAMBLES among the Musicians of Germany, with an account of the Operas of Munich, Dresden, Berlin, &c., by a Musical Professor. 8vo. London, 1828.

RAMSAY, ALBERT C. The Other Side, or Notes for the History of the War between Mexico and the United States, written in Mexico. From the Spanish, with Notes. 8vo. New York, 1850.

RAMSAY, DAVID. Life of George Washington. 8vo. New York, 1807.
Ditto. Ditto. 12mo. Boston, 1811.

RAMSAY, DAVID. The History of the American Revolution. 2 vols. 8vo. London, 1793.

RANDOLPH, JOHN. Life. (See Garland, Hugh A.)

RAPPORT au Roi des Canaux. 4to. Paris, 1826. *Presented through M. Alexandre Vattemare.*

RASPAIL, F. V. A New System of Organic Chemistry. From the French, with notes and additions, by William Henderson. 8vo. London, 1843.

RAYMOND, DANIEL. Elements of Political Economy. 2 vols. 8vo. Baltimore, 1823.

RAYMOND, DANIEL. Thoughts on Political Economy. 8vo. Baltimore, 1820.

RAYMOND, JAMES. Digested Chancery Cases, contained in the Court of Appeals of Maryland. 8vo. Baltimore, 1839.

RECHERCHES Historiques et Politiques sur les Etats-Unis. Par un Citoyen de Virginie. 12mo. A. Colle, 1788.

*RECORDS, PUBLIC. Report of the Commissioners on. Folio, London, 1837.

RECORDS, PUBLIC, OF IRELAND. Reports and Proceedings of the Commissioners of. Folio, London, 1810–1815.

RECUEIL DE DOCUMENTS STATISTIQUES. 4to. Paris, 1837. *Presented through M. Alexandre Vattemare.*

REESE, DAVID MEREDITH. Quakerism versus Christianity, being a reply to "Quakerism not Christianity." 12mo. New York, 1834.

REFORMATION. The Protestant Reformation in France; or, the History of the Huguenots. 2 vols. 8vo. London, 1847.

REGISTER of Arts, and Journal of Patent Inventions. Edited by L. Hebert. 7 vols. 8vo. London, 1828–1832.

REICH, G. C. Neuer und vollständiger Gartenkalender. 12mo. Nürnberg, 1798.

REICH, G. C. Rindviehseuche und die Inokulation derselben. 12mo. Nürnberg, 1798.

REID, THOMAS. Treatise on Clock and Watch Making. 8vo. Edinburgh, 1826.

REIDESEL, MADAME DE. Letters and Memoirs relating to the War of American Independence, and the Capture of the German Troops at Saratoga. 12mo. New York, 1827.

REINHARD, F. V. Plan of the Founder of Christianity. From the German, by O. A. Taylor. 12mo. New York, 1831.

REMARKABLE SHIPWRECKS, selected from Authentic Sources. 12mo. Hartford, 1813.

REMEDIES for some of the Evils which constitute the "Perils of the Nation." 12mo. London, 1844.

REMEMBRANCER, THE, or Impartial Repository of Public Events. 4 vols. 8vo. London, 1775–1778.

RENGGER AND LONGCHAMPS. The Reign of Doctor Joseph Gaspard Roderick De Francia in Paraguay. 8vo. London, 1827.

*REPERTORY, THE. 3 vols. folio, Boston, 1806–1807–1811, and 1812.

*Repertory of Arts and Manufactures. 12 vols. 8vo. London, 1794–1800.

*Repertory of Arts, Manufactures, and Agriculture. 7 vols. 8vo. Vols. 38, 41, 46. London, 1821–1825.

*Repertory of Patent Inventions. New Series. 12 vols. 8vo. London, 1836–1842.

*Repertory of Patent Inventions, and other Discoveries and Improvements in Arts, Manufactures and Agriculture. 6 vols. 8vo. London, 1826–1837, and 1851.

Reports, Annual, of the American Board of Commissioners for Foreign Missions, &c. 8vo. Boston, 1834.

Reports, Annual, of the American Institute. 5 vols. 8vo. Albany, 1843–1846–1850.

Reports, Annual, of the Royal Humane Society. 4 vols. 8vo. London, 1802–1808–1809–1811.

Report of the Cases of Stacey, Dewer, and Joseph Hendrickson vs. Thomas Shotwell. 8vo. Philadelphia, 1834.

Report on the Condition of the Police Department of New York. By F. R. Tillou and C. S. Woodhull. 8vo. New York, 1844.

Report of the Copy-Right Case of Wheaton v. Peters. 8vo. New York, 1834.

Report of the Debates and Proceedings of the Convention of the State of New York. By L. H. Clarke. 8vo. New York, 1821.

Report on the Funeral Ceremonies of Andrew Jackson. 8vo. New York, 1845.

Report on the Funeral Obsequies of William H. Harrison. With an Oration, by Theodore Frelinghuysen. 8vo. New York, 1841.

Report on Import Duties of Great Britain. 8vo. London, 1840. *Presented by Joseph Hume, Esq.*

Report of the Prison Discipline Society. 8vo. Boston, 1830.

Report of the Secretary of War on Indian Affairs, and of the Commissioner of Patents. 8vo. Washington, 1837.

Report on Spasmodic Cholera. 8vo. Boston, 1832.

Report on Steam Engines in the United States, by the Secretary of the Treasury. 8vo. Washington, 1838.

Republic of Letters. A Republication of Standard Literature, edited by Mrs. A. H. Nicholas. 8vo. New York, 1835.

Reuss, W. F. Calculations and Statements relative to the Trade between Great Britain and the United States. 8vo. London, 1833.

Revised Statutes of the State of New York. Vol. 3. 8vo. Albany, 1829.

Revue Horticole. Journal des Jardiniers et Amateurs. 4 vols. 12mo. Paris, 1832–1841.

Revue Scientifique et Industrielle, 1840 to 1851. 35 vols. 8vo. Paris.

Reynold, J. N. Voyage of the United States Frigate "Potomac." 8vo. New York, 1835.

Reynolds, Sir Joshua. Memoirs of. (See Farington, Joseph.)

Richardson, Charles James. Treatise on the Warming and Ventilation of Buildings. 8vo. London, 1837.

Richardson, James. Travels in the Great Desert of Sahara in 1845 and 1846. 2 vols. 8vo. London, 1848.

Richardson, M. A. The Borderer's Table Book, or Gatherings of the Local History and Romance of the English and Scottish Border. 4 vols. 8vo. London, 1846.

Rigg, Robert. Experimental Researches, Chemical and Agricultural. 8vo. London, 1844.

Riley, James. An Authentic Narrative of the Loss of the American Brig "Commerce." 8vo. New York, 1818.

Rimius, Henry. Memoirs of the House of Brunswick. 4to. London, 1790.

Ripley, R. S. The War with Mexico. 2 vols. 8vo. New York, 1849.

Robbins, Archibald. Journal of the Loss of the Brig Commerce. 12mo. Hartford, 1817. *Presented by Dr. Samuel Akerly.*

Robertson, William. An Historical Disquisition concerning the Knowledge the Ancients had of India. 4to. London, 1791.

Robertson, William. History of America. 2 vols. 8vo. Philadelphia, 1822.

Robertson, William. History of the Reign of Charles V. 4 vols. 18mo. Perth, 1812.

Robertson, William. Works. With an account of his Life and Writings, by Dugald Stuart. 8vo. London, 1835.

Robespierre. Life of. (See Lewis, G. H.)

Robinson, A. Life in California. With an Historical Account of the Origin, Customs, and Traditions of the Indians of Alta-California, from the Original Spanish Manuscript. 12mo. New York, 1846.

Robinson Crusoe. (See De Foe.)

Robinson, John. A System of Mechanical Philosophy. With Notes by David Brewster. 4 vols. 8vo. Edinburgh, 1822.

Robinson, William D. Memoirs of the Mexican Revolution. 8vo. Philadelphia, 1820.

Robison, John. Proofs of a Conspiracy against all the Religions and Governments of Europe. 8vo. New York, 1798.

Rochon, Abbe. Voyage to Madagascar and the East Indies. From the French, by Joseph Trapp. 8vo. London, 1793.

Rogers, Henry D. Description of the Geology of the State of New Jersey. 8vo. Philadelphia, 1840.

Rogers, John G. Specimen of Printing Types, from the Boston Type and Stereotype Foundry. 8vo. Boston, 1828.

Rollin, Charles. Ancient History. Vols. 2, 4, 6. 18mo. London, 1749.

Rollin, Charles. Ancient History. From the French. 4 vols. 8vo. New York, 1828.

Romer, Isabella F. A Pilgrimage to the Temples and Tombs of Egypt, Nubia, and Palestine in 1846. 2 vols. 8vo. London, 1846.

Romer, Isabella F. The Bird of Passage; or, Flying Glimpses of Many Lands. 3 vols. 8vo. London, 1849.

Romer, Isabella F. The Rhone, the Darro, and the Guadalquiver. 2 vols. 8vo. London, 1843.

Ronde, Lambertus de. The True Spiritual Religion. 12mo. New York, 1767.

Roscoe, Henry. Life of William Roscoe. 2 vols. 12mo. Boston, 1833.

Roscoe, Thomas. The Life of William the Conqueror. 8vo. Philadelphia, 1846.

Roscoe, William. The Life of Lorenzo de Medici. 2 vols. 8vo. Philadelphia, 1842.

Rose, Henry. A Manual of Analytical Chemistry. From the German, by John Griffin. 8vo. London, 1831.

Ross, Sir John. Memoirs and Correspondence of Admiral Lord de Saumarez. 2 vols. 8vo. London, 1838.

Rousseau, J. J. Eloisa, or a Series of Original Letters. 3 vols. 12mo. London, 1795.

Rowan, Archibald H. Autobiography. (See Drummond, W. H.)

Roy, Rammohun. Precepts of Jesus, together with the first and second Appeal to the Christian Public. 8vo. New York, 1825.

Royal Magazine. 8vo. London, 1762.

Royall, Anne. Southern Tour, or Second Series of the Black Book. 8vo. Washington, 1831.

Royer, C. E. Notes Economiques sur l'Administration des Richesses et la Statistique Agricole de la France. 8vo. Paris, 1843. *Presented through M. Alexandre Vattemare.*

Ruffin, Edmund. The Farmer's Register. 10 vols. 8vo. Petersburg, 1833–1842.

Ruins of Athens, with other Poems. By a Voyager. 8vo. Washington, 1831.

Rules and Regulations for the Field Exercise and Manœuvres of Infantry. 8vo. New York, 1815. *Presented by Gen. A. Chandler.*

Rules of the Supreme Court of the State of New York. 8vo. Albany, 1818.

Rumford, Benjamin, Count. Essays; Political, Economical, and Philosophical. 2 vols. 8vo. London, 1798.

Rupp, J. Daniel. An Original History of Religious Denominations in the United States. 8vo. Philadelphia, 1844.

Ruschenberger, W. S. W. The First Books of Natural History. 3 vols. 12mo. Philadelphia, 1844.

Elements of Botany.

" " Geology.

Third Book of Natural History.

Ruschenberger, W. S. W. Three Years in the Pacific, including Notices of Brazil, &c., &c. 8vo. Philadelphia, 1834.

Rush, Benjamin. Medical Inquiries and Observations. 8vo. Philadelphia, 1827–1828.

RUSH, BENJAMIN. Medical Inquiries and Observations upon the Disease of the Mind. 8vo. Philadelphia, 1830.

RUSH, RICHARD. Memoranda of a Residence at the Court of London. 8vo. Philadelphia, 1833.
Ditto. Ditto. 8vo. Philadelphia, 1845.

RUSKIN, JOHN. The Seven Lamps of Architecture. 8vo. New York, 1849.

RUSSELL, REV. MICHAEL. View of Ancient and Modern Egypt. 18mo. New York, 1833.

RUSSELL, WILLIAM. The History of Ancient Europe, with a View of the Revolutions in Asia and Africa. 2 vols. 8vo. Philadelphia, 1801.

RUSSELL, WILLIAM. The History of Modern Europe, with an Account of the Decline and Fall of the Roman Empire. 5 vols. 8vo. Philadelphia, 1802. *Presented by the Honorable James Tallmadge.*

RUXTON, GEORGE F. Adventures in Mexico and the Rocky Mountains. 12mo. New York, 1848.

SABINE, EDWARD. Narrative of an Expedition to the Polar Sea in 1820–1823, commanded by Admiral Ferdinand Von Wrangell. 12mo. London, 1846.

SACKVILLE, GEORGE, LORD. Trial. 8vo. London, 1760.

SAILOR'S CHRONICLE, or Interesting Narratives of Shipwrecks. 3 vols. 8vo. London.

SALE, GEORGE. The Koran, commonly called the Alcoran of Mohammed. A new edition, with a Memoir of the Translator. 8vo. Philadelphia, 1850.

SALMON, MR. A new Geographical and Historical Grammar. 8vo. London, 1760.

SALZMANN, G. C. Gymnastics for Youth. 8vo. Philadelphia, 1802.

SAMMES, AYLETT. Britannia Antiqua Illustrata, or the Antiquities of Ancient Britain. Vol. 1. Folio, London, 1676.

SANDERSON, JOHN. Biography of the Signers to the Declaration of Independence. 9 vols. 8vo. Philadelphia, 1823–1827.

SANDS, R. C. Writings in Prose and Verse. 2 vols. 8vo. New York, 1834.

SANFORD, EZEKIEL. A History of the United States before the Revolution, with some account of the Aborigines. 8vo. Philadelphia, 1819.

SANFORD, JOHN. Parochialia, or Church, School, and Parish. The Church System and Services practically considered. 8vo. London, 1845.

SANTAGNELLO, M. A. A Dictionary of the Peculiarities of the Italian Language. 8vo. London, 1820.

SARGENT, JR., JOHN. Memoir of the Rev. Henry Martin. 12mo. New York, 1821.

SATURDAY EVENING. By the Author of "the Natural History of Enthusiasm." 12mo. Hingham, 1833.

SAUMAREZ, ADMIRAL DE. Memoirs and Correspondence. (See Ross, Sir John.)

SAURIN, REV. JAMES. Sermons. From the French, by Robert Robinson. 8 vols. 8vo. Schenectady, 1813.

SAVAGE, MR. The Turkish History. 2 vols. 12mo. London, 1701.

SAVARY, M. The Universal Dictionary of Trade and Commerce. From the French, by M. Postlethwayt. Vol. 1. Folio, London, 1757.

SAXE-WEIMAR, DUKE OF. Travels through North America in 1825–1826. 8vo. Philadelphia, 1828.

SAY, JEAN BAPTISTE. Treatise on Political Economy. From the French, by C. R. Prinsep, with additional Notes, by C. C. Biddle. 8vo. Philadelphia, 1832.

SCENES on the Shores of the Atlantic. By the Author of "Souvenirs of a Summer in Germany," &c. 2 vols. 12mo. London, 1845.

SCENES where the Tempter has Triumphed. By the Author of the "Gaol Chaplain." 8vo. London, 1849.

SCHILLER, FREDERIC. Correspondence. (See Simpson, Leonard.)

SCHILLER, FREDERIC. History of the Thirty Years' War. From the German, by A. J. W. Morrison. 12mo. New York, 1846.

SCHILLER, FREDERIC. Life, &c. (See Carlyle, Thomas.)

SCHLIPF, J. A. Manuel Populaire d'Agriculture traduit de l'Allemand par Napoléon Nicklès. 8vo. Strasbourg et Paris, 1844.

SCHMITZ, L. A History of Rome, from the Earliest Times to the Death of Commodus, A. D. 192. 8vo. Andover, 1847.

SCHMUCKER, S. M. The Errors of Modern Infidelity. 12mo. Philadelphia, 1848.

SCHNITZLER, J. H. Sacred History of the Court and Government of Russia under the Emperors Alexander and Nicholas. 2 vols. 8vo. London, 1847.

SCHOBERL, FREDERIC. Persecutions of Popery. Historical Narratives of the Most Remarkable Persecutions, occasioned by the Intolerance of the Church of Rome. 2 vols. 8vo. London, 1844.

SCHOBEL, FREDERIC. Illyria and Dalmatia. 2 vols. 24mo. London.

SCHOLFIELD, NATHAN. Elements of Plane Geometry and Mensuration. 8vo. New York, 1845. *Presented by the Author.*

SCHOLFIELD, NATHAN. Higher Geometry and Trigonometry. 8vo. New York, 1845.

SCHOMANN, G. F. A Dissertation on the Assemblies of the Athenians. 8vo. Cambridge, 1838.

SCHOOLCRAFT, HENRY R. History, Rise, Condition, and Prospects of the Indian Tribes of the United States. 4to. Philadelphia, 1851. *Presented by the Commissioner of Indian Affairs.*

SCHOOLCRAFT, HENRY R. Narrative Journal of Travels through the North Western Regions of the United States. 8vo. Albany, 1821.

SCHOOLCRAFT, HENRY R. View of the Lead Mines of Missouri. 8vo. New York, 1819.

SCHOOLMASTER, THE. Essays on Practical Education, selected from the Works of Ascham, Milton, Locke, and Butler. 2 vols. 12mo. London, 1836.

SCHREVELI, CORNELII. Lexicon Manuale Grœco Latinum et Latino Grœcum. 8vo. New York, 1832.

SCHRÖDER, F. L. Reytrag zer deutschen Schaubuhne. 12mo. Berlin, 1786.

SCHROEDER, FRANCIS. Shores of the Mediterranean, with Sketches of Travels. 2 vols. 8vo. New York, 1846.

SCHACILER, A. Mary Schaciler, the Amber Witch; edited by Meinhold. From the German by Lady Duff Gordon; together with Undine, and Sintram and his Companions, from the German of F. De La Motte Fonqué. 12mo. New York, 1845.

SCHWERZ, J. N. Culture des Plantes Fourragères, traduit sur la seconde edition, par P. R. De Schauenburg. 8vo. Paris, 1840.

SCHWERZ, J. N. Culture des Plantes a Grains Farineux ou Cereales et Plantes a Cosses, traduit sur la seconde edition par P. R. De Schauenburg. 8vo. Paris, 1840.

SCHWERZ, J. N. Preceptes d'Agriculture Pratique, traduit sur la seconde edition par P. R. De Schauenburg. 8vo. Paris, 1839.

SCIENTIFIC TRACTS. Conducted by Josiah Holbrook and others. 2 vols. Boston, 1832–1833.

SCOTLAND. Enumeration of the Inhabitants of. 8vo. Glasgow, 1823.

SCOTT, DAVID. The History of Scotland. Folio, Westminster, 1728.

SCOTT, REV. A. J. D. D. Recollections of the Life of, Lord Nelson's Chaplain. 8vo. London, 1842.

SCOTT, JAMES. The Life, Letters and Remains of Robert Pollok. 12mo. New York, 1848.

SCOTT, SIR WALTER. Autobiography. 12mo. Philadelphia, 1831.

SCOTT, SIR WALTER. Letters on Demonology and Witchcraft. 18mo. New York, 1832.

SCOTT, SIR WALTER. Life, with a Critical Notice of his Writings, by George Allan. 8vo. Philadelphia, 1835.

SCOTT, SIR WALTER. Life of Napoleon Buonaparte. 3 vols. 8vo. New York, 1828.

SCOTT, SIR WALTER. Life of Napoleon Buonaparte. Abridged. 8vo. New York, 1827.

SCOTT, SIR WALTER. Quintin Durward, a Romance. 2 vols. 12mo. Philadelphia, 1823.

SCOTT, SIR WALTER. The Antiquary. 2 vols. 24mo. Exeter, 1824.

SCOTT, SIR WALTER. The History of Scotland. 2 vols. 12mo. Philadelphia, 1830.

SCOTT, SIR WALTER. The Works of. 7 vols. 8vo. New York, 1833.

Scott, William. New Spelling, Pronouncing and Explanatory Dictionary of the English Language. 12mo. Cork, 1810.

Scott, William. The Harmony of Phrenology with Scripture, shown in a Refutation of the Philosophical Errors contained in Mr. Combs' "Constitution of Man." 8vo. Edinburgh, 1837.

Scribe, Eugene. Victim of the Jesuits, or Piquillo Alliaga. From the French, by Charles Cocks. 3 vols. 8vo. London, 1848.

Seaman, Ezra C. Essays on the Progress of Nations. 8vo. Detroit, 1846.

Seances des Ecoles Normales recueillies par des Sténographes et revues par les Professeurs. Vols. 2 and 4. 8vo. Paris.

Secret History of the Armed Neutrality. By a German Nobleman. 8vo. London, 1792.

Secret History of the Lives and Reigns of the Kings and Queens of England. 2 vols. 12mo. London, 1725.

Seiler, George Frederic. Biblical Hermeneutics, or Scripture Interpretation. With Notes, &c., from the Dutch of J. Heringa. Translated from the Originals, with additional Notes and Observations, by the Rev. William Wright. 8vo. London, 1835.

Selectæ e Veteri Testamento Historie. 18mo. Philadelphia, 1827.

Semedo, F. Alvarez. The History of the Monarchy of China. 4to. London, 1655.

Sergent, John. Select Speeches. 8vo. Philadelphia, 1832.

Session of Parliament for 1825. 8vo. London, 1825.

Seward, Anna. Memoir of the Life of Dr. Erasmus Darwin. 8vo. Philadelphia, 1804.

Sewel, William. The History of the Christian People called Quakers, with a brief Memoir of the Author. 8vo. New York, 1844. *Presented by the Society of Friends.*

Seybert, Adam. Statistical Annals of the United States. 4to. Philadelphia, 1818.

*Shakspere, William. The Comedies, Histories, Tragedies, and Poems. Edited by Charles Knight. 9 vols. (From vol. 1 to 9.) 8vo. London, 1842–1843.

Shallus, Francis. Chronological Tables for Every Day in the Year. 12mo. Norwich, 1812.

SHARP, SAMUEL. A Critical Inquiry into the Present State of Surgery.

SHARSWOOD, GEORGE. The Public and General Statutes passed by Congress, from 1827 to 1847 inclusive. 8vo. Philadelphia, 1848.

SHATTUCK, LEMUEL. Census of Boston, for 1845. 8vo. Boston, 1846.

SHAW, EDWARD. Civil Architecture, or a Complete and Theoretical System of Building. 4to. Boston, 1836.

SHAW, THOMAS B. Outlines of English Literature. 8vo. Philadelphia, 1849.

SHEFFIELD, JOHN, LORD. Observations on the Commerce of the American States. 8vo. London, 1784.

SHEPARD, CHARLES UPHAM. Treatise on Mineralogy. 12mo. New Haven, 1832.

Ditto. Ditto. 12mo. New Haven, 1835. *Presented by Dr. John R. Chapin.*

SHEPARD AND STODDARD. Meditations and Spiritual Exercises. 12mo. Glasgow, 1791.

SHEPHERD, WILLIAM. The Life of Poggio Bracciolini. 8vo. Liverpool, 1837.

SHERIDAN, RICHARD B. Memoirs of his Life. (See Moore, Thomas.)

SHERIDAN, RICHARD B. Speeches, with a Sketch of his Life. Edited by a Constitutional Friend. 3 vols. 8vo. London, 1842.

*SHERIDAN, THOMAS. A General Dictionary of the English Language. 2 vols. 4to. London, 1780.

SHERLOCK, WILLIAM. Practical Discourses concerning Future Judgment. 12mo. London, 1695.

SHERWOOD, HENRY H. The Motive Power of Organic Life. 8vo. New York, 1841. *Presented by the Author.*

SHEYS, B. The American Bookkeeper. 8vo. New York, 1815. *Presented by Dr. Samuel Akerly.*

SHOEMAKERS, Lives of Distinguished. 12mo. Portland, 1849.

SHORT, CAPTAIN CHARLES. Two Expeditions into the Interior of Southern Australia during 1828–1829–1830–1834. 2 vols. 8vo. London, 1834.

SHORT Stories and Reminiscences of the Last Fifty Years. By an Old Traveller. 2 vols. 18mo. New York, 1842.

SIAMESE TWINS. A Satirical Tale of the Times; with other Poems, by the Author of "Pelham," &c. 12mo. New York, 1831.

SIDDONS, MRS. Life. (See Campbell, Thomas.)

SIDNEY, ALGERNON. Works. 4to.

SIDNEY, EDWIN. The Life and History of the Rev. Samuel Walker, B. A. 8vo. London, 1838.

SIDNEY, EDWIN. The Life of Richard Hill, Bart. 8vo. London, 1839.

SIDNEY, HENRY. Diary of the Times of Charles II., including his Correspondence with the Countess of Sunderland, &c. &c. Edited, with Notes, by R. W. Blencowe. 2 vols. 8vo. London, 1843.

SILK MANUFACTURE. A Treatise on the Origin, Progressive Improvement and Present State of. 12mo. Philadelphia, 1832.

SILLIMAN, BENJAMIN. American Journal of Science. 39 vols. 8vo. (vols. 26 and 30 missing,) New York and New Haven, 1819–1841.

SIMMS, J. R. History of Schoharie County, and Border Warfare of New York. 8vo. Albany, 1845. *Presented by the Author.*

SIMMS, W. GILMORE. The Life of Captain John Smith. 8vo. New York, 1846.

SIMOND, L. Switzerland, or a Journal of a Tour and Residence in that Country in 1817–1818–1819, with a Historical Sketch of the Manners and Customs of Ancient and Modern Helvetia. 2 vols. 8vo. London, 1823.

SIMPSON, ALEXANDER. The Life and Travels of Thomas Simpson, the Arctic Discoverer. 8vo. London, 1845.

SIMPSON, LEONARD. Correspondence of Schiller with Körner, comprising Sketches of Goethe, the Schlegel, Wieland and other Contemporaries, with Biographical Sketches and Notes. 3 vols. 8vo. London, 1849.

SIMPSON, THOMAS. Narrative of Discoveries on the North Coast of America. 8vo. London, 1843.

SINCLAIR, CATHERINE. Scotland and the Scotch, or the Western Circuit. 12mo. New York, 1840.

SINCLAIR, SIR JOHN. The Code of Agriculture. 8vo. Hartford, 1818.

SINCLAIR, SIR JOHN. The Code of Health and Longevity. 8vo. London, 1844.

Sinclair, Sir John. The Correspondence of. 2 vols. 8vo. London, 1831.

Sinclair, Sir John. The History of the Public Revenue of the British Empire. 3 vols. 8vo. London, 1803.

Sismondi, J. C. L. de. History of the Italian Republics. 12mo. Philadelphia, 1832.

Sismondi, J. C. L. de. Historical View of the Literature of the South of Europe, translated, &c., by Thomas Roscoe. 2 vols. 12mo. London.

Sister's Budget, (The) by the Author of the "Odd Volume," &c. Vol. 2. Baltimore, 1832.

Skeine, Henry. Two Successive Tours through Wales, &c. 8vo. London, 1798.

Sketch of Bolivar in his Camp. 12mo. New York, 1834.

Sketches of Venetian History. 2 vols. New York, 1832.

Sketches of the Resources of New York City. 8vo. New York, 1827.

Skillman's New York Police Reports. 8vo. New York, 1830.

Skinner, John S. The Monthly Journal of Agriculture. 8vo. New York, 1846. *Presented by Messrs. Greeley and McElrath.*

Skinner, Thomas H. Religion of the Bible. 12mo. New York, 1839.

Slater, Samuel. Memoirs of. (See White, George S.)

Smedley, Edward. The History of France, from the Final Partition of the Empire of Charlemagne, 843, to the Peace of Cambray, 1529. 8vo. London.

Smet, P. I. de. Oregon Missions and Travels over the Rocky Mountains in 1845–1846. 12mo. New York, 1847.

Smith, Aaron. Atrocities of the Pirates. 18mo. New York, 1824.

Smith, Adam. An Inquiry into the Nature and Causes of the Wealth of Nations. 8vo. Edinburgh, 1835.

Smith, Adam. The Theory of Moral Sentiment. 2 vols. 12mo. Edinburgh, 1822.

Smith, Admiral Sir W. S. Life, &c. (See Barrow, John.)

Smith, Augustus W. An Elementary Treatise on Mechanics, embracing the Theory of Statics and Dynamics and its Application to Solids and Fluids. 8vo. New York, 1849.

SMITH, CAPTAIN JOHN. Life. (See Simms, W. G.)

SMITH, CAPTAIN JOHN. Travels, Adventures and Observations of, in Europe, Asia, Africa, and America. 2 vols. 8vo. Richmond, 1819.

SMITH, ELIZABETH E. The Three Eras of Woman's Life. 12mo. New York, 1836.

SMITH, GEORGE. A Narrative of an Exploratory Visit to each of the Consular Cities of China, and to the Islands of Hong Kong and Chusan. 8vo. New York, 1847.

SMITH, G. The Laboratory, or School of Arts. 8vo. London, 1799.

SMITH, GEORGE. Essay on the Construction of Cottages. 8vo. Glasgow, 1834.

SMITH, JAMES. Panorama of Science and Art. 2 vols. 8vo. London. *Presented by J. W. Cochran, Esq.*

SMITH, JAMES T. The Northmen in New England, or America in the Tenth Century. 12mo. Boston, 1839.

SMITH, JEREMIAH. Life. (See Morrison, John H.)

SMITH, JEROME V. C. Natural History of the Fishes of Massachusetts, embracing a Practical Essay on Angling. 12mo. Boston, 1833.

SMITH, JOHN T. An Antiquarian Ramble in the Streets of London, with Anecdotes of their more celebrated Residents. Edited by Charles Mackay. 2 vols. 8vo. London, 1846.

SMITH, JOHN T. Nollekens and his Times. 2 vols. 8vo. London, 1829.

SMITH, JOSEPH A. The Farmer's Mine, or Source of Wealth. Revised and Corrected, by A. B. Allen. 12mo. New York, 1843.

SMITH, NATHAN. Medical and Surgical Memoirs. Edited, with Addenda, by N. R. Smith. 8vo. Baltimore, 1831.

SMITH, OLIVER. Outlines of Nature. 12mo. New York, 1847.

SMITH, REV. SIDNEY. Works. (See Modern British Essayists.)

SMITH, S. LOUISA P. Poems. 12mo. Providence, 1829.

*SMITH, WILLIAM. A Dictionary of Greek and Roman Antiquities. Revised, &c., by Charles Anthon. 8vo. New York, 1850.

*SMITH, WILLIAM. A New Classical Dictionary of Greek and Roman Biography, Mythology, and Geography. Revised, &c., by Charles Anthon. 8vo. New York, 1851.

Smith, William. History of New York. 8vo. Albany, 1814.

Smith, William. Journal of a Voyage to the Pacific Ocean. 12mo. New York, 1813. *Presented by Dr. Samuel Akerly.*

Smith, William A. List of Bankrupts, with Dividends, Certificates, &c. 8vo. London, 1806.

Smithgate, Horatio. Narrative of a Tour through Armenia, Kurdistan, Persia, and Mesopotamia. 2 vols. 8vo. London, 1850.

Smollett, Tobias. Adventures of Peregrine Pickle. 4 vols. 18mo. Philadelphia, 1825.

Smollett, Tobias. Expedition of Humphrey Clinker. Vol. 2. 18mo. Boston, 1818.

Smollett, Tobias. History of England. (See Hume, David.)

Smyth, J. F. D. A Tour in the United States of America. 2 vols. 8vo. London, 1784.

Snowden, Richard. History of North and South America. 12mo. Philadelphia, 1819.

Somerville, Thomas. History of Political Transactions, and of Parties, from the Restoration of Charles II. to the Death of King William. 4to. London, 1792.

Somerville, William C. Letters from Paris on the Causes and Consequences of the French Revolution. 8vo. Baltimore, 1822.

South America. The History of Don Francisco de Miranda's attempt to effect a Revolution in. By a Gentleman who was an Officer under that General; together with Sketches of the Life of Miranda, and Geographical Notices of Caraccas. 12mo. Boston, 1850.

Southern Review. 8 vols. 8vo. Charleston, 1828–1832.

Southey, Robert. Lives of Uneducated Poets, to which are added, Attempts in Verse, by John Jones, an old Servant. 8vo. London, 1836.

Southey, Robert. The Life of Nelson. 18mo. New York, 1833.

Southey, Robert. The Life of Wesley and the Rise and Progress of Methodism. 8vo. New York, 1820.

Southey's Common-Place Book. Edited by John W. Warter. 2 vols. 8vo. New York, 1849.

Spafford, Horatio G. Gazetteer of the State of New York. 8vo. Albany, 1824.

SPAFFORD, HORATIO G. General Geography, and Rudiments of Useful Knowledge. 12mo. Hudson, 1809. *Presented by Dr. Samuel Akerly.*

SPAIN AND PORTUGAL. History of. 4 vols. 12mo. Philadelphia, 1832.

SPARKS, JARED. Life of Gouverneur Morris. 3 vols. 8vo. Boston, 1832.

SPARKS, JARED. Life of John Ledyard, the American Traveller. 12mo. Cambridge, 1829.

SPARKS, JARED. The Library of American Biography. 15 vols. 12mo. Boston, 1844–1848.

SPARKS, JARED. The Works of Benjamin Franklin, with Notes and a Life of the Author. 10 vols. 8vo. Boston, 1840.

SPARKS, JARED. The Writings of George Washington, with a Life of the Author, Notes and Illustrations. 12 vols. 8vo. New York, 1847–1848.

*SPECTATOR, THE. 4 vols. fol. New York, 1797–1801.

SPECTATOR, THE. With Notes, and a General Index. 2 vols. 8vo. New York, 1826.

SPEECHES on the Passage of the Bill for the Removal of the Indians. 12mo. Boston, 1830.

SPELMAN, JOHANNES. Vita Alfredi Magni Anglorum Regis. Fol. Oxford, 1678.

SPENCER, J. A. The East. Sketches of Travels in Egypt and the Holy Land. 8vo. New York, 1850.

SPOHR, D. C. H. Veterinarisches Handbuch. 12mo. Nürnberg, 1798.

SPORTSMAN, THE, in Ireland, with his Summer Route through the Highlands of Scotland. By a Cosmopolite. 2 vols. 8vo. London, 1840.

SPORTSMAN'S DICTIONARY, or the Gentleman's Companion. 8vo. Dublin, 1780.

SPRAGUE, CHARLES. Writings of. 8vo. New York, 1841.

SPRAGUE, JOHN F. The Origin, Progress and Conclusion of the Florida War. 8vo. New York, 1848.

SPROUL, JOHN. Elements of Practical Agriculture. 8vo. London, 1844.

SPRY, HENRY H. Modern India, with Illustrations of the Resources and Capabilities of Hindustan. 2 vols. 8vo. London, 1837.

Stael, Madame de. A Treatise on the Influence of the Passions. 8vo. London, 1798.

Standish, Frank Hall. The Life of Voltaire, with interesting particulars respecting his Death, and Anecdotes and Characters of his Contemporaries. 8vo. London, 1821.

Stanford, John. The Christian Pocket Library. 2 vols. 12mo. New York, 1796–1800.

Stansbury, Daniel. Tables to Facilitate the Necessary Calculations in Nautical Astronomy. 4to. New York, 1821. *Presented by Dr. Samuel Akerly.*

Stanton, Sir George. An Account of an Embassy from Great Britain to China. 2 vols. 8vo. Philadelphia, 1799.

Stappleton, A. E. The Political Life of George Canning. 3 vols. 8vo. London, 1831.

Stark, General John. Life and Military Services, and Reminiscences of the French War. 12mo. Concord, 1831. *Presented by Caleb Stark, Esq.*

Stark, John. Elements of Natural History. 2 vols. 8vo. Edinburgh, 1828.

Starling, Elizabeth. Noble Deeds of Woman, or Examples of Female Courage and Virtue. 8vo. London, 1850.

State Triumvirate, a Political Tale, and the Epistles of Pindar Pugg. 18mo. New York, 1819.

Statistique des Routes Royales de France. 4to. Paris, 1844. *Presented through M. Alexandre Vattemare.*

Statutes relating to the Sewers within Westminster and Middlesex. 12mo. London, 1826.

St. Chrysostom. Life of. (See Neander, Augustus.)

Steel, John H. An Analysis of the Mineral Waters of Saratoga and Ballston. 18mo. Albany, 1819.

Steel, Sir Richard. A Remedy for Wandering Thoughts in the Worship of God. 12mo. New York, 1835.

Steel, Sir Richard. Epistolary Correspondence. (See Nichols, John.)

Steinmetz, Andrew. Voice in Ramah; or, Lament of the Poor African, a Fettered Exile afar from his Fatherland. A Poem. 12mo. London, 1842.

Steinmetz, Andrew. History of the Jesuits from the Foundation of their Society to its Suppression, by Pope Clement XIV. 2 vols. 8vo. Philadelphia, 1848.

Stephens, George. The Practical Irrigator. 8vo. Edinburgh, 1829.

Stephens, James. Essays. (See Modern British Essayists.)

Stephens, John L. Incidents of Travel in Yucatan. 2 vols. 8vo. New York, 1843.

Sterling, William Alexander, Earl of. Life. (See Duer, William A.)

Sterne, Laurence. Life and Opinions of Tristram Shandy. 2 vols. 12mo. New York, 1813.

Sterne, Laurence. Sentimental Journey, with Memoirs of his Life and Family. 18mo. New York, 1827.

Sterne, Laurence. Works. 4 vols. 12mo. Edinburgh, 1803.

Steuart, Sir Henry. The Planter's Guide. 8vo. New York, 1832.

Steuart, Sir James. An Inquiry into the Principles of Political Economy. 2 vols. 4to. London, 1767.

Stevenson, W. B. A Historical and Descriptive Narrative of Twenty Years Residence in South America. 3 vols. 8vo. London, 1825.

Stewart, Dugald. Philosophical Essays. 8vo. Edinburgh, 1818.

Stewart, John. Stable Economy, with Notes and Additions, adapting it to American Food and Climate, by A. B. Allen. 12mo. New York, 1845.

Stewart, J. W. Treble Almanac. 12mo. Dublin, 1824.

Stickney, Sarah. Home, or the Iron Rule. A Domestic Story. 12mo. New York, 1836.

St. John, Bayle. Adventures in the Lybian Desert, and the Oasis of Jupiter Ammon. 8vo. New York, 1849.

St. John, J. A. The Lives of Celebrated Travellers. 3 vols. 18mo. New York, 1832.

St. John, J. A. The History of the Manners and Customs of Ancient Greece. 3 vols. 8vo. London, 1842.

St. John, J. H. Letters from an American Farmer. 8vo. London, 1782.

St. John, John R. A True Description of the Lake Superior Country, its Rivers, Coasts, Bay, Harbors, Islands, and Commerce; also, a Minute Account of the Copper Mines of Working Companies. 12mo. New York, 1846.

St. John, Percy B. The Three Days of the French Revolution of February, 1848. 12mo. London, 1848.

St. Marie, Count. Algeria in 1845. A Visit to the French Possessions in Africa. 8vo. London, 1846.

Stocqueler, J. H. The Hand Book of India, or a Guide to the Stranger and the Traveller, and a Companion to the Resident. 8vo. London, 1844.

Stoltz, J. L. Manuel Elementaire du Cultivateur Alsacien. 12mo. Strasbourg, 1842.

Stone, Mrs. Chronicles of Fashion, from the Time of Elizabeth to the Early Part of the Nineteenth Century, in Manners, Amusements, Banquets, Costume, &c. 2 vols. 8vo. London, 1845.

Stone, William L. Life of Joseph Brant, (Thayendanegea,) including the Indian Wars of the American Revolution. 2 vols. 8vo. New York, 1838.

Stone, William L. Matthias and his Impostures. 12mo. New York, 1835.

Stone, William L. Tales and Sketches. Vol. 1. 12mo. New York, 1834.

Story, Joseph. Commentaries on the Constitution of the United States. 3 vols. 8vo. Boston, 1833.

Story, Joseph. Miscellaneous Writings, Literary, Critical, Judicial, and Political. 8vo. Boston, 1835.

Story, Joseph. The Public and General Statutes passed by Congress from 1789 to 1827 inclusive. 4 vols. 8vo. Boston, 1828.

St. Pierre, J. B. de. The Works of, comprising the Studies of Nature, the Indian Cottage, and Paul and Virginia; with a Memoir of the Author, and Explanatory Notes, by the Rev. E. Clarke. 2 vols. 18mo. London, 1846.

Strickland, Agnes. Lives of the Queens of England from the Norman Conquest, with Anecdotes of their Courts. 6 vols. 8vo. Philadelphia, 1850.

Strong, A. B. The American Flora, or History of Plants and Wild Flowers. 4 vols. 4to. New York, 1848–1850.

STRUVE, C. A. Practical Essay on the Art of Reviving Suspended Animation. 12mo. Albany, 1803.

STUART, GILBERT. View of Society in Europe. 8vo. London, 1813.

STUD BOOK FRANCAIS. Registre des Chevaux, de Par Sang. 3 vols. 8vo. Paris, 1838–1843.

SULLIVAN, WILLIAM. Political Class Book; with an Appendix, by George R. Emerson. 12mo. Boston, 1831.

SUPREME COURT. Minutes of, from August, 1701, to October, 1704. MS. folio.

SUTCLIFFE, JOHN. Treatise on Canals and Reservoirs. 8vo. Rochdale, 1816.

SVININE, PAUL. Some Details concerning General Moreau and his Last Moments. From the French. 12mo. Boston, 1814.

SWAN, ABRAHAM. A Collection of Designs in Architecture. Folio, London.

SWAN, ABRAHAM. The British Architect, or the Builder's Treasury of Staircases. Folio, Philadelphia, 1775.

SWEDEN AND GOTTLAND. Rambles in, with Etchings by the Way-side. By Sylvanus. 8vo. London, 1847.

SWEENEY, ROBERT. Odds and Ends. 12mo. New York, 1826.

SWIFT, JONATHAN. Interesting Miscellanies on a Variety of Subjects. 12mo. New York, 1816.

SWIFT, JONATHAN. Works. 2 vols. 8vo. London, 1843.

SWITZERLAND. History of. 12mo. Philadelphia, 1832.

TABLEAU HISTORIQUE et Politique de Marseille Ancienne et Moderne. 12mo. Marseilles, 1810.

TABLEAU ET RELEVÉS de Population, de Cultures, de Commerce, de Navigation, etc., sur les Colonies Françaises. 8vo. Paris, 1842.

TABLES of the Revenue, Population, Commerce, &c., of the United Kingdom and its Dependencies. Fol. London, 1834.

TACITUS, C. CORNELIUS. 18mo. Amstelædami, 1649.

TACITUS, C. CORNELIUS. Works, with an Essay on his Life and Genius, by Arthur Murphy. 6 vols. 8vo. New York, 1822.

TALFOURD, T. NOON. Writings. (See Modern British Essayists.)

TALLEYRAND, C. M. Memoirs of, by the Author of the Revolutionary Plutarch. 2 vols. 12mo. London, 1805.

TALLMADGE, JAMES. Speeches. 8vo.

TANNEHILL, WILKINS. Sketches of the History of Literature, from the Earliest Period to the Revival of Letters in the Fifteenth Century. 8vo. Nashville, 1827.

TANNER'S UNIVERSAL ATLAS. Accompaniment to. 12mo. Philadelphia, 1843.

TARIFFS. Examination of the New Tariff, proposed by Henry Baldwin. By One of the People. 8vo. New York, 1821.

TAVANTI, G. Trattato Teorico Pratico Completo Sull' Ulivo. 2 vols. 8vo. Firenze, 1819.

TAYLOR, C. B. Social Evils and their Remedy. The Mechanic. 18mo. New York, 1834.

TAYLOR, J. BAYARD. Pedestrian Tour in Europe. Views A-Foot, or Europe seen with a Knapsack and Staff. With a Preface, by N. P. Willis. 12mo. New York, 1841.

TAYLOR, JAMES. A View of the Money System in England. 8vo. London, 1828.

TAYLOR, JOHN. Tyranny Unmasked. 8vo. Washington, 1822.

TAYLOR, RICHARD. Scientific Memoirs. Vols. 2 and 3. 8vo. London, 1841–1843.

TAYLOR, RICHARD C. The Geology of East Norfolk. 8vo. London, 1827.

TAYLOR, W. B. S. The Origin, Progress and Present Condition of the Fine Arts in Great Britain and Ireland. 2 vols. 8vo. London, 1841.

TAYLOR, W. C. History of Ireland, from the Anglo-Norman Invasion, till the Union of the Countries with Great Britain. With Additions, by William Sampson. 2 vols. 18mo. New York, 1833.

TAYLOR, W. C. Illustrations of the Bible from the Monuments of Egypt. 12mo. London, 1838.

TAYLOR, W. C. The Modern British Plutarch, or Lives of Men distinguished in the Recent History of England for their Talents, Virtues or Achievements. 12mo. New York, 1846.

TEGG, THOMAS. Chronology, or the Historian's Companion. 12mo. London, 1826.

TEIGNMOUTH, LORD. Memoirs of the Life, Writings and Correspondence of Sir William Jones. 4to. London, 1800.

TEMPLE, EDWARD. Travels in Various Parts of Peru, including a Year's Residence in Potosi. 2 vols. 12mo. Philadelphia, 1833.

TEMPLE, SIR GREENVILLE. Travels in Greece and Turkey, and the Mediterranean. 2 vols. 8vo. London, 1843.

TEMPLE, THEODORE. Secret Discipline, mentioned in Ancient Ecclesiastical History, Explained. 12mo. New York, 1833.

TEMPLE, SIR WILLIAM. An Introduction to the History of England. 12mo. London, 1708.

TEMPLE, SIR WILLIAM. Works. 2 vols. 8vo. London, 1731.

TENNENT, J. E. Belgium. 2 vols. 8vo. London, 1841.

TERENTII PUBLII Comædiæ Sex Scholia Anonymi adjunxit, J. A. Giles. 8vo. London, 1837.

TERRY, ADRIAN R. Travels in the Equatorial Regions of South America in 1832. 12mo. Hartford, 1834.

TESTIMONY in the New Jersey Contested Election. 8vo. Washington, 1840.

THATCHER, B. B. Indian Biography. 2 vols. 18mo. New York, 1839.

THIERS, M. A. The History of the Consulate and Empire of Napoleon, from the last Paris edition, with Notes. 8vo. London, 1850.

THIERS, M. A. The History of the French Revolution, translated, &c., by Frederick Shoberl. 2 vols. 8vo. Philadelphia, 1844. *Presented by the Hon. James Tallmadge.*

THIMM, FRANZ L. J. The Literature of Germany, from its Earliest Period to the Present Time, edited by W. A. Farn. 12mo. London and Leipzig.

THINGS AS THEY ARE, or Notes of a Traveller through some of the Middle and Northern States. 12mo. New York, 1834.

THIRLWALL, BISHOP CONNOP. A History of Greece. 2 vols. 8vo. New York, 1845.

THOMAS, DAVID. Travels through the Western Country. 12mo. Auburn, 1819. *Presented by Dr. Samuel Akerly.*

THOMAS, ISAIAH. History of Printing in America, with a Biography of Printers, and an Account of Newspapers. 2 vols. 8vo. Worcester, 1810.

THOMAS, ISAIAH. The Perpetual Laws of the Commonwealth of Massachusetts. Vol. 2. 8vo. Worcester, 1799.

THOMAS, JOHN PENFORD. A Treatise on Universal Jurisprudence. 8vo. London, 1829.

THOMPSON, BENJAMIN F. History of Long Island. 8vo. New York, 1839.

THOMPSON, E. P. The Note-Book of a Naturalist. 8vo. London, 1845.

THOMPSON, HENRY. The Life of Hannah More, with Notices of her Sisters. 8vo. London, 1838.

THOMPSON, JOSEPH P. Memoir of David Hale, with Selections from his Miscellaneous Writings. 8vo. New York, 1850.

THOMPSON, WADDY. Recollections of Mexico. 8vo. London, 1846.

THOMPSON, ZADOCK. Gazetteer of the State of Vermont. 12mo. Montpelier, 1824.

THOMSON, ANTHONY. Occult Sciences. The Philosophy of Magic, Prodigies and Apparent Miracles. From the French of Eusebe Salverte, with Notes, Illustrative, Explanatory and Critical. 2 vols. 8vo. London, 1846.

THOMSON, JAMES. Letters on the Moral and Religious State of South America. 12mo. London, 1827.

THOMSON, MRS. Memoirs of the Jacobites of 1715 and 1745. 3 vols. 8vo. London, 1845.

THOMSON, MRS. A. T. Memoirs of the Life of Sir Walter Raleigh. 12mo. Philadelphia, 1831.

THORNTON, R. J. Elements of Botany. 2 vols. 8vo. London, 1812. *Presented by Charles Whitlaw, Esq.*

THORNTON, R. J. The British Flora. Vol. 2. Plates. 8vo. London, 1812. *Presented by Charles Whitlaw, Esq.*

THORNTON, W. Cadmus, or a Treatise on the Elements of Written Language. 8vo. Philadelphia, 1793.

THORESBY, RALPH. Diary, published from the Original Manuscript, by Rev. Joseph Hunter. 2 vols. 8vo. London, 1830.

THORESBY, RALPH. Letters of Eminent Men, addressed to. 2 vols. 8vo. London, 1832.

THYER, ROBERT. The Genuine Poetical Remains of Samuel Butler. 8vo. London, 1827.

TICKNOR, GEORGE. History of Spanish Literature. 3 vols. 8vo. New York, 1849.

TIME of the End Not Yet. 8vo. London, 1850.

TIMON. The Orators of France; with an Essay on the Rise of French Revolutionary Eloquence and the Orators of the Girondists, by J. T. Headly. Edited by G. H. Colton, with Notes, and Biographical Appendix. 8vo. New York, 1847.

TIMOUR. Institutes, Political and Military. Translated by Major Davy, with Notes, &c., by J. White. 4to. Oxford, 1783.

TIMPERLEY, C. H. A Dictionary of Printers and Printing, with the Progress of Literature, Ancient and Modern, Bibliographical Illustrations, etc. 8vo. London, 1839.

TIMPSON, THOMAS. Memoirs of British Female Missionaries. With an Introductory Essay on the Importance of Female Agency in Evangelising Pagan Nations, by Miss Thompson. 12mo. London, 1841.

TINDAL, MATTHEW. Christianity as Old as Creation, or the Gospel a Republication of the Religion of Nature. 8vo. Newburgh, 1798.

TINELLI, LEWIS. Hints on the Cultivation of the Mulberry and the Production of Silk. 12mo. New York, 1837.

TITHES. A New Treatise on the Laws concerning Tithes. 12mo. London, 1766.

TOCQUEVILLE, ALEXIS DE. Democracy in America. Translated by H. Reeve, with an Original Preface and Notes, by John C. Spencer. 2 vols. 8vo. New York, 1845.

TOKEN, THE. Christmas and New Years' Present. Edited by S. G. Goodrich. 18mo. Boston, 1830.

TOMLINE, GEORGE. Elements of Christian Theology. Fourteenth edition. With Additional Notes, and a Summary of Ecclesiastical History, by Henry Stebbins, D.D. 2 vols. 8vo. London, 1843.

TOOKE, JOHN HORNE. Diversions of Purley. 2 vols. 8vo. Philadelphia, 1806.

TOOKE'S Parthenon of the Heathen Gods and Illustrious Heroes. 12mo. Baltimore, 1817.

TOTT, BARON DE. Memoirs, containing the State of the Turkish Empire, during the War with Russia; with Anecdotes, Facts, and Observations on the Manners and Customs of the Turks and Tartars. From the French. 2 vols. 8vo. London, 1780.

TOUR. History of a Six Weeks' Tour through a part of France, Switzerland, Germany and Holland. 18mo. London, 1817.

TOWER, F. B. Illustrations of the Croton Aqueduct. 4to. New York, 1843.

TOWN and Country Magazine, or Universal Repository. 8vo. London, 1782.

TOWNSEND, P. S. An Account of the Yellow Fever. 8vo. New York, 1823.

TRANSACTIONS and Collections of the American Antiquarian Society. 8vo. Cambridge, 1836.

TRANSACTIONS of the American Institute. (See American Institute.)

TRANSACTIONS of the American Philosophical Society. 4to. Philadelphia, 1804.

TRANSACTIONS of the Highland Agricultural Society of Scotland. 2 vols. 8vo. Edinburgh, 1843–1847.

TRANSACTIONS of the Institution of Civil Engineers. 3 vols. 4to. London, 1836. *Presented by the Society.*

TRANSACTIONS of the Michigan State Agricultural Society, with Reports of County Agricultural Societies. 8vo. Lansing, 1850. *Presented by the Society.*

TRANSACTIONS of the New York State Agricultural Society. 10 vols. 8vo. Albany, 1842–1851.

TRANSACTIONS of the Royal Humane Society. By W. Hawes. Vol. 1. 8vo. London, 1774–1794.

TRANSACTIONS of the Society for the Encouragement of Arts, Manufactures, and Commerce. 55 vols. 8vo. London, 1789–1843.

TRANSACTIONS of the Society for the Encouragement of Arts, Manufactures, and Commerce. Vols. 19, 21, 22. 8vo. London, 1801–1803–1804.

TRANSACTIONS of the Society for the Promotion of Useful Arts in the State of New York. 8vo. Albany, 1807.

TRANSACTIONS of the Society for the Promotion of Agriculture, Arts, and Manufactures, instituted in the State of New York. 8vo. Albany, 1801.

TRAVANET, M. LE MIS. DE. Physiologie de la Terre, Etudes Geologiques et Agricoles. 8vo. Bourges et Paris, 1844.

TRAVANET, M. LE MIS. DE. Preservatif d'Agromanie Empirique ou Letters Agricoles. 8vo. Paris, 1845.

TRAVELLER'S Guide through Scotland. 2 vols. 12mo. Edinburgh, 1824.

TREASURY of Knowledge and Library of Reference. 2 vols. 12mo. New York, 1836.

Vol. 1. Brown, Gould. English Grammar.
Cobb, Lyman. English Dictionary.
Williams, Edwin. New Universal Gazetteer. Epitome of Chronology and History; Classical and Law Dictionary.
" 2. Moore, Hugh. Dictionary of Quotations.
Phillips, Sir R. Million of Facts.
Knapp, Samuel L. American Biography.

TREATISE on the Police of the Metropolis. By a Magistrate. 8vo. London, 1796.

Ditto. Ditto. Revised and Enlarged. 8vo. London, 1797.

TREATIES. A List of, between Great Britain and Other Powers, from 1788 to 1808. Alphabetically and Chronologically Arranged. 4to. MS.

TREDGOLD, THOMAS. Essay on the Strength of Cast Iron and other Metals. 8vo. London, 1831.

TREDGOLD, THOMAS. The Principles of Warming and Ventilating Public Buildings, &c. With an Appendix, by T. Bramah. 8vo. London, 1836.

TREMONT HOUSE. A Description of, with Architectural Illustrations. 4to. Boston, 1830.

TRENCK, BARON JAMES. Life of. 2 vols. 24mo. Exeter, 1828.

TROLLOPE, MRS. The Refugees in America: a Novel. 12mo. New York, 1833.

TRUMBULL, BENJAMIN. History of Connecticut. 2 vols. 8vo. Hartford, 1797.

TRUMBULL, HENRY. History of the Discovery of America, of the Landing of our Forefathers at Plymouth, &c. 12mo. Norwich, 1812.

TRUMBULL, JOHN. Autobiography, Reminiscences, and Letters, from 1756 to 1841. 8vo. New York, 1841.

TRUMBULL, JOHN. M'Fingal. A Poem. 12mo.

TRUMBULL, JOHN. Poetical Works. 8vo. Hartford, 1820.

TRUMBULL, WILLIAM. Treatise on the Strength and Stiffness of Timber. 8vo. London, 1833.

TRYXELL, ANDREW. The History of Sweden. From the Original, edited by Mary Howitt. 2 vols. 8vo. London, 1844.

TSCHUDI, J. J. VON. Travels in Peru, during the Years 1838–1842. From the German, by Thomasina Ross. 12mo. New York, 1848.

TUCKER, GEORGE. Progress of the United States in Population and Wealth in Fifty Years. 8vo. New York, 1843.

TUCKER, GEORGE. The Life of Thomas Jefferson. 2 vols. 8vo. London, 1838.

TUDOR, HENRY. Narrative of a Tour in North America. 2 vols. 8vo. London, 1834.

TUKE, HENRY. Memoirs of the Life of George Fox. 12mo. Philadelphia, 1815.

TURKEY. Sketches of, in 1831–1832. By an American. 8vo. New York, 1833.

TURNBULL, DAVID. Cuba, with Notices of Porto Rico, and the Slave Trade. 8vo. London, 1840.

TURNBULL, REV. ROBERT. The Genius of Italy, being Sketches of Italian Life, Literature and Religion. 8vo. New York, 1849.

TURNBULL, REV. ROBERT. The Genius of Scotland: a Sketch of Scottish Scenery, Literature and Religion. 8vo. New York, 1847.

TURNER, EDWARD. Elements of Chemistry. With Notes, &c., by Franklin Bache. 12mo. Philadelphia, 1835.

TURNER, SHARON. The Sacred History of the World. 18mo. New York, 1833.

TURNER, WILLIAM. Journal of a Tour in the Levant. 3 vols. 8vo. London, 1820.

TWISS, HORACE. The Public and Private Life of Lord Chancellor Eldon, with Selections from his Correspondence. 2 vols. 8vo. Philadelphia, 1844.

TWISS, TRAVERS. The Oregon Territory, its History and Discovery, &c. 12mo. New York, 1846.

TYFE, ANDREW. Elements of Chemistry. With Additions and Alterations, by John White Webster. 12mo. Boston, 1827.

TYLER, J. ENDELL. Henry of Monmouth; or Memoirs of the Life and Character of Henry V. as Prince of Wales and King of England. 2 vols. 8vo. London, 1838.

TYTLER, ALEXANDER F. Elements of General History. 12mo. Concord, 1825.

TYTLER, PATRICK F. England under the Reigns of Edward VI. and Mary, with Contemporary History of Europe, with Historical Introductions and Biographical and Critical Notes. 2 vols. 8vo. London, 1839.

UFFORD, HEZEKIAH G. An Elementary Treatise on Logic. 12mo. New York, 1823.

UNITED STATES of America as they are. 8vo. London, 1828.

UNITED STATES Form Book. By a Member of the New York Bar. 8vo. New York, 1845.

UNITED STATES. General Outline of. 8vo. Philadelphia, 1825.

UNITED STATES. History of, for 1796. 8vo. Philadelphia, 1797.

UNITED STATES Magazine and Democratic Review. Edited by Thomas P. Kettell. 2 vols. 8vo. New York, 1847.

UNITED STATES. Thrilling Incidents in the Wars of. By the Author of the Army and Navy of the United States. 8vo. Philadelphia, 1848.

UNIVERSAL Biographical Dictionary. 12mo. New York, 1825.

UNIVERSAL Biographical Dictionary. 8vo. Hartford, 1829.

UNIVERSAL Merchant, improved and enlarged, by W. J. Alldridge. 8vo. Philadelphia, 1798.

UNIVERSAL Pocket Gazetteer. 12mo. Boston, 1832.

*URE, ANDREW. A Dictionary of Arts, Manufactures, and Mines. 2 vols. 8vo. New York, 1843.

*URE, ANDREW. Recent Improvements, a Supplement to his Dictionary. 8vo. New York, 1845.

URE, ANDREW. Philosophy of Manufactures. 8vo. London, 1836.

URQUHART, DAVID. The Pillars of Hercules; or a Narrative of Travels in Spain and Morocco in 1848. 2 vols. 8vo. London, 1850.

UZTARIZ, DON G. DE. The Theory and Practice of Commerce and Maritime Affairs. From the Spanish, by John Kippax. Vol. 2. 8vo. London, 1751.

VADE MECUM, or Necessary Pocket Companion. 8vo. London, 1739.

VALENTINE, DAVID T. Manual of the Corporation of the City of New York. 7 vols. 18mo. and 12mo. 1842–1850. *Presented by the Compiler.*

VALENTINE, LEWIS. Voyages en Italie. 8vo. Paris, 1826.

VAN AMRINGE, W. F. An Investigation of the Theories of the Natural History of Man, by Lawrence Prichard and others. 8vo. New York, 1848.

VAN ESS, W. L. Life of Napoleon Buonaparte. 2 vols. 8vo. Philadelphia, 1809.

VAN RENSSELAER, J. Lectures on Geology. 8vo. New York, 1825.

VARLO, C. A New System of Husbandry. Vol. 2. 12mo. Philadelphia, 1785.

VAUGHAN, REV. DR. The History of England, under the House of Stuart, including the Commonwealth. 2 vols. 8vo. London.

VENEGAS, MIGUEL. A Natural and Civil History of California. 2 vols. 12mo. London, 1759.

VENICE under the Yoke of France and of Austria, with Memoirs of the Courts, Governments and People of Italy, by a Lady of Rank. 2 vols. 8vo. London, 1824.

VENTONILLAC, L. T. The French Librarian, a Literary Guide. 8vo. London, 1829.

VERICOUR, L. RAYMOND DE. Modern French Literature. Revised, &c., by W. S. Chase. 8vo. Boston, 1848.

VERMONT State Papers. 8vo. Middlebury, 1823.

VERNON, JAMES. Letters Illustrative of the Reign of William III. from 1696 to 1708, addressed to the Duke of Shrewsbury. Edited by G. P. R. James. 3 vols. 8vo. London, 1841.

VERPLANCK, GULIAN C. Discourse on the Advantages and Dangers of the American Scholar. 8vo. New York, 1836.

VERRI, ALESSANDRO. Roman Nights, or the Tomb of the Scipios. 2 vols. 12mo. New York, 1826.

VERTOT, ABBÉ. A Critical History of the Establishment of the Bretons among the Gauls. 12mo. London, 1722.

VERTOT, L'ABBE DE. The History of the Knights Hospitallers of St. John of Jerusalem, styled afterwards the Knights of Rhodes, and at Present the Knights of Malta. 3 vols. 8vo. Dublin, 1818.

VESTIGES of the Natural History of Creation. With an Introduction, by Rev. George B. Cheever. 8vo. New York, 1845.

VETERINARIAN, THE, or Monthly Journal of Veterinary Science. Edited by Messrs. Youatt and Percival. 8vo. London, 1844.

VICARY, REV. M. Notes of a Residence at Rome in 1846. 8vo. London, 1847.

*VIEYRA, ANTHONY. A Dictionary of the Portuguese and English Languages. 2 vols. 8vo. London, 1805. *Presented by James Green, Esq.*

VIEYRA, P. ANTONIO. Relaçaõ Exactissima do Procedimento das Inquiziçõis de Portugal. 12mo. Veneza, 1750.

VIGNE, GODFREY T. Six Months in America. 18mo. Philadelphia, 1833.

VIGNY, COUNT, ALFRED DE. Cinq Mars; or a Conspiracy under Louis XIII. An Historical Romance, translated by William Hazlitt. 12mo. London, 1847.

VIRGIL. Works. Translated by John Dryden. 2 vols. 24mo. New York, 1825.

VIRGILII, PUBLII MARONIS. Opera, or the Works of Virgil. With Copious Notes, by J. G. Cooper. 8vo. New York, 1832. *Presented by Gen. A. Chandler.*

VIRGINIA. First Settlers of. An Historical Novel. 12mo. New York, 1806.

VITRINGA, CAMPEGIUS. Korte Schets van de Christelyke Zeden. Leere ofte van het Geestelyk Leven, &c., uit Set Latyn vertaalt, door Johannes d'Outrein. 12mo. Amsterdam, 1724.

VOLNEY, C. F. View of the Soil and Climate of the United States of America. Translated by C. B. Brown. 8vo. Philadelphia, 1804.

VOLNEY, C. F. Volney's Ruins, or Meditations on the Revolution of Empires. 12mo. Dublin, 1811.

VOLTAIRE, F. M. AROUET DE. An Essay on the Manners and Spirit of Nations, and on the Principal Occurrences in History, from Charlemagne to Louis XIII. From the French, with Notes, Critical and Explanatory, by William Campbell, J. Johnson, and others, under the direction of W. Kenrick, LL. D. 4 vols. 8vo. London, 1779.

VOLTAIRE, F. M. AROUET DE. Letters on the English Nation. 8vo. London, 1733.

VOLTAIRE, F. M. AROUET DE. Life. (See Condorcet, Marquis de.)

VOLTAIRE, F. M. AROUET DE. Life. (See Standish, F. H.)

VOLTAIRE, F. M. AROUET DE. Philosophical Dictionary. 12mo. Catskill, 1805.

VOSGIEN. Dictionnaire Geographique. 8vo. Lyons, 1811.

VOYAGES and Discoveries. By Sir John Narbrough, F. Tasman, J. Wood, and F. Martin. 12mo. London, 1711.

WACHSMUTH, WILLIAM. The Historical Antiquities of the Greeks, with reference to their Political Institutions. From the German, by Edmund Woolrych. 2 vols. 8vo. Oxford, 1837.

*WADE, JOHN. British History, Chronologically arranged. 8vo. London, 1847.

WAGNER, RUDOLPH. Elements of Physiology. From the German, with Additions, by Robert Willis. 8vo. London, 1844.

WAKEMAN, WILLIAM T. Archæologia Hibernia. A Hand Book of Irish Antiquities, Pagan and Christian. 12mo. Dublin, 1848.

WALDO, S. PUTNAM. Tour of James Monroe through the Northern and Eastern States in 1817–1818, with a Sketch of his Life. 12mo. Hartford, 1820.

WALES, PRINCESS OF. "The Book," or Proceedings and Correspondence upon the Subject of the Inquiry into the Conduct of. 12mo. New York, 1813.

WALKER, EDWARD. The Art of Book Binding, its Rise and Progress, &c. 8vo. New York, 1850.

WALKER, GEORGE. Examples of English Prose, from the Reign of Elizabeth to the Present Time, with an Introduction. 8vo. London.

WALKER, JAMES. The Comparative Merits of Locomotive and Fixed Engines. With Observations, by Robert Stephenson and James Locke, and an Account of the Liverpool and Manchester Railways, by Henry Booth. 8vo. Philadelphia, 1831.

WALKER, JOHN. A Critical Pronouncing Dictionary and Expositor of the English Language. 4to. London, 1797.

WALKER, JOHN. Rhetorical Grammar. 8vo. Boston, 1822.

WALKER, REV. SAMUEL. Life. (See Sidney, Edwin.)

WALLER's Hibernian Magazine. 8vo. London, 1799.

WALLIS, S. T. Glimpses of Spain; or Notes of an Unfinished Tour in 1847. 12mo. New York, 1849.

WALPOLE, HORACE A Catalogue of the Royal and Noble Authors of England, with a List of their Works. 8vo. Edinburgh, 1796.

WALPOLE, HORACE. Historic Doubts on the Life and Reign of Richard III. 4to. London, 1748.

WALPOLE, HORACE. Letters of. 6 vols. 8vo. London, 1840.

WALPOLE, HORACE. Letters to Sir Horace Mann. 2 vols. 8vo. Philadelphia, 1844.

WALPOLE, HORACE. Letters to Sir Horace Mann. 4 vols. 8vo. London, 1843.

WALPOLE, HORACE. Letters addressed to the Countess of Ossory, from 1769 to 1797. Edited, with Notes, by the Right Honorable R. Vernon Smith. 2 vols. 8vo. London, 1848.

WALPOLE, HORACE. Memoirs of the Reign of George III. 2 vols. 8vo. Philadelphia, 1845.

WALSH. Letters on the Genius and Dispositions of the French Government. 8vo. Philadelphia, 1810.

WALSH, R. Notices of Brazil, in 1828–1829. 2 vols. 12mo. Boston, 1831.

WALSH, JR., ROBERT. An Appeal from the Judgments of Great Britain respecting the United States of America. 8vo. Philadelphia, 1819.

WALTON, IZAAC. The Lives of Dr. John Doane, Sir Henry Wotton, Mr. Richard Hooker, Mr. George Herbert, and Dr. Robert Sanderson. With some account of the Author and his Writings, by Thomas Zouch. 12mo. New York, 1846.

WALTON, IZAAC, AND CHARLES COTTON. The Complete Angler, or the Contemplative Man's Recreation. With Copious Notes, an Account of Fishing and Fishing Books, from the Earliest Antiquity to the Time of Walton, and a Notice of Cotton and his Writings, by the American Editor. 12mo. New York, 1848.

WANDERER in Washington. 12mo. Washington, 1827.

WANOSTROCHT, N. Recueil Choise de Traits Historique et de Countes Morceaux. 12mo. New York, 1820.

WAR INCONSISTENT with the Religion of Jesus Christ. 12mo. New York, 1815.

WARBURTON, ACTON. Rollo and his Race; or Footsteps of the Normans. 2 vols. 8vo. London, 1848.

WARBURTON, ELIOT. Hochelaga, or England in the New World. 12mo. New York, 1846.

WARBURTON, ELIOT. The Crescent and the Cross, or Romance and Realities of Eastern Travel. 12mo. New York, 1845.

WARD, GEORGE A. Journal and Letters of Samuel Curwen, Judge of Admiralty, etc.; and an American Refugee in England. 8vo. New York, 1842.

WARD, JAMES. Threatened Disorganization of France. Louis Blanc on the Working Classes. With corrected Notes, and a Refutation of his Destructive Plan. 12mo. London, 1848.

WARD, R. P. Pictures of the World, at Home and Abroad. 3 vols. 8vo. London, 1843.

WARD, R. PLUMER. A Historical Essay on the Revolution of 1688. 2 vols. 12mo. London, 1838.

WARD, WILLIAM. View of the History, Literature and Religion of the Hindoos, and their Manners and Customs. 12mo. Hartford, 1824.

WARD, W. G. The Ideal of a Christian Church, considered in Comparison with existing Practice. 8vo. London, 1844.

WARE, ISAAC. A Complete Body of Architecture. Fol. London, 1767.

WARING, GEORGE. Letters from Malta and Sicily addressed to a Young Naturalist. 12mo. London, 1843.

WARWICK, EDEN. Nasology, or Hints towards a Classification of Noses. 8vo. London, 1848.

WASHBURN, EMORY. Sketches of the Judicial History of Massachusetts. 8vo. Boston, 1840.

WASHINGTON, GEORGE. Letters on Agriculture. (See Knight, F.)

WASHINGTON, GEORGE. Life. (See Bancroft, Aaron.)

WASHINGTON, GEORGE. Life. (See Marshall, John.)

WASHINGTON, GEORGE. Life. (See Paulding, James K.)

WASHINGTON, GEORGE. Life. (See Ramsay, David.)

WASHINGTON, GEORGE. Life and Writings. (See Sparks, Jared.)

WASHINGTON, GEORGE. Official Letters to Congress. 2 vols. 12mo. New York, 1796.

WASHINGTON and the Generals of the American Revolution. 2 vols. 8vo. Philadelphia, 1848.

WASHINGTON'S Political Legacies. 12mo. New York, 1800.

*WATERSON, WILLIAM. A Cyclopædia of Commerce, Mercantile Law, Finance, Commercial Geography, and Navigation. 8vo. London, 1847.

WATSON, ELKANAH. History of the Western Canals in the State of New York, and an account of Modern Agricultural Societies. 8vo. Albany, 1820.

WATSON, J. F. Annals of Philadelphia. 8vo. Philadelphia, 1830.

WATSON, ROBERT. History of the Reign of Philip II. King of Spain. 2 vols. 8vo. New York, 1818.

WATTS, ISAAC. Logic, or the Right Use of Reason. 12mo. Walpole, 1809.

WATTS, ISAAC. The Improvement of the Mind. 8vo. London, 1815.

WATTS, JOSHUA. Remarkable Events in the History of Man. Vol. 2. 12mo. Philadelphia, 1826.

WEAVER, W. A. Blue Book. 12mo. Philadelphia, 1834.

WEBB, J. WATSON. Altowan, or Incidents of Life and Adventure in the Rocky Mountains, by an Amateur Traveller. 2 vols. 8vo. New York, 1846.

WEBSTER, DANIEL. The Changes and Modifications in the Commercial System of Nations, by Treaties, Duties on Import, and other Regulations. 8vo. Washington, 1842.

WEBSTER, DANIEL. Speeches, and Forensic Arguments. 8vo. Boston, 1833.

WEBSTER, JOHN WHITE. A Manual of Chemistry on the Basis of Professor Brande's. 8vo. Boston, 1828.

WEBSTER, NOAH. A Collection of Papers on Political Literature and Moral Subjects. 8vo. New York, 1843.

*WEBSTER, NOAH. Dictionary of the English Language. 2 vols. 4to. New York, 1828.

WEBSTER, NOAH. History of Epidemic and Pestilential Diseases. 8vo. Hartford, 1799.

WEBSTER, NOAH. Letters to a Young Gentleman commencing his Education. 8vo. New Haven, 1823.

WEBSTER, JR., NOAH. Dissertation on the English Language. 8vo. Boston, 1789. *Presented by Dr. Samuel Akerly.*

WEDGEWOOD, W. B. Science of Numbers. 12mo. New York, 1840. *Presented by Hon. Horace Greeley.*

WEEKS, JOHN M. A Manual, or an Easy Method of Managing Bees. 18mo. Middlebury, 1836.

WEIDLERI, D. JO. F. Institutiones Matheseos emendata, etc., cura Jo. Jacobi Eberti. 8vo. Leipzig, 1784.

WELLESLEY, RICHARD, MARQUIS. Memoirs and Correspondence. (See Pearce, Robert R.)

WELLINGTON, ARTHUR, DUKE OF. Dispatches during his various Campaigns, from 1799 to 1818. 8vo. London, 1834.

WELLINGTON, ARTHUR, DUKE OF. General Orders in Portugal, Spain and France. 8vo. London, 1832.

WELLS, NATHANIEL A. The Picturesque Antiquities of Spain. 8vo. London, 1846.

WELWOOD, JAMES. Memoirs of the Most Material Transactions in England. 12mo. London, 1700.

WEMYSS, THOMAS. Job and his Times. 8vo. London, 1839.

WERNE, FERDINAND. Expedition to Discover the Sources of the White Nile, in the years 1840–1841. From the German, by Charles W. O'Reilly. 2 vols. 8vo. London, 1849.

WESLEY, JOHN. Life of. (See Southey, Robert.)

WEST, BENJAMIN. Life and Studies of. (See Galt, John.)

WEST, MRS. FREDERIC. A Summer Visit to Ireland in 1846. 8vo. London, 1847.

WEST, MRS. Alicia de Lacy, an Historical Romance. 4 vols. 12mo. London, 1819.

WESTERN Agriculturist, and Practical Farmer's Guide. 12mo. Cincinnati, 1830.

WESTMINSTER REVIEW. 4 vols. 8vo. New York, 1834–1836–1841 and 1842.

WETMORE, ALPHONSO. Gazetteer of the State of Missouri. 8vo. St. Louis, 1837.

WHATELEY, RICHARD. Elements of Logic. 12mo. New York, 1839.

WHEATON, HENRY. An Address Pronounced at the Opening of the New York Athenæum. 8vo. New York, 1825.

WHEATON, HENRY. Digest of the Decisions of the Supreme Court of the United States, from 1789 to 1820. Continued to 1829, with Additions, by Two Gentlemen of the New York Bar. 2 vols. 8vo. New York, 1821–1829.

Wheaton, Henry. Life, Writings and Speeches of William Pinkney. 8vo. New York, 1826.

Wheeler, Henry G. History of Congress, Biographical and Political. 2 vols. 8vo. New York, 1848.

Whelpley, P. M. The Triangle; a discussion of Original Sin, Inability, and the Atonement. 8vo. New York, 1832.

Whewell, William. The Elements of Morality, including Polity. 2 vols. 12mo. New York, 1845.

Whipple, Edwin P. Essays and Reviews. 2 vols. 12mo. Boston, 1851.

Whipple, Edwin P. Lectures on Subjects connected with Literature and Life. 12mo. Boston, 1850.

Whishaw, Francis. The Railways of Great Britain and Ireland, practically described and Illustrated. 4to. London, 1842.

White, E. Specimens of Modern and Light Face Printing Types and Ornaments. 8vo. New York, 1831.

White, George S. Memoir of Samuel Slater, with a History of the Cotton Manufacture in England and America. 8vo. Philadelphia, 1836.

White, Henry. The Early History of New England. 12mo. Concord, 1845.

White, James. A New Century of Inventions. Designs and Descriptions of 100 Machines. 4to. Manchester, 1822.

White, P. S. and H. R. Pleasants. The War of 4000 Years, or the Efforts made to suppress the Vice of Intemperance in all Ages of the World. 12mo. Philadelphia, 1840.

Whitefield, George. Sermons on Various Important Subjects, with a Sermon by Joseph White. 12mo. Glasgow, 1795.

Whitelaw, James. An Essay on the Population of Dublin. 8vo. Dublin, 1815. *Presented by Dr. Samuel Akerly.*

Whitlaw, Charles. A Treatise on the Causes and Effects of Inflammation and Fever, &c., with Rules for Diet and Regimen, &c. 8vo. London, 1831.

Whitlaw, Charles. The Scriptural Code of Health, &c. 12mo. London, 1838.

WHITLAW, CHARLES. New Medical Discoveries, with a Defence of the Linnæan Doctrine, and a Translation of his Vegetable Materia Medica. 8vo. London, 1829. *Presented by the Author.*

WHITLING, H. J. Pictures of Nuremberg, and Rambles in the Hills and Valleys of Franconia. 2 vols. 8vo. London, 1850.

WHITMARSH, SAMUEL. Eight Years' Experience and Observation in the Culture of the Mulberry Tree and in the Care of the Silk Worm, with Remarks adapted to the American System of Producing Raw Silk for Exportation. 12mo. Northampton, 1839.

WHITON, JOHN M. Sketches of the History of New Hampshire. 12mo. Concord, 1834.

WHITTOCK, N. The Miniature Painter's Manual. 12mo. London, 1844.

WHYTE, JAMES C. History of the British Turf, from the Earliest Period to the Present Day. 2 vols. 8vo. London, 1840.

WICKHAM, H. L. AND J. A. CRAMER. A Dissertation on the Passage of Hannibal over the Alps. 8vo. London, 1828.

WIGGINS, FRANCIS S. The American Farmer's Instructor and Practical Agriculturist. 8vo. Philadelphia, 1840.

WILKIE, DAVID. Theory of Interest. 8vo. Edinburgh, 1794.

WILKES, CHARLES. Narrative of the United States Exploring Expedition. 5 vols. 8vo. Philadelphia, 1845.

WILLARD, EMMA. History of the United States, or Republic of America. 8vo. New York, 1831.

WILLARD, EMMA. Last Leaves of American History, comprising Histories of the Mexican War and California. 12mo. New York, 1849.

WILLIAMS, CHARLES. Missionary Gazetteer. 12mo. London, 1828.

WILLIAMS, DAVID. Lectures on the Spirit of Laws and the Constitution of England. 8vo. London, 1819. *Presented by Dr. Samuel Akerly.*

WILLIAMS, EDWIN. Book of the Constitution. 12mo. New York, 1833.

*WILLIAMS, EDWIN. New York Annual Register. 10 vols. 12mo. New York, 1830–1837–1840–1845.

*WILLIAMS, EDWIN. Statesman's Manual; or the Presidents' Messages; Inaugural, Annual and Special, from 1789 to 1846. 2 vols. 8vo. New York, 1846. *Presented by Edward Walker, Esq.*

WILLIAMS, EDWIN. United States Tariff, or Rates of Duties payable on Imports, alphabetically arranged. 8vo. New York, 1842.

WILLIAMS, EDWIN. United States Tariff, or Rates of Duties payable on Imports, alphabetically arranged. 8vo. New York, 1846.

WILLIAMS, HELEN M. Letters from France. 2 vols. 12mo. New York, 1794.

WILLIAMS, HELEN M. Political and Confidential Correspondence of Louis XVI. 3 vols. 8vo. New York, 1803.

WILLIAMS, J. The Rise, Progress and Present State of the Northern Governments. 2 vols. 4to. London, 1777.

WILLIAMS, REV. J. The Life and Actions of Alexander the Great. 18mo. New York, 1832.

WILLIAMS, JOHN. Narrative of the Missionary Enterprises in the South Sea Islands. 8vo. New York.

WILLIAMS, JOHN LEE. A View of West Florida. 8vo. Philadelphia, 1827.

WILLIAMS, SAMUEL. The Natural and Civil History of Vermont. 8vo. Walpole, 1794.

WILLIAMS, S. WELLS. The Middle Kingdom; a Survey of the Geography, Government, Education, Social Life, Arts, Religion, &c., of the Chinese Empire and its Inhabitants. 2 vols. 8vo. New York and London, 1848.

WILLIAMS, T. Academical Stenography. 8vo. London, 1821.

*WILLICH, A. F. M. Domestic Encyclopædia. Additions, by Thomas Cooper. 3 vols. 8vo. Philadelphia, 1821.

WILLISTON, E. B. Eloquence of the United States. 5 vols. 8vo. Middletown, 1827.

WILLOUGHBY, LADY. Diary, relating to her Domestic History, and the Eventful Period of the Reign of Charles I., together with Selections from the Works of Taylor, Latimer, Hall, Milton, Barrow, South, Brown, Fuller, and Bacon, by Basil Montagu. 12mo. New York, 1845.

WILSON, ALEXANDER, and Charles Lucian Buonaparte. American Ornithology. Edited by Robert Jameson. 4 vols. 18mo. Edinburgh, 1831.

WILSON, BERNARD. Thou's History of his Own Time. Fol. London, 1729.

Wilson, James. An Introduction to the Natural History of Birds. 4to. Edinburgh, 1839.

Ditto. Ditto. Of Fishes. 4to. Edinburgh, 1839.

Wilson, John. Recreations of Christopher North. (See Modern British Essayists.)

Wilson, John. Specimens of the British Critics, by Christopher North. 12mo. Philadelphia, 1846.

Windgate, Edward. An Abridgment of all the Statutes in Force and Use, from the Beginning of the Magna Charta. 12mo. London, 1689.

Winterbotham, W. A. View of the United States of America. 3 vols. 8vo. New York, 1796.

Winterbotham, W. A. Historical, Geographical, and Philosophical View of the Chinese Empire. 8vo. London.

Wirt, William. Memoirs of his Life. (See Kennedy, John P.)

Wirt, William. The Life of Patrick Henry. 8vo. Hartford, 1846.

Wolfe, Joseph. Researches and Missionary Labors among the Jews, Mahommedans, and other Sects. 12mo. Philadelphia, 1837.

Wolsey, Cardinal. Life. (See Galt, John.)

Wonders of the Universe, or Curiosities of Nature and Art. 8vo. New York, 1831.

Wood, John. History of the Administration of John Adams. 8vo. New York, 1802.

Wood, John George. Lectures on the Principles and Practice of Perspective. 4to. London, 1844.

Wood, Nicholas. A Practical Treatise on Railroads, &c. 8vo. London, 1838.

Wood, Nicholas. Treatise on Railroads. 8vo. Philadelphia, 1832.

Wood, Silas. A Sketch of the First Settlement of Long Island. 8vo. Brooklyn, 1828.

Wood, Thomas. Mosaic History of the Creation of the World. Revised and improved, by the Rev. J. P. Durbin. 8vo. New York, 1831.

Wood, Thomas. The Origin, Learning, Religion and Customs of the Ancient Britons. 8vo. London, 1846.

WOOD, WILLIAM M. Wandering Sketches of People and Things in South America, Polynesia, California and other places. 12mo. Philadelphia, 1849.

WOOD, W. W. Sketches of China. 12mo. Philadelphia, 1830.

WOODBRIDGE, WILLIAM C. American Annals of Education and Instruction. 3 vols. 8vo. Boston, 1832–1834.

WOODBRIDGE, WILLIAM C. Universal Geography. 12mo. Hartford, 1827.

WOODBRIDGE, WILLIAM C. Universal Geography, on the Principles of Comparison and Classification. 8vo. Hartford, 1831.

WOODBURY, LEVI. Report, as Secretary of the Treasury, on the Condition of the Several State Banks. 8vo. Washington, 1841.

WOODWORTH, SAMUEL. Melodies, Songs, and Ballads. 12mo. New York, 1830.

WORCESTER, J. E. A Comprehensive Pronouncing and Explanatory Dictionary of the English Language. 12mo. Boston, 1838.

WORCESTER, J. E. Gazetteer of the United States. 8vo. Andover, 1818. *Presented by Dr. Samuel Akerly.*

WORCESTER, J. E. Geographical Dictionary, or Universal Gazetteer, Ancient and Modern. 2 vols. 8vo. Boston, 1823.

WORDSWORTH, CHARLES. Sequel to Letters to M. Gondon on the Church of Rome, both in Religion and Polity. 8vo. London, 1848.

WORDSWORTH, CHRISTOPHER. Memoirs of William Wordsworth, edited by Henry Reed. 2 vols. 12mo. Boston, 1851.

WORKINGMAN'S COMPANION. Philadelphia, 1831–1832.

WORTMAN, TUNIS. Treatise concerning Political Inquiry and the Liberty of the Press. 8vo. New York, 1800.

WRAXALL, SIR N. W. Historical Memoirs of his Own Times. 8vo. Philadelphia, 1845.

WRAXALL, SIR N. W. Posthumous Memoirs of his Own Time. 8vo. Philadelphia, 1845.

WRIGHT, FRANCIS. A Few Days in Athens. 12mo. New York, 1831.

WRIGHT, J. American Negotiator; or the Various Currencies of the British Colonies in America. 8vo. London, 1761.

WRIGHT, THOMAS. England under the House of Hanover: its History and Condition during the Reigns of the Three Georges. 2 vols. 8vo. London, 1849.

WYATT, THOMAS. History of the Kings of France. 12mo. Philadelphia, 1846.

WYCLIFF, JOHN, D.D. Life. (See Cox, Margaret.)

WYNNE, MR. A General History of the British Empire in America. 2 vols. 8vo. London, 1770.

XENOPHON. The Complete Works of. 8vo. London, 1849.

YAZOO PAPERS. 8vo. *Presented by Dr. Samuel Akerly.*

YEAR BOOK. 8vo. London.

YEAR BOOK of Facts in Science and Art, exhibiting the most important Discoveries and Improvements of the Past Year, by the Editor of the "Arcana of Science." 7 vols. 12mo. London, 1839–1846.

YORKE, HENRY REDHEAD. Annals of Public Economy, containing Reports on the State of Agriculture, Commerce and Manufactures in the different Nations of Europe for 1802. 2 vols. 8vo. London, 1803.

YOUATT, WILLIAM. Every Man his own Cattle Doctor. With additions by John S. Skinner. 12mo. Philadelphia, 1844. *Presented by Joseph Catty, Esq.*

YOUATT, WILLIAM and W. C. L. Martin. Cattle. Edited by A. Stevens. 12mo. New York, 1851. *Presented by C. M. Saxton, Esq.*

YOUNG, ARTHUR. Course of Experimental Agriculture. 4 vols. 8vo. Dublin, 1771.

YOUNG, AUGUSTUS. Unity of Purpose, or Rational Analysis. 8vo. Boston, 1846. *Presented by the Author.*

YOUNG, EDWARD. Poetical Works. (See Milton.)

YOUNG, MARIA JULIA. Voltairiana. 4 vols. 18mo. London, 1805.

YOUNG MECHANIC, THE. Conducted by an Association of Practical Mechanics. 3 vols. 8vo. Boston, 1832–1833.

ZIELE, G. Vertroostingen. 18mo. t'Amsterdam, 1719.

ZIMMERMANN, J. G. Essay on National Pride, translated by S. H. Wilcock. 8vo. New York, 1799.

ZOOPHYTES. Structure and Classification of. By James D. Dana. 4to. Philadelphia, 1846.

SYNOPSIS

OF THE

ANALYTICAL CATALOGUE.

INDEX

TO THE

ANALYTICAL CATALOGUE.

ANALYTICAL CATALOGUE.

THEOLOGY.

Sacred Writings, Natural and Miscellaneous Theology, &c.

Addison, Joseph. Christian Religion.
Alden, T. Missions among the Senecas, &c.
Angeloni, B. Letters.
Aubigne, J. H. Merle, D'. Reformation.
Bakewell, F. C. Evidences of a Future State.
Barclay, Robert. An Apology.
Bennett, Rev. M. P. Lectures on Theology.
Bennett, T. Confutation of Quakerism.
Bentley, Richard. Works.
Biblia Sagrada, La.
Bingham. J. Antiquities of the Church.
Boecken des Nieuwen Testaments und Psalmen des Davids.
Boudinot, Elias. A Star in the West.
Brook, B. History of Religious Liberty.
Buchanan, C. Christian Researches.
Buck, Charles. Religious Anecdotes.
Burgess, G. Martyrdom of Peter and Paul.
Bush, Rev. George. Mohammed.
Butterworth, Rev. J. New Concordance.
Calmet's Dictionary of the Bible.
Chalmers, T. Discourses on Christianity.
Channing, William E. Discourses.
Christian Library, The.
Christelyke Bedenckingen.
Clarkson, Thomas. Portraiture of Quakerism.
Collection of Testimonies.
Collyer, W. B. Scripture Facts.
Confessional, The.
Cox, S. H. Quakerism not Christianity.
Dellon, M. Inquisition at Goa.
Dick, Thomas. Works.
Duffie, Rev. Cornelius R. Sermons.
Duncan, Henry. Sacred Philosophy.
Dwight, Timothy. Sermons on Theology.
Echard, L. Ecclesiastical History.
Edgar, Samuel. Variations of Popery.
Evans, J. Denominations of Christians.

Fellows, John. Ancient Mysteries.
Fowler, W. The Eastern Mirror.
Fox, George. Journal.
Freeman, James. Sermons and Charges.
Gallard, T. History of the Reformation.
General Delusion of Christians.
Gleig, G. R. History of the Bible.
Gulden-Spiegel, ofte Opweckinge tot Christelycke Deughden, &c.
Gurney, J. J. Views, &c. of the Quakers.
Hawks, Rev. F. L. Monuments of Egypt.
Holy Bible, with Mr. Ostervald's Notes.
Hopkins, Ezekiel. Works of.
Inchiquin. The Jesuits' Letters.
Isaacs, H. Ceremonies, &c., of the Jews.
Josephus, Flavius. Works.
Kelty, Mary Ann. Primitive Quakers.
Kersey, Jessy. Christian Religion.
Kitto, John. Palestine.
Kneeland, A. Review of Christianity.
Knibbe, David. Katechisatie.
Lathrop, Joseph. Sermons on Baptism.
Lane, E. W. Selections from the Kur-an.
Lawson, Joseph. Church of Scotland.
Legitimate Consequences of Reform.
Letters on the Writings of the Fathers.
Linn, William. Sermons.
List of the Lords Spiritual, &c.
Liturgie Française.
Macbean, A. Dictionary of the Bible.
Macgowan, Rev. J. Mirror for Professors.
Mackray, W. Effects of the Reformation.
Maffitt, J. N. Cabinet of Religion, &c.
Mason, John M. Sermons, Essays, &c.
Massillon, J. B. Sermons.
Missionary Herald.
More, Hannah. Sacred Dramas.
Murray, Lindley. Power of Religion.
Neale, W. H. Mohammedan Theology.
Nickelsburger, J. Jewish Religion.
Nuevo Testamento, El.
Osgood, Rev. David. Sermons.
O'Sullivan, M. A Guide to an Irish Gent.
Paine, Thomas. Age of Reason.

Paley, William. Works.
Priestley, Joseph. Christian Church.
Proceedings of the Missionary Society.
Psalms of David in the Nestorian Language.
Pulpit Cyclopædia.
Reese, D. M. Quakerism and Christianity.
Reformation. History of the Huguenots.
Reinhard, F. V. Plan of Christianity.
Robison, John. Proofs of a Conspiracy.
Ronde, L. de. The True Religion.
Roy, Rammohun. Precepts of Jesus.
Rupp, J. D. Religious Denominations.
Sale, George. The Koran, or Alcoran.
Sanford, John. Parochialia.
Saurin, Rev. James. Sermons.
Scenes where the Tempter has Triumphed.
Schmucker, S. M. Modern Infidelity.
Schoberl, Frederic. Popery.
Scott, W. The Harmony of Phrenology.
Seiler, George F. Biblical Hermeneutics.
Selectæ e Veteri Testamento Historie.
Sewel, William. History of the Quakers.
Shepard, &c. Meditations and Exercises.
Sherlock, Wm. Future Judgment.
Skinner, T. H. Religion of the Bible.
Smet, P. J. Oregon Missions.
Smith, Rev. S. Works.
Southey, Robert. Rise, &c., of Methodism.
Stanford, John. Christian Library.
Steinmets, Andrew. History of Jesuits.
Stone, Wm. L. Matthias and his Impostures.
Taylor, W. C. Illustrations of the Bible.
Temple, Theodore. Secret Discipline.
Thomas, J. Universal Jurisprudence.
Thomson, James. Letters.
Time of the End not yet.
Timpson, Thomas. Female Missionaries.
Tindal, Matthew. Religion of Nature.
Tomline, George. Elements of Theology.
Tooke, J. Parthenon.
Turnbull, Rev. R. Genius of Italy.
Turnbull, Rev. R. Genius of Scotland.
Turner, Sharon. Sacred History.
Vieyra, P. A. Inquizicõis de Portugal.
Vitringa, Campegius. Korte Schets.
Volney, C. F. Volney's Ruins.
Wakeman, W. T. Antiquities, Pagan, &c.
War Inconsistent with Religion.
Ward, Wm. Religion of the Hindoos.
Ward, W. G. The Ideal of a Church.
Wemyss, Thomas. Book of Job.
Whelpley, P. M. The Triangle.
Whitefield, George. Sermons.
Williams, John. Missionary Enterprises.
Wolfe, Joseph. Missionary Labors.
Wood, Thomas. Mosaic History.
Wordsworth, Charles. Sequel to Letters.

LAW.

National, Constitutional, Statute, Common, Mercantile and Military.

Adlington, John H. Cyclopædia of Law.
Amos, A. Trial of the Earl of Somerset.
Amos, A. & J. Ferard. Law of Fixtures.
American's Guide, The.
Bacon, Lord. Works.
Bayard, J. Constitution of the U. States.
Blackstone, Sir Wm. Commentaries.
Blue Laws of Connecticut.
Brady, I. H. Law of Debtor and Creditor.
Campbell, J. D., &c. American Chancery Digest.
Caroline, Queen. Trial of.
Chase, Samuel. Trial.
Chitty, Joseph. Bills of Exchange, &c.
Church, R. S. Index to the Reports.
Clark, Aaron. Parliamentary Practice.
Collection of Protests.
Collyer, John. Laws of Partnership.
Commercial Relations of United States.
Commercial Regulations of United States.
Comte et Dunoyer, M. M. Le Censeur ou Examen.
Comyn, S. Contracts and Agreements.
Cooper, Thomas. Law of Libel.
Duer, W. A. Constitutional Jurisprudence.
Elliot, J. Debates on the Constitution.
Farley, E. Imprisonment for Debt.
Fessenden, Thomas G. Laws of Patents.
Form Book. By a Member of the Bar.
Frederician Code, The.
Godwin, Wm. Political Justice.
Gordon, F. F. Treaties and Statutes.
Grim, Charles F. Register of Deeds.
Hamilton, A., &c. The Federalist.
Herty, T. Laws of the United States.
Hickey, W. Constitution of the U. S., &c.
Jackson, Wm. Constitution of Ind. States.
Jefferson, T. Parliamentary Practice.
Justice's Guide, or Digest for Justices.
Kent, James. Commentaries.
Lolme, I. L. de. Constitution of England.
Loosey, Charles F. Patent Laws.
Mably, Abbe de. Government and Laws.
Marshall, John. Federal Constitution.
Montesquieu, Charles. Spirit of Laws.
Mortimer, John. Trial of Mail Robbers.
Moulton, R. K. Constitutional Guide.
Neven, E. J. A. Lois Rurales.
O'Callaghan, J. Usury.
Oliver, Benj. L. Rights of an Am. Citizen.
Orders and Resolutions.
Paine, Jr., Elijah. Report of Cases.
Parke, Samuel. Laws relating to Salt.

Peace-Republican's Manual.
Pearce, R. R. Inns of Court and Chancery.
Philosophie. Les Crimes de la.
Pope, Charles. Laws of Customs, &c.
Raymond, J. Digested Chancery Cases.
Report of Cases.
Report of Copy-Right Cases.
Revised Statutes of the State of N. York.
Rules of the Supreme Court.
Sackville, George, Lord. Trial.
Schomann, G. F. Assemblies of Athenians.
Session of Parliament for 1825.
Sharswood, G. Public and Genl. Statutes.
Statutes relating to Sewers.
Story, Joseph. Commentaries.
Story, Joseph. Public and Genl. Statutes.
Supreme Court, Minutes of.
Thomas, Isaiah. Perpetual Laws.
Tithes. Treatise on.
Treasury of Knowledge.
Treaties. A List of.
Treaties of Great Britain, &c.
United States Form Book.
Wales, Princess of. "The Book."
Walsh, Jr., R. Appeal from Great Britain.
Washburn, E. Judicial History.
Waterson, Wm. Cyclopædia of Law.
Wellington, Duke of General Orders.
Wellington, Duke of. Dispatches of.
Wheaton, H. Decisions of Supreme Court.
Williams, David. Spirit of Laws, &c.
Williams, E. Book of the Constitution.
Windgate, E. Abridgment of Statutes.

SCIENCE.

Universal Science.

ENCYCLOPÆDIAS AND GENERAL DICTIONARIES.

American Encyclopædia of Arts and Sciences.
Appleton's Dictionary of Machines, &c.
Booth, J. C., &c. Encyclopædia of Chemistry.
Brande, W. T. Dictionary of Science.
Brewster, David. Edinburgh Encyclopædia.
Buys, E. Dictionary of Terms of Arts.
Dictionary of Arts and Sciences.
Encyclopædia Americana.
Encyclopædia Perthensis.
Gregory, G. Dictionary of Arts, Sciences.
Harris, John. Lexicon Technicum.
Hebert, Luke. Encyclopædia.
Jamieson, Alexander. Dictionary.
Johnson, Wm. M., &c. Imperial Encyclopædia.
London Encyclopædia.
Murry, W. R. Cyclopædia.
Nicholson, Wm. British Encyclopædia.
Penny Cyclopædia and Supplement.
Poppe, D. J. Technologisches Lexicon.
Ure, Andrew. A Dictionary of Arts, &c.
Ure, A. Supplement to Dictionary.
Willich, A. F. M. Domestic Encyclopædia.

Mental and Moral Science.

METAPHYSICS, ETHICS, LOGIC, AND EDUCATION.

Abercrombie, John. Intellectual Powers.
Abercrombie, John. Moral Feelings.
Akerly, Samuel. Elementary Exercises.
American Institute of Instruction. Discourse and Lectures.
Ansell, Charles. Friendly Societies.
Bacon, Francis, Lord. Essays.
Bakewell, Frederic C. Future Life.
Beattie, James. Moral Science.
Bolingbroke, H. St. John. Works.
Brisbane, Albert. Destiny of Man.
Brown, Dr. Civil Liberty, &c.
Brown, Thomas. Philosophy of Mind.
Back, C. Entertaining Anecdotes.
Burton, Robert. Anatomy of Melancholy.
Calmet, Augustine. Phantom World.
Central Society. Papers on Education.
Chalmers, Thomas. Affairs of Life.
Channing, W. E. Discourses.
Chapone, Mrs. Improvement of the Mind.
Chavannes, D. A. Methode Elementaire.
Coleridge, Samuel T. The Friend.
Colton, C. C. Lacon.
Cousin, V. Instruction in Prussia.
Cumberland, Richard. The Observer.
Darwin, Erasmus. Female Education.
Davis, A. J. Principles of Nature.
Dendy, W. C. Philosophy of Mystery.
Dick, Thomas. Improvement of Society.
Drelincourt, Charles. Doodts.
Dymond, J. Principles of Morality.
Educator, The. Prize Essays.
Foster, John. Popular Ignorance.
Franklin, Benjamin. Essays.
Frederic II. Works.
Gall, F. J. Moral Qualities, &c.
Good, John M. Book of Nature.
Gregoire, H. Moral Faculties of Negroes.
Hermit in London. English Manners.
Hill, Frederic. National Education.
Hume, David. Essays.
Infant Education. Remarks on.
Introductory Discourse and Lectures.
Lancaster, Joseph. Education.
Lavater, J. C. On Physiognomy.
Locke, John. Human Understanding.
Mackintosh, Sir J. Ethical Philosophy.
Martineau, Harriet. How to observe.
Millingen, J. G. History of Duelling.
Montaigne, M. Works.
Moore, John. Society and Manners.
More, Hannah. Works.

Morgan, Mr. Moral Philosopher.
Mudie, Robert. Popular Guide.
O'Callaghan, J. Usury.
Opie, A. Illustrations of Lying.
Paine, Thomas. Age of Reason.
Paley, Wm. Moral Philosophy.
Paley, Wm. Works.
Penscelwood Papers.
Phillips, R. Dialogues on Philosophy.
Phillips, Sir R. Social Philosophy.
Pinnock, W. Guide to Knowledge.
Poyntz, Albany. World of Wonders.
Preceptor, The. Course of Education.
Sanford, John. Parochialia.
Saturday Evening.
Schoolmaster, The. Essays on Education.
Scott, Sir W. Letters on Demonology.
Seances des Ecoles Normales.
Smith, Adam. Moral Sentiment.
Stael, Mme. de. Influence of the Passions.
Starling, E. Noble Deeds of Woman.
Steel, Sir R. Wandering Thoughts.
Stone, W. L. Matthias and his Impostures.
Stuart, Gilbert. Society in Europe.
Taylor, C. B. Social Evils.
Temple, Theodore. Secret Discipline.
Thomson, Anthony. Occult Sciences.
Turnbull, Rev. R. Genius of Italy.
Turnbull, Rev. R. Genius of Scotland.
Ufford, H. G. Treatise on Logic.
Van Amringe, W. F. History of Man.
Verplanck, Gulian C. American Scholar.
Vestiges of Creation.
Volney, C. F. Volney's Ruins.
Watts, I. Improvement of the Mind.
Watts, Isaac. Treatise on Logic.
Watts, Joshua. Remarkable Events.
Webster, Noah. Letters on Education.
Whateley, Richard. Elements of Logic.
Whewell, Wm. Elements of Morality.
White, P. S. and H. R. Pleasants. Intemperance.
Woodbridge, Wm. C. Annals of Education.
Young, M. J. Voltairiana.
Zimmermann, J. G. National Pride.

Political Science. I.

GOVERNMENT AND POLITICS.

Acherley, Roger. British Constitution.
Alberoni, Cardinal. Political Testament.
America. Political Situation.
American Annual Register.
American Institute. Journal.
American Institute. Reports.
American Register.
American Review.
American Remembrancer.
American's Guide, The.
Ames, Fisher. Works.
Analogies and Contrasts.
Angeloni, Baptista. Letters.
Annual Register.
Ansell, Charles. Friendly Societies.
Answer to "the Olive Branch."
Attempt to Rectify the Public Affairs.
Bacon, Francis, Lord. Works.
Barham, Francis. Cicero's Works.
Barnard, D. D. Speeches and Reports.
Bayard, J. Constitution of the U. States.
Bentham, J. Principles of Legislation.
Bolingbroke, Lord. Works.
Boyd, Hugh. Works.
Bradhurst, Lord. Speech.
Brougham, Lord. Political Philosophy.
Brown, Dr. Civil Liberty, &c.
Bulwer, E. L. England and the English.
Bulwer, H. L. France, Social, Literary, &c.
Burrish, Onslow. Policy of the Provinces.
Campbell, J. Survey of Great Britain.
Carey, Matthew. Miscellaneous Essays.
Carey, Matthew. The Olive Branch.
Carey, Mathew. Vindiciæ Hibernicæ.
Chalmers, G. Strength of Great Britain.
Chamberlayne, J. State of Great Britain.
Chatham, Burke, and Erskine. Speeches.
Chapman, N. Principles of Government.
Cicero, M. T. Political Works.
Cobbett's Monthly Sermons.
Commercial Regulations of the U. States.
Commercial Relations of the U. States.
Companion to the Newspaper.
Convention of 1821. Report of.
Cooper, J. F. American Democrat.
Copley, E. Slavery and Abolition.
Debate on the Seminole War.
Dickinson, John. Political Writings.
Diplomacy of the United States.
Diplomatic Correspondence of the U. S.
Diplomatic Correspondence of Revolution.
Discourses on Davila.
Dodd, Charles R. A Manual of Dignities.
Drummond, Henry. Agricultural Classes.
Duer, W. A. Constitutional Jurisprudence.
Dumas, A. The Progress of Democracy.
Dupin, Baron. Commercial Power.
Elliot, Jona. Debates on Constitution.
Fame and Glory of England Vindicated.
Federalist, The.
Fellows, J. Posthumous Works of Junius.
Force, P. National Calender.
Frederician Code, The.
Frederick II. Political Miscellanies.
Gallatin, A. North Eastern Boundary.
Godwin, W. Political Justice.
Gordon, Thomas F. Digest of Treatises.
Great Britain. Colonial Policy of.
Hamilton, A., &c. The Federalist.
Hamilton, A. Political Writings.
Hamilton, R. Debt of Great Britain.
Harper, R. G. Select Works.
Heron, R. Letters of Junius.
Hickey, W. The Constitution, &c.
Hinman, R. R. Letters to the Governors.
History of Passive Obedience, &c.
Humboldt, Alex. von. Political Essays.
Jackson, Wm. Constitution of Ind. States.
Jarvis, W. C. Policy, &c., of the Free States.

Jay, W. Review of the Mexican War.
Jefferson, T omas. Notes on Virginia.
Jefferson's Manual.
Johnson, J. F. Anti-Slavery Convention.
Journal of the Convention to Revise the Constitution.
Journal of the General Assembly.
Journal of the New York Convention.
Junius Identified.
Junius. Letters. (See Heron, Robert.)
Junius. Posthumous Works.
Knox, V. Spirit of Despotism.
Legaré, Hugh. Writings.
Leggett, Wm. Political Writings.
Legitimate Consequences of Reform.
Lemaire, M. L'Administration de la Police.
Letters on the Eastern States.
Letters, &c., in Favor of Public Liberty.
Lolme, J. L. de. Constitution of England.
Mac Allester, Oliver. Letters on France.
Macaulay, Thomas B. Essays.
Machiavelli, Nicholas. Works.
Marshall, John. Federal Constitution.
Mildmay, Wm. Political Treatises.
Milton, John. Works.
Monroe, J. View of the Foreign Affairs.
Moulton, B. K. Constitutional Guide.
New Whig Guide.
Oliver, B. L. Rights of an Am. Citizen.
Ouseley, Wm. G. Political Institutions.
Page, Richard. Critical Examination.
Paine, Thomas. Political Writings.
Paley, Wm. Political Philosophy.
Peace-Republican's Manual.
Petty, William. Political Arithmetic.
Pinkney, William. Writings.
Plowden, Francis. State of Ireland.
Political Magazine.
Politician's Code, or Political Extracts.
Porter, G. R. Progress of Nations.
Putt, Charles. Civil Policy.
Remedies for the "Perils of the Nation."
Report of the Convention of New York.
Rumford, Count. Political Essays.
Seaman, E. C. Progress of Nations.
Somerville, T. Political Transactions.
State Triumvirate. A Political Tale.
Story, Joseph. Political Writings.
Sullivan, Wm. Political Class Book.
Tallmadge, James. Speeches.
Taylor, John. Tyranny Unmasked.
Timour. Institutes, Political and Military.
Tocqueville, A. de. Democracy in Am.
United States Magazine and Dem. Review.
Voltaire, F. M. Letters on the English.
Walsh. French Government.
Walsh, Jr., R. Appeal from Great Britain
Ward, J. Threatened Disorganization.
Washburn, E. Judicial History of Mass.
Washington, George. Letters to Congress.
Washington's Political Legacies.
Webster, Daniel. Speeches.
Webster, Noah. Political Literature.
Williams, Edwin. Statesman's Manual.
Williams, H. M. Political Correspondence.
Williams, J. Northern Governments.
Wortman, T. Liberty of the Press.
Yazoo Papers.
Ziele, G. Vertroostingen.

Political Science. II.

POLITICAL ECONOMY, COMMERCE, MANUFACTURES, CURRENCY, STATISTICS, AND PUBLIC DOCUMENTS.

Academie der Kaufleute.
Adams, John Q. The Duplicate Letters.
Adams, John Q. Weights and Measures.
Addresses of the Philadelphia Society.
Agriculture Française.
American Almanac.
American Annual Register.
American Institute Journal.
American Institute Reports.
American State Papers.
Anderson, A. Origin of Commerce.
Ashley, John. Trade and Revenues.
Assembly Documents.
Atkinson, William. Political Economy.
Babbage, C. Economy of Machinery.
Baines, Edward. Cotton Manufactures.
Baldwin, Samuel. British Customs.
Banker's Magazine.
Barbarities of the Enemy Exposed.
Beaumont, G. de, &c. Systéme Pénitentaire.
Beman, David. Mysteries of Trade.
Bischoff, J. Woolen Manufactures, &c.
Blake, Rev. J. L. Political Economy.
Blue Book. Register of Officers, Agents, Civil, Military and Naval.
Bristed, J. Resources of the U. States.
Brissot, J. P., &c. Commerce of America.
British Almanac.
Brown, T. The Timber Measurer's, Merchant's and Shipmaster's Assistant.
Bulletin de la Societé Nationale.
Burrish, O. Commerce of the U. Provinces.
Campbell, John. Survey of Britain.
Cantillon, Philip. Analysis of Trade, &c.
Carey, H. C. Rate of Wages.
Cary, Matthew. Essay on Banking.
Cary, M. Miscellaneous Essays.
Cary, Matthew. Political Economy.
Catalogue of the Great Exhibition.
Census of the State of New York, 1835.
Census of the State of New York, 1845.
Chalmers, T. Political Economy.
Cobbett, William. Paper against Gold.
Collection of all the Protests.
Commercial Magazine.
Commercial Regulations.
Commercial Relations of the U. States.
Compendium of Inhabitants, &c., of U. S.
Congressional Documents.
Conseils Généraux de l'Agriculture, &c.
Convention of 1821. Reports of.
Cousin, Victor. Public Instruction.

Crouch, Henry. British Customs.
Crump, W. H. The World in a Pocket Book.
Dennis, Jr., J. Silk Manual.
De Quincey, Thomas. Political Economy.
D'Homergue, J., &c. American Silk.
Documents relatifs aux Canaux.
Dodd, George. British Manufactures.
Drummond, H. Agricultural Classes.
Dupin, Baron. Commercial Power.
Elliott, Wm. Patentee's Manual.
Ellis, Robert. British Tariff.
Ellsworth, H. L. Digest of Patents, 1790–1841.
England and America. Comparison of.
Everett, A. H. New Ideas on Population.
Exposition des Produits de l'Industrie 1844.
Fairman, W. Stocks Examined and Compared.
Federalist, The.
Forbes, F. Improvement of Waste Lands.
Fortune's Epitome of the Stocks, &c.
Franklin Institute. Journal of.
Frederician Code, The.
Ganilh, Charles. Political Economy.
Gilbart, James W. Treatise on Banking.
Gilroy, C. G. Silk, Cotton, Linen, Wool, &c.
Good, J. M. Maintaining the Poor.
Gordon, T. F. Commerce, Navigation, &c.
Gordon, T. F. Digest of Treaties.
Gregg, J. Commerce of the Prairies.
Grund, F. J. The Merchants' Assistant.
Guillet, Peter. Timber Merchant's Guide.
Hadley, W. H. Citizens' Manual.
Hagemerster, J. de. Report on Commerce.
Hart, N. C. House of Refuge.
Head, Sir G. Manufacturing Districts.
Heron, A. M. Des Metaux en France.
Holley, O. L. N. Y. State Register.
Houston, G. Manufacturer's Magazine.
Howard, J. Prisons in England and Wales.
Jacob, Wm. Production, &c., of Precious Metals.
Jefferson, Thomas. Manual.
Jefferson, Thomas. Notes on Virginia.
Johnson, J. F. Anti-Slavery Convention.
Johnson, Walter R. American Coal.
Journal of the General Assembly of N. Y.
Journal of the Convention of New York.
Journal of the Massachusetts Convention.
Kingsley, J. L. and J. P. Pirsson. Patent Laws.
Lambert, E. A Treatise on Dower.
Leake, Stephen M. English Money.
Legislative Documents.
Letters on Internal Resources of N. York.
Loosey, Charles F. Patent Laws.
Lord, E. Currency and Banking.
Lowndes, T. Duties, Drawbacks, &c.
Macgregor, John. Commercial Statistics.
Malthus, T. R. Additions to Essay.
Malthus, T. R. Essay on Population.
Manual for the Convention of New York.
Manual for the Legislature of New York.
Mapes, J. J. Repertory of Manufactures.
McCulloch, J. R. British Empire.
McCulloch, J. R. Dictionary of Commerce, &c.
McCulloch, J. R. Literature of Political Economy.
McCulloch, J. R. Political Economy.
Mercantile Calculation. A New System of.
Merchant's Magazine.
Message from the President of the U. S.
Messages of Gideon Lee.
Mill, John S. Political Economy.
Montefiore, J. Commercial Dictionary.
Montefiore, J. Traders' Companion.
Montgomery, J. Cotton Manufactures.
Morse, J. Report on Indian Affairs.
National Magazine and Industrial Record.
Newman, S. P. Political Economy.
New York City Directory.
Niles, Hezekiah. Domestic Industry.
Niles, Hezekiah. Weekly Register.
North American Review.
O'Callaghan, J. Usury or Interest.
Opdike, George. Political Economy.
Orders and Resolutions.
Ouseley, W. G. Statistics and Institutions.
Overman, Frederick. Iron and Steel.
Parliamentary Register.
Patents, List of American.
Patents. Commissioner's Reports of.
Patent Right Oppression Exposed.
Pebrer, Pablo. Taxation, Revenue, &c.
Perrine, Dr. Henry. Tropical Plants.
Philadelphia Society. Addresses of.
Phillips, Willard. The Inventor's Guide.
Phillips, Willard. Political Economy.
Pitkins, Timothy. Commerce of U. States.
Political Economy. Tracts on.
Political Magazine.
Poor Laws. Commissioners' Report.
Poor Laws. Extracts from the Report of.
Poor Laws. Reports on.
Pope, C. Laws of Customs and Excise.
Price, R. Reversionary Payments.
Prison Labor. Thoughts on.
Rapport au Roi des Canaux.
Raymond, Daniel. Political Economy.
Raymond, Daniel. Thoughts on Economy.
Records, Public, of Ireland. Commissioners' Reports, &c.
Records, Public. Commissioners' Report.
Recueil de Documents Statistiques.
Repertory of Arts, &c.
Repertory of Patent Inventions.
Report, &c., of the Convention of 1821.
Report on the Funeral Ceremonies of Andrew Jackson.
Report on the Funeral Obsequies of William H. Harrison.
Report on Import Duties of G. Britain.
Report on the N. Y. Police Department.
Report on Steam Engines in U. States.
Report of the Sec. of War on Ind. Affairs.
Reuss, W. F. Trade with Great Britain.
Royer, C. E. Notes Economiques.
Savary, M. Dictionary of Trade, &c.

Say, Jean B. Political Economy.
Scotland. Inhabitants of.
Senate Documents.
Seybert, Adam. Statistical Annals.
Shattuck, L. Census of Boston, for 1845.
Sheffield, John, Lord. Commerce.
Silk Manufacture. A Treatise on.
Sinclair, Sir John. Public Revenue.
Sketches of the Resources of N. York City.
Skillman's New York Police Reports.
Smith, Adam. Wealth of Nations.
Smith, Wm. A. List of Bankrupts, &c.
State Papers and Public Documents.
Statistique des Routes Royales de France.
Steuart, Sir James. Political Economy.
Stewart, J. W. Treble Almanac.
Tableau et Relevés de Population. etc.
Tables of Revenue, Population, etc.
Tariff. Examination of the New Tariff.
Taylor, J. Money System in England.
Testimony in the N. J. Contested Election.
Tinelli, Lewis. Production of Silk.
Transactions of the Society for the Encouragement of Arts, Manufactures and Commerce.
Transactions of the Society for the Promotion of Agriculture, Arts, and Manufactures.
Treatise on Police of the Metropolis.
U. S. Magazine and Democratic Review.
Universal Merchant.
Ure, A. Philosophy of Manufactures.
Uztaris, Don G. de. Commerce, &c.
Vade Mecum, or Pocket Companion.
Valentine, David T. Corporation Manual.
Vermont State Papers.
Waterson, W. Cyclopædia of Commerce.
Watson, Elkanah. Western Canals, &c.
Weaver, W. A. Blue Book.
Webster, Daniel. Commercial System.
White, G. S. Cotton Manufacture.
Whitelaw, James. Population of Dublin.
Wilkie, David. Theory of Interest.
Williams, E. Annual Register.
Williams, Edwin. Statesman's Manual.
Williams, Edwin. U. States Tariff.
Woodbury, Levi. State Banks.
Wright, J. American Negotiator.
Yazoo Papers.
Yorke, Henry R. Political Economy.

Exact Science.

ARITHMETIC, MATHEMATICS AND ASTRONOMY.

Bennett, John. Geometry.
Bradford, D. Wonders of the Heavens.
Bradley, T. Practical Geometry, &c.
DeMorgan, Augustus. Calculus.
Dick, Thomas. Practical Astronomer.
Dupin, Baron. Mathematics.
Euclid. Elements of.
Flint, Abel. Geometry, Trigonometry, &c.
Fontenelle, Bernard. Plurality of Worlds.
Hackley, C. W. Elements of Trigonometry.
Hackley, C. W. Treatise on Algebra.
Herschel, Sir J. F. W. Outlines of Astronomy.
Herschel, Sir J. F. W. Treatise on Astronomy.
Holtzapffel, C. Scales of Equal Parts.
Hutton, C. Course of Mathematics.
Hutton, C. Treatise on Mensuration.
Lacroix, S. F. Elements of Algebra.
Lardner, Dionysius. Elements of Euclid.
Le Blond, M. L'Arithmetique et Géométrie.
Loomis, Elias. Progress of Astronomy.
Mitchel, O. M. Planetary and Stellar Worlds.
Newton, Sir Isaac. Principia.
Nichol, J. P. Views of the Heavens.
Perceptor, The.
Pike, Nicholas. Arithmetic.
Scholfield, N. Geometry and Mensuration.
Scholfield, N. Geometry, Trigonometry, &c.
Stansbury, Daniel. Nautical Astronomy.
Wedgwood, W. B. Science of Numbers.
Weidleri, D. Jo. F. Institutiones Matheseos.

Natural Science. I.

NATURAL PHILOSOPHY AND CHEMISTRY.

Adams, George. Essay on Electricity.
American Philosophical Register.
American Railroad Journal.
American Repertory.
Appleton's Dictionary of Machines, &c.
Apprentice, The.
Arcana of Science and Art.
Arnott, Neil. Elements of Physics.
Artisan, The.
Babbage, C. Economy of Machinery, &c.
Bacon, Lord. Works.
Bailey, Alex. M. Mechanical Machines, &c.
Bain, Wm. Variation of the Compass.
Barlow, Peter. Strength, &c., of Timber.
Barrington, D. North Pole.
Beekman, Professor. Inventions and Discoveries.
Bibliotheque du Magnetisme Animal.
Booth, &c. Encyclopædia of Chemistry.
Boucharlat, M. Treatise on Mechanics.
Bourne, Oliver. Steam Engine.
Boyle, Robert. Works.
Brande, W. T. Manual of Chemistry.
Brewster, David. Natural Magic.
Brewster, David. Treatise on Optics.
Brown, T., &c. The Etherial Physician.
Bruce, John. Principles of Philosophy.
Bull, Marcus. Experiments on Fuel.
Capper, James. Winds and Monsoons.
Cavallo, Tiberius. Natural Philosophy.
Cavallo, T. Treatise on Electricity.
Chaptal, J. A. Chemistry applied to Ag.
Chemist, The.
Chemistry, Institutes of Experimental.
Christmas, Rev. H. Cradle of Science.
Civil Engineer and Architects' Journal.
Commentarii de Rebus in Scientia, etc.

Courtenay, E. Treatise on Mechanics.
Crell, D. L. Chemisches Annalen.
Crell, D. L. Chemisches Journal.
Cutbush, James. System of Pyrotechny.
Davis, A. J. Principles of Nature.
Davy, Sir H. Experimental Philosophy.
De la Fond, M. S. Traité de l'Electricité.
Dick, Thomas. Works.
Dictionary of Chemistry.
Discourse on the Advantages of Science.
Dumas, M. Chimie appliquee aux Arts.
Duncan, Henry. Sacred Philosophy.
Edinburgh New Philosophical Journal.
Espy, Jas. P. Philosophy of Storms.
Euler, Leonard. Natural Philosophy.
Ewbank, T. Hydraulic and other Machines.
Fischer, E. S. Natural Philosophy.
Franklin Institute Journal.
Gill, Thos. Technical Repository.
Green, Jacob. Chemical Philosophy.
Henry, Wm. Experimental Chemistry.
Higgins, W. M. Entertaining Philosopher.
Hoefer, F. Histoire de la Chimie.
Houston, Geo. Mechanics' Magazine.
Humboldt, Alex. von. Aspects of Nature.
Humboldt, Alex. von. Cosmos.
Johnston, J. F. W. Agricultural Chemistry.
Johnston, James F. W. Contributions to Scientific Agriculture.
Johnston, J. F. W. Science and Agriculture.
Journal of Science.
Joyce, J. Scientific Dialogues.
Kater, H. and Dion. Lardner. Mechanics.
Lardner, D. Hydrostatics and Pneumatics.
Lardner, D. Lectures on Science and Art.
Lardner, D. Lectures on the Steam Engine.
Lardner, Dion. The Steam Engine.
Lectures on Chemistry, &c.
Liebig, Justus. Chemistry.
Locke, John. Philosophical Works.
London Journal of Arts and Sciences.
Machines. Book of Plates of.
Magazine of Science.
Magnetisme Animal.
Main, T. J., &c. Marine Steam Engine.
Mapes, J. J. American Repertory.
Mechanics' Magazine.
Metcalf, S. L. Terrestrial Magnetism.
Natural Philosophy.
Newton, Sir Isaac. Principia.
Nicholson, Wm. Dictionary of Chemistry.
Overman, Frederick. Practical Mineralogy, &c.
Pambour, Chev. de. Locomotive Engines.
Petzholdt, A. Agricultural Chemistry.
Phillips, Sir R. Dialogues on Philosophy.
Phillips, Sir R. Material Phenomena.
Philosophical Pocket Dictionary.
Philosophical Transactions and Collections.
Pike, Jr., B. Catalogue of Instruments.
Pinnock, Wm. Guide to Knowledge.
Poyntz, Albany. World of Wonders.
Practical Mechanic and Engineers' Mag.
Rafinesque, C. S. Analyse de la Nature.
Raspail, F. W. Organic Chemistry.
Report on Steam Engines in U. States.
Revue Scientifique et Industrielle.
Richardson, C. J. Warming and Ventilation.
Rigg, Robert. Experimental Researches.
Robinson, John. Mechanical Philosophy.
Rose, Henry. Analytical Chemistry.
Rumford, Count. Philosophical Essays.
Scientific Tracts.
Silliman, Benjamin. Journal of Science.
Smith, A. W. Treatise on Mechanics.
Smith, James. Panorama of Science.
Smith, Oliver. Outlines of Nature.
Southey's Common Place Book.
Stuart, Dugald. Philosophical Essays.
Taylor, Richard. Scientific Memoirs.
Thomson, Anthony. Occult Sciences.
Transactions of the Am. Philo. Society.
Treasury of Knowledge.
Tredgold, T. Strength of Cast Iron, &c.
Tredgold, T. Warming and Ventilation.
Trumbull, Wm. Strength, &c., of Timber.
Turner, E. Elements of Chemistry.
Tyfe, Andrew. Elements of Chemistry.
Voltaire. Philosophical Dictionary.
Walker, J. Locomotive and Fixed Engines.
Webster, J. W. Manual of Chemistry.
White, Jas. Century of Invention.
Young, Augustus. Unity of Purpose.
Young, Maria Julia. Voltairiana.

Natural Science. II.

NATURAL HISTORY.

Ansted, D. T. The Ancient World.
Arnott, Neil. Elements of Physics.
Bakewell, R. Introduction to Geology.
Beck, Lewis C. Botany.
Bigland, J. Birds, Fishes, Reptiles, &c.
Botany. Principles of.
Broderip, W. J. Zoological Recreations.
Brown, Thos. Book of Butterflies, &c.
Cotton, Jr., Chas. Thirty-six Animals.
Chapin, Lorin D. Vegetable Kingdom.
Comstock, J. L. Introduction to Botany.
Conversations on Vegetable Physiology.
Cozzens, Jr., I. Geological History.
Cuvier, Baron. The Animal Kingdom.
Dana, James D. System of Mineralogy.
Darwin, Chas. Journal of Researches.
Darwin, E. Botanic Garden.
Darwin, E. Phytologia.
De la Beche, H. T. Geological Manual.
De la Beche, H. T. Geological Memoirs.
England Illustrated.
Etudes de Gites Minéraux.
Fleming, John. Molluscuous Animals.
Flint, Timothy. Natural History.
Geological Survey of New York.

Giraud, Jr., J. P. Birds of Long Island.
Goldsmith, Oliver. History of the Earth.
Good, John M Book of Nature.
Goodman, J. D. Natural History.
Goodman, John D. Rambles of a Naturalist.
Gray, Asa. Botanical Text Book.
Hall, John Chas. Animal Kingdom.
Henckel, J. F. Pyritologia.
Hitchcock, Edward. Elementary Geology.
Hitchcock, E. Report on the Geology, &c.
Humboldt, Alex. von. Aspects of Nature.
Humboldt, Alex. von. Cosmos.
Jackson, C. T. Geology of Maine.
Jackson, Charles T. Reports on Geology.
Jardine, Sir William. Natural History.
Johnston, J. F. W. Geology.
Kirwan, Richard. Mineralogie.
Latham, John. Birds.
Lectures on Geology.
Lempriere, Wm. Natural History, &c.
Lessons on Shells.
Letters on Natural History of New York.
Lindley, John. Vegetable Kingdom.
Lyell, Sir Chas. Second Visit.
Mantell, G. A. Geological Excursions.
Martyn, Thomas. Language of Botany.
Mather, Wm. W. Elements of Geology.
Maunder, Samuel. Natural History.
Moore, N. F. Ancient Mineralogy.
Mudie, Robert. Popular Guide.
Murray, W. R. Cyclopædia of Knowledge.
Natural History of Insects.
Nuttall, T. Manual of the Ornithology.
Penn, G. Mineral and Mosaical Geologies.
Perrine, Dr. H. Tropical Plants.
Phillips, W. Outline of Mineralogy, &c.
Pinnock, Wm. Guide to Knowledge.
Porter, George R. Sugar Cane.
Pursh, F. Plants of North America.
Rafinesque, C. S. Analyse de la Nature.
Rogers, Henry D. Geology of New Jersey.
Ruschenberger, W. S. W. Natural History.
Ruschenberger, W. S. W. Elements of Botany.
Ruschenberger, W. S. W. Elements of Geology.
Schoolcraft, H. R. Lead Mines of Missouri.
Shephard, C. U. Treatise on Mineralogy.
Smith, J. V. C. Fishes of Massachusetts.
Stark, John. Natural History.
St. John, John R. Lake Superior Country, Copper Mines, &c.
St. Pierre, J. B. de. Works of.
Strong, A. B. American Flora.
Taylor, Richard C. Geology of Norfolk.
Thompson, E. P. Note-Book of a Naturalist.
Thornton, R. J. The British Flora.
Thornton, R. J. Elements of Botany.
Travanet, M. de. Physiologie de la Terre.
Van Amringe, W. F. Natural History of Man.
Van Rensselaer, J. Lectures on Geology.
Venegas, M. Natural Hist. of California.

Vestiges of the Natural Hist. of Creation.
Waring, George. Letters to a Naturalist.
Williams, S. Natural History of Vermont.
Wilson, J. Natural Hist. of Birds.
Wilson, J. Natural History of Fishes.
Wilson and Buonaparte. Am. Ornithology.
Wonders of the Universe.
Year Book of Facts.
Zoophytes. Structure, &c., of.

Natural Science. III.

ANATOMY, PHYSIOLOGY, MEDICINE AND SURGERY.

American Journal of Medical Science.
American Lancet.
American Medical Recorder.
American Medical Register.
Anderson, Wm. System of Anatomy.
Arnott, Neil. Elements of Physics.
Beach, W. Practice of Medicine.
Blane, Gilbert. Diseases of Seamen.
Boston Medical Intelligencer.
Boston Medical and Surgical Journal.
Brown, Thomas. Etherial Physician.
Burke, Wm. Mineral Springs of Virginia.
Chemist, the.
Combe, George. Constitution of Man.
Commentarii de Rebus in Scientia Naturali et Medicina Gestis.
Corry, John. Detector of Quackery.
Cragie, David. Elements of Anatomy.
Donaldson, Peter. Medicine and Chirurgery.
Gilbert, J. E. Le Médecin Naturaliste.
Gilbert, J. E. Observations de Médecure, etc.
Hosack, D. Essays on Medical Science.
Hosack, David. Inaugural Discourses.
Inderwick, James. Surgical and Medical Practice.
Jennings, Isaac. Medical Reform.
Journal of Health.
Lavater, or the Science of Physiognomy.
Lefevre, Sir George. On Nerves.
Lowrie, W. F. Toxicologia.
Meckel, J. F. Manual of Anatomy.
Medical and Surgical Register.
Medical Intelligencer.
Medical Repository.
New England Journal.
Ouviere, F. P. Yellow Fever.
Paine, Martyn. Cholera Asphyxia.
Paris, John A. Medical Chemistry.
Parke, Samuel. Chemical Catechism.
Parmly, L. S. Nat'l History of the Teeth.
Pascalis, Felix A. Dangers of Interments.
Pharmacopœia of the United States.
Philadelphia Medical Museum.
Philip, A. P. W. Means of Preserving Health.
Pringle, John. Diseases of the Army.
Report on Spasmodic Cholera.
Reich, G. C. Rindviehseuche.

Rush, Benj. Disease of the Mind.
Scott, Wm. Phrenology.
Sharp, Samuel. The Present State of Surgery.
Sherwood, H. H. Motive Power of Org. Life.
Sinclair, Sir J. Health and Longevity.
Smith, N. Medical and Surgical Memoirs.
Steel, J. H. Mineral Waters of Saratoga.
Townsend, P. S. Yellow Fever.
Transactions of the Humane Society.
Wagner, R. Elements of Physiology.
Webster, Noah. Epidemic Diseases, &c.
Whitlaw, C. Inflammation and Fever, &c.
Whitlaw, C. New Medical Discoveries.
Whitlaw, C. Scriptural Code of Health, &c.

ARTS.

Mathematical Arts.

ENGINEERING, ART OF WAR, AND NAVIGATION.

Abstract of Infantry Tactics.
American Railroad Journal and Magazine.
Appleton's Dictionary of Engineering, &c.
Artisan, The. A Monthly Journal.
Bloodgood, S. Dewitt. Treatise on Roads.
Blunt, Edmund M. American Coast Pilot.
Blunt, E. M. Coast Pilot and Assistant.
Bourne, Oliver. Steam Engine.
Brady, Wm. The Kedge Anchor.
Budge, John. Practical Miner's Guide.
Campbell, E. S. N. Military Science.
Civil Engineer and Architect's Journal.
Cutbush, James. System of Pyrotechny.
Documents relatifs aux Canaux.
Dreury, C. Stewart. Suspension Bridges.
Dyckman, J. G. Militia Officer's Manual.
Fisher, Daniel. Military Tactics.
Franklin Institute Journal.
Fulton, Robert. Canal Navigation.
Furlong, L. American Coast Pilot.
Galloway, Elijah. Steam Engine.
Gray, Thos General Iron Railway.
Haupt, Herman. Bridge Construction.
Holtzapffel, Chas. Scales of Equal Parts.
Hughes, T. Making and Repairing Roads.
Infantry Tactics, Abstract of.
Infantry Tactics.
King, Chas. Memoirs of the Croton Aqueduct.
Knowles, John. Naval Architecture.
Lecount, Peter. Treatise on Railways.
Lescallier, C. Vocabulaire des Termes.
Lewis & Clark, Captains. The Navigator.
Mahan, D. H. Civil Engineering.
Memoirs, &c.; with a Military Dictionary.
Millingen, J. G. Duelling.
Moore, John. Practical Navigator.
Moore, John H. Seaman's Assistant.
Navigation of the United States.
New York Military Magazine.
Nicholson, Peter. Engineering Dictionary.
Pambour. Locomotive Engines, &c.
Phillips, I. History of Inland Navigation.
Pope, Thomas. Bridge Architecture.
Practical Engineer's Magazine.
Purdy, John. New Sailing Directory.
Rules and Regulations for Infantry.
Sutcliffe, John. Canals and Reservoirs.
Tower, F. B. Croton Aqueduct.
Transactions of Civil Engineers.
Walker, Jas. Locomotive Engines, &c.
Waterson, Wm. Cyclopædia of Navigation.
Watson, E. Western Canals.
Whishaw, F. Railways of Great Britain.
Wood, Nicholas. Treatise on Railroads, &c.

Natural Arts.

AGRICULTURE AND VETERINARY.

Agriculture Francaise.
Allen, R. L. Domestic Animals.
American Agriculturist.
American Husbandry.
Annales des Haras et de l'Agriculture.
Annales de la Société d'Horticulture.
Annals of Horticulture.
Armstrong, John. Treatise on Agriculture.
Bailey, A. M. Implements of Husbandry.
Barlow, Joel. Maize, or Indian Corn.
Barry, P. The Fruit Garden.
Berneaud, T. de. Vine Dresser's Manual.
Bischoff, James. History of the Sheep.
Blacklock, Ambrose. Treatise on Sheep.
Blake, Rev. J. L. Farmer's Every-day Book.
Boitard, M. Instruments d'Agriculture, etc.
Boitard, M. Manuel de l'Amateur des Roses.
Bridgeman, T. Gardener's Assistant.
Browne, D. J. American Poultry Yard.
Browne, D. J. Trees of America, Native and Foreign.
Buel, Jesse. Farmer's Companion.
Buist, Robert. Flower Garden Directory.
Busby, James. Vineyards of Spain.
Butler, Frederick. Farmer's Manual.
Canfield, Henry J. Breeds, &c., of Sheep.
Catalogue of Fruits, Ornamental Trees, &c.
Chaptal, J. A. Chemistry applied to Agr.
Child, David L. Culture of the Beet, &c.
Cobb, J. H. Manual of the Mulberry Tree.
Colman, Henry. European Agriculture.
Colman, Henry. Report of Agriculture.
Communications to the Board of Agricult.
Cultivator, The. A Monthly Publication.

Darwin, Erasmus. Botanic Garden.
Darwin, Erasmus. Phytologia.
Davies, David. Case of Laborers.
Davis, N. S. Text Book on Agriculture.
Davy, Sir H. Agricultural Chemistry.
Delafond, O. Maladie de Poitrine.
Dickson, A. Husbandry of the Ancients.
Dickson & Co. Catalogue of Plants.
Downing, A. J. Cottage Residences.
Downing, A. J. Fruits and Fruit Trees.
Downing, A. J. Landscape Gardening.
Doyle, Martin. Cyclopædia of Husbandry.
Doyle, Martin. The Flower Garden.
Drake, Daniel. Miami Country.
Drummond, H. Agricultural Classes.
Dufour, J. J. Vine Dresser's Guide.
Duhamel, M. Treatise of Husbandry.
Ellsworth, H. W. Upper Wabash.
Farmer's Cabinet. Philadelphia.
Farmer's Library. Animal Economy.
Farmer's Magazine.
Ferary, P. Florum Cultura.
Fessenden, T. G. Complete Farmer, &c.
Fleet, Samuel. The Rural Library.
Gardener and Practical Florist.
Gardner, D. P. The Farmer's Dictionary.
Gasparin, Cte de. Cours d'Agriculture.
Gera, Le Dr. Fo. Fabrication du Fromage.
Gill, Thos. Technical Repository.
Hanbury, Wm. Planting and Gardening.
Henderson, Andrew. Practical Grazier.
Hill, Isaac. Farmer's Monthly Visitor.
Hoffy, A. Orchardist's Companion.
Houel, Ephrem. L'Elève du Cheval.
Houston, Geo. Farmer's Magazine.
Hunter, James. Scotch Swing Plough.
Jacquemin, Emile. L'Allemagne, Agricole, &c.
Johnson, Geo. Dictionary of Gardening.
Johnson, G. W. The Gardener.
Johnson, S. W. Rural Economy.
Johnson, C. W. Farmer's Encyclopædia.
Johnston, James F. W. Lectures.
Johnston, J. F. W. Notes on North America.
Johnston, J. F. W. Scientific Agriculture.
Journal of the Agricultural Society.
Kent, N. Hints on Landed Property.
Knight, F. Washington's Letters on Agri.
Lathrop, L. E. The Farmer's Library.
Lectures on Agricultural Chemistry.
Lectures on Agriculture.
Liebig, J. Agricultural Chemistry.
Lindley, G. & J. Orchard and Fruit Garden.
Livingston, Robert R. Essay on Sheep.
Low, David. Practical Agriculture.
Magazine of Horticulture.
Maison Rustique de XIXe Siecle.
Manning, Robert. Book of Fruits.
Marshall, W. Planting, Rural Ornament, &c.
Marshall, W. Rural Economy.
Martinelli, Jules. Manuel d'Agriculture.
Massachusetts Agricultural Repository.
Memoires d'Agriculture, d'Economie, etc.
Memoirs of the Penn. Agricultural Soc.
Moll, L. Agriculture de l'Algêrie.
N. Y. Farmer's and Gardener's Magazine.
N. Y. Farmer and Mechanic.
N. Y. Farmer's, &c., Repository.
Normandie Agricole La. Journal d'Agriculture.
Observations on Modern Gardening.
Odart, Comte. Traité des Cepages.
Perrine, Dr. Henry. Tropical Plants.
Petzholdt, Alex. Agricultural Chemistry.
Picard, l'Abbe. L'Agriculture Raisonne.
Plough Boy, The.
Porter, Geo. R. Sugar Cane.
Prince, Wm. R. & Wm. Pomological Manual.
Prince, Wm. R. & Wm. Treatise on the Vine.
Rigg, Robert. Experimental Researches.
Reich, G. C Gartenkalender.
Revue Horticole.
Ruffin, Edmund. Farmer's Register.
Schlipf, I. A. Manuel d'Agriculture.
Schwerz, I. N. Plantes Fourragères.
Schwerz, I. N. Plantes a Grains Farineux.
Schwerz, I. N. Preceptes d'Agriculture.
Sinclair, Sir John. Code of Agriculture.
Skinner, John S. Journal of Agriculture.
Smith, Joseph A. Farmer's Mine.
Spohr, D. C. H. Veterinarisches Handbuch.
Sproul, John. Practical Agriculture.
Stephens, George. Practical Irrigator.
Steuart, Sir H. The Planter's Guide.
Stewart, John. Stable Economy.
Stoltz, J. L. Cultivateur Alsacian.
Stud Book Française, Registre, etc.
Tinelli, Lewis. Mulberry and Silk.
Transactions of the Agricultural Society.
Transactions of the American Institute.
Transactions of the Highland Society.
Transactions of the Michigan Society.
Transactions of the N. Y. State Society.
Travanet, M. de. Preservatif d'Agromanie.
Varlo, C. A New System of Husbandry.
Veterinarian, The. A Monthly Journal.
Volney, C. T. Soil and Climate of the U. S.
Washington, Geo. Letters on Agriculture.
Watson, E. Agricultural Societies.
Weeks, John M. Managing Bees.
Western Agriculturist and Prac. Guide.
Whitmarsh, Samuel. Mulberry Tree.
Wiggins, Francis S. Farmer's Instructer.
Youatt, Wm. Cattle Doctor.
Youatt, Wm., & W. C. L. Martin. Cattle.
Young, Arthur. Experimental Agricul.

Fine Arts.

DRAWING, PAINTING, ENGRAVING, SCULPTURE, ARCHITECTURE AND MUSIC.

Algarotte, Count. Essay on Painting.
American Art-Union. Bulletin of.
Architect's Journal.
Art-Journal, The.

Barnard, Henry. School Architecture.
Bradley, Thomas. Linear Perspective, &c.
Butler, C. Ancient and Modern Music.
Chapman, J. G. The American Drawing Book.
Civil Engineer's and Architect's Journal.
Dallaway, J. Architecture in England.
Downing, A. J. Cottage Residences.
Hay, D. R. Colors, Hues, Tints, and Shades.
Hoppus, E. Architecture Displayed.
Howard, Frank. Color as a Means of Art.
Langley, B. & T. Gothic Architecture.
Leoni, Jas. Designs for Buildings.
Nicholson, P. Architectural Dictionary.
Nicholson, P. Principles of Architecture.
Pain, William. The Builder's Companion.
Pain, Wm. & Jas. British Palladio.
Perceptor, The.
Pilkington, Jas. The Artist's Repository.
Pozzo, A. Rules, &c., of Perspective.
Pye, John. British Art.
Rambles among Musicians of Germany.
Ranlett, Wm. H. The Architect.
Ruskin, J. Seven Lamps of Architecture.
Shaw, Edward. Civil Architecture.
Smith, George. Construction of Cottages.
Swan, Abm. Designs in Architecture.
Swan, Abraham. The British Architect.
Taylor, W. B. S. Fine Arts in G. Britain.
Tremont House. Description of.
Ware, Isaac. Body of Architecture.
Whittock, N. Miniature Painter's Manual.
Wood, John Geo. Lectures on Perspective.

Miscellaneous Arts. I.

MECHANICAL, CHEMICAL, DOMESTIC, &C.

American Repertory.
Apprentice, The.
Arcana of Arts and Sciences.
Artisan, The. A Monthly Journal.
Babbage, Charles. Economy of Machinery, &c.
Bailey, A. M. Machines and Implements.
Baines, Edward. Cotton Manufactures.
Barlow, Peter. Strength, &c., of Timber.
Beekman, Prof. Inventions, &c.
Berthollet, C. L. and A. B. Art of Dyeing.
Berthollet, C. L. Method of Bleaching.
Bion, M. Mathematical Instruments.
Bischoff, James. Woolen and Worsted.
Boucharlat, M. Treatise on Mechanics.
Bourne, Oliver. Steam Engine.
Browne, J. R. Whale Fishery.
Carding and Spinning Master's Assistant.
Chemist, The.
Chesterfield. The American Chesterfield.
Cobb, J. H. Manual of the Mulberry Tree.
Cooper, T. Dyeing and Calico Printing.
Coppinger, J. Brewer and Tanner.
Cassigny, J. F. C. Fabrication de la Poudre.
Cotton Spinner's Manual.
Courtenay, E. Treatise on Mechanics.
Cutbush, James. System of Pyrotechny.
Dennis, Jr., Jona. Silk Manual.
D'Homergue, John, &c. Essays on Silk.
Dickinson, S. N. Help to Printers, &c., and Publisher.
Dodd, G. British Manufactures.
Dolbear's Science of Penmanship.
Emporium of Arts, &c.
Ewbank, T. Hydraulic and other Machines.
Fessenden, T. G. Register of Arts.
Frost, J. Art of Swimming.
Gallier, J. Price Book and Estimator.
Gera, Le Dr. Fo. Fabrication du Fromage.
Gilroy, C. G. Dyeing and Calico Printing.
Gilroy, Clinton G. Art of Weaving.
Gilroy, C. G. Silk, Cotton, Linen, Wool, &c.
Gray, Andrew. Spinning Machinery.
Hall, J. Sparker. The Book of the Feet.
Handmaid to the Arts.
Hansard, T. C. Printing and Type-Founding.
History of Wonderful Inventions.
Holtzapffel, Chas. Turning, &c.
Hughes, Thomas. On Roads.
Hunter, James. Scotch Swing Plough, &c.
Imison, John. Schools of Arts.
Jacob, Wm. Precious Metals.
Jenkins, John. Art of Writing.
Johnson, Walter R. American Coal.
Journal of the Arts.
Kerr, Robt. Method of Bleaching.
Lasteyrie, C. P. Pastel on Wood.
London Journal of Arts.
Machines. Book of Plates of.
Magazine of Domestic Economy.
Magazine of Science and School of Arts.
Mapes, J. J. Repertory of Arts.
Massy, W. Origin, &c., of Letters.
Mechanic's Magazine.
Metal. Manufactures in.
Miles, P. Mnemotechny, the Art of Memory.
Millingen, J. G. History of Duelling.
Montgomery, Jas. Cotton Manufacture.
Morin, Arthur. Roues Hydrauliques.
Morin, Arthur. Tirage des Voitures.
Murphy, John. Art of Weaving.
Nicholson, P. The Mechanic's Companion.
Overman, F. Assaying and Mining.
Overman, F. Manufacture of Iron.
Pain, Wm. and Jas. British Palladio.
Pain, Wm. The Builder's Companion.
Pain, Wm. The Carpenter's Repository.
Partridge, Wm. Treatise on Dyeing, &c.
Phillips, Sir R. Familiar Cyclopædia.
Phillips, Willard. The Inventor's Guide.
Pilkington, James. Mechanic's Repository.
Pitman, Isaac. Manual of Phonography.
Porter, G. R. Sugar Cane.
Register of Arts.
Reid, Thos. Clock and Watch Making.
Repertory, The.
Richardson, C. J. Warming and Ventilation.
Rogers, John G. Printing Types.

Sheys, B. American Bookkeeper.
Silk Manufacture.
Smith, G. Construction of Cottages.
Smith, G. The Laboratory.
Travanti, G. Trattato Completo Sull' Ulivo.
Thomas, Isaiah. Printing in America.
Timperley, C. H. Printers and Printing.
Tinelli, Lewis. Mulberry and Silk.
Walker, Edward. Art of Book Binding.
Warwick, Eden. Nasology.
Weeks, John M. Managing Bees.
White, E. Printing Types and Ornaments.
White, Jas. Century of Inventions.
Whitmarsh, Samuel. Mulberry Tree.
Williams, T. Academical Stenography.
Willich, A. F. M. Domestic Encyclopædia.
Wonders of the Universe.
Workingman's Companion.
Year Book of Facts.
Young Mechanic, The.

Miscellaneous Arts. II.

GAMES AND SPORTS.

Arrian on Coursing.
Beckford, Peter. Thoughts on Hunting.
Chronicles of the Seasons.
Edgar, Patrick N. American Race, Turf Register, Sportsman's Herald, and General Stud Book.
Frost, J. Art of Swimming.
Hieover, A. Stable Talk and Table Talk.
Houston, Geo. Sportsman's Magazine.
Hoyle's Fashionable Games.
Maxwell, W. H. Wild Sports of the West.
Millingen, J. G. History of Duelling.
Salzmann, G. C. Gymnastics for Youth.
Smith, J. V. C. Essay on Angling.
Sportsman's Dictionary.
Sportsman, The, in Ireland.
Walton, Izaac, and Chas. Cotton. The Complete Angler.
Whyte, Jas. C. British Turf.

BELLES LETTRES.

Elementary.

DICTIONARIES AND GRAMMARS.

Ainsworth's Dictionary. Abridged.
Alberti, Francois. Grand Dictionnaire.
Bailey, N. Dictionarium Britannicum.
Bailey, N. Etymological Dictionary.
Boyer, A. Dictionary, French, &c.
Crabbe, George. English Synonyms.
Dictionnaire de l'Academie Françoise.
Fowler, Wm. C. English Grammar.
Kenrick, Wm. English Dictionary.
Lasteyrie, C. P. Abhandlung.
Martin, Benj. Bibliotheca Technologica.
Martin, John. Dictionnaire de Poche.
Martin, John. French Homonynas.
Murray, Lindley. English Grammar.
Neuman and Baretti's Dictionary, Spanish and Portuguese.
Oudin, Cæsar. Langues Françoise, etc.
Parker, R. G. Aids to English Composition.
Polyglot Lexicon.
Priestly, Joseph. English Grammar.
Santagnello, M. A. Italian Language.
Schreveli, Cornelii. Lexicon Manuale.
Scott, Wm. English Dictionary.
Sheridan, Thos. English Dictionary.
Tooke, J. H. Diversions of Purley.
Treasury of Knowledge.
Vieyra, Anthony. Portuguese Dictionary.
Walker, John. English Dictionary.
Walker, John. Rhetorical Grammar.
Webster, Noah. English Dictionary.
Worcester, J. E. English Dictionary.

Elementary and Theoretical.

RHETORIC, ORATORY, POESY, PHILOLOGY AND CRITICISM.

Ansley, E. A. Elements of Literature.
Aristotle. Treatise on Poetry.
Athenæum, The.
Blair, H. Rhetoric and Belles Lettres.
Bouterwek, F. Spanish Literature.
Brerewood, E. Diversity of Languages.
Campbell, Geo. Philosophy of Rhetoric.
Corticelli, Salvadore. Lingua Toscana.
Guthrie, Wm. Cicero de Oratore.
Hazlitt, Wm. Dramatic Literature.
Hazlitt, Wm. English Comic Writers.
Home, Henry. Elements of Criticism.
Hunt, L. English Poets.
Olney, Sarah H. Extracts from Blair.
Parker, R. G. English Composition.
Porny, Mark A. Models of Letters.
Sismondi, J. C. L. de. Italian Literature.
Shaw, Thos. B. English Literature.
Tannehill, Wilkins. History of Literature.
Thimm, Franz L. J. Literature of Germany.
Thornton, W. Cadmus. Written Language.
Ticknor, George. Spanish Literature.
Timon. Eloquence.
Timperley, C. H. Progress of Literature.
Tooke, J. H. Diversions of Purley.
Vericour, L. R. de. French Literature.
Walker, George. English Prose.
Walker, John. Rhetorical Grammar.
Webster, Jr., Noah. English Language.

Belles Lettres Proper. I.

POETRY AND THE DRAMA.

Aiken, John. British Poets.
Alden, T. Epitaphs and Inscriptions.
Bailey, Philip Jas. Festus. A Poem.
Barlow, J. The Hasty Pudding. A Poem.
Beattie, James. Poetical Works.
Browning, Robert Poems.
Burgess, Geo. Peter & Paul. A Poem.
Burns, Robert. Poetical Works.
Bulter, Samuel. Poetical Remains.
Byron, Lord. Marino Faliero. A Tragedy.
Byron, George Gordon, Lord. Works.
Caffaro, Father. Defence of the Drama.
Cary, H. F. French Poets and Poetry.
Chalmers, George. Poetic Remains.
Churchill, C. Poems.
Collins, William. Poetical Works.
Courtenay, Thos. P. Plays of Shakspere.
Cowper, William. Poems.
Cowper, William. Works.
Crabbe, Rev. George. Poems, Tales, &c.
Croker, T. C. Popular Songs of Ireland.
Dante, A. Vision; or, Hell, Purgatory, &c.
Dawes, Rufus. Athenia of Damascus. A Tragedy.
Dennis, Mr. Remarks on Prince Arthur.
Dwight, Timothy. Conquest of Canaan.
Emerson, Ralph Waldo. Poems.
Emmons, Richard. Battle of Bunker Hill.
Faber, F. W. Styrian Lake, and other Poems.
Fairfield, S. L. Abaddon, and other Poems.
Fairfield, S. L. Last Nights of Pompeii.
Fairfield, Sumner L. Poems, &c.
Fessenden, T. G. Ladies' Monitor. A Poem.
Freneau, Philip. Collection of Poems.
Gibson, H. S. Miscellaneous Poems.
Gray, Thomas. Poetical Works.
Griswold, Rufus W. Poets and Poetry of America.
Hagedorn, F. von. Samtliche Poetische Werke.
Hazlitt, Wm. Dramatic Literature.
Hazlitt, Wm. English Comic Writers, &c.
Heber, Reginald. Poetical Works.
Hemans, Heber, & Pollok. Poetical Works.
Hillhouse, Jas. A. Hadad. A Dramatic Poem.
Howitt, W. Homes, &c., of British Poets.
Ifflands, A. W. Dramatische Werke.
Milton, John. Poetical Works.
Milton, Young, Gray, Beattie, and Collins. Poetical Works.
Minstrel, The; or, a Selection of Songs.
Moore, Thomas. Lalla Rookh.
Moore, Thomas. Poetical Works.
More, Hannah. Sacred Dramas.
Morris, George P. Deserted Bride, &c.
Ossian. Poems, by James Macpherson.
Paine, Jr., R. T. Works.
Poe, Edgar A. Works.
Poems, by a Collegian.
Poems, by a Proser.
Pollok, Robert. Poetical Works.
Pope, Alexander. Works.
Ruins of Athens, with other Poems.
Sands, R. C. Writings.
Schobel, Fred. Illyria and Dalmatia.
Scott, Sir Walter. Poetical Works.
Shakspere, Wm. The Works of.
Siamese Twins, with other Poems.
Smith, S. Louisa P. Poems.
Southey's Common Place Book.
Southey, Robert. Uneducated Poets.
Steinmetz, Andrew. A Voice in Ramah.
Terentii Publii Comediœ Sex.
Thyer, Robert. Remains of Sam'l Butler.
Trumbull, John. M'Fingal.
Trumbull, John. Poetical Works.
Virgil. Works.
Woodworth, S. Melodies, Songs & Ballads.
Young, Edward. Poetical Works.

Belles Lettres Proper. II.

ROMANCE AND FACETIÆ.

Adams' Anecdotes.
Arabian Nights' Entertainments.
Boccaccio, Giovane. The Decameron.
Cervantes, Miguel De. Don Quixote.
Cervantes, Miguel De. El Buscapié.
Colton, Rev. W. Deck and Port.
Colton, Rev. W. Ship and Shore.
Cramer, Carl G. Rasereien der Liebe.
Defoe, Daniel. Robinson Crusoe.
Dickens, Charles. Works.
Don Quixote. (See Cervantes.)
Edgeworth, Maria. Popular Tales.
Fielding, Henry. Tom Jones.
Fielding, Henry. History of Amelia.
Fouqué, F. De La Motte. Undine and Sintram.
Fume, Joseph. A Paper—of Tobacco.
Gil Blas. (See Le Sage.)
Haliburton, Thos. C. The Attaché.
Hawthorne, N. Mosses from an old Manse.
Hawthorne, Nath'l. The Scarlet Letter.
Holcroft, T. Caroline of Lichtfield.
Irving, Washington. Works.
Lane, E. W. The Thousand and One Nights.
Last of the Plantagenets. An Historical Romance.
Le Gros, W. B Fables, &c.
Le Sage, Alain René. Gil Blas.
Le Sage. The Devil upon Two Sticks.
Lytton, Sir Edward Bulwer. Harold.
Maxwell, W. H. Legends of Cheviots.
Moore, Thomas. Lalla Rookh.
Neal, John. The Down Easters, &c. &c.
Oxberry, W. The Actor's Budget of Wit, &c.
Parkman, Jr., Francis. Oregon Trail.
Paulding, J. K. The Dutchman's Fireside.
Percy Anecdotes. The Revised Edition.
Robinson Crusoe. (See Defoe.)
Schweiler A. Amber Witch and Undine.
Scott, Sir W. The Antiquary.
Scott, Sir Walter. Quintin Durward.

Scribe, Eugene. Victim of the Jesuits.
Smollett, Tobias. Humphrey Clinker.
Smollett, Tobias. Peregrine Pickle.
Sterne, Lawrence. Tristram Shandy.
Stone, Wm. L. Tales and Sketches.
Vigny, Count, Alfred de. Cinq Mars.

Belles Lettres Proper. III.

LITERARY ESSAYS, LETTERS AND ORATIONS.

Adams, Mrs. John. Letters, &c.
Addison, Joseph. Works.
Alison, Archibald. Essays.
American Common Place Book of Prose.
Andrews, Wm. W. Correspondence.
Angeleni, Baptista. Letters on England.
Anniversary, The, for 1829.
Anonymiana, or 1,000 years of Observations.
Arblay, Madame d'. Diary and Letters.
Barnard, D. D. Speeches, &c.
Barrington, Daines. Miscellanies.
Beauties of the British Classics.
British Essayists. The Spectator, &c.
Browne, A. Sketches or Hints for Essays.
Buckingham, Jos. Newspaper Literature.
Cameron, Mrs. Englishwomen.
Cardonne, M. A. Eastern Learning.
Carlyle, Thomas. Cromwell's Letters, &c.
Carlyle, Thomas. Essays.
Carpenter, S. C. American Speeches.
Chatham, Earl of. Correspondence.
Chatham, Earl of. Letters.
Chatham, Burke, and Erskine. Speeches.
Cicero, M. T. Select Orations.
Cicero, M. T The Letters of.
Clinton, De Witt. Discourse.
Coleridge, Samuel T. Letters, &c.
Collingwood, G. L. Correspondence.
Colton, C. C. Lacon.
Correspondence between the Countess of Hartford, and Pomfret.
Corsair, The.
Cowper, Wm. Correspondence.
Critical Review.
Cromwell, Oliver. Letters and Speeches.
Crump, W. H The World in a Pocket Book.
Cumberland, Richard. The Observer.
Curwen, Samuel. Journal and Letters.
Dagley, Richard Death's Doings.
Davis, J. B. More Subjects than One.
Discourse on Advantages of Science.
D'Israeli, J. Curiosities of Literature.
D'Israeli, J. Miscellanies of Literature.
Duncan, Wm. Cicero's Select Orations.
Eldon, Lord. Correspondence.
Emerson, James. Letters from the Ægean.
Evans, John. Shakspere's Seven Ages.
Fairfax, Lord. Correspondence.
Fenn, John. Paston Letters.
Fitz-Adam, Adam. The World.
Foster, John. Popular Ignorance.
Foscolo, Ugo. Essays on Petrarch.
Foster, Mrs. M. E. European Literature.
Fugitive Pieces by Several Authors.
Golovine, Ivan. Russian Sketch Book.
Great Metropolis, The.
Greene, Geo. W. Historical Studies.
Gregory, Jacob. Dissertatio Inauguralis.
Griswold, R. W. Prose Writers of Am.
Hamilton, Alex. Correspondence.
Hazlitt, Wm. Table Talk.
Headly, J. T. Letters from Italy.
Hedge, F. H. Prose Writers of Germany.
Herbert, Charles. Italian Literature.
Hinman, R. R. Letters to the Governors.
Hints and Sketches.
Hippisley, Sir John Cox. Correspondence.
Hosack, David. Discourses.
Humboldt, Alex. von. Essays.
Hume, David. Essays and Treatises.
Hume, David. Private Correspondence.
Hunt, Leigh. Imagination and Fancy.
Inchiquin, The Jesuit's Letters.
Irving, Washington. Works.
Jeffrey. Lord. Contributions to the Edinburgh Review.
Jones, W. A. Literary Studies.
Jones, Sir Wm. Correspondence.
Junius. Letters.
Kavanagh, Julia. Woman in France.
Knapp, Samuel L. American Literature.
Knight, Chas. Half Hours.
Knight, F. Fac Similes of Letters.
Knox, Vicesimus. Elegant Extracts.
Korner, Carl F. Correspondence.
Letters of the British Spy.
Letters from Buenos Ayres and Chili.
Letters from the Danube.
Letters on the Eastern States.
Letters and Essays.
Letters between John Locke and Friends.
Letters of a Mother to her Daughter.
Letters from the Old World.
Letters from Virginia.
Macaulay, Thos. B. Essays, Critical, &c.
Maintenon, Madame de. Correspondence.
Martineau, Harriet. How to Observe.
Matthisson, F. Letters.
Miscellanies by G. C. Verplanck, &c.
Mitford, Mary Russell. Our Village.
Modern British Essayists.
Moise, Miss Penina. Fancy's Sketch Book.
Morgan, Lady. Woman and Her Master.
Much Instruction from Little Reading.
Nelson, Lord. Letters to Lady Hamilton.
Newton, John. Letters.
Nichols, John. Corresp. of Sir R. Steel.
No Fiction ; a Narrative.
Observations on Lord Bradhurst's Speech.
Our Neighborhood, &c.
Pazos, Vicente. Letters.
Pearce, R. R. Wellesley's Correspondence.
Pepys, Samuel. Correspondence.
Perkins, Nathan. Discourses.
Petrarch. Essays on.
Petty, Wm. Essays.

Philips, Curran, and Grattan. Speeches.
Pinkney, Wm. Speeches.
Potalis, M. Speech.
Prescott, Wm. H. Miscellanies.
Reidesel, Madame de. Letters, &c.
Republic of Letters. Standard Literature.
Ross, Sir J. Corresp. of Lord Saumarez.
Rumford, Benjamin, Count. Essays.
Schiller, Frederic. Correspondence.
Schomann, G. F. Dissertation.
Schröder, F. L. Reytrag.
Scott, James. Letters and Remains.
Sergent, John. Select Speeches.
Sheridan, Richard B. Speeches.
Sidney, H. Correspondence of Charles II.
Simpson, L. Correspondence of Schiller.
Sinclair, Sir John. Correspondence.
Smith, Sir W. S. Correspondence.
Spectator, with Notes.
Speeches in Congress.
Steel, Sir Richard. Correspondence.
Stephens, James. Essays.
St. John, J. H. Letters from a Farmer.
Sweeney, Robert. Odds and Ends.
Swift, Jona. Interesting Miscellanies.
Tallmadge, James. Speeches.
Thomson, James. Letters.
Thoresby, R. Letters from Eminent Men.
Timon. The Orators of France.
Token, The. A Christmas Present.
Trumbull, John. Letters.
Turnbull, Rev. R. Genius of Italy.
Turnbull, Rev. R. Genius of Scotland.
Ventonillac, L. T. The French Librarian.
Vericour, L. R. de. French Literature.
Vernon, James. Letters.
Verplanck, Gulian C. American Scholar.
Voltaire, F. M. Letters on the English.
Walker, George. English Prose.
Walpole, Horace. Letters of.
Walpole, Sir H. Letters to Sir Horace Mann.
Walpole, Sir Horace. Letters to Ossory.
Walpole, Horace. Noble Authors.
Ward, George. A Journal and Letters.
Washington, Geo. Letters to Young, &c.
Washington, Geo. Official Letters.
Webster, Noah. Collection of Papers.
Webster, D. Speeches and Arguments.

Belles Lettres Proper. IV.

GREEK AND LATIN CLASSICS AND TRANSLATIONS.

Aristotles Poetics.
Cicero, M. T. Orations.
Cicero, M. T. Works.
Herodotus. Lexicon to.
Homer. Illiad and Odyssy.
Horatii, Q. Flacci. Carminum, etc.
Horatii, Quinti Flacci. Opera.
Josephus, Flavius. Works.
Livius, T. P. By Baker.
Livius, T. P. Roman History.
Philo Judæus. Opera exegetica in Libros Mosis.
Plutarchus, by Langhorne.
Tacitus, C. C. Opera.
Terentii Publii Comædiæ Sex Scholia Anonymi adjunxit, J. A. Giles.
Virgilius. Opera.
Xenophon. Anabasis.

GEOGRAPHY, VOYAGES AND TRAVELS.

Geography, Voyages, Travels, &c. I.

UNIVERSAL.

Accompaniment to Tanner's Atlas.
Adalbert, Prince. Travels.
Bell, James. System of Geography.
Bigland, John. View of the World.
Brookes, R., &c. Dictionary of the World.
Browne, I. R. Etchings of a Whaling Cruise.
Clarke, Edward Daniel. Travels.
Cook, James. Voyages round the World.
Coreal, Francois Voyages aux Indes.
Darby, William. Universal Gazetteer.
Delano, Amasa. Voyages and Travels.
Ewing, Thomas. Geography for Schools.
Geography for Youth.
Goldsmith, J. General View of Nations.
Goldsmith, J. View of the World.
Goodman, J. D. Rambles.
Gordon, Pat. Geography Anatomatized.
Guthrie, Wm. Modern Geography.
Heron, Robert. Universal Geography.
Kelly, Christopher. Universal Geography.
Kippis, Dr. A. Narrative of Voyages.
Lardner, Dion. Maritime and Inland Discovery.
Lester, C. Edwards, & Andrew Foster. The Life and Voyages of Americus Vespucius.
Malhan, Rev. John. Naval Gazetteer.
Malte Brun, M. Universal Geography.
Mavor, Wm. The British Tourists.
Mavor, Wm. Voyages, Travels and Discoveries.
Maxwell, W. H. Rambling Recollections.
McCulloch, J. R. Universal Gazetteer.
Miller, E. A Companion to the Atlas.
Mitchel's Map. An Accompaniment to.
Modern Gazetteer, or Geographical Dict'y.
Modern Traveller, The.
Moore, S. S. The Traveller's Dictionary.
Murray, H. Encyclopædia of Geography.
Museum of History.
Payne, John. Universal Geography.
Perceptor, The.
Piquot, A. General Gazetteer.

Poole, John. Sketches and Recollections.
Portlock and Dixon's Voyage, Abridged.
Reynolds, J. N. Voyage of the Potomac.
Salmon, Mr. Geographical Grammar.
Short Stories and Reminiscences.
Simpson, Alex. Travels of Thos. Simpson.
Smith, Capt. J. Travels, Adventures, &c.
Smith, Wm. Geography.
Spafford, Horatio G. General Geography.
Tanner's Atlas. Accompaniment to.
Treasury of Knowledge.
Universal Pocket Gazette.
Vosgien. Dictionnaire Geographique.
Voyages and Discoveries.
Voyages of Drake, Cavendish and Dampier.
Ward, R. P. Pictures of the World.
Waterson, Wm. Cyclopædia of Geography.
Williams, Chas. Missionary Gazetteer.
Wolfe, Jas. Researches, &c.
Woodbridge, W. C. Universal Geography.
Worcester, J. E. Geographical Dictionary.

Geography, Voyages, Travels, &c. I.

EUROPE, ASIA, AND AFRICA.

Ali Bey. Travels in Africa, &c.
Allen, W. H., &c. Expedition to the Niger
Allen, Z. Practical Tourist.
American in England.
Anderson, Æ. British Embassy to China.
Anthon, Chas. Pilgrimage to Treves.
Arrian's Voyage round the Euxine Sea.
Aubigne, J. H. Merle d'. Germany, England and Scotland.
Australia, Picture of.
Austria and the Austrians.
Baines, Edward. County Palatine.
Baretti, J. Manners and Customs of Italy.
Barnard, Lieut. Three Years' Cruise.
Barrow, Jr., John. North of Europe.
Barrow, Sir John. Arctic Regions.
Barrow, Sir John. Pitcairn's Island.
Barthelemi, Abbé. Travels of Anacharsis.
Beckford, Wm. Italy, Spain and Portugal.
Bell, Robert. Wayside Pictures.
Beltrami, J. C. A Pilgrimage in Europe.
Berrian, W. Travels in France and Italy.
Bigelow, A. Travels in Malta and Sicily.
Blessington, Countess of. Idler in Italy.
Blessington, Countess of. Idler in France.
Boys, Edward. Captivity and Adventures.
Brockedon, Wm. Excursions in the Alps.
Brydone, P. Sicily and Malta.
Buchanan, C. Researches in Asia.
Bulkeley, J., &c. Voyage to Southern Seas.
Busby, J. Vineyards of Spain and France.
Byrne, J. C. British Colonies.
Carr, Sir John. Tour through Holland.
Carter, N. H. Letters from Europe.
Chatterton, Lady. Rambles in Ireland.
Cheever, H. T. Island World.
Johnston, Charles. Southern Abyssinia.
Keppell, Henry. Expedition to Borneo.

Clarke, Andrew. Tour in France, &c.
Clarke, E. D. Travels in Europe, Asia, &c.
Clarke, Edward Daniel. Travels.
Cobbett, Jas. P. A Ride of 800 miles in France.
Colman, H. European Life and Manners.
Colton, Rev. Walter. Ship and Shore.
Conway, Derwent. Switzerland, &c.
Coxe, Wm. Travels into Poland, &c.
Crawfurd, J. Courts of Siam and China.
Crawfurd, J. Embassy to the Court of Ava.
Crosley, M. A. Tour to London.
Dalrymple, Wm. Travels thro' Spain, &c.
Damer, Mrs. G. L. D. Tour in Greece, &c.
Dellon, M. Inquisition at Goa.
Discovery and Adventure in Africa.
Discovery, &c., in the Polar Regions.
Ditson, George L. Circassia.
Dumas, Alexandre. Travels in Egypt, &c.
Dwight, Henry E. Travels in Germany.
East India Sketch-Book.
Ellis, Henry. Embassy to China.
Ellis, Wm. Polynesian Researches.
Emerson, Jas. Letters from the Ægean.
England Illustrated.
English, Geo. B. Dongola and Sennaar.
Erman, Adolph. Travels in Siberia.
Eustace, John C. Tour through Italy.
Fisk, Wilbur. Travels in Europe.
Fletcher, Rev. J. P. Notes from Nineveh.
Forbes, F. E. Five Years in China.
Forbes, Major. Eleven Years in Ceylon.
Ford, R. Spaniards and their Country.
French in Algiers.
Furniss, Wm. The Old World.
Furniss, Wm. Waraga.
Germany. Rambles among the Musicians of.
Gliddon, George R. Ancient Egypt.
Golovine, Ivan. Russian Sketch Book.
Goodman, J. D. Rambles of a Naturalist
Granville, A. B. The Spas of England.
Granville, A. B. The Spas of Germany.
Great Metropolis, The.
Greece. Sketches of Modern Greece.
Griscom, John. A Year in Europe.
Hamilton, Wm. Remarks on Turkey.
Haussez, Baron. Great Britain in 1833.
Hawks, Rev. F. L. Monuments of Egypt.
Hawthorne, Nath'l. Journal of a Cruiser.
Head, Sir George. A Home Tour.
Herbert, Charles. Italy.
Hermit in London.
Holcroft, Thos. Travels to Paris.
Holmes, Wm. R. Shores of the Caspian.
Howitt, Wm. German Experiences.
Howitt, W. Homes and Haunts of Poets.
Hunter, W. P. Expedition to Syria.
India. Picture of.
Inglis, Henry D. Journey thro' Ireland.
Ireland. The Irish Tourist.
Jacquemin, Emile. L'Allemagne.
Janes, John. Sketches of Travels.

Keysler, John Geo. Travels.
Kotzebue, M. von. Journey into Persia.
Laign, Samuel. Notes of a Traveller.
Lander, R. & J. Expedition to the Niger.
Leake, Wm. M. Travels in Morea.
Lewald. Fanny. Italians at Home.
Mantell, Gideon A. Geological Excursions.
Martin, R. M. British Colonial Library.
Layard, A. H. Nineveh and its Remains.
Low, Hugh. Sarawak.
Lowe, Jos. Present State of England.
MacFarlane, C. Turkey and its Destiny.
Macnevin, W. J. Ramble thro' Switzerland.
Martin, R. Montgomery. China.
Mas, Pocco. Scenes, &c., in Spain.
Mavor, Wm. British Tourists.
Maxwell, J. S. Czar, his Court and People.
Miller, Jona. P. The Condition of Greece.
Moll, L. Colonization, etc., de l'Algérie.
Montgomery, James. South Sea Islands.
Moore, John. View of Society, &c.
Morgan, Lady. France in 1829-30.
Mügge, Theodore. Switzerland in 1847.
Murray, John F. The World of London.
Musgrave, G. M. Excursions to Paris, &c.
Musgrave, G. M. Parson, Pen, and Pencil.
Niebuhr, C. Travels through Arabia, &c.
Noah, M. M. Travels in England, &c.
Park, M. Journal of a Mission to Africa.
Park, Mungo. Travels in Africa.
Parrot, Frederick. Journey to Ararat.
Pennant, T. Journey to the Isle of Wight.
Perdicaris, G. A. Greece of the Greeks.
Rambles among the Musicians of Germany.
Rich, Claudius J Site of Babylon.
Richardson, James. Travels in Sahara.
Rochon, Abbe. Voyage to Madagascar.
Romer, Isabella F. Temples and Tombs.
Romer, Isabella F. The Bird of Passage.
Romer, I. F. The Rhone, the Darro, &c.
Royall, Anne. Southern Tour.
Ruschenberger, W. S. W. Three years in the Pacific.
Rush, Richard. Court of London.
Sabine, E. Expedition to the Polar Sea.
Schroeder, Francis. Mediterranean.
Scotland, Travelers' Guide through
Short, Capt. Chas. Southern Australia.
Simond, L. Switzerland.
Sinclair, C. Scotland and the Scotch.
Skeine, H. Two Tours thro' Wales, &c.
Smith, A. Atrocities of the Pirates.
Smith, George. Visit to China.
Smith, John T. Antiquarian Ramble.
Smith, Wm. Voyage.
Smithgate, H. Tour thro' Armenia, &c.
Spencer, J. A. Egypt and the Holy Land.
Spry, H. H. Modern India.
Stanton, Sir George. Embassy to China.
St. John, Bayle. Lybian Desert.
St. Marie, Count. Algeria in 1845.
Stocqueler, J. H. Hand Book of India.
Sweden and Gottland. Rambles in.
Taylor, J. Bayard. Views Afoot.
Taylor, W. C. Monuments of Egypt.
Temple, Sir G. Travels in Greece, &c.
Tour. History of a Six Weeks' Tour.
Traveller's Guide through Scotland.
Turkey. Sketches of, in 1831-32.
Turnbull, Rev. Robt. Genius of Italy.
Turnbull, Rev. R. The Genius of Scotland.
Turner, Wm. Tour in the Levant.
Urquhart, D. The Pillars of Hercules.
Valentine, Lewis. Voyages en Italie.
Vicary, Rev.M. Residence at Rome in 1846.
Volney, C. F. Volney's Ruins.
Von Wrangell, F. Exp. to the Polar Sea.
Wallis, S. T. Glimpses of Spain.
Warburton, Eliot. Crescent and the Cross.
Waring, Geo. Letters from Malta, &c.
Werne, Ferd. Sources of the White Nile.
West, Mrs. Frederic. Visit to Ireland.
Whitling, H. J. Pictures of Nuremberg.
Williams, H. M. Letters from France.
Williams, John. South Sea Islands.
Winterbotham, W. A. Chinese Empire.
Wood, W. W. Sketches of China.

Geography, Voyages, Travels, &c. II.

AMERICA.

Abbott, A. Cuba and the Cubans.
Alden, Timothy. Sundry Missions.
Alexander, J. E. Transatlantic Sketches.
America and the Americans.
Baird, R. Impressions and Experiences.
Barrow, Sir John. Arctic Regions.
Bartram, W. Travels thro' Carolina, &c.
Beck, L. C. Gazetteer of Ill. and Missouri.
Beltrami, J. C. Pilgrimage in America.
Beltrami, J. C. Sources du Mississippi.
Bigly, C. A. Gold Regions.
Bonnycastle, R. H. Newfoundland.
Bonnycastle, R. H. Spanish America.
Bonneyville's Adventures. (See W. Irving.)
Bossu, Capt. Travels thro' Louisiana.
Bouchette, Joseph A. Lower Canada, &c.
Brackenridge, H. M. Persons and Places.
Brackenridge, H. M. South America.
Bryant, Edwin. California.
Bulkeley, John, &c. South Seas.
Burr, David H. Atlas of New York.
Carey, Martin. American Pocket Atlas.
Carver, J. Travels thro' North America.
Catlin, George. North American Indians.
Chappell, Edward. Hudson's Bay.
Chastellux. Travels in North America.
Cheever, H. T. The Island World.
Christmas, Rev. H. Canada in 1849.
Clark, E. D. Travels.
Colton, Rev. Walter. Deck and Port.
Colton, Rev. W. Three Years in California.
Columbus, Christ'r. Voyage to America.
Cox, Ross. Columbia River.
Darby, Wm. Tour from N. Y. to Detroit.
Davalos, J. E. Limina, apud Peruvianos.
Del Rio, Antonio. Ruins in Guatimala.
Discovery, &c., in the Polar Seas.
Dixon, Geo. Voyage Autour du Monde.
Drake, Samuel G. Indian Captivities.

Duane, Wm. A Visit to Columbia.
Dwight, T. Travels in N. England and N. Y.
Ebelings, C. D. Nordamerika.
Edwards, W. H. Voyage up the Amazon.
Eastern States. Letters on.
Featherstonhaugh, G. W. Minnay Sotor.
Flint, Timothy. Mississippi Valley.
Flint, Timothy. Western States, &c.
Fowler, John. Tour in New York.
Fremont, J. C. Exploring Expedition.
Gass, Patrick. Travels in North America.
Gazetteer of the State of New York.
Gordon, T. F. Gazetteer, &c., of N. Jersey.
Gordon, Thos. F. Gazetteer of N. York.
Gordon, Thos. F. Gazetteer of Penn.
Graham, J. A. Sketch of Vermont.
Gregg, J. Commerce of the Prairies.
Grund, F. J. Aristocracy in America.
Grund, Francis J. The Americans.
Gurney, J. J. Winter in the West Indies.
Haliburton, Thos. C. Nova Scotia.
Hall, Basil. Extracts from his Journal.
Hall, Basil. Travels in America.
Hall, Basil. Voyage of Discovery.
Hall, Francis. Travels in Canada, &c.
Hardie, Jas. Description of New York.
Haskell and Smith. Gazetteer of U. States.
Head, Sir F. B. A Narrative.
Hodgson, A. Journey thro' N. America.
Holley, Mrs. Observations on Texas.
Humboldt, Alexander von. Travels, &c.
Hunter, J. D. Manners of Indian Tribes.
Inlay, Gilbert. Western Territory.
Irving, Washington. Astoria.
Irving, W. Bonnyville's Adventures.
Irving, Washington. Rocky Mountains.
Irving, W. Voyages of Columbus.
Johnson, Theodore T. Gold Regions.
Johnston, J. F. W. Notes on N. America.
Juan & De Ulloa. Voyage to S. America.
Jukes, J. B. Excursions in Newfoundland.
Kalm, P. Travels into North America.
Keating, W. H. Long's Expedition.
Kendall, E. Travels in United States.
Kendall, G. W. Santa Fé Expedition.
Kerr, H. Travels in the United States.
Kilbourn, John. Ohio Gazetteer.
Latrobe, Chas. J. Rambles in Mexico.
Letters on the Eastern States.
Long, Geo. Geography of America, &c.
Long, Stephen H Expedition.
Lyell, Sir C. 2d Visit to the U. States.
Lynch, W. F. Expedition to the Dead Sea.
Macgillivray, W. Humboldt's Travels.
Martin, Jos. Gazetteer of Virginia.
Martin, R. M. Colonial Library.
McKenney, Thomas. Tour to the Lakes.
McLean, John. Hudson's Bay Territory.
Mease, Jas., &c. Picture of Philadelphia.
Melish, John. Travels thro' U. States.
Merrill, E. Gazetteer of New Hampshire.
Molina, J. I. Geography, &c., of Chili.
Monroe, James. Tour of Observation.
Morse, J. Am. Universal Geography.
Morse, Jedidiah. The American Gazetteer.
Murat, Achilles. The United States.
New York. Gazetteer of the State of.
Ogden, John C. Tour through Canada.
O'Reilly, B. Greenland, &c.
Parkinson, Richard. Tour in America.
Parkman, Jr., F. California and Oregon.
Parry, William E North West Passage.
Parry, Wm. E. Second Voyage.
Pattie, James O. Personal Narrative of.
Pazos, V. Letters on South America.
Pearce, J. C. and J. H. Niles. Gazetteer of Connecticut and Rhode Island.
Pinkerton, John. Voyages and Travels.
Porter, David. Cruise to the Pacific.
Rainsford, M. Black Empire of Hayti.
Robinson, A. Life in California.
Royall, A. Southern Tour.
Ruschenberger, W. S. W. Three years in the Pacific.
Ruxton, Geo. F. Adventures in Mexico.
Saxe-Weimar, Duke of. Travels.
Schoolcraft, H. R. Lead Mines of Missouri.
Schoolcraft, H. R. N. Western Regions.
Simpson, T. Narrative of Discoveries.
Smet, P. J. de. Oregon Missions, &c.
Smith, A. Atrocities of the Pirates.
Smith, Capt. John. Travels in America.
Smith, J. T. Northmen in New England.
Smith, William. A Voyage to the Pacific.
Smyth, J. F. D. Tour in the United States.
Spafford, Horatio G. Gazetteer of N. Y.
Stephens, John L. Travel in Yucatan.
Stevenson, W. B. South America.
St. John, John R. Lake Superior, &c.
Temple, Edward. Travels in Peru.
Terry, A. R. Travels in South America.
Things as they are, or Notes of a Traveller.
Thomas, D. Travels thro' Western Country.
Thompson, W. Recollections of Mexico.
Thompson, Zadock. Gazetteer of Vermont.
Thomson, Jas. South America.
Trumbull, Henry. Discovery of America.
Tschudi, J. J. von. Travels in Peru.
Tudor, Henry. Tour in North America.
Turnbull, David. Cuba, Porto Rico, &c.
Turner, William. Tour in the Levant.
Twiss, Travers. Oregon Territory, &c.
United States of America as they are.
Vigne, G. T. Six Months in America.
Volney, C. F. View of the United States.
Waldo, S. Putnam. Tour of Jas. Monroe.
Walsh, R. Notices of Brazil.
Wanderer in Washington.
Warburton, Eliot. Hochelaga.
Webb, J. Watson. Altowan.
Wetmore, A Gazetteer of Missouri.
Wilkes, Charles. Exploring Expedition.
Williams, John. South Sea Islands.
Williams, J. L. View of West Florida.
Wilson, Prof. John. British Critics.
Wilson, John. Recreations.
Winterbotham, W. View of the U. States.
Wood, Wm. M. Wandering Sketches
Worcester, J. E. Gazetteer of the U. S.
Year Book.

HISTORY.

History.

ANCIENT, UNIVERSAL, &C.

Adam, Alex. Roman Antiquities.
Banks, T. C. Genealogical and Heraldic Gleanings.
Barrington, A. Introduction to Heraldry.
Beekman, Prof. Ancient Institutions, &c.
Bigland, John. A View of the World.
British India. Account of.
Brookes and Collyer. Dictionary.
Brown, William. Antiquities of the Jews.
Burke. Encyclopædia of Heraldry.
Carr, Thomas L. Roman Antiquities.
Cary, Henry. Lexicon to Herodotus.
Christmas, Rev. Henry. The Cradle of History.
Chronology, or an Introduction, &c.
Echard, L. Ecclesiastical History.
Ferguson, Adam. Roman Republic.
Gibbon, Edward. Roman Empire.
Gillies, John. Ancient Greece.
Gliddon, George. Ancient Egypt.
Goldsmith, J. View of Nations.
Hebbe, Gustavus C. Universal History. (Ancient.)
Heeren, A. H. L. Ancient Greece.
Heylin, Peter. Cosmographie.
Isaacs, Hyam. Traditions, &c., of the Jews.
James, G. P. R. Dark Scenes of History.
James, G. P. R. History of Chivalry.
Josephus, Flavius. The Works of.
Keightley, Thomas. History of Rome.
Kitto, John. History of Palestine.
Lardner, Dion. History of Discovery.
Layard, A. H. Nineveh.
Leland, Thos. Philip, King of Macedon.
Livius, Titus. History of Rome, by Baker.
Livius, Titus. Roman History.
Malte Brun, M. Tableau de la Pologne.
Maunder, Samuel. Treasury of History.
McCulloch, W. T. The Use, &c., of History.
Memoirs of what has Passed in Christen dom, from 1672 to 1679.
Michelet, M. Roman Republic.
Milman, H. H. History of the Jews.
Mitford, Wm. The History of Greece.
Montagu, Edward W. Ancient Republics.
Muller, John von. Universal History.
Museum of History.
Niebuhr, B. G. History of Rome.
Nuttall, P. A. Classical Dictionary.
Outlines of History.
Percy Anecdotes.
Porny, M. A. Elements of Heraldry.
Plutarch's Lives. Langhorne.
Prideaux, M. An Introduction to History.
Robertson, Wm. Ancients and India.
Rollin, Chas. Ancient History.
Russel, Wm. Ancient Europe.
Russel, Wm. Roman Empire.
Salmon, Mr. Historical Grammar.
Savage, Mr. Turkish History.
Schmitz, L. A History of Rome.
Schomann, G. F. Assemblies of the Athenians.
Seaman, E. C. Progress of Nations.
Shallus, F. Chronological Tables.
Smith, William. Classical Dictionary.
Smith, Wm. Dictionary of Antiquities.
Southey, Robert. Common Place Book.
St. John, J. A. Ancient Greece.
Tegg, Thomas. Chronology.
Thirlwall, Bishop. History of Greece.
Treasury of Knowledge.
Turner, S. History of the World.
Tytler, A. F. Elements of History.
Vertot, L'Abbé de. Knights of Malta.
Voltaire, F. M. de. The Manners, &c., of Nations.
Wachsmuth, W. Antiquities of the Greeks.
Ward, R. P. Pictures of the World.
Watts, Joshua. Remarkable Events.
Wemyss, Thos. Job and his Times.
Wickham, H. L. and J. A. Cramer. Passage of Hannibal over the Alps.
Wood, Thos. Mosaic History.

History.

EUROPE, ASIA AND AFRICA.

Alexander, A. Colonization in Africa.
Alison, Archibald. History of Europe.
Andrews, John. History of the War.
Anthing, F. Campaigns of Suwarrow.
Aubigne, J. H. Merle, d'. Reformation.
Bancks, John. History of Germany.
Bertrand, A. F. Memoirs of Louis XVI.
Blanc, L. France under Louis Philippe.
Blanc, L. French Revolution of 1789.
Bourrienne, M. Life of Napoleon.
Bresciano, G. Z. Lezioni di Storia.
British India. Account of.
Browning, W. S. History of the Huguenots.
Buonaparte, Napoleon. History of.
Camden, Theophilus. History of the War.
Campbell, Thomas. Frederick the Great.
Cass, Lewis. France, its King, &c.
Caussidiere, Citizen. Memoirs of.
Chateaubriand, F. A. de. Congress of Verona.
Chateaubriand, F. A. de. Portrait of Bonaparte.
Comstock, John L. Greek Revolution.
Conway, D. Switzerland, France, &c.
Corkran, J. F. National Assembly.
Costello, Louisa Stuart. Jacques Cœur.
Crowe, E. E. History of France.

Cushing, C. Review of the Revolution.
Dow, Alexander. Hist. of Hindostan.
Duncan, J. Dukes of Normandy.
Duncan, J. Religious Wars of France.
Dupan, Mallet. Helvetic Union, &c.
Dwight, T. The Roman Republic of 1849.
Elphinstone, M. Kingdom of Caubul.
England and France. Comparative View of.
Europe. Secret History of.
Fain, Baron. Invasion of France.
Fletcher, James. History of Poland.
Florian, M. Consalvo of Cordova.
France Arcana Gallica.
Frederick II. His Court and Times.
Frederick II. Life, &c.
Froissart, Sir John. Chronicles of.
Gaillard, T. History of the Reformation.
George, Anita. Queens of Spain.
Gordon, Thomas. Greek Revolution.
Grattan, T. C. History of the Netherlands.
Grimm, Baron de. Historical Memoirs, &c.
Guinea. An Historical Account of.
Guizot, F. History of Civilization.
Hallam, Henry. State of Europe.
Hazlitt, Wm. Napoleon Buonaparte.
Heiss, Sieu'r. History of the Empire.
Hordynski, Jos. Polish Revolution.
India. Historical Picture of.
Irving, W. Mahomet and his Successors.
James, G. P. R. History of Charlemagne.
James, Wm. Naval Occurrences.
James, Wm. Nader Shah, King of Persia.
Kelly, Christopher. French Revolution, &c.
Kohlrausch, F. History of Germany.
Kugler, Francis History of Germany.
Lamartine. History of the Girondists.
L'Ardeche, Laurent. History of Napoleon.
Layard, Austin H. Nineveh.
Liberia. The History, &c., of the Colony.
Linquet, M. Memoirs sur la Bastille.
Louis the Fourteenth. Memoirs of.
Lockhart, J. G. History of Bonaparte.
Low, Hugh. Sarawak.
Mac Farlane, Chas. Turkey.
Marseille. Historique, et Politique.
Martin, R. M. China.
Martin, R. M. British Possessions.
Martin, R. M. History of the East India Company.
Martin, R. M. History of Southern Africa.
Maxwell, J. S. The Czar, his Court, &c.
Memoirs of the Royal Family of France.
Merimee, Prosper. Peter the Cruel.
Michelet, M. History of France.
Mignet, F. A. French Revolution, from 1789 to 1814.
Miller, Jona. P. Greece.
Mills, Charles. History of the Crusades.
Milman, H. H. The History of the Jews.
Mirabeau. A Life History.
Moll, L. L'Algerie.
Monstrelet, E. Chronicles.
Moore, John. View of the French Revolution.
Morgan, Lady. France.
Mügge, Theodore. Switzerland.
Napoleon. History of.
Pardoe, Miss. City of the Magyar.
Pardoe, Miss. Francis the First.
Perdicaris, G. A. Greece.
Picture of Australia.
Playfair, Wm. History of Jacobinism.
Poore, B. P. Rise, &c., of Louis Philippe.
Portugal. Civil War in, &c.
Pradt, M. de. Europe after the Congress.
Prescott, Wm H. Ferdinand and Isabella.
Raffles, Sir Thos. S. History of Java.
Ranken, Alex. History of France
Reformation. History of the Huguenots.
Robertson, Wm. Historical Disquisition.
Russel, Rev. M. Ancient and Modern Egypt.
Russell, Wm. Ancient Europe.
Russell, Wm. Modern Europe.
Savage, Mr. Turkish History.
Schiller, Frederick. Thirty Years' War.
Schnitzler, J. H. Court, &c., of Russia.
Schoberl, F. Persecutions of Popery.
Secret History of the Armed Neutrality.
Semedo, F. Alvarez. Monarchy of China.
Shallus, F. Chronological Tables.
Simond. L. Switzerland.
Sismondi, J. C. L. de. Italian Republics.
Sketches of Venetian History.
Smedley, Edward. History of France.
Somerville, W. C. French Revolution.
Spain and Portugal. History of.
Spry, Henry H. Modern India.
St. John, Percy B. French Revolution of 1848.
Svinine, P. Moreau and his last Moments.
Switzerland. History of
Tableau Historique et Politique.
Tennent, J. E. Belgium.
Thiers, M. A. Consulate and Empire.
Thiers, M. A. French Revolution.
Thomson, Mrs. Jacobites of 1715 and 1745.
Tott, Baron de. Memoirs of the Turkish Empire.
Tryxell, Andrew. History of Sweden.
Turkey. Sketches of.
Venice under the Yoke of France, &c.
Voltaire, F. M. Occurrences in History.
Wanostrocht, N. Traits Historique, etc.
Warburton, A. Footsteps of the Normans.
Ward, Wm View of the Hindoos.
Watson, Robt. Reign of Philip II.
Wellington, Arthur, Duke of. General Orders.
Wells, N. A. Antiquities of Spain.
Williams, J. Northern Governments.
Williams, S. Wells. The Middle Kingdom.
Wilson, Bernard. Thou's History.
Winterbotham, A. A. Chinese Empire.
Wyatt, Thomas. Kings of France.

History.

ENGLAND, SCOTLAND, AND IRELAND.

Adams, Nath'l. Annals of Portsmouth.
Aikin, Lucy. Court of Charles I.

Andrews, John. History of the war.
Ashburnham, J. Attendance on Charles I.
Ashmole, Elias. Order of the Garters.
Aspen, J. Naval and Military Exploits.
Aubigne, J. H. Merle d'. The Protector.
Baines, E. History, &c., of the Co. Palatine.
British Chronologist, The.
British Empire. The History of.
Brodie, George. British Empire.
Brougham, Lord. Sketches of Statesmen.
Burton, Richard. Remarks on London, &c.
Camden, William. Camden's Britannia.
Carrel, Armand. Counter Revolution in England.
Cary, Henry. Great Civil War.
Chambers, Robert. History of Scotland.
Chronicles of London Bridge.
Clarendon, Lord. Rebellion and Wars.
Clarke, W. History of England.
Clarkson, T. Abolition of Slave Trade.
Cook, A. Life, &c., of Charles I.
Cooke, Geo. W. History of Party.
Copley, E. Slavery, and its Abolition.
Cumberland, Duke of. Historical Memoirs of.
Dales, Major S. Study of the History of England.
Dawson, Thos. Memoirs of St. George.
Echard, L. History of the Revolution.
England. Critical History of.
England and France. Comparative View of.
England Illustrated.
Entick, John. A History of London, &c.
Europe. Secret History of.
Fairfax, Lord. Charles I., and Civil War.
Fenn, John. Paston Letters.
Froissart, Sir J. Chronicles.
George IV. Diary of the Times of.
Goldsmith, Oliver. History of England.
Goodman, Dr. Court of James I.
Great Metropolis, The.
Grimshaw, Wm. History of England.
Guizot, F. English Revolution of 1640.
Guthrie, Wm. History of England.
Hallam, Henry. Constitutional History.
Halliday, Sir Andrew. House of Hanover.
Halsted, Caroline A. Richard III.
Harrop. History of the Irish Rebellion.
Haussez, Baron. Great Britain.
Henry V. Life and Character.
Hume, David. History of England.
Imperial Annual Register.
Ireland, The Annals of.
Ireland and its Rulers since 1829.
James, G. P. R. Henry IV.
James, William. Naval Occurrences.
Jesse, J. H. Court of England, from 1688.
Jesse, J. H. Memorials of London.
Jesse, J. H. Pretenders and Adherents.
Jesse, J. H. Reign of the Stuarts.
Jesse, J. H. Selwyn and Contemporaries.
Kemble, J. M. Saxons in England.
King, Robt. Covenanters in the North.
Knight, Charles. London.
Lathbury, Thomas. Guy Fawkes.
Lincoln, Wm. History of Worcester.
Lingard, John. History of England.
Liverpool, History, &c., of.
London. (See Knight, Charles.)
Lowe, Jos. State of England.
Macaulay, Thos. B. History of England.
Mackintosh, Sir James. History of England.
Memoirs of the House of Bradenburgh.
Monstrelet, Euguerraud. Chronicles of.
Montgaillard, M. Mir. England in 1811.
Morell, Thomas. Studies in History.
Murray, J. F. World of London.
Nicholas, Sir Harris. Royal Navy.
Nichols, John. Reign of George III.
Peerage of England.
Plowden, Francis. History of Ireland.
Plowden, Francis. State of Ireland.
Porter, G. R. The Progress of the Nation.
Prestwick's Respublica.
Prevost, The Abbe. Margaret of Anjou.
Pye, John. Historical Sketch.
Richardson, M. A. Borderer's Table Book.
Rimius, Henry. House of Brunswick.
Robertson, Wm. Reign of Charles V.
Roscoe, Thomas. William the Conqueror.
Russell, Wm. Ancient Europe.
Russell, Wm. Modern Europe.
Sammes, Aylett. Britannia Antique.
Scott, David. History of Scotland.
Scott, Sir Walter. The Antiquary.
Scott, Sir Walter. History of Scotland.
Secret History of England.
Shallus, F. Chronological Tables.
Sidney, H. Times of Charles II.
Smith, John T. Anecdotes of London.
Smollett, T. History of England.
Somerville, Thomas. History of Parties.
Spelman, J. Vita Alfredi Magni.
Stone, Mrs. Chronicles of Fashion.
Strickland, Agnes. Queens of England.
Taylor, W. C. History of Ireland.
Temple, Sir Wm. An Introduction to the History of England.
Tyler, J. E. Henry V.
Tytler, P. F. Reigns of Edward VI. and Mary.
Vaughan, Rev. Dr. History of England.
Vernon, Jas. Reign of William III.
Vertot, Abbé. Bretons among the Gauls.
Vertot, L'Abbé. Knights of Malta.
Wade, John. British History.
Wakeman, Wm. T. Archæologia Hibernia.
Walpole, Horace. Historic Doubts.
Walpole, Horace. Reign of George III.
Warburton, Acton. Rollo and his Race.
Ward, R. Plumer. Revolution of 1688.
Wellington, Arthur, Duke of. Dispatches.
Wellington, Duke of. Orders.
Welwood, James. Transactions in England.
Willoughby, Lady. Diary and Selections.
Wood, Thomas. Ancient Britons.
Wraxall, Sir N. W. Historical Memoirs.

Wraxall, Sir N. W. Posthumous Memoirs.
Wright, Thomas. History of England.

History.

AMERICA.

Abbott, A. Cuba.
Adams, Hannah. History of New England.
Agapida, Fray A. Conquest of Granada.
Allen, Paul. American Revolution.
American Annual Register.
American Register.
Amerique Histoire Pittoresque.
Andrews, John. History of the War.
Baldwin, E. Annals of Yale College.
Bancroft, Aaron. Life of Washington.
Bancroft, G. History of the U. States.
Barber, J. W., &c. Historical Collections of N. York.
Belknap, J. Hist. of New Hampshire.
Benson, Egbert. Memoir.
Bolton, Jr., Robt. County of Westchester.
Bonnycastle, R. H. Spanish America.
Boston Tea Party. Retrospect of.
Botta, Charles. Revolutionary War.
Boucher, Jonathan. American Revolution.
Bradford, A. Hist. of Massachusetts.
Buckingham, Joseph S. America.
Buckingham, J. S. Eastern and Western States.
Buckingham, Joseph S. Slave States.
Burnet, Jacob. North Western Territory.
Campbell, Mrs. Life of Gen. Wm. Hull.
Campbell, W. W. Annals of Tryon County.
Castillo, Dias Del. Conquest of Mexico, &c.
Catlin, George. North American Indians.
Chalmers, George. Revolt of the Colonies.
Cist, Charles. Cincinnati in 1841.
Colden, C. Five Indian Nations.
Connecticut. History of.
Cooper, J. F. Navy of the United States.
Cortez, F. Conquete du Mexique.
Cressé, A. de. Catastrophie de St. Domingue.
Debate on the Seminole War.
Drake, Samuel G. History of the Indians.
Dunn, Henry. Guatimala.
Dwight, Theodore. Hartford Convention.
Earthquake at Lima. Relation of.
Elliot, J. Debates on the Constitution.
Elliot, Jonathan. District of Columbia.
Fellows, John. The Veil Removed.
Flint, Timothy. Mississippi Valley.
Flint, Timothy. Western States.
Force, P. Annals of United States.
Gallatin, A. North Eastern Boundary.
Gibbs, Geo. Washington and John Adams.
Graham, J. A. Vermont.
Griffith, Wm. American Colonies.
Haliburton, T. C. Nova Scotia.
Hamilton, A. Documents on his Death.
Head, Sir F. B. Narrative.
Henderson, J. History of the Brazils.
Hildreth, R. History of United States.
Hinman, R. R. Letters to the Governors.
Historical Register of the U. States.
Holley, Mrs. M. A. Texas.
Holmes, Abiel. American Annals.
Hutchinson, Thos. Province of Mass. Bay.
Irving, Theodore. Conquest of Florida.
Irving, Washington. Astoria.
Irving, W. Columbus and his Companions.
Irving, W. Conquest of Granada.
Jay, Wm. Review of the Mexican War.
Jefferson, Thomas. Notes on Virginia.
Jeffreys, Thomas. French Dominions.
Jones, I. Seawell. Revolutionary History.
Kendall, George W. War with Mexico.
Knapp, Samuel L. Library of History.
Knapp, S. L. Remarks on Am. History.
Lee, Henry. Campaigns in Carolina.
Lee, Henry. Memoirs of the War.
Letters on the Eastern States.
Letters, with a History of Chili.
Lossing, Benson J. Pictorial Field Book.
Lossing, Benson J. Revolutionary War.
Macauley, James. History of New York.
Marbois, Barbe. History of Louisiana.
Marshall, H. History of Kentucky.
Marshall, John. Life of Washington.
Martin, Jos. History, &c., of Virginia.
Martin, R M. History of Nova Scotia.
Martin, R. M. Hist. of the West Indies.
McCartney, W. Origin, &c., of the States.
Memoirs, Historical and Military.
Minot, George R. Insurrections in Mass.
Miranda's Revolutionary Attempt.
Morse, J. Annals of the Revolution.
Morse, J., &c. History of New England.
Murat, A. United States of N. America.
Narrative. Capture of the Olive Branch.
Niles, Hezekiah. Weekly Register.
North American Review.
Onderdonk, Jr., H. Revolutionary Incidents of Queens County.
Page, M. Le. Hist. of Louisiana, &c.
Pazos, Vicente. United Provinces.
Perkins, Samuel. Historical Sketches.
Perkins, T. Hist'y of the U. States.
Porter, David. Cruise to the Pacific.
Prescott, Wm. H. Conquest of Mexico.
Prescott, Wm. H. Conquest of Peru.
Priest, Josiah. American Antiquities, &c.
Proceedings of the Historical Society.
Proud, Robt. Hist. of Pennsylvania.
Putnam, Geo. P. American Facts.
Rainsford, M. Black Empire of Hayti.
Ramsay, A. C. Notes on the Mexican War.
Ramsay, David. American Revolution.
Recherches Historiques et Politiques.
Reidesel, Mme. de. Letters and Memoirs.
Remembrancer, The.
Rengger, &c. The Reign of De Francia.
Ripley, R. S. The War with Mexico.
Robbins, Archibald. Journal.
Robertson, Wm. History of America.
Robinson, A. California.
Robinson, Wm. D. Mexican Revolution.
Rupp, J. D. Religious Denominations.
Sanford, Ezekiel. United States.

Schoolcraft, Henry R. Indian Tribes.
Shallus, F. Chronological Tables.
Simms, J. R. Schoharie County, &c.
Smith, A. Atrocities of the Pirates.
Smith, J. T. Northmen in N. England.
Smith, William. History of New York.
Snowden, R. North and South America.
South America. Miranda's Revolution.
Sprague, John T. Florida War.
Stark, John. French War.
Starling, E. Noble Deeds of Woman.
Stevenson, W. B. Historical Narrative.
Stone, Wm. L. Indian Wars.
Thomas, Isaiah. History of Printing.
Thompson, B. F. History of Long Island.
Thomson, Jas. State of South America.
Transactions, &c., of the American Antiquarian Society.
Trumbull, B. History of Connecticut.
Trumbull, David. Cuba, &c.
Trumbull, Henry. Discovery of America.
Tucker, Geo. Progress of the U. States.
Twiss, Travers. Oregon Territory.
United States. General Outline of.
United States, History of, for 1796.
United States. Incidents in the Wars of.
Venegas, Miguel. Hist. of California.
Vermont State Papers.
Vertot, L'Abbé. Knights of Malta.
Volney, C. F. View of the United States.
Washburn, Emory. Judicial History.
Washington and his Generals.
Watson, J F. Annals of Philadelphia.
Wheeler, H. G. History of Congress.
White, Henry. History of New England.
Whiton, John M. Hist. of N. Hampshire.
Willard, Emma. Last Leaves of History.
Willard, Emma. Republic of America.
Williams, E. Annual Register.
Williams, J. L. West Florida.
Williams, Samuel. History of Vermont.
Winterbotham, W. United States.
Wood, John. Administration of Adams.
Wood, S. First Settlement of L. Island.
Winne, Mr. British Empire in America.

BIOGRAPHY.

Biography.

FOREIGN AND UNIVERSAL.

Allen, William. Biography.
Belisarius. Life of. (See Mahon, Lord.)
Bertrand, A F. Memoirs of Louis XVI.
Biographie Moderne.
Blake, J. L. Biographical Dictionary.
Bombet, L. A. C. Lives of Haydn and Mozart.
Bonaparte Life. (See Hazlitt, William.)
Bonaparte. Life. (See Scott, Sir Walter.)
Bonaparte. Life. (See Van Ess, W. L.)
Bonaparte. Memoirs. (See Bourrienne.)
Bonaparte, Joseph Napoleon. Sketch of.
Bourrienne, M. Life of Napoleon.
Brookes and Collyer Dictionary.
Brougham, Lord. Men of Letters, &c.
Brougham, Lord. Sketches of Statesmen.
Bush, Rev. George. Life of Mohammed.
Campbell, Thomas. Life of Petrarch.
Carlyle, Thomas. Life of Schiller.
Cary, Henry T. The French Poets.
Chateaubriand. Portrait of Bonaparte.
Cicero, M. T. Life.
Cicero, M. T. Life and Letters.
Condorcet, Marquis de. Life of Voltaire.
Costello, Louisa S. Jacques Cœur.
Dobson, Mrs. The Life of Petrarch.
Francis, G. H. Orators of the Age.
Frederick II. of Prussia. Life, &c.
Genlis, Madame la Comtesse de. Memoirs.
Grimm, Baron de. Memoirs and Anecdotes.
Haydn. Life. (See Bombet, L. A. C.)
Hazlitt, Wm. Life of Napoleon.
Headley, P. C. Life of Josephine.
Holstein, H. D. Memoirs of La Fayette.
Hunter, H. Sacred Biography.
Irving, W. Columbus and his Companions.
Irving, W. Mahomet and his Successors.
Jones, Sir Wm. Life of Nader Shah.
Josephine, Life of. (See Headley, P. C.)
Knapp, S. L. Biographical Sketches.
Knapp, S. L. Female Biography.
Korner, Carl Theodor. Life of.
Lafayette, Marquis de. Memoirs of
Langallerie, Marquis de. Memoirs of.
Langhorne, J. and Wm. Plutarch's Lives.
L'Ardeche, L. History of Napoleon.
Las Cases. Life, &c., of Napoleon.
Lee, Mrs R. Memoirs of Baron Cuvier.
Lempriere, J. Universal Biography
Lester, C. Edward, &c. Life of Americus Vespucius.
Lewis, G. H Life of Robespierre.
Lockhart, J. G. History of Bonaparte.
Louis XIV. Memoirs of Himself.
Mahon, Lord. Life of Belisarius.
Marmontel, J. F. Memoirs of.
Memoirs, Secret, of the Royal Family.
Michelet, M. The Life of Luther.
Middleton, Conyers. Life of Cicero.
Mirabeau; a Life History.
Mozart. Life. (See Bombet, L. A. C.)
Naturalist's Library. Memoirs of Celebrated Naturalists.
Neander, A. Life of St. Chrysostrom.
Ney, Marshal. Memoirs of.

Pepé, General. Memoirs.
Percival, C. G. Misfortunes of the Dauphin.
Percy Anecdotes.
Petrarch. Life of. (See Campbell, T.)
Petrarch. Life of. (See Dobson, Mrs.)
Plutarch's Lives.
Pulzsky, T. Memoirs of a Hungarian Lady.
Robespierre. Life of.
Roscoe, Wm. Life of Lorenzo de Medici.
Ross, Sir John. Memoirs of Saumarez.
Saumarez, Admiral de. Memoirs of.
Schiller, Frederic. Life, &c.
Scott, Sir Walter. Life of Napoleon.
Shepherd, Wm. Life of Poggio Bracciolini.
Shoemakers, Lives of Distinguished.
Simpson, Leonard. Biographical Sketches.
Smith, Wm. Biography.
Southey, Robt. Common Place Book.
Standish, Frank H. The Life of Voltaire.
Starling, E. Noble Deeds of Women.
St. Chrysostrom, Life of.
St. John, J. A. Lives of Travellers.
Tacitus, C. Cornelius.
Talleyrand, C. M. Memoirs of.
Treasury of Knowledge.
Universal Biographical Dictionary.
Van Ess, W. L. Life of Napoleon.
Voltaire. Life. (See Condorcet, M. de.)
Voltaire. Life. (See Standish, F H.)
Wemyss, Thomas. Job and his Times.
Williams, Rev. J. Alexander the Great.

Biography. II.

ENGLISH.

Addison, Joseph. Life of.
Ashburnham, J. Attendance on Charles I.
Aubigne, J. H. Merle d'. The Protector.
Autobiography of a Country Curate.
Autobiography of a Workingman.
Barrow, J. Life, &c., of Admiral Smith.
Barrow, John. Writings of Macartney.
Beattie, James. Life and Writings.
Bell, Robert. Life of George Canning.
Benson, R. Memoirs of Arthur Collier.
Berwick, James Fitzjames, Duke of. Life.
Boaden, James. Memoir of Mrs. Inchbald.
Bolingbroke, Lord. Life and Works.
Bonner, Edmund. Life and Defence.
Boswell, Jas. Life of Samuel Johnson.
Brewster, D. Life of Sir Isaac Newton.
Budgell, Eustace. Life, &c.
Butler, Charles. Reminiscences of.
Byron, George Gordon, Lord. Life.
Camden, T. Memoirs of Wellington.
Campbell, John. The British Admirals.
Campbell, John. The Chief Justices.
Campbell, John. The Lord Chancellors.
Campbell, Thomas Life of Mrs. Siddons.
Canning, George. Life.
Canning, George. Memoirs of.
Canning, George. Political Life of
Cary, Henry T. Lives of the Poets.

Chatham, Lord. Life and Speeches.
Cibber, Colley. Apology for his Life.
Clarke, E. Daniel. Life and Remains.
Coleridge, S. T. Biographia Literaria.
Combe. G. Life, &c., of Andrew Combe.
Costello, L. Eminent English Women.
Coxe, M. Life of John Wycliffe.
Cumberland, Duke of. Memoirs of.
Cunningham, A. Painters and Sculptors.
Currie, W. W. Life, &c., of James Currie.
D'Arblay, Madame. (See Arblay, D'.)
Daunt, W. Recollections of O'Connell.
Davies, Thos. Life of Garrick.
Dawson, Thos. Memoirs of St. George.
Dickson, W. S. Confinement and Exile.
Drummond, Wm. H. Autobiography of Rowan.
Edgeworth, Richard L. Memoirs.
Eldon, Lord Chancellor. Life.
Emmet, Thomas Addis. Memoirs of.
Fairfax, Lord. Charles the First.
Farington, Joseph. Memoirs of
Fanshawe, Lady Memoirs of Herself.
Felton, S. English Authors.
Forbes, Sir W. Life, &c., of James Beattie.
Fox, George. Memoirs of his Life.
Fox, Maria. Memoirs of.
Galt, John. Life of Byron.
Galt, John. Life of Wolsey.
Garrick, David. Life.
George the Fourth. Diary, &c.
Gleig, G. R. Life of Warren Hastings.
Goldsmith, Oliver. Life.
Graydon, A. Memoirs of his own Time.
Haines, Charles G. Memoir of Emmet.
Halliwell, Jas. O. Autobiography, &c., of D'Ewes.
Halsted, Caroline A. Richard the Third.
Hastings, Warren. Memoirs of.
Hatton, Sir C. Memoirs of his Life.
Hawkins, Sir J. Life of Samuel Johnson.
Heber, Reginald. Life of.
Henry V. Life and Character.
Hill, Richard. Life.
Huish, Robert. Memoirs of the Princess of Wales, &c., and Prince Leopold.
Huntington, Countess of. Life of.
Inchbald, Mrs. Memoir.
Irving, Washington. Oliver Goldsmith.
James, G. P. R. Life of Henry IV.
Jenner, Edward. The Life of.
Jesse, J. H. Memoirs of George Selwyn, &c.
Johnson, Samuel, D.D. Life.
Johnson, Samuel, LL.D. Life.
Jones, Sir William. Life and Writings.
Kent, Edward, Duke of. Life.
Kippis, Dr. A. Life of Capt. Cook.
Knighton, Lady. Memoir of Sir Wm. Knighton.
Lewis, M. G. Life and Correspondence.
Lives of Drake, Cavendish, and Dampier.
Lives of Eminent Scotsmen.
Lives of Leland, Hearne, and A. Wood.
Memoirs of the House of Bradenburg.
Military Memoirs of Four Brothers.

Moore, Thomas. Memoirs of Sheridan.
More, Hannah. Life, &c.
Neale, E. Life Book of a Laborer.
Neale, E. Life of the Duke of Kent.
Nelson, Horatio, Lord. Life.
Newton, Sir Isaac. Life.
Nicholas, Sir Harris. Memoirs of Hatton.
O'Connell, Daniel. Personal Recollections.
O'Connell, John. Recollections and Experiences.
Ormonde, James, Duke of. The Life of.
Otter, Wm. Life and Remains of Clarke.
Pearce, R. R. Memoirs, &c., of Wellesley.
Penn, Granville. Life of Penn.
Pepys, Samuel. Life and Correspondence.
Pitt, William. (See Chatham.)
Pollok, Robert. Life and Remains.
Poole, J. Sketches and Recollections.
Powell, Thomas. Authors of England.
Priestley, Joseph. Memoirs of.
Prior, Jas. Life of Goldsmith.
Raffles, Sir Thomas S. Memoirs of.
Raleigh, Sir Walter. Memoirs of his Life.
Reynolds, Sir Joshua. Memoirs of.
Rimius, Henry. House of Brunswick.
Roscoe, Henry. Life of Wm. Roscoe.
Roscoe, Thomas. William the Conqueror.
Rowan, Archibald H. Autobiography.
Sackville, Lord. Trial.
Scott, Rev. A. J. Recollections of.
Scott, James. Life, &c., of Robert Pollok.
Scott, Sir Walter. Autobiography.
Scott, Sir Walter. Life.
Sheridan, R. B. Memoir of his Life.
Siddons, Mrs. Life.
Sidney, Edwin. Life of Richard Hill.
Sidney, E. Life, &c., of Samuel Walker.
Sidney, Henry. Diary, &c.
Simms, W. G. Life of Captain Smith.
Simpson, Thomas. Life, &c.
Smith, Admiral Sir W. S. Life, &c.
Smith, Captain John. Life.
Smith, John T. Nollekens and his Times.
Southey, Robert. Life of Nelson.
Southey, Robert. Life of Wesley.
Southey, R. Lives of Uneducated Poets.
Spelman, Johannes. Vita Alfredi Magni.
Stappleton, A. E. Life of Canning.
Sterne, L. Sentimental Journey.
Strickland, Agnes. Lives of the Queens.
Taylor, W. C. Modern British Plutarch.
Teignmouth. Memoirs of Sir Wm. Jones
Thompson, Henry. Life of Hannah More.
Thomson, Mrs. Memoirs of Sir W. Raleigh.
Thoresby, Ralph. Diary.
Thompson, T. Memoirs of Missionaries.
Trenck, James Baron. Life of.
Tuke, Henry. Memoirs of George Fox.
Twiss, Horace. Life of Eldon.
Tyler, J. E. Henry of Monmouth.
Wales, Princess of. Inquiry into her Conduct.
Walker, Rev. Samuel. Life.
Walpole, Horace. George the Third.
Walpole, Horace. Noble Authors.
Walton, I. Lives of Doane, Wotton, &c.
Wellesley, Richard, Marquis. Memoirs of.
Wesley, John. Life, &c.
Willoughby, Lady. Diary.
Wolsey, Cardinal. Life.
Wycliff, John, D.D. Life.

Biography. III.

AMERICAN.

Adams, J. Q. Lives of Madison & Monroe.
Adams, Mrs., Wife of John. Letters, &c.
Austin, J. T. Life of Elbridge Gerry.
Bancroft, Aaron. Life of Washington.
Barclay, H. A Volume from the Life of.
Black Hawk. Life of.
Bowen, H. L. Memoir of Tristam Burges.
Brainerd, Rev. David. Memoirs of.
Brant, Joseph. (Thayendangea.) Life.
Buckingham, J. T. Memoirs, Anecdotes, &c.
Burr, Aaron. Examination, &c.
Burr, Aaron. Private Journal.
Caldwell, C. Genius of Rev. H. Holley.
Campbell, J. W. Biographical Sketches.
Campbell, Mrs. M. Life, &c., of Gen. Hull.
Chalmers, Thomas. Memoirs of his Life.
Chandler, T. B. Life of S. Johnson, D.D.
Clay, Henry. Biography of.
Clay, Henry. Life and Speeches.
Clinton, DeWitt. Memoirs of.
Clinton, DeWitt. Tribute to his Memory.
Colden, C. D. Life of Robert Fulton.
Darwin, Dr. Erasmus. Memoirs of his Life.
Davis, M. L. Journal of Aaron Burr.
Drake, S. G. Biography, &c. of the Indians.
Duer, Wm. A. Life of Sterling.
Durand, T. Memoirs, &c., of an Only Son.
Dwight, N. Sketches of the Lives of the Signers of the Declaration.
Eaton, John H. Life of Andrew Jackson.
Eaton, William. The Life of.
Eddy, Thomas. Life.
Edward, J. Memoirs of David Brainerd.
Elmwood, E. An Autobiography.
Fox, George. Life, Travels, &c.
Franklin, Benjamin. Life and Writings.
Franklin, Benj. Memoirs of his Life, &c.
Franklin, Benj. Works, with his Life.
Fulton, Robert. Life.
Galt, John. Life, &c., of Benj. West.
Garland, Hugh A. Life of Randolph.
Gibbs, George. Washington and Adams.
Greene, N. Sketches of his Life, &c.
Hall, David. Memoir of.
Hamilton, A. Collection of Facts, &c.
Hanna, Rev. W. Life, &c., of Thomas Chalmers.
Hardie, James. Biographical Dictionary.
Henry, Patrick. Life.
Hewes, George R. T. Memoir of.
Holland, W. M. Life, &c., of Martin Van Buren.
Holley, Horace. Genius and Character.
Hosack, D. Memoir of DeWitt Clinton.

Howe, Henry. Memoirs of Mechanics.
Hull, General William. Life, &c.
Humphreys, D. Miscellaneous Works.
Irving, W. Biography of M. M. Davidson.
Jackson, Andrew. Life.
Jackson, James. Memoir of His Son.
Jay, Wm. Life of John Jay.
Jefferson, T. Life. (See Linn, William.)
Jefferson T. Life. (See Tucker, George.)
Jefferson, Thos. Memoir, &c.
Johnson, W. Life, &c., of General Greene.
Kennedy, J. P Memoirs of William Wirt.
Knapp, Samuel L. Life of Thomas Eddy.
Ledyard, John. Life.
Lee, Gen. Charles. Life and Memoirs of.
Lee, Richard Henry. Life of Arthur Lee.
Linn, William. Life of Thomas Jefferson.
Mallory. D. The Life, &c., of Henry Clay.
Marshall, John. Life of Washington.
Martin, Rev. Henry. Memoir of.
Memoirs of a Nullifier. Written by Himself.
Miller, John. Memoirs of General Miller.
Morris, Gouverneur. Life.
Muhlenburg, General Peter. Life of.
Paulding, J. K. Life of Washington.
Pinkney, William. Life, Writings, &c.
Prescott, W. H. Biographical Miscellanies.
Poe, Edgar A. Life and Genius.
Ramsay, David. Life of Washington.
Randolph, John Life.
Sanderson, J. Biography of the Signers to the Declaration of Independence.
Sargent, Jr., J. Memoir of Rev. H. Martin.
Seward, A. Memoir of Dr. E. Darwin.
Sketch of Bolivar in his Camp.
Slater, Samuel. Memoirs of.
Smith, Jeremiah. Life.
Sparks, J. American Biography.
Sparks, Jared. Life of Franklin.
Sparks, J. Life of Gouverneur Morris.
Sparks, J. Life of John Ledyard.
Sparks, Jared. Life of Washington.
Stark, General John. Life, &c.
Sterling, Wm. Alexander, Earl of. Life.
Stone, Wm. L. Life of Joseph Brant.
Thatcher, B. B. Indian Biography.
Thomas, Isaiah. Biography of Printers.
Thompson, J. P. Memoir of David Hale.
Trumbull, John. Autobiography, &c.
Tucker, George. Life of Jefferson.
Ward, G. A. Journal, &c., of Samuel Curwen.
Washington, G. Life. (See Bancroft, A.)
Washington, G. Life. (See Marshall, J.)
Washington, G. Life. (See Paulding, J. K.)
Washington, G. Life. (See Ramsay, D.)
Washington, G. Life, &c. (See Sparks, Jared.)
Washington and the Generals of the Revolution.
West, Benjamin. Life and Studies.
Wheaton, H. Life, &c., of W. Pinkney.
Wheeler, H. G. Biographical Sketches.
White, G. S. Memoir of Slater.
Wirt, W. Life of Patrick Henry.
Wirt, William. Memoirs of His Life.
Wordsworth, C. Memoirs of Wm. Wordsworth.

TRANSACTIONS.

Memoirs and Transactions of Literary and Scientific Institutions.

Addresses of the Philadelphia Society for the Promotion of National Industry.
American Institute Journal.
American Institute Reports.
Asiatic Researches; or, Transactions of the Society in Bengal.
Collections of the N. Y. Historical Society.
Journal of the Royal Agricul. Society.
Memoirs of the Academy of Arts, &c.
Memoirs of the Board of Agriculture.
Memoirs of the Philadelphia Agr. Society.
Memoirs of the Penn. Agricultural Society.
Minutes and Proceedings of the Institution of the Civil Engineers.
Philosophical Transactions, &c.
Proceedings of the Historical Society.
Proceedings of the Missionary Society.
Reports of the American Institute.
Reports of the Board of Commissioners.
Report of the Prison Discipline Society.
Reports of the Royal Humane Society.
Transactions, &c., of the American Antiquarian Society.
Transactions of the American Institute.
Transactions of the Am. Philosoph. Society.
Transactions of the Highland Agr. Soc.
Transactions of the Institution of Civil Engineers.
Transactions of the Michigan State Agricultural Society.
Transactions of the Royal Humane Society.
Transactions of the Society of Arts, &c.
Transactions of the Society for the Promotion of Agriculture, &c.
Transactions of the Society for the Promotion of Useful Arts.
Transactions of the N. Y. State Agr. Soc.

PERIODICAL WORKS.

Periodical Works. I.

REGISTERS, REVIEWS, AND MAGAZINES.

Agriculture Francaise.
American Advertising Directory.
American Agriculturalist.
American Almanac.
American Annual Register.
American Art-Union. Bulletin of.
American Institute, Journal of.
American Journal of Medical Science.
American Lancet, The.
American Magazine, 1787.
American Magazine and Review.
American Magazine of Useful Knowledge.
American Medical and Philos. Register.
American Medical Recorder.
American Museum. By Matthew Carey.
American Quarterly Review.
American Rail Road Journal.
American Register.
American Repertory of Arts, Sciences, &c.
American Review, or History of Politics, Literature, &c.
American (Whig) Review.
Analectic Magazine.
Annales des Haras et de l'Agriculture.
Annales de la Société Royale d'Horticulture de Paris.
Annals of Horticulture.
Anniversary, The. By A. Cunningham.
Annual Register.
Apprentice, The. A Weekly Journal.
Arcana of Science and Art.
Artisan, The. A Monthly Journal.
Art Journal, The.
Athenæum, The.
Banker's Magazine.
Bentley's Miscellany.
Blackwood's Edinburgh Magazine.
Blue Book.
Boston Medical Intelligencer.
Boston Medical and Surgical Journal.
Christian Library.
Civil Engineer and Architect's Journal.
Corsair, The. A Gazette of Literature, &c.
Crell, D. Loreng. Chemisches Annalen.
Crell, D. Loreng Chemisches Journal.
Critical Review, or Annals of Literature.
Cultivator, The. A Monthly Journal.
Doggett, J. New York Directory.
Dwight, Jr. American Penny Magazine.
Eclectic Repository and Review.
Edinburgh Annual Register.
Edinburgh New Philosophical Journal.
Edinburgh Review.
Emporium of Arts and Sciences.
European Magazine and London Review.
Examiner, The. By Barnet Gardiner.
Farmer's Cabinet.
Farmer's Library. Animal Economy.
Farmer's Magazine.
Farmer's Register, The.
Fessenden, Thomas G. Register of Arts.
Force, Peter. The National Calendar.
Foreign Quarterly Review.
Franklin Institute. Journal of.
Gentleman's Magazine and Chronicle.
Gill, Thomas. The Technical Repository.
Grand Magazine, The.
Greenbank's Periodical Library.
Hadley, W. Hobart. Manual of Reference.
Harper's New Monthly Magazine.
Hill, Isaac. The Farmer's Visitor.
Historical Register of the United States.
Hoppy, A. The Orchardist's Companion.
Holden's Triennial Directory, for 1805-6-7.
Holley, O. L. N. Y. State Register, 1845.
Homans, J. Smith. Banker's Magazine.
Houston, George. Farmer's Mazazine, &c.
Imperial Annual Register for 1810.
Imperial Magazine
Inventor's Advocate and Patentee's Recorder.
Journal of the American Institute.
Journal of Civilization.
Journal of the Franklin Institute.
Journal of Health.
Journal of the Royal Ag. Society.
Journal of Science and the Arts.
Kimball & James' Business Directory.
Knickerbocker Magazine.
Lady's Magazine.
London Journal of Arts and Sciences.
London Quarterly Review.
London and Westminster Review.
Longworth, D. Almanac, Directory, &c.
Longworth, T. Register and Directory.
Maandelyke Wittreksels of Boekzaal der Geleerde Waerelt.
Magazine of Domestic Economy.
Magazine of Horticulture.
Magazine of Science, and School of Arts.
Mapes, James J. American Repertory.
Massachusetts Repository, &c.
Mechanics' Magazine. By J. C. Robertson.
Mechanics' Magazine, Museum, &c.
Mechanics' Magazine and Register.
Medical Intelligencer. By J. V. C. Smith.
Medical Repository, The. By Samuel L. Mitchell.
Medical and Surgical Register.
Merchants' Magazine. By Freeman Hunt.
Metropolitan Magazine.
Minerva, The, or Literary Journal.
Missionary Herald for 1821.
Monthly Magazine, or British Register.
Monthly Review, or Literary Journal.
National Magazine. By R. Fisher.
Newcastle Magazine.
N. E. Journal of Medicine.
New Monthly Magazine.

New York Business Directory for 1841.
New York Farmer and Gardener's Magazine. Edited by D. K. Miner.
New York Farmer and Horticultural Repository. Samuel Fleet, Editor.
New York Farmer and Mechanic.
New York Military Magazine.
New York Review.
New York Review and Athenæum Magazine.
New York Weekly Museum.
Niles, Hezekiah. Weekly Register.
North American Review.
Olive Branch, Simon. The Looker-on.
Parliamentary Register.
Penny Magazine.
Philadelphia Medical Museum.
Pigot & Sons, Directory of Manchester, &c., for 1830.
Plough Boy, The.
Political Magazine, 1785–1786.
Port Folio. A Monthly Magazine.
Practical Mechanic's and Engineer's Mag.
Practical Mechanics' Journal.
Register of Arts and Journal of Patent Inventions.
Remembrancer, The.
Repertory of Arts, Manufactures, &c.
Repertory of Patent Inventions.
Revue Horticole, Journal des Jardiniers et Amateurs.
Revue Scientifique et Industrielle.
Royal Magazine, 1762.
Ruffin, Edmund. The Farmer's Register.
Sailor's Chronicle, or Narratives of Shipwrecks.
Scientific Tracts.
Silliman, B. American Jour. of Science.
Skinner, J. S. Journal of Agriculture.
Smith, G Laboratory, or School of Arts.
Southern Review.
Spectator, The.
Stanford, John. Christian Library.
Stewart, John. Treble Almanac, 1824.
Town and Country Magazine.
U. S. Magazine and Democratic Review.
Waller's Hibernian Magazine.
Westminster Review.
Williams, Edwin. Annual Register.
Year Book of Facts.
Young Mechanic, The.

Periodical Works. II.

NEWSPAPERS.

Albany Argus. A Daily Newspaper.
Albion, The A Journal of News, &c.
American & Commercial Daily Advertiser.
Atlas, The. A General Newspaper.
Chronicle Express. Semi-weekly Paper.
City Gazette and Daily Advertiser.
Commercial Journal. New Haven.
Connecticut Courant, &c.
Connecticut Herald.
Connecticut Journal. A Weekly Newspaper.
Gazette and Phila. Daily Advertiser.
Herald, The. A Gazette for the Country.
Massachusetts Mercury.
Miscellaneous Newspapers, 1802–3.
Miscellaneous Newspapers, 1823–24.
National Intelligencer, 1819–25–31–51.
N. E. Palladium & Russell's Gazette.
New York American, 1827–29.
N. Y. Chronicle Express, 1802–04.
N. Y. Evening Post, 1801–03.
N. Y. Gazette and General Advertiser.
N. Y. Herald and Weekly Register.
N. Y. Journal and State Gazette.
N. Y. Tribune, 1841–43.
Patron of Industry, 1820.
Repertory, The, 1806–7–11 and 12.
Spectator, The, 1797–1801.

POLYGRAPHY.

Polygraphy.

COLLECTED WORKS OF MISCELLANEOUS WRITERS.

Addison, Joseph. The Works of.
Ames, Fisher. Works, &c.
Ayscough, G. E. Works of Lord Lyttleton.
Bacon, Francis, Lord. The Works of.
Barham, Francis. Works of Cicero.
Barrington, D. Miscellanies.
Bentley, Richard. The Works of.
Bolingbroke, H. St. John, Lord. Works.
Boyd, Hugh. Works.
Boyle, Robert. Works, Epitomized.
Burns, Robert. The Works of.
Byron, George Gordon, Lord. Works.
Campbell, L. D. Works of Hugh Boyd.
Chambers, R. Cyclopædia of Literature.
Chambers, Wm. & Rob't. Information for the People.
Channing, W. E. Discourses, Reviews, &c.
Chesterfield, Lord. Works.
Cicero, M. T. Works.
Clark, W. G. Literary Remains.
Colman, George. The Works of.
Cowper, William. The Works of.
Davenant, Sir William. Works.
Dick, Thomas. The Works of.
Dickinson, John. Political Writings
Fellows, John. Works of Junius.
Franklin, B. Works of
Frederick II. Posthumous Works.
Goldsmith, O. Miscellaneous Works.
Hale, David. Miscellaneous Writings.
Hamilton, Alexander. Works.

Harper, Robert G. Select Works.
Hopkins, Ezekiel. The Whole Works of.
Johnson, Samuel. The Works of.
Josephus, Flavius. Works.
Legare, Hugh S. Writings of.
Legget, Wm. Political Writings.
Machiavelli, Nicholas. Works.
Mackintosh, Sir James. Works.
Maty, M. Works of Lord Chesterfield.
Montagu, Mary W. Letters and Works.
Montaigne, M. de. The Works of.
More, Hannah. The Works of.
Osborne, Francis. Miscellaneous Works.
Painė, Jr., Robert Treat. Works.
Paine, Thomas. Political Writings.
Paley, Wm. Complete Works.
Pinkney, Wm. Writings.
Poe, Edgar A. The Works of.
Pope, Alexander. The Works of.
Robertson, William. Works.
Sands, R. C. Writings.
Scott, Sir Walter. The Works of.
Sidney, Algernon. Works.
Smith, Rev. Sidney. Works.
Sparks, Jared. Works of.
Sprague, Charles. Writings of.
Sterne, Lawrence. Works.
Story, Joseph. Miscellaneous Writings.
Swift, Jonathan. Works.
Tacitus, C. Cornelius. Works.
Talfourd, T. Noon. Writings.
Temple, Sir William. Works.
Virgil, Publius. Works. By John Dryden.
Virgil, Publius. Opera.
Washington, G. Writings.
Wheaton, H. Writings, &c., of William Pinkney.
Xenophon. The Complete Works of.

BIBLIOGRAPHY.

Catalogue of Books.

Appleton's Library Manual.
Apprentice's Library, Catalogue of. 1833.
Bohn, H. C. Catalogue of Books.
Catalogue of Engravings.
Catalogue of the Library of the Corporation of London.
Catalogue of Lib'y of the Historical Society.
Catalogue of the Mercantile Library, 1830.
Catalogue of the Mercantile Library, 1844.
Catalogue of the Mercantile Library, 1851.
Catalogue of the Society Library, 1813.
Catalogue of the Society Library, 1851.
Dibdin, Thomas F. Introduction to the Greek and Latin Classics.
Doyle, John. Catalogue of Books.
Gibbings, Richard. Index Expurgatorius.
Mendham, J. Index of Prohibited Books.
New York Mercantile Library Catalogues.
New York Society Library Catalogues.
Walpole, Horace. Catalogue of Authors.

NOVELS, ROMANCES, AND TALES.

Adventures of Hajji Baba. 2 vols.
Alhambra. By Washington Irving.
Alice de Lacy. By Mrs. West. 4 vols.
Alice Paulet. By the Author of "Sydenham." 2 vols.
Alonzo and Melissa. By D. Jackson, Jr.
Altowan. 2 vols.
Amber Witch.
Amelia. By H. Fielding. 2 vols.
American in England. 2 vols.
Anastasius, or Memoirs of a Greek. By T. Hope. 2 vols.
Antiquary. By Sir Walter Scott.
Arabian Nights' Entertainments.
Arlington. By the Author of "Granby."
Attaché, The. By Haliburton. 4 vols.
Aurifodina, or Adventures in the Gold Regions.
Austen, Miss. Mansfield Park. 2 vols.
Austen, Miss. Northanger Abbey. 2 vols.
Austen, Miss. Sense and Sensibility. 2 vols.
Authorship. A Tale.
Ayesha, the Maid of Kars. By J. Morier. 2 vols.
Bachelor and Other Tales. By S. L. Knapp.
Barony, The. By A. M. Porter. 2 vols.
Bentley's Miscellany. 10 vols.
Boccaccio's Decameron.
Bracebridge Hall By W. Irving.
Brown, Chas. B. Wieland, or the Transformation.
Buccaneers, The. 2 vols.
Bulwer, E. L. England and the English. 2 vols.
Bulwer, E. L. Last Days of Pompeii. 2 vols.
Bulwer. (See Lytton.)
Burney, Miss. Camilla. 5 vols.
Camilla. By Miss Burney. 5 vols.
Caroline of Lichtfield. By Thos. Holcroft. 2 vols.
Cervantes, Miguel de. Don Quixote.
Christmas Carol. By Charles Dickens.

Cinq Mars. By Alfred de Vigny.
Cloudesley. By Wm. Godwin. 2 vols.
Colton, Rev. W. Deck and Port.
Colton, Rev. W. Ship and Shore.
Conquest of Granada. By Wash. Irving.
Cooper, J. Fennimore. The Spy. 2 vols.
Country Curate. By G. R. Gleig. 2 vols.
Crayon Miscellany. By Wash. Irving.
Cricket on the Hearth. By C. Dickens.
Croly, G. Salathiel. 2 vols.
Cramer, Carl G. Rasereien der Liebe.
Debtor's Prison.
Decameron. By Boccaccio.
Deck and Port. By Rev. W. Colton.
Defoe, Daniel. Robinson Crusoe.
Delaware, or the Ruined Family. 2 vols.
Dickens, Chas. Christmas Carol, Chimes, and Cricket on the Hearth.
Don Quixote. By Cervantes.
Down-Easters, &c., &c. By John Neal. 2 vols.
Dreams and Reveries of a Quiet Man. By T. S. Fay 2 vols.
Dutchman's Fireside. By J. K. Paulding.
Ecarté, or the Salons of Paris. 2 vols.
Edgar Huntley. By Brown. 3 vols.
Edgeworth, Maria. Popular Tales. 2 vols.
Elizabeth de Bruce.
Eloisa. By J. J. Rousseau. 3 vols.
England and the English. By E. L. Bulwer. 2 vols.
Entertaining and Marvellous Repository.
Few Days in Athens. By F. Wright.
Fielding, Henry. Amelia. 2 vols.
Fielding, Henry. Tom Jones. 4 vols.
Fitz-Adam, Adam. The World. 4 vols.
Fitzgeorge. A Novel. 2 vols.
Five Nights of St. Albans. By the Author of "First and Last." 2 vols.
Fouqué, F. de la Motte. Undine and Sintram.
Francis Berrian, or the Mexican Patriot. 2 vols.
French in Algiers.
Fume, Jos. A Paper of Tobacco.
Gaston de Blondeville. By Anne Radcliffe. 2 vols.
Gil Blas. By Le Sage. 3 vols.
Gleig, G. R. Country Curate. 2 vols.
Goldsmith, Oliver. Works. 4 vols.
Golovine, Ivan. Russian Sketch Book.
Gonsalvo de Cordova. From Florian.
Guide to an Irish Gentleman. By M. O'-Sullivan
Guy Rivers. By W. G. Simms. 2 vols.
Hajji Baba. Adventures of. By J. Morier. 2 vols.
Haliburton, Thos. C. The Attaché. 4 vols.
Haverhill. By James A. Jones. 2 vols.
Hawthorne, Nathaniel. Mosses from an Old Manse.
Hawthorne, N. Scarlet Letter.
Heiress, The. Vol. 1.
Hermit in London.
Hermit, The, or Philip Quarll.
History of an Irish Family.
Holcroft, T. Caroline of Lichtfield. 2 vols.
Home, or the Iron Rule. By Sarah Stickney.
Hope, Thomas. Anastasius. 2 vols.
Horse-Shoe Robinson. By J. P. Kennedy. 2 vols.
How to Observe. By Harriet Martineau.
Humphrey Clinker. By Tobias Smollett.
Insurgents, The. By Ralph R. Lockwood. 2 vols.
Irving, W. Alhambra.
Irving, W. Bracebridge Hall.
Irving, W. Conquest of Granada.
Irving, W. Crayon Miscellany,
Irving, W. Knickerbocker's New York.
Irving, W. Sketch Book.
Irving, W. Tales of a Traveller.
Jackson, Jr., D. Alonzo and Melissa.
Jacob Faithful. By Capt. Marryat. 3 vols.
Johnston, A. G. Memoirs of a Nullifier.
Kennedy, J. P. Horse Shoe Robinson. 2 vols.
Knapp, Saml. L. The Bachelor and other Tales.
Knickerbocker's New York. By W. Irving.
Koningsmarke. By J. K. Paulding. 2 vols.
Lane, E. W. The Thousand and One Nights.
Last Days of Pompeii. By E. L. Bulwer. 2 vols.
Last of the Plantagenets. An Historical Romance.
Legend of Cheviots. By W. H. Maxwell.
Legends of the Library at Lilies. 2 vols.
Le Gros, W. B. Fables and Tales.
Le Sage. Adventures of Gil Blas. 3 vols.
Le Sage. Devil on Two Sticks.
Life's Lessons.
Lindmark, J. The Vigilant Farmer.
Lives and Exploits of Banditti and Robbers. By C. MacFarlane. 2 vols.
Lockwood, Ralph R. The Insurgents; an Historical Novel. 2 vols.
Lytton, Sir E. B. Harold. 3 vols.
Lytton. (See Bulwer.)
Mansfield Park. By Miss Austen. 2 vols.
Marmondel, J. F. Moral Tales. 2 vols.
Marryat, F. Jacob Faithful. 3 vols.
Marryat, F. Midshipman Easy. 2 vols.
Martineau, Harriet. How to Observe.
Maxwell, W. H. Legends of Cheviots.
Maxwell, W. H. Soldier of Fortune.
Maxwell, W. H. Wild Sports of the West.
Memoirs of a Nullifier. By A. J. Johnston.
Merchant's Clerk. By Samuel Warren.
Midshipman Easy. By Capt. Marryat.
Mitford, Mary R. Our Village. 2 vols.
Moore, Thomas. Lalla Rookh.
Morell, Sir C. Tales of the Genii. 2 vols.
Morgan, Lady. Florence Macarthy. 2 vols.
Morier, J. Ayesha, the Maid of Kars. 2 vols.

Morier, J. Hajji Baba. 2 vols.
Mosses from an Old Manse. By Hawthorne.
Mysteries of Udolpho. By Anne Radcliff. Vols. 2 & 3.
National Tales. 2 vols.
Neal, John. Rachel Dyer.
Neal, John. The Down Easter. 2 vols.
Newton, Foster. By Capt. Marryat. 2 vols.
Northanger Abbey. By Miss Austen. 2 vols.
Ocean and the Desert. By a Madras Officer.
Oran the Outcast. 2 vols.
Our Village. By M. R. Mitford. 2 vols.
Parkman, Jr., Francis. Oregon and California Trail.
Paulding, J. K. Koningsmarke. 2 vols.
Paulding, J. K. The Dutchman's Fireside.
Peregrine Pickle. By Tobias Smollett. 4 vols.
Piquillo Alliaga. By Eugene Scribe.
Poe, Edgar A. Tales.
Popular Tales. By Maria Edgeworth. 2 vols.
Porter, A. M. The Barony. 2 vols.
Quentin Durward. By Sir Walter Scott. 2 vols.
Rachel Dyer. By John Neal.
Radcliffe, Anne. Mysteries of Udolpho. Vols. 2 & 3.
Rambler in North America. By C. J. Latrobe. 2 vols.
Refugees in America. By Mrs. Trollope. 2 vols.
Remarkable Shipwrecks.
Robinson Crusoe. By Daniel Defoe.
Roman Nights. By A. Verri. Vol. 2.
Romance of Real Life. 2 vols.
Romantic Facts. Vol 2.
Rombert. A Tale of Carolina. 2 vols.
Rousseau, J. J. Eloisa. 3 vols.
Russian Sketch Book. By Ivan Golovine.
Salathiel. By Rev. G. Croly.
Sayings and Doings at the Tremont House in 1832. 2 vols.
Scarlet Letter. By N. Hawthorne.
Scenes on the Shores of the Atlantic.
Schweiler, A. Amber Witch, and Undine.
Scott, Sir W. Quentin Durward. 2 vols.
Scott, Sir Walter. The Antiquary.
Scott, Sir Walter. Works.
Scribe, Eugene. Victim of the Jesuits. 3 vols.
Sense and Sensibility. By Miss Austen. 2 vols.
She Lives in Hope. By Miss Hatfield. 2 vols.
Ship and Shore. By Rev. W. Colton.
Siamese Twins. By E. L. Bulwer.
Sister's Budget, The. Vol. 2.
Sketch-Book. By Washington Irving.
Smollett, Tobias. Humphrey Clinker.
Smollett, Tobias. Peregrine Pickle. 4 vols.
Spy, The. By J. Fennimore Cooper. 2 vols.
Staff-Officer. By Oliver Moore. 2 vols.
Sterne, Lawrence. Tristam Shandy. 2 vols.
Stone, W. L. Tales and Sketches. Vol. 1.
Subaltern in America. 12mo.
Tales of the Genii. By Sir Chas. Morell. 2 vols.
Tales of Passion. 2 vols. 12mo.
Tales and Sketches. By W. L. Stone.
Tales of a Traveller. By Wash. Irving.
Three Eras of Woman's Life. By E. E. Smith.
Tokeah, or the White Rose. 2 vols.
Tom Jones. By Henry Fielding. 4 vols.
Traits and Stories of the Irish Peasantry. 2 vols.
Tristam Shandy. By L. Shreve. 2 vols.
Two Years and a Half in the Navy. By E. E. Wines. 2 vols.
Undine and Sintram, and his Companions.
Victim of the Jesuits. By Eugene Scribe. 3 vols.
Vigny, Alfred de. Cinq Mars.
Virginia. First Settlers of. An Historical Novel.
Wanderer in Washington.
West, Mrs. Alice de Lacy. 4 vols.
Wieland, or the Transformation. By C. B. Brown.
Wild Sports of the West. By W. H. Maxwell.
World. By Adam Fitz-Adam. 4 vols.

PAMPHLETS, &c.

Vol. 1. Select Pamphlets. By Mathew Carey.

" 2. Select Pamphlets. By Mathew Carey.

" 3. 1. Report of a Committee of the Citizens of Boston and vicinity, opposed to a further increase of Duties on Importations.
2. Medical Repository. Vol. 4, No. 3.
3. Proceedings of the General Convention of the Baptists at Philadelphia, 1817.
4. 1st Report of the American Society for Ameliorating the Condition of the Jews. 1823.
5. Constitution and By-Laws of the National Academy of Design.
6. The Universal Traveller. 1821.
7. Annual Review, or Register of Literature. 1802.
8. Address before the Newark Female Bible Society. By the Rev. L. P. Bayard. 1816.
9. The Universal Traveller. 1825.
10. 1st Report of the United Domestic Missionary Society. 1823.
11. Proceedings of the General Convention of the Baptists at Philadelphia. 1817.
12. 4th Annual Report of the New-York Eye Infirmary.

" 4. 1. New York City Hall Reporter. 1823.
2. Proceedings on a Suit brought by the U. S. against Daniel D. Tompkins. 1832.
3. Trial of Lieut. Joel Abbot on Allegations made against him by Capt. David R. Porter.
4. Opinion of Judge Bland, on the right of the Judiciary to declare an Act of Assembly Unconstitutional, &c.
5. Herttell's Remarks on the Law of Imprisonment for Debt.
6. An Examination of the case of the People vs. Edward Robbins and John Sheffield.
7. A Valedictory, delivered at the Forum. By J. P. C. Sampson.
8. Trial of Moore, Mullen, Lowry, and Rush, for an Assault and Battery on James Murray.
9. Report of the Committee to inquire into the official conduct of Hon. Wm. W. Van Ness.
10. Report of the Trial brought by Sylvanus Miller against M. M. Noah, for an alleged Libel.

" 5. 1. Speech of Mr. Archer on the Removal of the Deposites. 1834.
2. Speech of Hon. Horace Binney, on the Removal of the Deposites. 1834.
3. Speech of Hon. John C. Calhoun, on the Removal of the Deposites. 1834.
4. Speech of Hon. Henry Clay, on the Removal of the Deposites. 1834.
5. Report of the Secretary of War. 1833.
6. Report of the Secretary of the Navy. 1833.
7. Report of the Secretary of the Treasury. 1833.
8. Views of the minority on the Payment of Pensions.
9. Report made by Mr. Webster on the Removal of the Deposites. 1834.

" 6. 1. New York City Hall Recorder.
2. Letters to Archibald McIntyre, Esq.

26

Vol. 6. 3. Letter to Daniel D. Tompkins, late Governor of the State of New York.

4. Address of the Albany Republican Corresponding Committee, transmitted by the late Governor Tompkins to the Committee of Ways and Means, and to the House of Assembly.

5. An Account of Abimelech Coody, and other celebrated writers of New York, in a letter from a traveller to his friend in South Carolina.

6. The Address of Epaminondas to the citizens of the State of New York.

7. Letters addressed to De Witt Clinton, Esq., Mayor of the city of New York. By Marcus.

8. The Martling Man, or, Says I to Myself, How is This.

9. Address to the Republican Electors of the Southern District by the General Committee, friendly to the general Government and State Administration.

10. Two letters by Solomon Southwick, anti-caucus candidate for Senator for the middle district at the election in 1819.

11. Considerations against the appointment of Rufus King to the Senate of the United States.

12. Address of Republican Members of the Senate and Assembly.

13. Proceedings of the committee appointed to inquire into the official conduct of Wm. W. Van Ness, Esq., one of the Justices of the Supreme Court of the State of New York.

14. Message of Governor Clinton to the House of Assembly. 1821.

15. The Constitution defended, &c.

" 7. 1. Report of the Secretary of the Treasury, (Alexander Hamilton,) on the subject of a National Bank.

2. Report of the Committee appointed on the 30th Nov., 1818, to inspect the books and examine into the proceedings of the United States Bank.

3. National Currency.

4. A Brief Review of the Origin, Progress, and Administration of the Bank of the United States.

5. Letters to Albert Gallatin, Esq., on the Doctrine of Gold and Silver, and the evils of the present Banking System in effect and tendency.

6. Address from the President and Directors of the Pennsylvania Company for Insurance on Lives and Granting Annuities to the inhabitants of the United States.

7. First Report of the Trustees of the Bank for Savings in the City of New York.

8. Petition of Marinus Willett and others—Applicants for "the New York Interest Bank."

9. An Appeal to the Hon. the Members of the Senate and House of Assembly of the State of New York. By Civis.

10. An Appeal to the Public, on the conduct of the Banks in the City of New York. By a Citizen.

" 8. 1. Henry R. Storr's Address to the Electors of the 16th Congressional District.

2. On the Expediency and Constitutionality of prohibiting Slavery in Missouri.

Vol. 8. 3. Free Remarks respecting the exclusion of Slavery from the Territories and New States.
4. The Missouri Question.
5. An Appeal to the people of Illinois on the Question of a Convention.
6. An Oration. By Gouverneur Morris, in Celebration of the Recent Deliverance of Europe from the yoke of Military Despotism.
7. Speech of Robert G. Harper, Esq., at the Celebration of the Russian Victories. June 5, 1813.
8. An Oration. By Isaac M. Ely. Delivered before the Washington Benevolent Society.
9. Speech of De Witt Clinton, to the Legislature of the State of New York, 2d January, 1822.
10. Speech of Gov. Clinton, to the Legislature of the State of New York.

" 9. 1. Message from the President of the United States, in relation to the Seminole War, &c.
2. Speech of the Hon. James Tallmadge, Jr., on the Seminole War.
3. A Vindication, &c.
4. Message from the President of the United States, transmitting a Report of the Secretary of State, with the Documents relating to a Misunderstanding between Andrew Jackson, while acting as Governor of the Floridas, and Elijius Fromentin, Judge of a Court therein; and correspondence between the Secretary of State and the Minister of Spain, on certain Proceedings in that Territory, &c. &c.
5. Documents Accompanying the Message of the President of the United States to both Houses at the opening of the 7th Congress.

" 10. 1. Private Life and Character of the Marquis of Londonderry.
2. Remarks on the Consumption of Public Wealth, by the Clergy of every Christian Nation.
3. System of Voluntary, National Revenue combined with the Right of Suffrage.
4. Cobbett's Weekly Register, February 22, 1823, containing the Leader of the Blind.
5. Cobbett's Weekly Register, February 15, 1823. Address to the Yeomen of the County of Surrey.
6. Erskine's Letter to the Earl of Liverpool, on the subject of the Greeks. 1822.
7. The Spirit of Despotism, dedicated to Lord Castlereagh. London. 1821.
8. The Total Eclipse, a grand Politico-Astronomical Phenomenon which occurred in the year 1820.
9. The Cock of Cotton Walk, and Maid of all Work, a poem. 1820.
10. The Indicator, a weekly Paper.
11. The Gridiron, or Cook's Weekly Register.
12. Jack, and the Queen Killers, a tale of the times.
13. Riddle's Observations on the present state of Nautical Astronomy, &c.

" 11. 1. The Monthly Review for August, 1823.
2. The " " " October, 1824.
3. Letter from the Secretary of the Treasury, with his Report on the State of the Finances of the U. S. 1825.
4. Report of Wright and Sullivan, Engineers, on the proposed Canal from the Hudson to the head waters of the Lackawaxen River.

Vol. 11. 5. Catalogue of the Officers and Graduates of the Brown University, Providence, 1827.

6. The United Brethren's Missionary Intelligencer, for the year 1822, for the third and fourth quarter of 1823, and for the year 1824.

" 12. 1. Hull's Memoirs of the Campaign of the North Western Army of the United States in 1812.

2. Documents accompanying the President's Message to Congress, 1st Session, 19th Congress. 1825.

3. Minutes of Evidence taken before the Committee on Manufactures, the 1st Session, 20th Congress. 1828.

" 13. 1. Message from the President U. S., &c., &c.

2. Organization of the Army. 1818.

3. Message from the President United States, transmitting a copy of the Rules and Regulations for the Naval service of the United States.

4. Letter from the Secretary of the Treasury, transmitting an Estimate of the Appropriations proposed for 1820.

5. Message from the President United States, transmitting sundry papers in relation to the merchants of the United States, for their property seized, and confiscated under the authority of the King of Naples.

6. Letter from the Secretary of War, with statements of the sums awarded by the Commissioners of Claims.

7. Message from the President United States, transmitting the Correspondence which led to the treaty of Ghent.

8. Report of the Secretary of War, of a plan to reduce the Army of the United States.

9. Report of the Secretary of War, upon the subject of the reduction of the expenses of the military peace establishment of the U. S.

" 14. 1. Fourth Annual Report of the Managers of the Society for the prevention of Pauperism.

2. An Expose of the causes of Intemperate Drinking, and the means by which it may be obviated.

3. Second Annual Report of the Managers of the Society for the prevention of Pauperism.

4. Address delivered before the Auxiliary New York Bible and Common Prayer Book Society. 1817.

5. First Report of the Managers of the Auxiliary New York Bible and Common Prayer Book Society. 1817.

6. Journal of the Proceedings of the Bishops, Clergy, and Laity, of the Protestant Episcopal Church in the United States, in a General Convention.

7. Constitution of the American Bible Society.

8. Bishop Hobart's Address before the Auxiliary New York Bible and Common Prayer Book Society. 1816.

9. Constitution of the Auxiliary New York Bible and Common Prayer Book Society.

10 An act to incorporate the Members of the New York Institution for the Deaf and Dumb, with the By-Laws.

11. Pastoral Letter to the members of the Protestant Episcopal Church in the United States of America. 1817.

12. Christian Mourning, a sermon occasioned by the death of Mrs. Isabella Graham, by J. M. Mason, D. D.

Vol. 14. 13. A Dialogue between a Clergyman and a Layman, on the subject of Bible Societies.

14. Christ's warning to the churches. A Sermon, by the Rev. A. V. Griswold.

15. Hints on the Establishment and Regulation of Sunday Schools.

16. First Report and Constitution of the Sunday School Union. 1817.

" 15. 1. Message from the President United States, at the commencement of the first session. 1817.

2. Letter from the Secretary of the Treasury, transmitting the amount of tonnage, &c. 1816.

3. Message of the President in relation with Spain.

4. Statement submitted to the Honorable Henry Baldwin, relating to imposing "a duty on Sales by auction."

5. Foreign Commerce of the United States from 1789 to 1818.

6. The Beneficial Tendency of Auctioneering and the danger of restraining it.

7. A Cursory Review of the Schuylkill Coal.

8. History, &c., of the Berkshire Agricultural Society, Mass.

9. A Letter on the Commerce of the Western Waters.

10. A Serious Appeal on the subject of a Canal Communication between the great Western Lakes and the Hudson.

11. An Examination into the expediency of establishing a Board of Agriculture in the State of New York.

" 16. 1. Beltrami to the public of New York and United States.

2. McDonald's description of two new Instruments, by the assistance of which Astronomers and Nautical men may ascertain Longitude.

3. Dwight's Address before the Greek Committee on the Greek Revolution, Boston. 1824.

4. Beecher's Sermon at the Ordination of the Rev. Loammi Ives Hoadley, Worcester. 1823.

5. Wickliffe's Speech against the bill to repeal the law organizing a court of appeals, and to reorganize a court of appeals.

6. Strong's Speech on the Tariff Bill. 1824.

7. Page's Nature's Oracle, the Word of God.

8. Constitution, &c., of the New York State Horticultural Society.

9. Carey's Reflections on the proposed plan for establishing a College in Philadelphia. 1826.

10. Essay on Free Trade, from Blackwood's Magazine, May, 1825.

11. Statement of the objections to the Passage of the Bill entitled an act to regulate the Sale of Lottery Tickets. Yates and McIntyre. 1827.

12. Report of the Commissioners on the controversy with the State of New York, respecting the Eastern Boundary of the State of New Jersey. 1807.

13. Monthly extracts of the American Bible Society. April, 1823.

14. An Address of the Gardiner Lyceum, "Immediate not Gradual Abolition of West Indian Slavery." 1824.

15. Johnson's Address to the Utica Forum. 1824.

16. The State of Business in the Supreme Court of the State of New York.

17. Strictures addressed to James Madison on the celebrated Report of William H. Crawford, recommending the intermarriage of Americans with the Indian Tribes, ascribed to Judge Cooper.

Vol. 16. 18. Proceedings in the city of Philadelphia, respecting the Nomination of Henry Clay as a Candidate for the Presidency of the U. S.

19. Answer to Vindicatory Address, and Appeal of Lieut. Weaver to the public, from the opinion of Chancellor Sanford. 1824.

20. A Sketch of several distinguished members of the Woodbee Family. 1823.

21. Johnson's Oration commemorative of American Independence, delivered at Utica. July 5th, 1824.

22. Nixon's Oration, delivered in the Presbyterian Church in Litchfield. 1821.

23. Darling's Oration, delivered before the Washington Benevolent Society, Canaan, New York. February 22, 1816.

24. Argument in the Supreme Court of the United States, in the case of Ogden vs. Saunders, involving the Constitutionality of the State Bankrupt Laws. 1824.

" 17. 1. The First Annual Report of the American Society for the Promotion of Temperance. 1827.

2. The Opinions of a Layman on the method of treating the Marriage of a deceased Wife's Sister.

3. United States Law Journal for April, 1826.

4. Sharp's Discourse before the Legislature of Massachusetts. May 26, 1824.

5. Williston's Sermon on Revivals of Religion.

6. Appendix to the documentary evidence relative to the controversy between the Regents of the University of the State of New York and the Trustees of Union College.

7. Report of the Committee on Literature, relative to Common Schools and Academies. 1827.

8. Wm. Jay's Letter to Bishop Hobart, in reply to the pamphlet addressed by him to the author under the signature of Corrector.

9. Eighth Annual Report of the Presbyterian Education Society. 1826.

10. Seventh Report of the directors of the American Asylum at Hartford. 1823.

11. Ninth Annual Report of the directors of the American Asylum at Hartford. 1825.

12. The report of the Secretary of the Treasury, (Alexander Hamilton) on the subject of a National Bank. 1790.

13. The Acts and Proceedings of the General Synod of the Reformed Dutch Church in North America, at New Brunswick. 1825.

14. Anniversary Poem, delivered at New Haven, before the Connecticut Alpha of the Phi Beta Kappa, by James G. Brooks. 1826.

15. Catalogue of the Professors and Students of the Theological Seminary, at Andover, Mass., 1823.

16. Governor's (Ohio) Message, transmitting the Report of the Canal Engineer, on the subject of a canal at the Falls of Ohio. 1824.

17. The Constitution and By-Laws of the New York Historical Society.

18. Eighth Annual Report of the Presbyterian Education Society. May 11, 1826.

19. The Third Report of the United Domestic Missionary Society. 1825.

20. First Annual Report of the Auxiliary Foreign Mission Society of New York and Brooklyn. 1828.

Vol. 18.
1. Dwight's Greenfield Hill, a Poem.
2. Observations on the Emigration of Dr. Joseph Priestley.
3. Lee's Funeral Oration in honor of the memory of George Washington.
4. Morris's Oration upon the death of General Washington.
5. Democracy, an Epic Poem.
6. Minutes of the proceedings of the Fifth Convention of Delegates from the Abolition Societies.
7. Miln's Plan of Instruction by private classes.
8. Well's Oration, delivered on the 4th of July, 1798.

" 19.
1. Observations by Dr. Price, on the Nature of Civil Liberty.
2. Price's Discourse on the Love of our Country.
3. Harper's Economy of Health.
4. Fordyce on the Digestion of Food.

" 20.
1. Adet Reponse au Priestley sur la Doctrine du Philogistique.
2. Maclean's two Lectures on Combustion.
3. Bay's Inaugural Dissertation on the Dysentery.
4. Townsend on Pot and Pearl Ash.
5. Constitution of the Dunfermline Weaver's Society.
6. Logan on Rotation of Crops.
7. Walker's Inquiry into the causes of Sterility.
8. Dewitt on Oxygen.
9. Johnson on Fixed Air.
10. Thomas Paine's Trial.
11. Proudfit de Variola.
12. Statement of the Resignation of the Artillery Officers of New York, in 1797.

" 21.
1. English Review for December, 1789.
2. English Review for August, 1794.
3. English Review for May, 1795.
4. English Review for July, 1795.
5. English Review for August, 1795.
6. English Review for September, 1796.
7. Considerations on the Scotch Broadcloth Manufacture.
8. Letters concerning the Trade and Manufactures of Scotland.
9. Essay on the high price of provisions. London, 1773.

" 22.
1. Price's Supplement on Reversionary Payments, &c.
2. Mitchell on Soap and Manufactures. 1797.
3. Charles Webster on the Stomach.
4. Ledyard's Essays on Matter.
5. Priestley's second part of the Observations on Phlogiston.
6. Barron on the Plough.
7. Dickson's Sketch of Lectures on Medical Philosophy.
8. Sheet of Irish Pharmacopœia.
9. President Blair Smith's Oratio de Institutione Juventutis, in Schenectady College, 1796.
10. Warner's Oration. 4th July, 1797.
11. Catalogue of Books in the Library of the Massachusetts Historical Society.
12. Lathrop's Dudleian Lecture on the Errors of Popery.
13. Hamilton's Vindication from the Charge of Speculation.
14. Goetz Lied der Freude.

Vol. 22. 15. Goez Predigt.
16. James Hutton on Coal and Culm.

" 23. 1. Act of Incorporation, Laws, &c., of the Massachusetts Historical Society.
2. Selecta ex Theocrite Idylliis.
3. Blacklock's Analysis of a Sentence in Verse.
4. Duncan on a Public Dispensary.
5. Mason's Sermon before the Missionary Society. Nov. 7, 1797.
6. Hamilton's Reply to Gregory.
7. Minutes of the 4th Convention of Delegates for Abolishing Slavery. 1797.
8. Monthly Magazine for August, 1797.
9. Pott on Fistula Lachrymalis.
10. Monthly Review for February 7, 1797.

" 24. 1. Beatson on horizontal and vertical windmills.
2. Priestley's Observations on Phlogiston, part second.
3. Lent's Inaugural Dissertation on Pestilential Vapors.
4. Gallatin's Speech on the Foreign Intercourse Bill.
5. Hill's Sermon on the Happiness of Great Britain.
6. Gleig's Fasting and Humiliation Sermon.
7. Miller's Fasting and Humiliation Sermon.
8. Monthly Magazine for March, 1797.
9. Monthly Magazine for October, 1797.
10. Monthly Magazine for November, 1797.
11. Monthly Magazine for December, 1797.
12. Dermody's Rational Liberty.

" 25. 1. Horsefield on the three Sumach.
2. Miller's Discourse before the Manumission Society.
3. Well's Oration to the young men.
4. Insolvent Act, which passed the Assembly at Albany, 1798, but not the Senate.
5. Delabigane on Silk-Worms.
6. Robespierre's Political Morality.
7. Paine's Common Sense.
8. Livre Rouge.
9. Johnson's Discourse July 4th, 1798. Albany.
10. T. Dwight's Oration July 4th, 1798. Hartford.
11. Beaufoy's Speech.
12. T. P. Smith's Revolutions in Chemistry.
13. Burrell's Medical Advices.

" 26. 1. Albert de Luis Bovillæ Origine et Natura. Erlangæ, 1797.
2. Reich Mantissæ Insectorum fasciculus I. (Genus Curculio.)
3. Miller's Thanksgiving Sermon.
4. Report of the Committee of the New York Medical Society. 1798.
5. Letters from the Health Office.
6. Hardie's Account of the Malignant Fever of 1798, in New York.
7. Browne's Treatise on the Yellow Fever.
8. Constitution of the Lying-in Hospital.
9. Archer on the Croup or Hives.
10. Monthly Magazine for May, 1797.

" 27. 1. Kirwan on Manure.

Vol. 27. 2. Mitchell, Miller, and Smith's Address, &c.
3. Priestley on Phlogiston.
4. Ramsay's Sketch of South Carolina.
5. Certificates of the efficacy of Metallic Points in removing pain, and evidences respecting the same.
6. Turnbull, on the Philadelphia Prison.
7. Minutes of the Convention of Delegates, for the Abolition of Slavery.
8. Constitution of the New York Manumission Society.
9. Ouviere on Yellow Fever.
10. Beddoes' Select Cases.
11. Ideas on Yellow Fever.
12. Child on Brewing.
13. Clerke on the Epidemic Fevers of Manchester.
14. Condict's Dissertation on Contagion.

" 28. 1. Smith's Edwin and Angelina.
2. Cullen's Letter to Cathcart.
3. Romish Doctrine of breaking faith with heretics.
4. Memorial on the State of Poland for 1791.
5. Paine's Prospects on the War and Paper Currency for 1793.
6. Address to the People of Scotland on the Slave Trade, 1792.
7. McNeill on the Treatment of Negroes in Jamaica.
8. Proceedings of the General Assembly of the Presbyterian Church for 1792.
9. Patton's Attempt to establish the Basis of Freedom.

" 29. 1. Mitchell's Address to the citizens of New York, on July 4, 1799.
2. Miller's Sermon on the death of George Washington, December 29, 1799.
3. Linn's Funeral Eulogy on Washington.
4. Mason's Funeral Oration on Washington.
5. Proceedings of the Virginia Assembly on the answer of sundry States to their Resolutions of 1798.
6. Johnson's Eulogy on George Washington.
7. Commercial, Agricultural, &c., Magazine, No. 1.
8. Commercial, Agricultural, &c., Magazine, No. 2.
9. Annual Report of Hawes to the London Humane Society. 1797.
10. Annual Report of Hawes to the London Humane Society. 1798.
11. Annual Report of Hawes to the London Humane Society. 1799.
12. Harrison's Anniversary Sermon to do. 1799.
13. Wright's Art of Floating Land.

" 30. 1. Cooper's Political Essays. 1800.
2. Case of Charles Pigott. 1793.
3. Warning of the Judges, &c., on State Trials.
4. The True Churchman. 1794.
5. Eaton's Indictment for selling Paine's Rights of Man.
6. State Criminals brought to the bar of Public Justice.
7. Cooper's Reply to Burke's Invective. 1792.
8. Letters to the People of Great Britain.
9. Blake's Letter to the Clergy of the Church of Scotland. 1794.
10. Commercial Magazine for January, 1808.

" 31. 1. Philosophical Magazine for June, 1799.
2. Rules and Orders of the New York German Society.

Vol. 31. 3. Menzie's Tentamen Physiologicum Inaugurale de Respiratione. 1790.
4. Charter of the City of New York, passed by the Attorney General Bradley, January 15th, 1730, during John Montgomerie's Administration.
5. Blanchet's Recherches sur la Medecine.
6. Catalogue of Dr. Black's Library, sold 1800.
7. Wilson de Cynanche Maligna.

" 32. 1. Randolph de Respiratione.
2. Weekes de flava febre.
3. Macdonald de necrossi et callo.
4. Birkbeck de Sanguine.
5. Blake de dentium formatione.
6. Tringham de absorbentium systemate.

" 33. 1. Spalding's Nomenclature of Chemistry.
2. Laws and Ordinances of the City of New York, to 29th April, 1799.
3. Report of the Inspectors of the State Prison—1798-99.
4. Act for the assessment and collection of Taxes. 1799.
5. Facts and Observations on the Pestilential Fever of 1798, by the College of Physicians of Philadelphia.
6. Caldwell's Eulogium on Dr. Cooper.
7. Condie and Folwell on the Philadelphia Pestilence of 1798.
8. G. Nicholas's letter on Kentucky Politics for 1799.
9. Adams on the Principles of Animation.

" 34. 1. Annual Report of the Canal Commissioners of the State of New York, January 19, 1828.
2. American Journal of Education, February, 1828.
3. Catalogus Collegii Columbiani neo-eboracensis. 1814.
4. Catalogue of the Organic Remains, &c., presented to the New York Lyceum of Natural History, by Samuel L. Mitchell.
5. Sketch of the Life and Military services of General La Fayette.
6. Reports relative to the Chenango Canal, by Messrs. Roberts and Hutchinson, January 5, 1822.
7. Cobbett's Weekly Register.
8. Sixth Annual Report of the Missionary Society of the Reformed Dutch Church. 1828.
9. Literary Magazine and American Register, October, 1804.
10. Plan of the Theological Seminary of the Protestant Episcopal Church of the United States.
11. Lindsay's Essays on the Human Mind.
12. Entzucking des Las Casas.

" 35. 1. Waterhouse's Lecture against Tobacco and Rum.
2. Proposals of the Sunfire office, London.
3. Account of Coal-Tar.
4. Peale's Guide to the Philadelphia Museum.
5. List of Trumbull's Paintings at New York.
6. London Kine-pock Institution in favor of Vaccination.
7. Mann's Dissertation on Cholera Infantum.
8. Lettsom's Appeal to the Critical Reviews.
9. Brickell on the Immortality of the Soul.
10. Ramsay's Oration on the Cession of Louisiana to the United States.
11. Liverpool-men in praise of Cheshire Salt.

Vol. 35. 12. Thornton on Political Economy.
13. Report of the London Humane Society. 1774.
14. Valpy's Sermon to the Humane Society. 1804.
15. Girle on Hasty Interments.
16. Barry's Sermon to the Humane Society.

" 36. 1. Boys's General View of the Agriculture of the County of Kent.
2. Monthly Magazine for August, 1796.
3. Monthly Magazine for October, 1796.
4. Monthly Magazine for January, 1797.
5. Thomas Hardy's Trial for High Treason, at the Session House in Clerkenwell, 1794.

" 37. 1. Masonic Constitutions in the State of New York. 5801.
2. Deed of Settlement of the Washington Mutual Assurance Co. 1801.
3. Act to Incorporate the Stockholders of the Columbian Insurance Co. 1801.
4. Facts and Observations relative to Kine-pock.
5. Joseph Bayley's dissertation on Yellow Fever.
6. Logan's Fourteen Agricultural Experiments. 1797.
7. Logan's Address to the Philadelphia Tammany Society.
8. Logan's Letter to the Pennsylvanians on promoting Agriculture, Manufactures and Useful Arts.
9. Caldwell's reply to Haygarth's letter to the College of Physicians, Philadelphia.
10. Woodward on the Government of the Territory of Columbia. 1802.
11. Morgan's view of the Finances of Great Britain. 1801.
12. Annals of the Corporation of New York relative to the contested Elections for Aldermen and Assistants in 1801.

" 38. 1. Barton on the Fascinating Power of the Rattlesnake and other Serpents.
2. Seaman on the New York Yellow Fever of 1795.
3. Principles of Aerostation.
4. Blanchard's Journal of his 45th Ascension.
5. Acts of the General Assembly of the Presbyterian Church for 1795–96.
6 Linn's Discourse on Thanksgiving-day, Nov. 26, 1795.
7. Wortman's Tammanial Oration.
8. Noel Dissertatis de Angina Tracheali.
9. Review of Original German Books, No. 1.
10. Humphrey's Poem on Industry.
11. Bard on the Angina Suffocativa.
12. Giraud's Universal Salt for Syphilis.

" 39. 1. Miller's Independence Sermon.
2. Miller's Masonic Sermon. 1795.
3. French Constitution for 1793.
4. Remarks on the Scotch Salt Laws.
5. Rules of the Edinburgh Lying-in Hospital.
6. Addoms on the Malignant Fever, New York, 1791.
7. Creech's Letters to Sinclair.
8. Smith on Watering Grounds.
9. Harvard College Laws. 1790.
10. Arden's Syllabus of Lectures.
11. Address of Great Britain to America. 1775.

Vol. 39. 12. Prior on Irish Linen Manufacture.
13. Process of Flax-husbandry in Scotland.
14. Stephenson on Irish Linen. 1760–61.
15. Dublin Society on Flax and Lint Seed.

" 40. 1. Harper's Case of the Yazoo Lands (Georgia.)
2. Anderson and Hobby's view of the Georgia Sales.
3. Hare on the Hydraulic Blow Pipe.
4. Quackenbos on Dysentery.
5. Walker on the Perspirable Fluids.
6. New York Book of Prices for Cabinet and Chair work. 1802.
7. President Jefferson's Regulations for the Navy of the U. States. 1802.
8. Constitution of the United States and Amendments thereto.
9. Webster's Oration on the Anniversary of the Declaration of Independence, July, 1802.
10. Hints on the Health and Cleanliness of New York.
11. Perkins on Fever.

" 41. 1. Constitution of the State of New York.
2. Ordinance of Convention of the State of New York.
3. Duane's Decree in the Case of the Catharine.
4. Rotheram's Vindication of the Sexes of Plants.
5. Adair de Hæmorrhœa petechiali.
6. Description de L'Hôpital general du Cap François.
7. Dissertation sur le Tetanos.
8. Observations sur les Lois concernant la Médecine et la Chirurgie dans la Colonil de St. Domingue.
9. Hoffman's Friars Oratory.

" 42. 1. Knox on Extinguishing Fire.
2. Mitchell's Report on the State of Learning in Columbia College. 1794.
3. Priestley on the Generation of Air from Water.
4. Outlines of a State Society of Agriculture in Pennsylvania.
5. Democracy; an Epic Poem.
6. ——'s Remarks on Witherspoon.
7. McKnight's Sermon to the Democratic Society. 1794.
8. Edwards' Sermon on the Slave Trade.
9. Dwight's Oration on Slavery.
10. Wedgwood's Catalogue.
11. Clarkson on Slave Trade.
12. Brissot de Warville's Oration upon the necessity of establishing at Paris a Society to co-operate towards the abolition of the Slave Trade.
13. Woodhouse on the Persimmon Trees.
14. Walkeri Delineateo Fossiliam.
15. Wyche's Oration on Party Spirit.

" 43. 1. Gregory's Answer to Hamilton.
2. Waterhouse's Discourse on the rise, progress, and present state of Medicine.
3. Catalogus Collegii Yalensis. 1793.
4. Sweeting's Narrative on the Murder of Darius Quimby.
5. Bard's Discourse on the Duties of a Physician.
6. White on the Regeneration of Animal Substances.
7. Rush on the Impolicy of punishing Murder by Death.

Vol. 43. 8. Minutes of the Proceedings of the Philadelphia Committee during the prevalence of the Malignant Fever in 1793.

" 44. 1. Report of Proceedings at a Court of Oyer and Terminer, appointed for the Investigation of Cases from the Indian Territories at Quebec, 1819.

2. Administration of the affairs of Great Britain, Ireland, &c. 1823.
3. An Exposition of the Administrative Labors of the Peruvian Government. 1823.
4. A Letter relative to Banking Institutions in Canada. 1823.
5. Constitution of the Spanish Monarchy. 1814.
6. Constitution of the United Provinces of South America.

" 45. 1. Speech of the Hon. Morris S. Miller on the Army Bill. 1814.

2. Speech of Mr. Pitkin on the Loan Bill. 1814.
3. Speech of the Hon. Daniel Sheffey on the Loan Bill. 1814.
4. Speech of Mr. Ingersoll on the Loan Bill. 1814.
5. Speech of the Hon. William Gaston on the Loan Bill. 1814.
6. Case of the Merchants considered.
7. Speeches of Messrs. Homes, Findley, and Young, on the War. 1814.
8. Stevens' Discourse on the duty of Union in a Just War. 1814.
9. Reply to the criticism on Inchiquin's Letters.
10. Irving's Oration on the 4th of July, 1809.
11. Wood's correct statement of the various sources from which the History of the Administration of John Quincy Adams was compiled.
12. Correct statement of the Affair of Honor between Gen. Hamilton and Col. Burr. 1804.
13. Examination of the various charges exhibited against Aaron Burr.

" 46. 1. Kent's Introductory Law-Lecture.

2. Fowler's Experiments on Animal Electricity.
3. Pennsylvania Penal Laws. 1794.
4. Gloag's Christian Knowledge Sermon.
5. Laws of New Jersey College. 1794.
6. Maywood de Actione Mercurii.
7. Keir de Attractione Chemica.
8. Campbell de Acido Vitriolico.
9. Old Statutes of Columbia College, (obsolete.)
10. Milns' plan of Instruction.

" 47. 1. Philosophical Magazine, July, 1799.

2. Brown's Treatise on Yellow Fever.
3. Bishop's Oration on Political Delusion.
4. Rush's Lecture on Animal Life.
5. Trent on the effects of Sight upon Perspiration.
6. Frobisher on the Manufacture of Potash.
7. Hosack on Medical Education.
8. Mease on Rabies versus Rush.
9. Best's Dissertation on Oratory.

" 48. 1. Voight's account of the management of the poor in Hamburgh. 1795.

2. Hosack's Botanical Syllabus.
3. Kent's Law Dissertations.
4. Catalogue of the Library to the Writers of the Signet of Edinburgh.
5. Randolph's Vindication.
6. Letters on Emigration. 1794.

Vol. 48. 7. Aberdour on Smallpox.

" 49. 1. Saltonstall's Dissertation on Septon Azote or Nitrogene.
2. Burke's Letters on the Duke of Bedford's Attack.
3. Abstract of the Corn-Act.
4. Observations on the Scotch Fisheries, Emigration, &c.
5. Prize Questions proposed by the Harveian Society of Edinburgh.
6. Memoire sur Charles Bonnet par Jean Trembley.
7. Anderson's Dissertation on Chronic Mania.
8. Caldwell's Dissertation on Fever.
9. Otto's Dissertation on Epilepsy.
10. Jones' Dissertation on Pneumonia.
11. Chisholm on Hydrocephalus Internus.
12. Dunn's Discourse before the New York Emigration Society.

" 50. 1. Mitchell's Oration on Patriotism.
2. Dingley's Oration on Medicine.
3. Webster on French Revolution.
4. Seaman on Saratoga Waters.
5. Mease on Rabies Canina.
6. Dana on African Slave Trade.
7. Themmen De Mensibus.

" 51. 1. Washington's Last Will. 1800.
2. Smith's economical plan of Family Medical Instruction.
3. Fraser on Party Spirit.
4. Constitution of the Society in New York for the Relief of poor Widows with small Children.
5. Act of Incorporation of the Mutual Assurance Company in New York.
6. Perkins' Evidences in favor of the Metallic Tractors.
7. Bradley on the Plague of Marseilles and London.
8. Catalogue of Books belonging to the Albany Library, with the Act of Incorporation and By-Laws.
9. Bacon's Remarks on Robison's Proofs of a Conspiracy.
10. Thomas Paine's Letter to Erskine on the prosecution of Williams for publishing the Age of Reason—with Paine's Discourse to the Theophilanthropists.

" 52. 1. New-Oxford Guide.
2. Votes and Proceedings of the American Continental Congress. 1774.
3. Middleton's Medical Discourse.
4. Dialogue on African Slavery.
5. Allum's Speech in Coachmakers' Hall on abstaining from West India Produce.
6. Address to Great Britain on the same subject.
7. Summary of the Evidence before the Committee of the English House of Commons, on the Slave Trade.
8. Clinton's Friars-Oration.
9. Priestley's Letters to the French Philosophers.
10. Hughes's Complete Horseman.

" 53. 1. Barlow's Privileged Orders (2d part.)
2. Paine on the English System of Finance.
3. Noble on Maple Sugar.
4. Priestley on a Chart of History.
5 Mardevall's Practice in Malignant Fever.

Vol. 53. 6. Constitution of Tennessee.
7. Essay on Comparative Anatomy.
8. Perkins' Evidences on Metallic Points.
9. Wheaton's Friars-Oration for 1796.
10. Observations on the Distilleries of Scotland.

" 54. 1. Report of the Directors of the Sierra Leone Company. 1795.
2. Report of the Directors of the Western Inland Lock-Navigation Co. to the Legislature. 1798.
3. State of the National Debt, by John Earl of Stair.
4. Gov. Johnston's Speech on American Affairs.
5. Longevity, being an account of various persons who have lived to an extraordinary age.
6. La Sagesse.
7. The Young Mason's Monitor and Vocal Companion.
8. Essay on the efficacy and safety of Sir John Hills' Balsam of Honey.
9. Nisbet's syllabus of a course of Lectures.
10. Spaulding's dissertation on the production of Animal Heat.
11. Allen's treatise on the Scarlatina, Anginosa, and Dysentery.

" 55. 1. Report of the Commissioners, Madison, Gallatin, and Lincoln, on the Georgia controversy, Feb. 1, 1803, with Documents.
2. Documents accompanying the said report.
3. Rutledge's defence against the charges in the Geoffroy letters.
4. Gallatin's explanation of the conduct of the Commissioners of the Sinking Fund.
5. Plan of the Infirmary at New Castle upon Tyne.
6. Niderburg's Improved Galvanismus.
7. Sea Bathing Infirmary at Margate.
8. Proposals to make Paper from Gunny Bags.
9. Dispensary of New Castle upon Tyne.
10. Tytler's Criticism on Pinkerton's Geography.
11. Constitution of the Protestant Episcopal Society in New York for promoting Religion and Learning.
12. Hebert's Air Pump Vapor Bath.
13. Memoirs of Dr. Hawes of London.
14. Logan on Promoting Agriculture, Manufactures, and Useful Arts in Pennsylvania.
15. Woodward on the Government of the Territory of Columbia.
16. Convention of 1801 between the French Republic and the United States of America.

" 56. 1. Mitchell's Synopsis of Chemical Nomenclature.
2. Waterhouse on Kine-pock, (Part 2.)
3. Hamilton's bar against Yellow Fever.
4. Percival's Medical Jurisprudence.
5. Percival's Sermon at Liverpool on Hospital Duties.
6. Memoirs of Baron Drinsdale.
7. Baltzell on the sweet spring of Virginia.
8. Kentish de Corporis partibus adustis earumque Curatione.
9. Woodhouse's Experiments on the Vegetation of Plants.
10. Vaughan of the Wilmington Fever of 1802.
11. Constitution of the Cancer Society of London. 1801.
12. Willan on Dram Drinking.

Vol. 56. 13. Minutes of the Abolition Convention held in Philadelphia for 1803.
14. John Dickinson's Address to Congress and Citizens of Freedom, on French Politics.
15. Hargrove's New Jerusalem Sermons preached in the Capitol at Washington in December, 1802.
16. Du Buc Marentille's Insubmersible Boat.
17. Mitchill's proposal of Generic Names, &c.
18. Fredish Song for July 4, 1803.

" 57. 1. Aristides on the various charges exhibited against Aaron Burr. 1803.
2. Cheetham's reply to Aristides.
3. Morse's Sermon before the Artillery Company of Boston.
4. Pollock's supplementary representation to Congress.
5. Manley's Dissertation on Yellow Fever.
6. Albers's American Annals (Part 3.)
7. Constitution of the New York Society for promoting the Manumission of Slaves.
8. Minutes of the Constitution held at Philadelphia for bettering the condition of the Negroes. 1804.
9. Letters of Sicilius (Gov. Jackson) to the people of Georgia on the Yazoo proceedings.
10. Philadelphia Communication on Manufactures, &c.
11. Scofield's Dissertation upon Smallpox.

" 58. 1. Massachusetts papers on Agriculture for 1803.
2. Walker's Dissertation on the Cornus, Florida and Sericea.
3. New York Directions for the Kine-pock Inoculation.
4. Constitution of the New York Kine-pock Institution.
5. Moyes' (the Blind Philosopher) Syllabus of his course of Lectures.
6. Johnson's Farewell Sermon to the Albanians, September, 1802.
7. Leigh on Opium.
8. Cowdrey's Oration to the Tammany Society, May 12th, 1803.
9. Hamblin's Republic of Reason (A Poem.)
10. Brothers' Revealed Knowledge.
11. Dwight's discourse on the authenticity of the New Testament.
15. Pearson on the Influenza of 1703, as it appeared in England.

" 59. 1. Firth on the non-contagiousness of Malignant Fever.
2. Account of the First Festival of the Royal Jennerian Society.
3. Priestley's doctrine of Phlogiston established (2nd Edition, 1803.)
4. Peale's historical disquisition on the Mammoth.
5. Duvall's experimental Botanic Medical Essay on the "Pride of China."
6. Archer's Inaugural Essay on the effects and modus operandi of the carbonates of Lime, Magnesia, and Potash.
7. Brief account of the New York Hospital.
8. British new excise law for 1803.
9. Darlington's dissertation on Habits and Disease.
10. Constitution of the Mississippi Society for the acquirement and dissemination of Useful Knowledge.
11. Essay on the Manufacturing Interests of the United States.
12. Act to provide against Infectious and Pestilential Diseases. 1801.
13. Walter's Inaugural dissertation on Inflammation.

ALPHABETICAL AND ANALYTICAL

CATALOGUE

OF THE

AMERICAN INSTITUTE LIBRARY.

FIRST

SUPPLEMENT.

New-York:

JOHN W. AMERMAN, PRINTER,

No. 60 William-street.

1857.

INTRODUCTORY NOTE.

The Alphabetical and Analytical Catalogue of the American Institute Library was printed in 1852. In the Introduction to that Catalogue a brief historical sketch of the origin and progress of the Library was given, together with the By-Laws of the Institute relating to the Library, and the Rules and Regulations adopted for its government. As no changes or alterations have been made either in these By-Laws or in the Rules and Regulations, it will be sufficient to refer those desirous of information on these points to the Catalogue.

The Library contained on the 1st of January, 1852, five thousand eight hundred and sixty (5,860) volumes; the number of volumes in the Library at the present time is seven thousand seven hundred and fifty, (7,750.) There have been added to the Library, therefore, since the publication of the Catalogue, one thousand eight hundred and ninety (1,890) volumes. Of these an Alphabetical and an Analytical Catalogue are given in the present Supplement, which has been carefully prepared by the Librarian, Mr. Ezekiel A. Harris, who also prepared the Catalogue.

The Library, as a glance at the Catalogue will show, is quite general or miscellaneous in its character. Of such libraries, large and easily accessible, there are many in New York, which are an honor and an ornament to the city. There are also extremely valuable collections devoted to law, medicine and theology. On the other hand, the agriculturist, the mechanic and the manufacturer, whose pursuits have now attained a scientific basis and taken their place among the learned professions, have hitherto had their wants but imperfectly provided for. Something, indeed, has been done.

It will be seen that while many important additions have been made to the Library of the Institute in works of general interest, numerous valuable works have been procured on the subjects falling more directly within its scope and sphere. It is believed that in no other way can the American Institute promote those great industrial interests for which it has labored unremittingly during more than a quarter of a century, than by making its collection of books worthy to take its place by the side of our Libraries of Law, Medicine and Theology, as the great Scientific Library of the country.

By steadily adhering to system, with this object in view, in the purchase of works upon science—those in particular giving the latest results of scientific investigation, the new discoveries and processes which modern genius is constantly producing, the history of invention, the rights of inventors, the records of patents, the influence and history of industrial exhibitions and all kindred topics—the collection of the American Institute may be rendered a library of the highest value to the engineer, mechanic and farmer, as well as to men of abstract science. It is hoped that when another Supplement shall be found necessary, it will exhibit satisfactory progress towards so desirable a result.

WILLIAM HIBBARD,
RALPH LOCKWOOD,
DAVID R. JAQUES,
WILLIAM H. BROWNE,
BAILEY J. HATHAWAY,
WILLIAM B. LEONARD,
Ex-officio,
} Library Committee.

NEW YORK, *April* 1, 1857.

SUPPLEMENTARY

ALPHABETICAL CATALOGUE.

Abeja Argentina. 8vo. Buenos Ayres, 1822.

Abernethy, John. Memoirs of, with a View of his Lectures, Writings and Character. 8vo. New York, 1853.

Addison, Joseph. Dramatic Works. 12mo. Boston, 1808.

Agriculture Française. Par M. M. les Inspecteurs de l'Agriculture. 6 vols. 8vo. Paris, 1843–1847.

Agriculture of Massachusetts. Charles L. Flint. 3 vols. 8vo. Boston, 1853–1855.

Aiken, Arthur. Arts and Manufactures Illustrated. 8vo. London, 1831–1845.

Aiken, J. Letters on Various Topics relative to Literature and the Conduct of Life. 8vo. Philadelphia, 1794.

Alban, Ernest. The High Pressure Steam Engine. 2 vols. 8vo. London, 1847–1848.

Alcantara, Father. Golden Treatise of Mental Prayer, translated by Giles Willoughby. 18mo. Liverpool, 1843.

Allen, Lewis F. Farm Houses, Cottages and Out Buildings. 8vo. New York, 1852.

Allen, Zachariah. Philosophy of the Mechanics of Nature. 8vo. New York, 1852.

Allen, Zachariah. Science of Mechanics. 8vo. Providence, 1829.

Almanak Administrativo Mercantil e Industrial. 8vo. Rio Janeiro, 1851.

Alms House. Annual Reports of the Governors. 8vo. New York.

AMERICAN AGRICULTURIST. 2 vols. 8vo. New York, 1850–1851.

*AMERICAN ALMANAC and Repository of Useful Knowledge. 7 vols. 12mo Boston, 1851–1857.

*AMERICAN ARCHIVES. A Documentary History of the American Colonies. By Peter Force. 9 vols. 4th and 5th series. Fol. Washington, 1837–53.

AMERICAN BIBLE SOCIETY. Reports, from 1820 to 1835. 4 vols. 8vo. New York.

AMERICAN BOARD OF COMMISSIONERS FOR FOREIGN MISSIONS. Reports, from 1821 to 1851. 4 vols. 8vo. New York.

AMERICAN HOME MISSIONARY SOCIETY. Reports, from 1827 to 1834. 8vo. New York.

AMERICAN MONTHLY MAGAZINE and Critical Review. 8vo. New York, 1818.

AMERICAN POLYTECHNIC JOURNAL. Conducted by Messrs. Page, Greenough and Fleischmann. 4 vols. 8vo. New York, 1853–1854.

AMERICAN RAIL-ROAD JOURNAL. Henry V. Poor, Editor. 6 vols. 4to. New York, 1850–1856.

AMERICAN REVIEW; a Whig Journal of Politics and General Repository of Literature and State Papers. 6 vols. 8vo. New York, 1850–1852.

AMERICAN ROSE CULTURIST. 12mo. New York, 1852. *Presented by C. M. Saxton, Esq.*

AMERICAN TRACT SOCIETY. Reports, from 1827 to 1834. 8vo. New York.

ANDERSON, WILLIAM. System of Surgical Anatomy. 4to. New York, 1822. *Presented by Dr. McComb.*

ANDREWS, ISRAEL D. Report on the Trade and Commerce of the British North American Colonies, and upon the Trade of the Great Lakes and Rivers. 8vo. Washington, 1853.

ANGELL, J. K. and THOMAS DURFEE. Reports of Cases in the Supreme Court of Rhode Island. 2 vols. 8vo. Providence, 1847–1852.

ANIMAL BIOGRAPHY; a Supplement to Buffon's Natural History. 8vo. London, 1840.

ANNALS OF HORTICULTURE and Year Book of Information on Practical Gardening. 4 vols. 8vo. London, 1846–1850.

ANNALS of the Lyceum of Natural History of New York. Vol. 1, 8vo. New York, 1824.

ANNALS of the Massachusetts Charitable Mechanics' Association; compiled by Joseph T. Buckingham. 8vo. Boston, 1853.

ANNUAIRE des Deux Mondes. 2 vols. 8vo. Paris, 1850–1852.

Annual Report of the Croton Aqueduct Department, 1851. 8vo. New York, 1852.

Annual Report of the State Engineer and Surveyor on the Rail-Roads. 8vo. Albany, 1854.

Annual of Scientific Discovery. (See Year Book of Facts.)

Anquetil, M. A Summary of Universal History. 9 vols. 8vo. London, 1800.

Answeise über den Handel von Desterveisch. Fol. Vienna, 1851.

Antiquarian and Architectural Year Book for 1844. 8vo. London, 1845.

Apuleius. The Works of. 12mo. London, 1853.

Arnault, M. F., and others. Memoirs of Napoleon Bonaparte. 2 vols. 18mo. Boston, 1839.

Arnot, D. H. Gothic Architecture applied to Modern Residences. 4to. New York, 1851.

Arnott, Neil. Smokeless Fire Places, Chimney Valves, &c. 8vo. London, 1855.

Arthur, T. S. and W. H. Carpenter. History of Georgia. 12mo. Philadelphia, 1852.

Arthur, T. S. and W. H. Carpenter. History of Kentucky. 12mo. Philadelphia, 1852.

Arthur, T. S. and W. H. Carpenter. History of Virginia. 12mo. Philadelphia, 1852.

Artisan, The. A Monthly Journal of the Operative Arts. 6 vols. 4to. London, 1851–1856.

*Art-Journal, The. 3 vols. 4to. London, 1849–1852.

*Art-Journal. Illustrated Catalogue of the Great Exhibition. 4to. London, 1851.

*Art-Union, The. 2 vols. 4to. London, 1847–1848.

Ashburner, John. Physico-Physiological Researches on the Dynamics of Magnetism, Electricity, &c., in their Relations to Vital Force. 8vo. New York, 1851.

*Astor Library. Alphabetical and Analytical Index, or Catalogue of the Books collected and of the Proposed Additions. 8vo. New York, 1851.

Athenæum, The. 10 vols. 4to. London, 1847–1856.

Audubon and Bachman. Quadrupeds of America. Vols. 2 and 3, 8vo. New York, 1851–1854.

Auxiliador da Industria Nacional. 5 vols. 8vo. Rio Janeiro, 1844–1851.

Bache, A. D. Annual Reports of the United States Coast Survey. 2 vols. 8vo. and 3 vols. 4to. Washington, 1847, 1851–1853. *Presented by Prof. Bache.*

Bagay, V. Nouvelles, Tables Astronomiques et Hydrographiques. 4to. Paris, 1829.

Bailey, Samuel. Discourses on Various Subjects. 8vo. London, 1852.

Bainbridge, William. Life and Services of, by Thomas Harris. 8vo. Philadelphia, 1837.

Baird, Robert H. American Cotton Spinner. 12mo. Philadelphia, 1851.

*Baker, Richard. A Chronicle of the Kings of England. Fol. London, 1694.

Baldwin, J. G. Party Leaders; Sketches of Jefferson, Hamilton, Jackson, Clay, Randolph, &c. 8vo. New York, 1855.

Balfour, J. H. Class Book of Botany. 8vo. Edinburgh, 1852.

Balfour, J. H. Manual of Botany. 8vo. London, 1851.

Bancroft, George. History of the United States. 7 vols. 8vo. Boston, 1850–56.

Bankers' Magazine and Financial Register. 7 vols. 8vo. Baltimore, 1849 to 1850.

Barclay, James. Complete and Universal English Dictionary. 4to.

Barlow, Peter. Treatise on the Manufactures and Machinery of Great Britain. 2 vols. 4to. London, 1836.

Barrington, A. Treatise on Physical Geography; edited by Charles Burdett. 12mo. New York, 1851.

Bartol, R. H. Treatise on the Marine Boilers of the United States. 8vo. Philadelphia, 1851.

Baucher, F. A Method of Horsemanship, and Breaking and Training of Horses. 12mo. Philadelphia, 1852.

*Bayle, Peter. Historical and Critical Dictionary, revised, &c., by Mr. Des Maizeaux. 5 vols. fol. London, 1734.

Beames, Thomas. Rookeries of London; Past, Present and Prospective. 8vo. London, 1852. *Presented by John A. Bunting, Esq.*

Beattie, James. Essay on the Nature and Immutability of Truth. 8vo. Edinburgh, 1771.

Beaumont, William. Physiology of Digestion, with Experiments on the Gastric Juice. 12mo. Burlington, 1847.

BECK, THEODORE R. and JOHN B. Elements of Medical Jurisprudence. 5 vols. 8vo. Albany, 1850.

BECKET, ANDREW. Dramatic and Prose Miscellanies. 2 vols. 8vo. London. 1838.

BECQUEREL, M. Des Engrais Inorganiques. 12mo. Paris, 1848.

BEECHER, HENRY WARD. Star Papers; or Experiences of Art and Nature, 8vo. New York, 1855.

BELCHER, EDWARD. Treatise on Nautical Surveying. 8vo. London, 1835.

BELTRAMI, J. C. Le Mexique. 8vo. Paris, 1830.

BENSLEY, BENJAMIN. Henry the Eighth and his Contemporaries. 12mo. London, 1847.

BENTON, THOMAS H. Abridgement of the Debates of Congress, from 1789 to 1856. 8vo. New York.

BENTON, THOMAS H. Thirty Years' View; or a History of the Working of the American Government from 1820 to 1850. 2 vols. 8vo. New York, 1854–1856.

BERKELEY, GEORGE. The Works of. By Rev. G. N. Wright. 2 vols. 8vo. London, 1843.

BERNARD, HENRY. Discourse on the Life and Character of Rev. Thomas Gallaudet. 8vo. Hartford, 1852.

BERRINGTON, JOSEPH. Literary History of the Middle Ages. 8vo. London, 1846.

BIOGRAPHICAL DICTIONARY of Eminent Persons of Every Nation, &c. 18mo. London, 1809.

BLACK, WILLIAM. Practical Treatise on Brewing. 8vo. London, 1849.

BLACKWOOD'S EDINBURGH MAGAZINE, from 1841 to 1856. 27 vols. 8vo. New York.

BLAKE, JOHN L. Agriculture for Schools. 12mo. New York, 1851.

BLAKE, JOHN L. The Farmer's Cyclopædia of Modern Agriculture. 8vo. New York, 1852.

BLAKE, JOHN L. The Farmer's Every Day Book. 8vo. Auburn, 1850.

BLAKELY, ROBERT. Historical Sketch of Logic. 8vo. London, 1851.

BLOOMINGDALE ASYLUM for the Insane. (See New York Hospital.)

BOARDMAN, A. Defence of Phrenology. 12mo. New York, 1850. *Presented by Messrs. Fowler & Wells.*

BODIN, FELIX. Summary of the History of France. 12mo. London, 1840.

Bogue, David. Theological Lectures; edited by Rev. J. S. C. F. Frey. 2 vols. New York, 1849.

Bonelli, L. Hugh, de. Travels in Bolivia, &c. 2 vols. 12mo. London 1854.

Bon Jardinier Almanach. 4 vols. 12mo. Paris, 1851, 1854–1855.

Bonomi, Joseph. Nineveh and its Palaces. 8vo. London, 1853.

Bonynge, Francis. Future Wealth of America. 12mo. New York, 1852.

Bourne, John. A Catechism of the Steam Engine. 12mo. London, 1850.

Bourne, John. Treatise on the Screw Propeller. 4to. London, 1852.

Boyd, Sir William. History of Literature. 3 vols. 8vo. London, 1843.

Boyle, Henry. Universal Chronologist and Historical Register. 2 vols. 8vo. London, 1826.

Brande, William T. Manual of Chemistry. 2 vols. 8vo. London, 1848.

Brandon, R. and J. A. Open Timber Roofs of the Middle Ages. 4to. London, 1849.

Brees, S. C. Second Series of Railway Practice. 4to. London, 1840.

Brees, S. C. Fourth Series of Railway Practice. 4to. London, 1847.

Bremer, Frederika. Homes of the New World. Translated by Mary Howitt. 2 vols. 12mo. New York, 1853.

Brewster, Sir David. Popular Treatise on Magnetism. 8vo. Edinburgh, 1851.

Brewster, Sir David. More Worlds than One. 12mo. New York, 1854.

British Gazeteer and Travelling Road Book. 9 vols. 8vo. London.

Britton, John. The Union of Architecture, Sculpture and Painting. 4to. London, 1827.

Brooks, S. H. City, Town and Country Architecture. Fol. London, 1847.

Brown, Henry. History of Illinois. 8vo. New York, 1844.

Brown, Thomas. Illustrations of the Land and Fresh Water Conchology of Great Britain and Ireland. 8vo. London, 1845.

Browne, D. J. The American Muck Book. 8vo. New York, 1851. *Presented by the Author.*

Browne, J. Ross. Yusef; or the Journey of the Frangi. 8vo. New York, 1853.

Bryan, Michael. Biographical and Critical Dictionary of Painters and Engravers. 8vo. London, 1849.

BRYANT, WILLIAM C. Poems. 2 vols. 12mo. New York, 1855.

BUCHANAN, ROBERT. Culture of the Grape and Wine Making: and the Cultivation of the Strawberry, by N. Longworth. 12mo. Cincinnati, 1852. *Presented by J. A. Carman, Esq.*

BUCKINGHAM, JOSEPH T. Annals of the Massachusetts Charitable Mechanics' Association. 8vo. Boston, 1853.

BULLETIN de la Société d'Encouragement pour L'Industrie Nationale. 12 vols. 4to. Paris, 1833, 1840–1853.

BULLOCK, JOHN. History and Rudiments of Architecture. 12mo. New York, 1853. *Presented by the Editor.*

BULLOCK, JOHN. Rudiments of the Art of Building. 12mo. New York, 1853. *Presented by the Editor.*

BURNET, JOHN. Discourses of Sir Joshua Reynolds. 4to. London, 1842.

BURNET, JOHN. Landscape Painting in Oil Colors. 4to. London, 1849.

BURNET, JOHN. Practical Essays on Various Branches of the Fine Arts. 8vo. London, 1848.

BURNET, JOHN. An Essay of the Education of the Eye with reference to Painting. 4to. London, 1837.

BURNHAM, GEORGE P. The History of the Hen Fever. 12mo. Boston, 1855.

BURR, AARON. (See Davis, Matthew L.)

BURTON, RICHARD F. Sindh, and the Races that inhabit the Valley of the Indus. 8vo. London, 1851.

BURY, T. TALBOT. Rudimentary Architecture. 12mo. London, 1853.

BUSHMAN, J. S. Cholera and its Cures; an Historical Sketch. 8vo. London, 1850.

BUTLER, CHARLES. Life of Hugo Grotius. 8vo. London, 1826.

BUTLER, CHARLES. Memoirs of the Life of Henry Francis D'Aguesseau. 8vo. London, 1830.

BUTLER, CHARLES. Reminiscences of. 2 vols. 8vo. London, 1824.

BYRNE, OLIVER. Practical Cotton Spinner and Manufacturer. 8vo. Philadelphia, 1851.

BYRNE, OLIVER. Practical Model Calculator. 8vo. Philadelphia, 1852.

Cabot, Sebastian. Memoir of, with a Review of the History of Maritime Discovery. 8vo. London, 1832.

Campan, Madame. Journal Anecdotique de. 8vo. Paris, 1825.

Campbell, Thomas. Life and Letters of, edited by William Beattie. 3 vols. 8vo. London, 1827.

Canada. Tables of the Trade and Navigation of. 4 vols. 8vo. Quebec, 1851, 1852, 1853, 1855.

Carpentry and Joinery; a Comprehensive Guide Book. 2 vols. 4to. London, 1849.

Catalogue of the Apprentices' and the Demilt Libraries. 12mo. New York, 1855.

Catalogue of the Astor Library. 8vo. New York, 1851.

Catalogue of the Great Exhibition of the Industry of all Nations. 3 vols. 8vo. London, 1851.

Catalogue of the Library Company of Philadelphia. 2 vols. 8vo. Philadelphia, 1835 and 1856. *Presented by the Company.*

Catalogue of the Library of Harvard University. 5 vols. 8vo. Cambridge, 1830–1834.

Catalogue of the Library of the Salfour Borough Royal Museum. 8vo. Manchester, 1851.

Catalogue of the Mercantile Library Company of Philadelphia. 8vo. Philadelphia, 1850.

Cavendish, Henry. Life of; including Abstracts of his more important Scientific Papers, by George Wilson. 8vo. London, 1851.

Census. The Seventh Census of the United States. 1850. 4to. Washington, 1852.

Cervantes, Miguel de. El Buscapié, with Notes of Alfolgo De Castro. Translated by T. Ross. 8vo. London, 1849.

Chalmers, Thomas. (See Hanna, William.)

Chandler, P. W. American Criminal Trials. 2 vols. 8vo. Boston, 1841.

Channing, William E. Memoir of, with Extracts from his Correspondence and Manuscripts. 3 vols. 8vo. Boston, 1848.

Chapman, John R. Improved American Rifle. 12mo. New York, 1848.

Charrel, J. Traité de la Culture du Murier. 8vo. Grenoble, 1840.

Charrel, J. Traité des Magnaneries. 8vo. Paris, 1848.

CHAUCER, GEOFFREY. Selections from his Poetical Works, by Charles D. Deshler. 8vo. New York, 1850.

CHAUCHARD, M. Description of Germany, Holland, the Netherlands, Switzerland, Prussia, Italy, Sicily, Corsica and Sardinia. 4to. London, 1800.

CHINA, with some Account of Ava and the Burmese, Siam and Anam. 12mo. London, 1853.

CHORLTON, WILLIAM. The Cold Grapery. 12mo. New York, 1853. *Presented by the Author.*

CIST, CHARLES. Sketches and Statistics of Cincinnati in 1851. 8vo. Cincinnati, 1851.

CLARK, AARON. Manual of Parliamentary Practice. 12mo. New York, 1826.

CLARKSON, THOMAS. Biographical Sketch of Thomas Taylor. 12mo. London, 1847.

CLINTON, DE WITT. Discourse before the New York Historical Society. 8vo. New York, 1812.

CLINTON, DE WITT. Life of, by James Renwick. 12mo. New York, 1840.

COCKBURN, HENRY. Memorials of his Time. 8vo. New York, 1856.

COLLECTIONS of the Georgia Historical Society. Vol. 2, 8vo. Savannah, 1842.

COLLECTIONS of the New York Historical Society. Vol. 2, 8vo. New York, 1849.

COLLIER, J. PAYNE. Notes and Emendations to the Text of Shakespeare's Plays. 8vo. New York, 1853.

COLLINS, LEWIS. Historical Sketches of Kentucky. 8vo. Cincinnati, 1850.

COLTON, CALVIN. Life and Times of Henry Clay. 2 vols. 8vo. New York, 1846.

COMBE, GEORGE. Constitution of Man. 8vo. New York, 1852.

COMBE, GEORGE, R. Cox and others. Moral and Intellectual Science. 8vo. New York, 1848. *Presented by Messrs. Fowler & Wells.*

COMSTOCK, J. L. History of the Precious Metals. 12mo. Hartford, 1849.

CONCOURS D'Animaux de Boucherie en 1853. 8vo. Paris, 1853.

Congress of the United States.

American Archives, Fourth Series. A Documentary History of the English Colonies in North America, from 1774 to 1776. 6 vols. fol. Washington, 1837–1848.

American Archives, Fifth Series. A Documentary History of the United States of North America, from 1776 to 1783. 3 vols. fol. Washington, 1848–1853.

Andrews, Israel D. Report on the Trade and Commerce of the British North American Colonies, and upon the Trade of the Great Lakes and Rivers. 8vo. Washington, 1853.

Bache, A. D. Report of the United States Coast Survey. 2 vols. 8vo. and 3 vols. 4to. Washington, 1847, 1851–1853. *Presented by Professor Bache.*

Census. Seventh Census of the United States. 4to. Washington, 1852.

Census. Abstract of the Seventh Census of the United States. 8vo. Washington, 1853. *Presented by D. J. Browne, Esq.*

Census. Compendium of the Seventh Census of the United States. 8vo. Washington, 1854.

Commerce and Navigation of the United States. Reports of the Secretary of the Treasury. 21 vols. 8vo. Washington, 1823–1855.

Finances. Reports of the Secretary of the Treasury on the State of the Finances. 3 vols. 8vo. Washington, 1852–1855.

Foster, J. W., and J. D. Whitney. Report on the Geology of the Lake Superior Land District. 2 vols. 8vo. Washington, 1851. *Presented by Hon. Hamilton Fish.*

Emmons, George F. Statistical History of the Navy of the United States. 4to. Washington, 1853. *Presented by Hon. J. C. Dobbin.*

Herndon, William L., and L. Gibson. Exploration of the Valley of the Amazon. 2 vols. 8vo. Washington, 1853. *Presented by Hon. William A. Walker.*

History of the Rise, &c., of the Indian Tribes. (See Schoolcraft, H. R.)

Lee, S. P. Report and Charts of the Cruise of the United States Brig Dolphin. 2 vols. 8vo. Washington, 1854. *Presented by Hon. Hamilton Fish.*

Congress of the United States—Continued.

Light Houses. Report of the Light House Board upon the Condition of the Light House Establishments of the United States. 8vo. Washington, 1852.

Messages of the Presidents of the United States, and Accompanying Documents. 16 vols. 8vo. Washington, 1849–1856.

Reports of the Commissioner of Patents. 12 vols. 8vo. Washington.

Agricultural, 5 vols. 1850–1854.
Mechanical, 7 vols. 1851–1855.

Sabine, Lorenzo. Report on the Principal Fisheries of the American Seas. 8vo. Washington, 1853.

Sitgreaves, L. Report of an Expedition down the Zuni and Colorado Rivers. 8vo. Washington, 1853. *Presented by Hon. Hamilton Fish.*

Smithsonian Institution. Contribution to Knowledge. (See Smithsonian Institution.)

Smithsonian Institution. Tenth Annual Report of the Board of Regents. 8vo. Washington, 1856.

Stansbury, Howard. Exploration and Survey of the Valley of the Great Salt Lake of Utah. 2 vols. 8vo. Washington, 1853. *Presented by Hon. William A. Walker.*

United States Naval Astronomical Expedition to the Southern Hemisphere. (See Gilliss, J. M.)

Congressional Globe. Edited by John C. Rives. 12 vols. 4to. 1851–1855.

Constantinople and its Environs. By an American. Vol. 1, 12mo. New York, 1835.

Cormenin, Louis Marie de. History of the Popes, from St. Peter to Pius 9th. 2 vols. 8vo. Philadelphia, 1851.

Correspondence between John Adams and William Cunningham. 8vo. Boston, 1823.

Coste, M. Instructions Pratiques sur la Pisciculture. 12mo. Paris, 1853.

Coues, S. E. Outlines of Mechanical Philosophy. 8vo. Boston, 1851.

Country House. Poultry Yard, Piggery, the Ox and the Dairy. 12mo. London.

Coxe, William. Account of the Russian Discoveries between Asia and America. 4to. London, 1780.

CRABB, GEORGE. Technical Dictionary, or a Dictionary of the Terms used in all Arts and Sciences. 8vo. London, 1851.

CRAIK, GEORGE L. Outlines of the History of the English Language 12mo. London, 1851.

CRAYON, THE. A Monthly Journal of Art and Literature. 4to. New York, 1855.

CURTIS, GEORGE T. History of the Constitution of the United States. Vol. 1, 8vo. New York, 1854.

CURTIS, WILLIAM. Practical Observations on the British Grasses, &c. 8vo. London, 1805.

D'AGINCOURT, SEROUX. History of Art by its Monuments. 3 vols. in 1, fol. London, 1847.

Vol. 1.	Architecture,	73 plates.
" 2.	Sculpture,	51 "
" 3.	Painting,	204 "

DANA, JAMES D. Structure and Classification of Zoophytes. 4to. Philadelphia, 1846.

DANA, JR., R. H. Two Years before the Mast. 12mo. New York, 1840.

DANIEL, JAMES. Ship-owners' and Ship-masters' Directory to the Port Charges, Depths of Water, &c. 8vo. Aberdeen, 1843.

DARLINGTON, WILLIAM. Agricultural Botany. 12mo. Philadelphia, 1847.

DARLINGTON, WILLIAM. Memorials of John Bertram and Humphrey Marshall. 8vo. Philadelphia, 1849.

DARWIN, CHARLES. Geological Observations on South America. 8vo. London, 1846.

DARWIN, CHARLES. Geological Observations on Coral Reefs, Volcanic Islands, and on South America. 8vo. London, 1851.

DARWIN, CHARLES. The Structure and Distribution of Coral Reefs. 8vo. London, 1842.

D'AUBUISSON, J. F. Treatise on Hydraulics for the use of Engineers. Translated by Joseph Bennett. 8vo. Boston, 1852.

DAVIES, C. M. History of Holland and the Dutch Nation. 3 vols. 8vo. London, 1851.

DAVIS, JOHN FRANCIS. The Chinese; or the History of China and its Inhabitants. 2 vols. 12mo. New York, 1836.

DAVIS, MATTHEW L. Memoirs of Aaron Burr, with Selections from his Correspondence. 2 vols. 8vo. New York, 1855.

DAVY, JOHN T. Devon Herd Book. 8vo. New York, 1855. *Presented by Lewis G. Morris, Esq.*

DEBOW, J. D. B. Statistical View of the United States. (Compendium of the Seventh Census.) 8vo. Washington, 1854.

DE LA BACHE, SIR H. T. Geological Observer. 8vo. Philadelphia, 1851.

DE ONIS, D. LUIS. Memoir upon the Negotiations between Spain and the United States. Translated from the Spanish by Tobias Watkins. 8vo. Baltimore, 1821.

DE QUINCEY, THOMAS. Memorials and Other Papers. 2 vols. 8vo. Boston, 1856.

DEW, THOMAS. Digest of the Laws, Customs, Manners and Institutions of Ancient and Modern Nations. 8vo. New York, 1853.

DICKENS, CHARLES. Works of. 9 vols. 8vo. Philadelphia, 1853, viz.:

Pickwick Papers,	Bleak House,
Barnaby Rudge,	Sketches,
Martin Chuzzlewit,	Christmas Stories,
Oliver Twist,	Dombey & Son,
David Copperfield,	Hard Times.

DICTIONNAIRE Raisonné Universel des Arts et Metiers. 5 vols. 12mo. Paris, 1773.

DIDIER, FRANKLIN J. Letters from Paris and other Cities. 8vo. New York, 1821.

DIE ENTDECKUNG des Naturselbstdruckes oder die crfindung. (Natural Printing Process.) 2 vols. 4to. and 6 vols. fol. Vienna, 1854–1856. *Presented through Charles F. Loosey, Esq., Austrian Charge d'Affairs.*

DIRECTIONS for taking Meterological Observations. 8vo. New York, 1844.

DISSERTATION on the Numbers of Mankind in Ancient and Modern Times. 8vo. Edinburgh, 1753.

DODD, GEORGE. Manufactures of Great Britain. 3 vols. 12mo. London, 1844.

DONALDSON, JOHN. Treatise on Manures. 8vo. London, 1846.

DONNEGAN, JAMES. Greek and English Lexicon. 8vo. Boston, 1838. *Presented by F. W. Geissenhainer, Jr., Esq.*

DOUBLEDAY, THOMAS. Mundane Moral Government. 8vo. Edinburgh, 1852.

DOWNING, A. J. Architecture of Country Houses. 8vo. New York, 1851.

DRAINAGE. Lois et Documents relatifs au. 4to. Paris, 1854.

DUJEUX, M. J. B. C. Lois et Réglements en Vigueur, sur les Brevets, D'Intervention. 8vo. Bruxelles, 1846.

DUMAS, COUNT MATTHIEU. Memoirs of his Own Time. 2 vols. 8vo. Philadelphia, 1839.

DUNCAN, JONATHAN. The Religions of Profane Antiquity. 12mo. London.

DUNLAP, THOMAS. History of the New Netherlands. (New York.) 2 vols. 8vo. New York, 1839.

DUNLAP, WILLIAM. Memoirs of George Frederick Cooke. 2 vols. 18mo. New York, 1813.

DUTENS, LOUIS. An Inquiry into the Origin of the Discoveries attributed to the Moderns. 8vo. London, 1769.

DYCKE'S Dictionary of the English Language. 8vo.

DYER and Color Maker's Companion. 18mo. Manchester, 1850.

EADIE, JOHN. Early Oriental History. 12mo. London, 1852.

EATON, AMOS. Geological Text Book. 8vo. Albany, 1830.

ECKFELDT, JACOB R., and W. E. Dubois. Manual of Gold and Silver Coins of all Nations. 4to. Philadelphia, 1851.

EDINBURGH NEW PHILOSOPHICAL JOURNAL. 6 vols. 8vo. Edinburgh, 1848–1850.

EDINBURGH REVIEW; from 1834 to 1856. 20 vols. 8vo. New York.

EGAN, PIERCE. Boxiana, or Sketches of Ancient and Modern Pugilism. 3 vols. 8vo. London.

ELIZABETH, CHARLOTTE. The Seige of Derby, or the Sufferings of the Protestants. 12mo. New York, 1841.

ELLIS, GEORGE. Irish Ethnology, embracing an Outline of the Celtic and Saxon Races. 12mo. Dublin, 1852.

ELLIS, SARAH. Family Monitor; comprising the Women of England, the Daughters of England, the Wives of England, and the Mothers of England. 8vo. New York.

ELLIS, SARAH. Guide to Social Happiness, Pictures of Private Life, and a Voice from the Vintage. 8vo. New York. *Presented by E. Walker, Esq.*

EMMONS, GEORGE F. The Navy of the United States, from 1775 to 1853. 4to. Washington, 1853.

EMORY, W. H. Notes of a Military Reconnoissance from Fort Leavenworth to California. 8vo. Washington, 1848.

*ENCYCLOPÆDIA of Domestic Economy. 8vo. New York, 1849.

ENGLAND, Pictorial History of. 4 vols. 8vo. New York, 1846.

ENTERTAINING NATURALIST; or Popular Descriptions of Quadrupeds, Birds, Fishes, Reptiles and Insects. 12mo. London, 1851.

ESDAILE, JAMES. Natural and Mesmeric Clairvoyance. 12mo. London, 1852.

ESPY, JAMES P. Report on Meteorology. 4to. Washington, 1851. *Presented by Hon. William H. Seward.*

ESSAYS upon Art. The Old Masters and Modern Artists. 12mo. New York, 1849.

ETUDES sur les Colonies Agricoles. 8vo. Paris, 1854.

EXPOSITION Nationale des Produits de L'Industrie, Agricole et Manufacturiere, 1849.

FARADAY, MICHAEL. Lectures on the Non-Metallic Elements. Arranged, &c., by J. Scoffern. 12mo. London, 1853.

*FARMERS' DICTIONARY, or Cyclopædia of Agriculture. 2 vols. 8vo. Edinburgh, 1850.

*FARMERS' FRIEND; a Record of Recent Discoveries, Improvements and Practical Suggestions in Agriculture. 8vo. London, 1847.

FARMERS' MAGAZINE. 26 vols. 8vo. London, 1844–1856.

FARRIERS' MAGAZINE. Edited by James Carver. 8vo. Philadelphia, 1818.

FERGUSON, JAMES. Lectures on Select Scientific Subjects. Revised &c., by David Brewster and Robert Patterson. Vol. 2, 8vo. Philadelphia, 1814.

FERGUSSON, JAMES. An Inquiry into the True Principles of Beauty in Art. 8vo. London, 1849.

Fessenden, Thomas G. The Complete Farmer. 8vo. New York, 1851.

Fisher, Richard S. Book of the World. 2 vols. 8vo. New York, 1852.

Flint, Charles L. Agriculture of Massachusetts. 3 vols. 8vo. Boston, 1853–1855.

Fortune, Robert. Voyage Agricole et Horticole en Chine. 8vo. Paris, 1853.

Foster, J. W. and J. D. Whitney. Report on the Geology of the Lake Superior Land District. 2 vols. 8vo. Washington, 1851. *Presented by Hon. Hamilton Fish.*

Foster, Thomas C. Letters on the Condition of the People of Ireland. 8vo. London, 1847.

Fowler, O. S. Hereditary Descent; its Laws and Facts. 12mo. New York, 1851. *Presented by Messrs. Fowler & Wells.*

Fowler, O. S. Home for All; the Gravel Wall and Octagonal Mode of Building. 12mo. New York, 1854.

Fowler, O. S. Memory and Intellectual Improvement. 8vo. New York, 1852. *Presented by Messrs. Fowler & Wells.*

Fowler, O. S. Physiology; Animal and Mental. 12mo. New York, 1852. *Presented by Messrs. Fowler & Wells.*

Fowler, O. S. Practical Phrenology. 8vo. New York, 1853. *Presented by Messrs. Fowler & Wells.*

Fowler, O. S. Self-Culture and Perfection of Character. 8vo. New York, 1852. *Presented by Messrs. Fowler & Wells.*

Fowler, O. S. and L. N. Illustrated Self-Instructor. 12mo. New York, 1853. *Presented by Messrs. Fowler & Wells.*

Fox, Charles James. Speeches in the House of Commons. Edited by a Barrister. 8vo. London, 1853.

France. Compte Général de L'Administration de la Justice Criminelle. 2 vols. 4to. Paris, 1828–1831.

France. Statistique de Agricole. 4to. Paris, 1840.

France. Tableau Général du Commerce de la. 4 vols. 4to. Paris, 1831–1837.

*Franklin Institute. The Journal of. 60 vols. 8vo. Philadelphia, 1826–1856.

FREEMAN, EDWARD A. History of Architecture. 8vo. London, 1849.

FRENCH, B. F. Historical Collections of Louisiana. 8vo. Redfield, 1852.

GALLATIN, ALBERT. Sketch of the Finances of the United States. 8vo. New York, 1796.

GARVEY, M. A. The Silent Revolution; or, the Future Effects of Steam and Electricity. 12mo. London, 1852.

GASPARIN, CTE. DE. Cours D'Agriculture. 8vo. Paris.

GAY, JOHN. Poems on Several Occasions. 2 vols. 4to. London, 1720.

GEIJER, ERIC G. History of the Swedes. Translated by J. H. Turner. 8vo. London, 1850.

GENESEE FARMER; a Monthly Journal of Agriculture. 8 vols. 8vo. Rochester, 1845–1852. *Presented by W. H. Allis, Esq.*

GENIN, SYLVESTER. Selections from his Works. 8vo. New York, 1855.

GERVAIS, PAUL. Atlas de Zoologie. 8vo. Paris, 1844.

GILBART, J. W. Elements of Banking. 12mo. London, 1852.

GILBART, J. W. Lectures on Ancient Commerce. 12mo. London, 1853.

GILLESPIE, W. M. Manual of Road Making. 8vo. New York, 1851.

GILLIES, JOHN. History of the World. 3 vols. 8vo. New York, 1809.

GLENNY, GEORGE. Hand Book of Practical Gardening. 8vo. London, 1850.

GLYNN, JOSEPH. Rudimentary Treatise on the Power of Water. 12mo. London, 1853.

GODDARD, T. H. General History of Banking Institutions in Europe and America. 8vo. New York, 1831.

GOLD. (See Lectures.)

GORDON, THOMAS F. History of New Jersey. 8vo. Trenton, 1834.

GORDON, WILLIAM. History of the Independence of the United States. 4 vols. 8vo. London, 1788.

GRAHAM, THOMAS. Elements of Chemistry. 2 vols. 8vo. London, 1850.

GRANT, GEORGE. Life of Robert Bruce. 12mo. Dublin, 1849.

GRANT, ROBERT. History of Physical Astronomy. 8vo. London, 1852.

Great Britain. Tables of the Revenue, Population, Commerce, &c., of the United Kingdom and its Dependencies. Fol. London, 1834.

Green, Frances H. Analytical Class Book of Botany. 4to. New York, 1855.

Griffin, William N. Treatise on the Motion of a Rigid Body. 8vo. Cambridge, 1847.

Griffiths, John W. Treatise on Marine and Naval Architecture. 4to. New York, 1850. *Presented by the Author.*

Grove, W. R. Correlation of Physical Forces. 8vo. London, 1850.

Grover, Captain. The Bokhara Victims. 8vo. London, 1845.

Guide to Knowledge; or, Repertory of Facts. Edited by Robert Sears. 8vo. New York, 1852.

Guizot, M. Corneille and his Times. 8vo. London, 1852.

Gurowski, Count A. de. Russia as it is. 12mo. New York, 1854.

Gutzlaff, Charles. Sketch of Chinese History, Ancient and Modern. 2 vols. 12mo. New York, 1834.

*Gwilt, Joseph. Encyclopædia of Architecture. 8vo. London, 1851.

Gwilt, Joseph. Treatise on the Equilibrium of Arches. 8vo. London, 1839.

Haliburton, Thomas C. Rule and Misrule of the English in America. 8vo. New York, 1851.

Hall, S. C. Ireland; its Scenery, Character, &c. 3 vols. 8vo. London, 1850.

Hallez, Theophile. Memoires Secrets pour Servir a L'Histoire de la Cours de Russie. 8vo. Paris, 1853.

Hamilton, Alexander. Works. Edited by John C. Hamilton. 5 vols. 8vo. New York, 1851.

Hamilton, Sir William. Philosophy. Edited by O. W. Wright. 8vo. New York, 1853.

Hammond, Jabez D. History of Political Parties in the State of New York, and the Life and Times of Silas Wright. 3 vols. 8vo. Syracuse, 1848.

HANNA, WILLIAM. Memoirs of the Life, &c., of Thomas Chalmers. 8vo. New York, 1851.

HARCOURT, L. VERNON. Doctrine of the Deluge. 2 vols. 8vo. London, 1835.

HARDY, R. SPENCE. Manual of Budhism in its Modern Development. 8vo. London, 1853.

HARPER'S New Monthly Magazine. 13 vols. 8vo. New York, 1850–1856.

HARRIS, GEORGE. The Life of Lord Chancellor Hardwick. 3 vols. 8vo. London, 1847.

HARRIS, THADDEUS W. Treatise on Insects injurious to Vegetation. 8vo. Boston, 1852.

HARRIS, THOMAS. Life and Services of Commodore William Bainbridge. 8vo. Philadelphia, 1837.

HARTLEY, ROBERT M. Intemperance in Cities and Large Towns. 12mo. New York, 1851.

HASE, CHARLES. History of the Christian Church. 8vo. New York, 1855.

HASKOLL, W. D. The Clerk of Works and Young Architects' Guide. 18mo. London, 1849.

HAZEN, EDWARD. Popular Technology; or, Professions and Trades. 2 vols. 18mo. New York, 1850.

HEAD, SIR FRANCIS. A Faggot of French Sticks; or, Paris in 1851. 8vo. New York, 1854.

HEADLEY, J. T. The Lives of Winfield Scott and Andrew Jackson. 12mo. New York, 1852.

HEDLEY, JOHN. Practical Treatise on the Working and Ventilation of Coal Mines, with Suggestions on Mining. 8vo. London, 1851.

HENDERSON, E. The Vaudois; or, a Tour to the Valley of the Piedmont. 8vo. London, 1845.

HENFREY, ARTHUR. The Vegetation of Europe, its Condition and Causes. 12mo. London, 1851.

HENRY, JR., JAMES. Family and School Monitor and Educational Catechism. 12mo. New York, 1853.

HERBERT, EDWARD, LORD. Life and Reign of Henry the Eighth. 4to. London, 1672.

HERNDON, WILLIAM L. Exploration of the Valley of the Amazon. 2 vols. 8vo. Washington, 1853.

Herschel, Sir John F. W. The Admiralty Manual of Scientific Inquiry. 8vo. London, 1851.

Hildreth, S. P. Pioneer History. 8vo. Cincinnati, 1848.

History of an Irish Family. 18mo. Haddington, 1822.

History of the Imperial and Government Printing Establishment at Vienna. By one of its Members. 8vo. Vienna, 1851.

Hobart, Nathaniel. Life of Swedenborg. 12mo. Boston, 1845.

Hobhouse, M. Substance of Letters written at Paris during the Last Reign of the Emperor Napoleon. 8vo. Philadelphia, 1816.

Hoblyn, Richard D. Dictionary of Scientific Terms. 12mo. New York, 1850.

Hoby, James. Memoir of William Yates, with an Abridgment of his Life by W. H. Pearce. 8vo. London, 1847.

Hodge, Paul R. Analytical Principles and Practical Applications of the Expansive Steam Engine. 4to. London, 1839.

Holland, Henry R., Lord. Foreign Reminiscences. 12mo. New York, 1851.

Holmboe, C. A. Det norske Sprogs væsentligste Ordforraad sammenlignet med Sanskrit og andre Sprog af samme Æt. 4to. Vienna, 1852.

Homer. The Iliad. Translated by Theodore A. Buckley. 8vo. New York, 1856.

Hood, Edwin P. The Literature of Labor. 12mo. London, 1851.

Hooker, Worthington. Lessons from the History of Medical Delusions. 12mo. New York, 1850.

Horne, Thomas H. Diplomacy. 8vo. London, 1848. (See Polson, Archer.)

Hosking, William, Thomas Tredgold and Thomas Young. Treatise on Architecture, Building, Masonry, Joinery and Carpentry. 4to. New York, 1852.

Hoste, P. Paul. Treatise on Naval Tactics. Translated by J. D. Boswall. 4to. Edinburgh, 1834.

Hotchkin, James H. History of Western New York and of the Presbyterian Church. 8vo. New York, 1848.

Houssaye, Arsene. Men and Women of the Eighteenth Century. 2 vols. 8vo. New York, 1852.

Hovey, C. M. The Fruits of America. 4to. Boston, 1852. *Presented by the Editor.*

Howe, Henry. Historical Collections of Virginia. 8vo. Charleston, 1852.

Howison, Robert R. History of Virginia. 2 vols. 8vo. Philadelphia, 1846.

Huc, M. Journey through Tartary, Thibet and China. 2 vols. 12mo. New York, 1852.

Hughes, William. Manual of Geography, Physical, Industrial and Political. 8vo. London, 1852.

Hunt, Robert. Photography; a Treatise on the Chemical Changes produced by Solar Radiation. 8vo. London, 1851.

Hunt, T. F. Examplars of Tudor Architecture. 4to. London, 1841.

Hunt's Merchants' Magazine. 10 vols. 8vo. New York, 1852–1856.

Hunt's Universal Yacht List for 1850. 12mo. London.

Hurlbut, E. P. Essays on Human Rights and their Political Guarantees. 12mo. New York, 1850.

*Illustrated London News. 3 vols. fol. London, 1851–1852.

Importance of Literature to Men of Business. 12mo. London, 1852.

Ingersoll, Charles J. History of the Second War with Great Britain. 2 vols. 8vo. Philadelphia, 1852.

Inkersley, Thomas. An Inquiry concerning the Romanesque and Painted Architecture in France. 8vo. London, 1850.

Inquiry into the Difference of Styles in Ancient Glass Paintings, with Hints by an Amateur. 2 vols. 8vo. Oxford, 1847.

Institution for the Instruction of the Deaf and Dumb. Annual Reports, &c. 6 vols. 8vo. New York, 1821–1852.

International Monthly Magazine of Literature, Science and Art. 5 vols. 8vo. New York, 1850–1852.

Irving, Washington. Life of George Washington. 3 vols. 8vo. New York, 1855–1856.

Irving, Washington. Wolfert's Roost and other Papers. 8vo. New York, 1855.

James, Charles. Military Dictionary. 8vo. London, 1802.

Jameson, Robert. Mineralogy according to the Natural History System. 8vo. Edinburgh, 1837.

Jarves, James J. Italian Sights and Papal Principalities. 8vo. New York, 1856.

Jefferson, Thomas. The Writings of. Edited by H. A. Washington. 5 vols. 8vo. New York, 1853.

Jobard, J. B. A. M. Exposition de L'Industrie Belge. 8vo. Bruxelles, 1847.

Johnson, Jeremiah. Discourse on the Life of. By Samuel R. Johnson. 8vo. Brooklyn, 1854.

Johnston, J. F. Chemistry of Common Life. 2 vols. 8vo. New York, 1855.

Jones, Alexander. Historical Sketch of the Electric Telegraph. 8vo. New York, 1852.

Jones' Views of the Seats, Castles, &c., in Scotland. 4to. London.

Journal of Agriculture. 7 vols. 8vo. Edinburgh, 1849–1856.

Journal of Agriculture. Edited by John S. Skinner. Vol. 3, 8vo. New York, 1848.

*Journal of Design and Manufactures. 8 vols. 8vo. London, 1849–1852.

*Journal of the Franklin Institute. 13 vols. 8vo. Philadelphia, 1846–1852.

Journal of the Royal Agricultural Society of England. 2 vols. (6 and 8) 8vo. London.

Kaerle, Joseph. Lexicon Chrestomathiæ Targumico-Chaldaicæ. 8vo. Vienna, 1852.

Kane, Elisha K. The United States Grinnell Expedition in Search of Sir John Franklin. 8vo. New York, 1854.

Kane, Elisha K. Arctic Explorations. The Second Grinnell Expedition in Search of Sir John Franklin. 2 vols. 8vo. Philadelphia, 1856.

Keating, Jeoffry. History of Ireland. Translated by Dermo'd O'Connor. 8vo. Dublin, 1841.

Kellogg, Edward. Labor and other Capital. 8vo. New York, 1846.

KELLY, P. The Universal Cambist and Commercial Instructor. 4to. London, 1835.

KENRICK, JOHN. Ancient Egypt under the Pharaohs. 2 vols. 8vo. London, 1850.

KING, WILLIAM R. Obituary Addresses on the Death of. 8vo. Washington, 1854.

KINGSLEY, JR., CHARLES. Hypatia; or, New Foes with an Old Face. 8vo. Boston, 1855.

KIP, W. J. Early Jesuit Missions in North America. 8vo. New York, 1847.

KIRKLAND, C. M. Garden Walks with the Poets. 8vo. New York, 1852.

KLENCKE, M. Lives of Alexander and William von Humboldt. 8vo. London, 1852.

KNICKERBOCKER MAGAZINE. Edited by Lewis Gaylord Clark. 48 vols. 8vo. New York, 1833–1856.

KNAPP, F. Chemistry applied to the Arts and Manufactures. 3 vols. 8vo. London, 1848–1851.

KNIGHT, CHARLES. Cyclopædia of the Industry of all Nations. 8vo. New York, 1851.

KNIGHT, T. A. Treatise on the Culture of the Apple and Pear, and on the Manufacture of Cider and Perry. 12mo. London, 1813.

KNOX, R. Great Artists and Great Anatomists: a Biographical and Philosophical Study. 8vo. London, 1852.

KNOX, ROBERT. The Races of Men. 12mo. London, 1850.

KNOX, VICESIMUS. Christian Philosophy; or, the Evidence and Excellence of Revealed Religion. 8vo. London, 1824.

KOSSUTH, LOUIS. Kossuth in New England. 8vo. Boston, 1852.

LAING, SAMUEL. Observations on the Social and Political State of the European People. 8vo. London, 1850.

LAMARTINE, ALPHONSE DE. History of the Restoration of Monarchy in France. 4 vols. 8vo. New York, 1851.

LAMB, JOHN. Memoir of the Life and Times of. By Isaac Q. Leake. 8vo. Albany, 1850.

Lardner, Dionysius. Railway Economy. 8vo. New York, 1850.

Lardner, Dionysius. The Steam Engine, Steam Navigation, Roads and Railways. 8vo. London, 1851.

Lascallier, Baron. Trône Enchante, Conte Indien traduit du Persan. 8vo. New York, 1817.

Latham, R. G. Ethnology of the British Colonies and Dependencies. 12mo. London, 1851.

Latham, R. G. Ethnology of the British Islands. 12mo. London, 1852.

Latham, R. G. Ethnology of Europe. 12mo. London, 1852.

Lawrence, Richard M. Medical Electricity and Galvanism. 12mo. London, 1853.

Lawrence, Sir Thomas. Life and Correspondence. Edited by D. E. Williams. 2 vols. 8vo. London, 1831.

Laws and Treaties of the United States. A Synoptical Index of. 8vo. Boston, 1852.

Layard, Austen H. Discoveries in the Ruins of Nineveh and Babylon. 8vo. New York, 1853.

Lectures on Gold; for the Instruction of Emigrants to Australia. 8vo. London, 1852.

Lectures on the Results of the Great Exhibition of 1851. 8vo. London, 1852.

Lee, Samuel P. Reports and Charts of the Cruise of the Brig Dolphin. 2 vols. 8vo. Washington, 1854.

Lefebvre-St.Marie, M. G. Race Bovine Courte corne ameliorce dite Race de Durham. 4to. Paris, 1849.

Legaré, Hugh S. Writings of. 2 vols. 8vo. Charleston, 1846.

Lepsius, Richard. Discoveries in Egypt, Ethiopia and the Peninsula of Sinai. 8vo. London, 1852.

Leuchars, Robert B. Practical Treatise on Hot Houses. 8vo. Boston, 1851.

Lewis, George C. Treatise on the Methods of Observation and Reasoning in Politics. 2 vols. 8vo. London, 1852.

Lewis, Taylor. The Six Days of Creation. 8vo. Schenectady, 1855.

Lieber, Oscar M. The Assayer's Guide. 12mo. Philadelphia, 1852.

Liebig, Justus. Familiar Letters on Chemistry. 12mo. London, 1851.

LIEBIG, JUSTUS. Principles of Agricultural Chemistry. 8vo. New York, 1855.

LIEBIG, JUSTUS and H. KOPP. Annual Report of the Progress of Chemistry, &c. 3 vols. 8vo. London, 1847–1849.

LINCOLN, R. W. Lives of the Presidents. 8vo. New York, 1844.

LINDLEY, JOHN. The Vegetable Kingdom. 8vo. London, 1846.

LLOYD, HENRY. Lectures on the Wave Theory of Light. 8vo. Dublin, 1841.

LOBSTEIN, J. F. DANIEL. Treatise on the Semeiology of the Eye. 8vo. New York, 1830.

LOCKE, JOHN. Reasonableness of Christianity. 12mo. London.

LONDON JOURNAL. Edited by William Newton. 11 vols. 8vo. London, 1851–1856.

LONDON QUARTERLY REVIEW; from 1834 to 1856. 20 vols. 8vo. New York.

LONG, GEORGE. France and its Revolutions, 1789–1848. 4to. London, 1850.

LONGFELLOW, HENRY W. The Song of Hiawatha. 12mo. Boston, 1856.

LOSSING, B. J. Pictorial Field-Book of the Revolution. Vol. 2, 8vo. New York, 1852.

LOW, DAVID. Domesticated Animals of the British Islands. 8vo. London, 1845.

LYELL, SIR CHARLES. Principles of Geology. 8vo. London, 1850.

LYSTRUS, ALEXANDER. The Poetic Rambler, (in Greek.) 12mo. Athens, 1839.

MACAULAY, THOMAS B. History of England. Vols. 3 and 4, 8vo. 1855.

MACAULEY, M. Tales of the Drama. 12mo. Hartford, 1850.

MACFARLANE, CHARLES. A Geographical and Historical Account of Japan. 8vo. London, 1852.

MACFARLANE, CHARLES. Popular Customs, Sports and Recollections of the South of Italy. 12mo. London, 1846.

MACGILLIVRAY, WILLIAM. History of the Molluscous Animals of Scotland. 12mo. London, 1844.

MACHINERY. Collection of Drawings of American Machinery. By the American Engineering Society. Folio, New York, 1852.

MACNEIL, SIR JOHN. Progress and Present Position of Russia in the East. 8vo. London, 1838.

MAGAZINE of Horticulture, Botany, &c. Edited by C. M. Hovey. 3 vols. 8vo. Boston, 1850–1852.

MAGAZINE of Science and School of Arts. 12 vols. 8vo. London, 1844–1851.

MAISTRE, COUNT JOSEPH DE. The Pope considered in his Relations with the Church. 12mo. London, 1850.

MALCOLM, JAMES P. Miscellaneous Anecdotes of the Manners and History of Europe. 8vo. London, 1811.

MALTON, THOMAS. Complete Treatise on Perspective. Fol. London, 1776.

MANGLES, JAMES. Papers and Dispatches relating to the Arctic Searching Expeditions of 1850, 1851, 1852. 8vo. London, 1852.

MANN, JAMES. Bird-Keeper's Manual. 18mo. Boston, 1848.

MANSFIELD, EDWARD D. American Education; its Principles and Elements. 8vo. New York, 1851.

MANSFIELD, EDWARD D. Political Grammar of the United States. 12mo. New York, 1836.

MANTELL, GIDEON A. The Geology of the South East of England. 8vo. London, 1833.

MANTELL, GIDEON A. The Medals of Creation; or, First Lessons in Geology. 2 vols. 12mo. London, 1844.

MAPS. A Collection of Maps of the British Colonies. 8vo. London, 1776.

MAPS of the District of Columbia and City of Washington. 4to. Washington, 1852. *Presented by Hon. E. B. Hart.*

MARCOU, JULES. Geological Map of the United States. 2 vols. 8vo. Boston, 1853.

MARSHALL, JOHN. Royal Naval Biography. 12 vols. 8vo. London, 1823–1830.

MARTIN, R. M. Australasia. 4to. London, 1850.

MARYLAND Historical Society. Discourses and Addresses. 8vo. Baltimore.

MASSACHUSETTS Charitable Mechanics' Association. (See Transactions.)

MATHER, J. H. and L. P. Brockett. Geography of the State of New York. 12mo. Hartford, 1847.

MATTHEWS, J. M. The Bible and Civil Government. 12mo. New York, 1851. *Presented by H. Meigs, Esq.*

MAURY, M. F. The Physical Geography of the Sea. 8vo. New York, 1855.

MAURY, SARAH M. An Englishwoman in America. 8vo. London, 1848.

MCCORMICK, JR., R. C. Visit to the Camp before Sevastopol. 12mo. New York, 1855.

MCMULLEN, THOMAS. Hand-Book of Wines. 12mo. New York, 1852.

MCSHERRY, JAMES. History of Maryland. 8vo. Baltimore, 1849.

MECHANICS' MAGAZINE. Edited by J. C. Robertson and R. A. Brooman. 34 vols. 8vo. London, 1823–1856.

MEIGS, HENRY. List of Members of the National Institute of France, and also of the American Institute. Folio, 1853.

MEMOIRS of the Geological Survey of Great Britain. 3 vols. 8vo. London, 1846–1848.

MERCHANTS' MAGAZINE and Commercial Review. Conducted by Freeman Hunt. 8 vols. 8vo. New York, 1848–1852.

MERRIFIELD, M. P. The Art of Fresco Painting. 8vo. London, 1846.

MERRIWEATHER, F. SEYMOUR. Lives and Anecdotes of Misers. 12mo. London, 1850.

MERYON, EDWARD. The Physical and Intellectual Constitution of Man Considered. 8vo. London, 1836.

METROPOLITAN Catholic Almanac and Laity's Directory for 1850. 12mo. Baltimore, 1849.

MICHAUX, F. ANDREW. North American Sylva. 2 vols. 8vo. Paris, 1819.

MIDDLETON, HENRY. The Government and the Currency. 12mo. New York, 1850.

MIGNET, M. Notices Historiques. 2 vols. 8vo. Paris, 1853.

MILES, H. A. Lowell as it Was and Is. 18mo. Lowell, 1845.

MILLER, SAMUEL. Retrospect of the Eighteenth Century. 2 vols. 8vo. New York, 1803.

MILLER, THOMAS. History of the Anglo-Saxons from the Earliest Period to the Conquest. 8vo. London, 1848.

MILNOR, JAMES. Memoir of the Life of. By Rev. John S. Stone. 8vo. New York.

MINER, CHARLES. History of Wyoming. 8vo. Philadelphia, 1845.

MITCHELL, DONALD G. Dream Life; a Fable of the Seasons. 12mo. New York, 1852.

MITCHELL, JOHN. Treatise on the Falsification of Food. 12mo. London, 1848.

MITCHELL'S New Universal Atlas. Fol. Philadelphia, 1852.

MODERN GEOGRAPHY and General Gazetteer. By a Society. 3 vols. 8vo. Berwick, 1811.

MONTHLY JOURNAL of Agriculture. Edited by John S. Skinner. 2 vols. 8vo. New York, 1846–1848.

MONTHLY JOURNAL of Foreign Medicine. Edited by Squire Littell, Jr. 2 vols. 8vo. Philadelphia, 1828.

MORGAN, LEWIS H. League of the Iroquois. 8vo. Rochester, 1851.

MORTIMER, G. W. Pyrotechny; or, a Familiar System of Recreative Fire-works. 12mo. London.

MOSES, HENRY. Sketches of India. 8vo. London, 1850.

MOWATT, ANNA C. Autobiography of an Actress; or, Eight Years on the Stage. 12mo. Boston, 1854.

MULLER, J. Principles of Physics and Meteorology. 8vo. London, 1847.

MUNN, B. Practical Land Drainer. 12mo. New York, 1855.

MURPHY, JOHN G. Review of Chemistry for Students. 8vo. Philadelphia, 1851.

MURRAY, AMELIA M. Letters on the United States, Cuba and Canada. 8vo. New York, 1856.

NAPIER, JAMES. Manual of the Art of Dyeing. 8vo. Glasgow, 1853.

NAPOLEON DYNASTY; or, the History of the Bonaparte Family. By the Berkeley Men. 8vo. New York, 1852. *Presented by Messrs. Cornish and Lamport.*

NATIONAL MAGAZINE. Edited by Abel Stevens. 9 vols. 8vo. New York, 1852–1856. *Presented by the Publishers.*

NAUTICAL MAGAZINE and Quarterly Review. 3 vols. 8vo. New York, 1854–1856.

NAVY OF THE UNITED STATES. (See Emmons, George F.)

NEALE, F. A. Narrative of a Residence in the Kingdom of Siam. 8vo. London, 1852.

NEWMAN, FRANCIS W. Lectures on Political Economy. 12mo. London, 1851.

NEWTH, SAMUEL. Elements of Statics, Dynamics and Hydrostatics. 8vo. London, 1850.

NEW YORK CITY.

Alms House. Annual Reports of the Governors; from 1849–1855. 5 vols. 8vo. New York.

Reports of the Comptroller of the City of New York. 1826–1850. 8vo. New York.

Rode, Charles R. New York City Directory for 1853–1854, and 1854–1855. 2 vols. 8vo. New York.

Topographical Map of the City and County. 8vo. New York, 1855.

Valentine, David T. Manual of the Corporation of the City of New York. 1851–1856. 6 vols. 12mo. New York. *Presented by D. T. Valentine, Esq.*

Wilson, H. Trow's New York City Directory for 1853–1854, 1854–1855, 1855–1856. 3 vols. 8vo. New York.

NEW YORK ECCLESIOLOGIST. 3 vols. 8vo. New York, 1848–1852.

NEW YORK HOSPITAL. An Account of, together with the Charter, By-Laws and Regulations of that Institution, and those of the Bloomingdale Asylum for the Insane. 8vo. New York, 1856.

NEW YORK MEDICAL GAZETTE and Journal of Health. Edited by D. Meredith Reese. Vol. 1, 4to. New York, 1850.

NEW YORK MEDICAL and Physical Journal. Vols. 3, 4 and 5. 8vo. New York, 1824–1826.

NEW YORK REVIEW and Quarterly Church Journal. 10 vols. 8vo. New York, 1837–1842.

New York State.

Agriculture and Palæontology. Natural History of New York. 3 vols. 4to. Albany, 1853.

Documents of the Senate.

72d Session.	4 vols.	1849.
73d "	4 "	1850.
77th "	3 "	1854.
78th "	4 "	1855.
79th "	3 "	1856.

Documents of the Assembly.

72d Session.	4 vols.	1849.
73d "	10 "	1850.
77th "	7 "	1854.
78th "	9 "	1855.
79th "	7 "	1856.

Laws of the State.

77th Session.	8vo. 1854.
78th "	8vo. 1855.
79th "	8vo. 1856.

Nichol, J. P. Architecture of the Heavens. 8vo. London, 1851.

Niebuhr, B. G. Life and Letters of, with Essays on his Character and Influence. By the Chevalier Bunson and others. 8vo. New York, 1852.

Niles, Hezekiah. Principles and Acts of the American Revolution. 8vo. Baltimore, 1822.

Niles, Hezekiah. Weekly Register. 64 vols. (52 vols. 8vo. and 12 vols. 4to.) Baltimore, 1811–1848.

Noah, Henry M. Lectures on Electricity. 8vo. London, 1849.

Normandy, A. Commercial Hand-Book of Chemical Analysis. 12mo. London, 1850.

Normandy, A. Farmers' Manual of Agricultural Chemistry. 8vo. London, 1853.

Norris, Septimus. Hand-Book for Locomotive Engineers and Machinists. 12mo. Philadelphia, 1851.

Notes on the Roman Provinces. (Latin.) 4to. Published by Froben, at Basle, in 1552. *Presented by Alanson Nash, Esq.*

North American Review. General Index to, from 1815 to 1827. 8vo. Boston, 1829.

North British Review; from 1847 to 1856. 10 vols. 8vo. New York.

O'Callaghan, E. B. Documentary History of the State of New York. 4 vols. 8vo. Albany, 1849.

Odd Fellows' Offering for 1853. 8vo. New York. *Presented by E. Walker, Esq.*

Ohio State Board of Agriculture. Annual Reports from 1848 to 1854. 6 vols. 8vo. Columbus.

Oliphant, Laurence. The Russian Shores of the Black Sea. 12mo. New York, 1854.

Olmsted, Frederick L. A Journey in the Sea-Board Slave States. 8vo. New York, 1856.

O'Meara, Barry. Napoleon in Exile; or, a Voice from St. Helena. 2 vols. 8vo. London, 1827.

Oxberry's Dramatic Biography and Histrionic Anecdotes. 6 vols. 18mo. London, 1835.

Overman, Frederick. Mechanics for Millwright, Machinist, Engineer, Civil Engineer, Architect and Student. 12mo. Philadelphia, 1851.

Overman, Frederick. Treatise on Metallurgy. 8vo. New York, 1852.

Owen, David Dale. Report of a Geological Survey of Wisconsin, Iowa and Minnesota. 2 vols. 4to. Philadelphia, 1852.

Owen, Madden D. Revelations of Ireland in the Past Generation. 8vo. Dublin, 1848.

Owen, Robert Dale. Hints on Public Architecture. 4to. New York, 1849.

Pain, W. Carpenters' and Joiners' Repository. Fol. London, 1787.

Paine, Martyn. Discourses on the Soul and Instinct, and upon Organic Life. 12mo. New York, 1849. *Presented by the Author.*

Paine, Martyn. Institutes of Medicine. 8vo. New York, 1847. *Presented by the Author.*

Paine, Martyn. Materia Medica and Therapeutics. 12mo. New York, 1848. *Presented by the Author.*

Paine, Martyn. Medical and Physiological Commentaries. 3 vols. 8vo. New York, 1840. *Presented by the Author.*

Paine, Robert T. Writings, &c. of, with a Memoir by his Parents. 4to. New York, 1852. *Presented by his Parents.*

Palmer, John. Journal of Travels in the United States and Canada. 8vo. London, 1818.

Papers on Subjects connected with the Duties of the Corps of Royal Engineers. Vol. 10, 4to. London, 1849.

Pardee, R. G. Complete Manual of the Strawberry. 12mo. New York, 1854.

Parliament of Great Britain.

Parliamentary Reports. Catalogue of, from 1696 to 1834. Fol. London, 1834.

Reports upon Hand-Loom Weavers, Joint-Stock Banks, and the Commerce and Manufactures of Switzerland. Fol. London, 1836–1841.

Report on Import Duties. Fol. London, 1840.

Report on the Penitentiaries of the United States. By William Crawford. Fol. London, 1834.

Report on the Police of the Metropolis. Fol. London, 1828.

Parnell, Edward A. Elements of Chemical Analyses. 8vo. London, 1845.

*Patents. Commissioners' Reports of, from 1848 to 1855. 9 vols. 8vo. Washington. *Presented by the Commissioners.*

Peck, George W. Melbourne and the Chincha Islands, with Sketches of Lima and other places. 8vo. New York, 1854.

Peirce, Charles. Meteorological Account of the Weather. 12mo. Philadelphia, 1847.

Pellew, George. Life and Correspondence of Henry Addington, First Viscount Sidmouth. 3 vols. 8vo. London, 1847.

Perry, Matthew C. Japan Expedition. 8vo. New York, 1856.

Peter Schlemihl in America. 8vo. Philadelphia, 1848.

Peyton, George. How to Detect Counterfeit Bank Notes. 8vo. New York, 1856.

Pfeiffer, Ida. A Woman's Journey round the World. 8vo. London, 1852.

Pfeiffer, Ida. A Second Journey round the World. 8vo. New York, 1856.

PFEIFFER, IDA. Visit to the Holy Land, Egypt and Italy. Translated by H. W. Dulcken. 12mo. London, 1852.

PFEIFFER, IDA. Visit to Iceland and the Scandinavian North. 8vo. London, 1852.

PHILIP, ROBERT. The Hannahs; or, Maternal Influence on Sons. 12mo. London, 1846.

PHILIP, ROBERT. The Lydias; or, the Development of Female Character. 12mo. London, 1840.

PHILIP, ROBERT. The Marthas; or, the Varieties of Female Piety. 12mo. London, 1841.

PHILLIPS, HENRY. Companion for the Orchard. 8vo. London, 1831.

PHILLIPS, J. A. Metallurgy. 8vo. London, 1852.

PHILLIPS, WILLARD. Propositions concerning Protection and Free Trade. 12mo. Boston, 1850.

PHILOSOPHICAL MAGAZINE AND JOURNAL. Alexander Tilloch. Vol. 47, 8vo. London.

PICKERING, CHARLES. The Races of Man; with a Synopsis by John C. Hall. 12mo. London, 1851.

PICKETT, ALBERT J. History of Alabama; and also of Georgia and Mississippi. 2 vols. 8vo. Charleston, 1851.

PICKETT, WILLIAM VOSE. New System of Architecture. 8vo. London, 1845. *Presented by the Author.*

PICTORIAL History of England. By George L. Craik, Charles MacFarlane and others. 4 vols. 8vo. New York, 1846.

PIGOTT, CHARLES. Political Dictionary, explaining the True Meaning of Words. 8vo. London, 1795.

PINKERTON, J. Recollections of Paris in 1802, 1803, 1804, 1805. 2 vols. 8vo. London, 1806.

PITMAN, SIR G. Review of Great Britain. 8vo. New York, 1822.

PLAUTUS, Comedies of. Translated by H. T. Riley. 2 vols. 8vo. London, 1852.

PLOUGH, LOOM AND THE ANVIL. A Monthly Journal of the Industrial Arts. 3 vols. 8vo. New York, 1849–1851.

POITEAU ,A. Cours d'Horticulture. 8vo. Paris, 1848.

POLSON, ARCHER. Principles of the Law of Nations. 8vo. London, 1848.

Porter, Jane. Thaddeus of Warsaw. 8vo. London, 1845.

Porter, Jane. The Pastor's Fireside. 8vo. London, 1850.

Positive Medical Agents; a Treatise on the New Alkaloid Resinoid. 8vo. New York, 1855. *Presented by B. Keith, Esq.*

Postans, T. Personal Observations on Sindh. 8vo. London, 1843.

Potter, Alonzo, and George B. Emerson. The School and the Schoolmaster. 12mo. New York, 1854.

Potter, Joseph. Specimens of Ancient English Architecture. Fol. London, 1848.

Powell, Baden. View of the Undulatory Theory as applied to the Dispersion of Light. 8vo. London, 1851.

Practical Mechanic and Engineers' Magazine; from 1841 to 1847. 5 vols. 4to. London.

Practical Mechanics' Journal. 10 vols. 4to. London, 1848–1856.

Pratt, Anne. The Field, the Garden and the Woodland. 18mo. London, 1847.

Prescott, W. H. Robertson's History of Charles the Fifth. 3 vols. 8vo. Boston, 1856.

Prescott, W. H. The Reign of Phillip the Second, King of Spain. 2 vols. 8vo. New York, 1856.

Prichard, J. C. Six Ethnographical Maps, with Letter-press. Fol. London.

Pugin, M. Designs for Gold and Silver Smiths. 4to. London, 1836.

Putnam's Monthly Magazine of American Literature, Science and Art. 8 vols. 8vo. New York, 1853-1856.

Quarterly Journal of the Geological Society of London. 5 vols. 8vo. 1846–1850.

Queckett, John. Lectures on Histology. 8vo. London, 1852.

Queckett, John. Practical Treatise on the Use of the Microscope. 8vo. London, 1852.

Quimby, M. Mysteries of Bee-Keeping Explained. 8vo. New York, 1855.

RACHEL and the New World. A Trip to the United States and to Cuba. Translated from the French of Léon Beauvellet. 12mo. New York, 1856.

RAMSAY, J. G. M. Annals of Tennesee. 8vo. Philadelphia, 1853.

RANLETT, W. H. The Architect; a Series of Original Designs for Domestic and Ornamental Cottages and Villas. 2 vols. 4to. New York, 1847.

RAZ RAM. Essay on the Architecture of the Hindus. 4to. London, 1834.

READE, CHARLES. Peg Woffington. A Novel. 12mo. Boston, 1845.

RECORDS of the School of Mines, and of Science applied to the Arts. 2 vols. 8vo. London, 1852–1853.

RECUEIL des Lois et des Réglements en Vigueur, sur les Brevets d'Invention. By M. J. B. C. Dujeux. 8vo. Bruxelles, 1846.

REED, JOSEPH. Life and Correspondence of. By William B. Reed. 8vo. Philadelphia, 1847.

REGISTER of Officers and Agents in the Service of the United States. 8vo. Washington, 1853.

RENDELL, E. D. Antedeluvian History. 12mo. London, 1850.

RENDU, COMPTE. Concours d'Animaux de Boucherie. 8vo. Paris, 1849.

RENDU, VICTOR. Maladie de la Vigne. 8vo. Paris, 1853.

RENNIE, JAMES. Alphabet of Gardening. 12mo. London, 1836.

*REPERTORY of Patent Inventions. 11 vols. 8vo. London, 1851–1856.

REPORTS of Agricultural and other Societies. (See Transactions.)

REPORT of the British Association for the Advancement of Science. 8vo. London, 1845.

REPORTS of Cases in the Supreme Court of Rhode Island. By J. R. Angell and Thomas Durfee. 2 vols. 8vo. Boston, 1847.

REPORTS of the Commissioners of Patents. (See Patents.)

REPORT of the Commissioners upon the Application of Iron to Railway Structures. Fol. London, 1849.

REPORT on the Epidemic Yellow Fever, by the Sanitary Commission of New Orleans. 8vo. New Orleans, 1853.

REPORTS of the Committee of Arrangements concerning the New York Volunteers. 8vo. New York, 1851.

REPORTS of Explorations and Surveys for a Rail-Road Route from the Mississippi to the Pacific. 4to. Washington, 1855.

Reports by the Juries of the World's Fair, London, 1851. 8vo. London, 1852. *Presented by Her Majesty's Commissioners for the Exhibition.*

Reports of the Massachusetts Charitable Mechanics' Association. (See Transactions.)

Reports of the Ohio State Board of Agriculture. 6 vols. 8vo. Columbus, 1846–1854.

*Revised Statutes of the State of New York. Prepared by Hiram Denio and William Tracy. 2 vols. 8vo. Albany, 1852.

Rham, W. L. Dictionary of the Farm. Revised, &c., by W. and H. Raynbird. 12mo. London, 1853.

Rhode Island. Acts and Resolves of the General Assembly. 4 vols. 8vo. Providence, 1850–1856. *Presented by the Secretary of State of Rhode Island.*

Rhode Island. Public Laws of the State of Rhode Island and the Providence Plantations. 2 vols. 8vo. Providence, 1844–1852.

Rhode Island. Reports of Cases in the Supreme Court. By J. K. Angell and Thomas Durfee. 2 vols. 8vo. Providence, 1847–1854. *Presented by the Secretary of State of Rhode Island.*

Ricauti, T. J. Sketches for Rustic Work. 4to. London, 1848.

Richardson, Sir John. Arctic Expedition in Search of Sir John Franklin. 8vo. New York, 1852.

Rivero, M. E. and J. J. von Tschudi. Peruvian Antiquities. Translated by Rev. F. L. Hawks. 8vo. New York, 1853.

Robinson, Conway. Account of Discoveries in the West, and of Voyages to and along the Atlantic Coast of North America. 8vo. Richmond, 1848.

Robinson, P. F. Designs for Ornamental Villas. 4to. London, 1836.

Robinson, Samuel. Catalogue of American Minerals. 8vo. Boston, 1825.

Robson, Thomas C. Treatise on Marine Surveying. 8vo. London, 1834.

Roget, Peter M. The Sources of English Words and Phrases. 8vo. Boston, 1853.

Rordansz, C. W. European Commerce; or, Complete Mercantile Guide to the Continent of Europe. 8vo. London, 1818.

Ross, David. Opinions of the European Press on the Eastern Question. 8vo. London, 1836.

Ross, Joel H. What I saw in New York. 12mo. Auburn, 1851.

Roy, General. Military Antiquities of the Romans in North Britain. Fol. London, 1794.

Royer, M. L'Agriculture Allemande. 8vo. Paris, 1847.

*Rural Cyclopædia; or, a General Dictionary of Agriculture, &c. Edited by Rev. John M. Wilson. 4 vols. 8vo. Edinburgh, 1852.

Russell, John. Tour in Germany. 8vo. Boston, 1825.

Russell, John S. Steam and Steam Navigation. 12mo. Edinburgh, 1841.

Ryland, Arthur. The Assay of Gold and Silver Wares. 12mo. London, 1852.

Sabine, Lorenzo. Report on the Principal Fisheries of the American Seas. 8vo. Washington, 1852.

Sagra, Ramon de la. Anales de Ciencias, Agricultura, Comercio y Artes. 8vo. Havana, 1829–1831.

St. Fargeau, G. Histoire Litteraire. 12mo. Paris, 1852.

St. John, Samuel. Elements of Geology. 12mo. New York, 1851.

Salad for the Solitary. By an Epicure. 8vo. New York, 1853.

Sarmiento, D. F. Civilization et Barbarie. 12mo. Paris, 1853.

Schlegel, Frederick von. Philosophy of History; with a Memoir by J. B. Robertson. 8vo. Boston, 1855.

Schleiden, M. J. The Plant; a Biography in a Series of Lectures. Translated by A. Henfrey. 8vo. London, 1848.

Schoedler, F. The Book of Nature. 8vo. London, 1851.

*Schoolcraft, H. R. History, &c., of the Indian Tribes of the United States. 5 vols. 4to. Philadelphia, 1851–1855. *Presented by the Commissioner of Indian Affairs.*

Schouw, J. F. The Earth, Plants and Man, and Sketches from the Mineral Kingdom. By F. von Kobell. 8vo. London, 1852.

Selkirk, James. Recollections of Ceylon. 8vo. London, 1844.

Semmes, Raphael. Service Afloat and Ashore during the Mexican War. 8vo. Cincinnati, 1851.

SENIOR, NASSAU W. Four Introductory Lectures on Political Economy. 8vo. London, 1852.

SERINGE, N. C. Le Petit Agriculteur ou Elements de Botanique. 18mo. Lyons, 1841.

SGANZIN, M. J. Elementary Course of Civil Engineering. 8vo. Boston, 1837.

SHAW, HENRY. Book of Sundry Draughts; principally for Glaziers. 8vo. London, 1848.

SHEEP; their Breeds, Management and Diseases. 8vo. London, 1837. *Presented by Col. Thomas F. Devoe.*

SHEW, JOEL. Tobacco; its History, Nature and Effect on the Body and Mind. 12mo. New York, 1850.

SHIP MASTERS' Guide to the Baltic. 12mo. London, 1845.

SIBORNE, W. History of the War in France and Belgium in 1815. 8vo. Philadelphia, 1845.

SIDNEY, SAMUEL. The Three Colonies of Australia. 8vo. London, 1852.

SILLIMAN, BENJAMIN. American Journal of Science and Art. 74 vols. 8vo. New Haven, 1819–1856.

SILLIMAN, BENJAMIN. Journal of Travels in England, Holland and Scotland. 2 vols. New Haven, 1820.

SILLIMAN, BENJAMIN. Visit to Europe in 1851. 2 vols. 12mo. New York, 1854.

SIMPSON, JAMES H. Journal of a Military Reconnaissance from Santa Fé to the Navajo Country. 8vo. Philadelphia, 1852.

SITGREAVES, L. Expedition down the Zuni and Colarado Rivers. 8vo. Washington, 1853.

SITUATIM Economique et Agricole de l'Angleterre. 8vo. Paris, 1854.

SKETCHES and Tales of Barbadoes. 12mo. London, 1840.

SKINNER, JOHN S. (See Monthly Journal of Agriculture.)

SMEATON, A. C. Builder's Pocket Companion. 12mo. Philadelphia, 1850.

SMEE, ALFRED. Elements of Electro-Metallurgy. 8vo. New York, 1852.

SMITH, ADAM. An Inquiry into the Nature and Causes of the Wealth of Nations. 2 vols. 4to. London, 1776.

SMITH, CHARLES H. J. Parks and Pleasure Grounds. 8vo. London, 1852.

SMITH, GEORGE. Laboratory; or, School of Arts. 2 vols. 8vo. London, 1799.

SMITH, JOHN. Treatise on Cucumbers, Melons, &c. 12mo. Ipswich, 1833.

SMITH, SIDNEY. Wit and Wisdom of. By E. A. Duyckinck. 8vo. New York, 1856.

SMITH, THOMAS. Scientific Library. 6 vols. 24mo. New York, 1818.

SMITH, WILLIAM. Strategraphical System of Organized Fossils. 4to. London, 1817.

SMITHSONIAN INSTITUTION. Annual Reports. 2 vols. 8vo. Washington, 1854–1855.

SMITHSONIAN INSTITUTION. Contributions to Knowledge. 6 vols. 4to. Washington, 1851–1855.

SMOLLETT, TOBIAS. History of England. 15 vols. 8vo. London, 1758–1791.

SOPHOCLES. Tragedies, in English Prose. 8vo. New York, 1855.

SOUTHEY, THOMAS. Rise, Progress and Present State of Colonial Wools. 8vo. London, 1848.

SPALDING, M. J. Early Catholic Missions of Kentucky. 12mo. Louisville, 1844.

SPARKS, JARED. Replies to the Strictures of Lord Mahon and others. 8vo. Cambridge, 1852.

SPEECHES of Chatham, Sheridan, Erskine and Burke. Edited by a Barrister. 8vo. London, 1853.

*SPEED, JOHN. The History of Great Britain. Fol. London, 1611.

*SPIER'S and Surenne's French and English Pronouncing Dictionary. 8vo. New York, 1853.

SPIRITUALISM. By John W. Edmonds and George T. Dexter. With an Appendix by N. P. Tallmadge. 2 vols. 8vo. New York, 1853.

SPOONER, ALDEN. Cultivation of American Grape Vines and Making of Wine. 12mo. Brooklyn, 1846.

SPOONER, W. C. Veterinary Art. 8vo. London, 1851.

SPRAGUE, W. B. Visit to European Celebrities. 12mo. Boston, 1855.

SPURZHEIM, J. G. Education; its Elementary Principles. 12mo. New York, 1852. *Presented by Messrs. Fowler & Wells.*

SQUIER, E. G. Antiquities of the State of New York and the West. 8vo. Buffalo, 1851.

SQUIER, E. G. Nicaragua; its People, Scenery, Monuments, &c. 8vo. New York, 1853.

STANSBURY, HOWARD. Exploration and Survey of the Valley of the Great Salt Lake of Utah. 2 vols. 8vo. Washington, 1853.

STATESMAN'S MANUAL. The Addresses and Messages of the Presidents, &c. Compiled by Edwin Williams. 4 vols. 8vo. New York, 1852.

STEAM ENGINE INDICATOR and Improved Manometer, Steam and Vacuum Gauges; their Utility and Application. 12mo. New York, 1851.

STEEL'S SHIPMASTER'S ASSISTANT. Edited by Graham Willmore, George Clements and William Tate. 8vo. London, 1850.

STEPHENS, HENRY. The Book of the Farm; with Notes, &c., by John S. Skinner. 8vo. New York, 1847.

STEPHENS, JOHN L. Incidents of Travel in Central America, Chiapas and Yucatan. 2 vols. 8vo. New York, 1855.

STEPHENS, JOHN L. Incidents of Travel in Egypt, Arabia Petrea and the Holy Land. 2 vols. 12mo. New York, 1837.

STEPHENS, JOHN L. Incidents of Travel in Greece, Turkey, Russia and Poland. 2 vols. 12mo. New York, 1854.

STEWART, F. CAMPBELL. Hospitals and Surgeons of Paris. 8vo. New York, 1843.

STOCKHARDT, J. A. Chemical Field Lectures for Agriculturists. Edited by J. E. Teschemacker. 12mo. Cambridge, 1853.

STOCQUELER, J. H. India; its History, Climate, Productions and Field Sports. 12mo. London, 1853.

*STOCQUELER, J. H. Military Encyclopædia. 8vo. London, 1853.

STODDART, RICHARD. Tables for Computing the Solid Contents of Timber. 12mo. Edinburgh.

STRABO. The Geography of. Translated, &c., by H. C. Hamilton and W. Falconer. Vol. 1, 8vo. London, 1854.

STRAIN, ISAAC G. Sketches of a Journey in Chili and the Argentine Provinces in 1849. 8vo. New York, 1853.

STRYKER'S AMERICAN REGISTER. 3 vols. 8vo. New York, 1848 and 1851.

*STUART, ROBERT. Dictionary of Architecture. 2 vols. 8vo. Philadelphia, 1851.

STURGEON, WILLIAM. Scientific Researches in Electricity, Magnetism and Galvanism. 4to. London, 1852.

SULLIVAN, WILLIAM. Historical Causes and Effects, from 476 to 1517. 8vo. Boston, 1838.

SULLIVAN, WILLIAM. Public Men of the Revolution. 8vo. Philadelphia, 1847.

SUMMARY of the Principal Chinese Treatises upon the Culture of the Mulberry and the Rearing of Silk Worms. 8vo. Washington, 1838.

SWEDENBORG, EMANUEL. Divine Love and Power. 8vo. New York, 1851. *Presented by Charles Reed, Esq.*

SWEDENBORG, EMANUEL. Divine Providence. 8vo. New York, 1851. *Presented by Charles Reed, Esq.*

SWEDENBORG, EMANUEL. Heaven and Hell. 12mo. Boston, 1837. *Presented by Charles Reed, Esq.*

SWEDENBORG, EMANUEL. Life of, by Nathaniel Hobart. 12mo. Boston, 1845. *Presented by Charles Reed, Esq.*

SWEDENBORG, EMANUEL. Miscellaneous Observations. 8vo. London, 1847. *Presented by Charles Reed, Esq.*

SWEDENBORG, EMANUEL. Outlines on the Infinite. 8vo. London, 1847. *Presented by Charles Reed, Esq.*

SWEDENBORG, EMANUEL. Posthumous Tracts. 8vo. London, 1847. *Presented by Charles Reed, Esq.*

SWEDENBORG, EMANUEL. Principles of Chemistry. 8vo. London, 1847. *Presented by Charles Reed, Esq.*

SWEDENBORG, EMANUEL. True Christian Religion. 8vo. Boston, 1851. *Presented by Charles Reed, Esq.*

SYMONS, J. C. Arts and Artisans at Home and Abroad. 12mo. Edinburgh, 1839.

TALLIS' DRAMATIC MAGAZINE. 8vo. London and New York, 1850.

TAYLOR, BAYARD. Encyclopædia of Modern Travel. 8vo. New York and Cincinnati, 1856.

Taylor, Bayard. Eldorado; or, Adventures in the Path of Empire. 8vo. New York, 1854.

Taylor, Bayard. Journey to Central Africa. 8vo. New York, 1854.

Taylor, Bayard. Lands of the Saracen. 8vo. New York, 1855.

Taylor, James N. Sketch of the Geography, Political Economy and Statistics of France. 8vo. Washington, 1815.

Taylor, W. B. S. Manual of Fresco and Encaustic Painting. 12mo. London, 1843.

Teflen zur Statistik der Osterreischischen Monarchée, 1845–1846. Fol. Vienna, 1851.

Tennent, Sir James E. History of Modern Greece. 2 vols. 8vo. London, 1845.

TerReehorst, K. P. Polyglot Marine Dictionary, in Ten Languages. 4to. London, 1850.

Thaer, Albert D. The Principles of Agriculture. Translated by W. Shaw and C. W. Johnson. 8vo. New York, 1846.

Theophrastus. The Characters of; or, Physiognomical Sketches. 12mo. Boston, 1831.

Thompson, Zadoc. History of Vermont. 8vo. Burlington, 1842.

Thorpe, Charles. British Marine Conchology. 12mo. London, 1844.

Thomson, Thomas. History of Chemistry. 2 vols. 12mo. London, 1830.

Thomson, Thomas. Travels in Western Himalaya and Thibet. 8vo. London, 1852.

Thorburn, Grant. Life and Writings of. Prepared by Himself. 12mo. New York, 1852.

Thou, M. de. History of his Own Time. Translated by Bernard Wilson. Fol. London, 1729.

Thucydides. History of the Peloponnesian War. Translated by Rev. H. Dale. 2 vols. 8vo. London. 1854.

Timbs, John. Year-Book of Facts in Science and Art. 2 vols. 12mo. London, 1851 and 1853.

Tizard, W. L. Theory and Practice of Brewing. 8vo. London, 1850.

Torrey, John. A Flora of the Northern and Middle Sections of the United States. Vol. 1, 8vo. New York, 1824.

TRAITÉ de la Taille et de la Culture des Arbres Fruitiers. 12mo. Gand. 1851.

TRALL, R. T. Hydropathic Encyclopædia; a System of Hydropathy and Hygiene. 2 vols. 8vo. New York, 1853.

TRANSACTIONS of the Agricultural Societies of Massachusetts, from 1845 to 1855. 7 vols. 8vo. Boston.

TRANSACTIONS of the American Institute. 6 vols. 8vo. Albany, 1851–1855.

TRANSACTIONS of the Central Agricultural Society of Bavaria. 8vo. Munchen, 1855. *Presented by the Society.*

TRANSACTIONS of the Highland Agricultural Society of Scotland. 5 vols. 8vo. Edinburgh, 1851–1856.

TRANSACTIONS of the Manchester Geological Society. 8vo. London, 1841.

TRANSACTIONS of the Massachusetts Charitable Mechanics' Association, from 1837 to 1855. 2 vols. 8vo. Boston.

TRANSACTIONS of the Michigan Agricultural Society. 6 vols. 8vo. Lansing, 1849–1854.

TRANSACTIONS of the New York State Agricultural Society. 6 vols. 8vo. Albany, 1851–1855.

TRANSACTIONS of the Ohio State Board of Agriculture. (See Reports.)

TRANSACTIONS of the Pennsylvania State Agricultural Society. 8vo. Harrisburgh, 1854.

TRANSACTIONS of the Wisconsin State Agricultural Society. 2 vols. 8vo. Madison, 1851–1852.

TREDGOLD, THOMAS. Elementary Principles of Carpentry. 4to. Philadelphia, 1837.

TREDGOLD, THOMAS. Illustrations of Steam Machinery and Steam Naval Architecture. Fol. London, 1839.

TROLLOPE, T. A. A Summer in Brittany. 2 vols. 8vo. London, 1840.

TRUMAN, MATTHEW. Food and its Influence on Health and Disease. 12mo. London, 1842.

TURNBULL, WILLIAM. Treatise on Cast-Iron Beams and Columns. 8vo. London, 1832.

TYNG, STEPHEN H. Recollections of England. 12mo. London, 1847.

United States Commercial Register. By George Prior. 8vo. New York, 1851.

United States Economist. Thomas P. Kettell, Editor. 6 vols. 4to. New York, 1852–1856.

United States Magazine and Democratic Review, from 1847 to 1856. 18 vols. 8vo. New York.

United States Naval Astronomical Expedition to the Southern Hemisphere in 1849, 1850, 1851 and 1852.

Urquhardt, David. Progress of Russia in the North, South and West. 12mo. London, 1853.

Valentine, David T. Manual of the Corporation of the City of New York, from 1851 to 1856. 6 vols. 12mo. New York.

Van Santvoord, George. Lives and Judicial Services of the Chief Justices. 8vo. New York, 1854.

Vasey, George. Delineations of the Ox Tribe. 8vo. London, 1851.

Vericour, M. de. Historical Analysis of Christian Civilization. 8vo. London, 1850.

Veterinarian; or, Monthly Journal of Veterinary Science. Edited by Youatt and Percival. 7 vols. 8vo. London, 1844–1850.

Veterinary Record and Transactions of the Veterinary Medical Association. 2 vols. 8vo. London, 1849–1850.

Village and Farm Cottages. By William and Samuel D. Backus. 8vo. New York, 1855.

Villeroy, Felix. Manuel de l'Eleveur de Bêtes a Cornes. 12mo. Paris.

Vicat, L. J. Treatise on Mortars and Cements. Translated by J. T. Smith. 8vo. London, 1837.

Virgil. The Æneid of; with Notes, &c., by Charles Anthon. 8vo. New York, 1848.

Virgilii Maronis Carmina. 12mo. Philadephia, 1852.

WAISTELL, CHARLES. Designs for Agricultural Buildings. 4to. London, 1837.

WAIT, BENJAMIN. Letters from Van Dieman's Land. 12mo. Buffalo, 1843.

WALKER, B. J. Code of Signals for the Use of the Mercantile Navy. 2 vols. 8vo. London, 1851.

WASHINGTON, GEORGE. Life of. (See Irving, Washington.)

WASHINGTON, GEORGE. Revolutionary Orders of. Selected by Henry Whitney. 8vo. New York, 1844.

WATTERSTON, GEORGE, and N. B. Van Zandt. Tabular Statistical View of the United States. 4to. Washington, 1828.

WEALE, JOHN. Quarterly Papers on Engineering. Vol. 1, 4to. London, 1844.

WEBSTER, DANIEL. Obituary Addresses. 8vo. Washington, 1853.

WEBSTER, DANIEL. The Works of, with a Memoir. By Edward Everett. 6 vols. 8vo. Boston, 1853.

WEISBACH, JULIUS. Principles of the Mechanics of Machinery and Engineering. 2 vols. 8vo. Philadelphia, 1849.

WELLINGTON, DUKE of. Maxims and Opinions of; with a Biographical Memoir by G. H. Francis. 8vo. London, 1845.

WELLS, DAVID A. Year-Book of Agriculture. 8vo. Philadelphia, 1856.

WESTMINSTER REVIEW, from 1834 to 1856. 21 vols. 8vo. New York.

WHITE, GEORGE. Historical Collections of Georgia. 8vo. New York, 1855.

WHITE, GEORGE. Statistics of Georgia, &c. 8vo. Savannah, 1849. *Presented by Messrs. Pudney & Russell.*

WHITLOCK, N. Picture of London. 18mo. London.

WIGHTWICK, GEORGE. Palace of Architecture. 8vo. London, 1840.

WILKES, CHARLES. Voyage round the World. 8vo. New York, 1851.

WILKES, JOHN. Memoirs and Correspondence of, by John Almon. 5 vols. 12mo. London, 1805.

WILKES, JOHN. Speeches in the House of Commons. 8vo. London, 1786.

WILLAN, ROBERT. Vaccine Inoculation. 4to. London, 1806. *Presented by Dr. McComb.*

Williams, J. J. The Isthmus of Tehuantepec. 2 vols. 8vo. New York, 1852.

Williams, W. S. American Medical Biography. 8vo. Greenfield, Mass., 1845.

Williamson, W. D. History of the State of Maine. 2 vols. 8vo. Hallowell, 1839.

Wilson, James. Works of. 3 vols. 8vo. Philadelphia, 1804.

Wilson, John M. The Potato; an Essay on its Constitution, Diseases, Varieties, Cultivation and Uses. 12mo. Edinburgh, 1850.

With, Emile. Railroad Accidents; their Causes and the Means of Preventing them. Translated by G. F. Barstow. 12mo. Boston, 1856.

Woehler, Friederich. Analytical Chemists' Assistant, with Additions, &c., by Oscar M. Lieber. 12mo. Philadelphia, 1852.

Wonders of the World. Compiled by Robert Sears. 8vo. New York, 1851.

Wood, George B. Treatise on the Practice of Medicine. 2 vols. 8vo. Philadelphia, 1852.

Wood, Henry. Designs for Modern Furniture. Fol. London.

Woodward, Charles. Familiar Introduction to the Study of Polarized Light. 8vo. London, 1851.

Worcester, H. A. Sermons on the Lord's Prayer. 12mo. Philadelphia, 1850.

Worcester, Samuel. Sermons. 12mo. Boston, 1851.

Working Farmer, The. Edited by James J. Mapes. 4 vols. 4to. New York, 1849–1856.

World's Fair.

Art-Journal Illustrated Catalogue of the Great Exhibition. 4to. London, 1851.

Canada at the Universal Exhibition of 1855. 8vo. Toronto, 1856. *Presented by L. A. Huguet-Latour, N. P.*

Exhibition of 1851. First Report of the Commissioners. 4to. London, 1852.

General Report of the British Commissioners upon the New York Industrial Exhibition. 4to. London, 1854.

Reports of the Juries of the World's Fair. 8vo. London, 1852.

WORLD'S FAIR.

Official Descriptive and Illustrated Catalogue of the Great Exhibition of the Works of Industry of all Nations. 3 vols. 8vo. London, 1851.

Official Catalogue of the Great Exhibition. 4to. London, 1851.

Official Catalogue of the Articles from the German Zoll-Verein and Northern Germany. 12mo. London, 1851.

WORSAAE, J. J. A. An Account of the Danes and Norwegians. 8vo. London, 1852.

WORTLEY, EMMELINE S. Travels in the United States. 8vo. New York, 1851.

WRIGHT, G. N. Life and Campaigns of the Duke of Wellington. 4 vols. 8vo. London.

WRIGHT, SILAS. Life and Times of. By J. D. Hammond. 8vo. Syracuse, 1848.

WRIGHT, THOMAS. The Celt, the Roman and the Saxon. 8vo. London, 1852.

WYATT, THOMAS. Synopsis of Natural History, from the French of C. Lemmonnier. 8vo. Philadelphia, 1839.

YEAR-BOOK OF FACTS. Edited by David A. Wells and George Bliss, Jr. 3 vols. 8vo. Boston, 1850–1852.

YEAR-BOOK OF FACTS. (See Timbs, John.)

YOUATT, WILLIAM. The Horse, and an Essay on the Ass and the Mule, by John S. Skinner. 8vo. Philadelphia, 1843.

YOUATT, W. and W. C. L. Martin. Cattle; their Breeds, Management and Diseases. 8vo. New York, 1851. *Presented by Charles M. Saxton, Esq.*

YOUNG, J. R. Elements of the Integral Calculus. 12mo. London, 1831.

ZEITSCHRISF des niederasterreichischen Gewerb-Bereins. 4to. Vienna, 1849.

SYNOPSIS

OF THE

SUPPLEMENTARY

ANALYTICAL CATALOGUE.

INDEX

TO THE

SUPPLEMENTARY

ANALYTICAL CATALOGUE.

INDEX.

SUPPLEMENTARY

ANALYTICAL CATALOGUE.

THEOLOGY.

Sacred Writings, Natural and Miscellaneous Theology, &c.

Alcantara, Father. Treatise of Mental Prayer.
American Bible Society Reports.
American Board of Commissioners for Foreign Missions. Reports.
American Home Missionary Society Rep.
American Tract Society Reports.
Beattie, James. Immutability of Truth.
Berkeley, George. Works of.
Bogue, David. Theological Lectures.
Brewster, Sir D. More Worlds than One.
Combe, George. Constitution of Man.
Cormenin, Louis Marie de. History of the Popes.
Doubleday, T. Mundane Moral Governm't.
Duncan, J. Religions of Profane Antiquity.
Edmonds, John W. Spiritualism.
Harcourt, L. V. Doctrine of the Deluge.
Hardy, R. Spence. Manual of Budhism.
Hase, C. History of the Christian Church.
Hotchkin, J. H. The Presbyterian Church.
Kip, W. J. Early Jesuit Missions.
Knox, Vicesimus. Christian Philosophy.
Lewis, T. The Six Days of Creation.
Locke, J. Reasonableness of Christianity.
Maistre, Jos. de. The Pope Considered.
Matthews, J. M. Bible and Civil Governm't.
Meryon, Edward. Constitution of Man.
Metropolitan Catholic Almanac for 1850.
New York Ecclesiologist.
Philip, R. The Varieties of Female Piety.
Spalding, M. J. Early Catholic Missions.
Spiritualism. By John W. Edmonds.
Swedenborg, E. Divine Love and Power.
Swedenborg, E. Divine Providence.
Swedenborg, E. Heaven and Hell.
Swedenborg, E. Miscell. Observations.
Swedenborg, E. Outlines on the Infinite.
Swedenborg, E. Posthumous Tracts.
Swedenborg, E. True Christian Religion.
Vericour, M. de. Christian Civilization.
Worcester, Samuel. Sermons.
Worcester, H. A. The Lord's Prayer.

LAW.

National, Constitutional, Statute, Common, Mercantile and Military.

Acts and Resolves of the General Assembly of Rhode Island.
Angell, J. K. Reports of Cases.
Beck, T. R. Medical Jurisprudence.
Chandler, P. W. American Criminal Trials.
Clark, Aaron. Parliamentary Practice.
Curtis, G. T. History of the Constitution.
Dujeux, M. J. B. C. Lois et Réglements.
France. L'Administration de la Justice Criminelle.
Laws and Treaties of the United States. A Synoptical Index of.
Niles, Hezekiah. Principles and Acts.
Polson, A. Principles of National Law.
Public Laws of Rhode Island and the Providence Plantations.
Recueil des Lois et des Réglements en Vigueur, sur les Brevets d'Invention.
Reports of Cases in the Supreme Court.
Revised Statutes of State of New York.

SCIENCE.

Mental and Moral.

METAPHYSICS, ETHICS, LOGIC AND EDUCATION.

Beattie, James. Immutability of Truth.
Blake, J. L. Agriculture for Schools.
Blakeley, R. Historical Sketch of Logic.
Boardman, A. Defence of Phrenology.
Combe, George. Constitution of Man.
Combe, G. Moral and Intellectual Science.
Doubleday, T. Mundane Moral Governm't.
Edmonds, John W. Spiritualism.
Esdaile, James. Clairvoyance.
Fowler, O. S. Hereditary Descent.
Fowler, O. S. Intellectual Improvement.
Fowler, O. S. Physiology, Animal & Ment'l.
Fowler, O. S. Practical Phrenology.
Fowler, O. S. Self-Culture, &c.
Fowler, O. S. and L. N. Self-Instructor.
Hamilton, Sir William. Philosophy.
Hartley, R. M. Intemperance in Cities.
Henry, Jr., J. Family and School Monitor.
Hurlbut, E. P. Essays on Human Rights.
Institution for the Instruction of the Deaf and Dumb. Annual Reports, &c.
Lewis, G. C. Observation and Reasoning.
Locke, J. Reasonableness of Christianity.
Mansfield, E. D. American Education.
Meryon, Edward. Constitution of Man.
Paine, Martyn. The Soul and Instinct.
Philip, R. Lydias; or, Female Character.
Philip R. Hannahs; or, Maternal Influence on Sons.
Philip, R. Marthas; or, Female Piety.
Potter, A. The School and Schoolmaster.
Schlegel, F. Philosophy of History.
Shew, J. Effects of Tobacco on the Mind.
Spiritualism. By John W. Edmonds.
Spurzheim, J. G. Principles of Education.
Swedenborg, E. Divine Love and Power.
Swedenborg, E. Miscellaneous Observat'ns.
Swedenborg, E. Outlines on the Infinite.
Swedenborg, E. Posthumous Tracts.
Theophrastus. The Characters of.

Political Science. I.

GOVERNMENT AND POLITICS.

American Almanac.
American Review; a Whig Journal.
Annuaire des Deux Mondes.
Baldwin, J. G. Party Leaders.
Benton, Thos. H. Debates of Congress.
Benton, Thos. H. Thirty Years' View.
Bonynge, F. Future Wealth of America.
Congressional Globe. By J. C. Rives.
Democratic Review. By T. P. Kettell.
DeOnis, D. Luis. Negotiations between Spain and the United States.
Didier, F. G. Letters from Paris.
Doubleday, T. Mundane Moral Governm't.
Emmons, G. F. Navy of the U. States.
Foster, Thomas C. Condition of Ireland.
France. L'Administration de la Justice Criminelle.
Gurowski, Count. Russia as it Is.
Haliburton, T. C. Rule and Misrule in Am.
Hamilton, Alexander. Works of.
Hammond, J. D. Political Parties of N. Y.
Hobhouse, M. Letters written at Paris.
Holland, Lord. Foreign Reminiscences.
Horne, Thomas H. Diplomacy.
Houssaye, Arsene. Men and Women.
Hurlbut, E. P. Human Rights.
Jefferson, Thomas. Writings of.
Laing, Samuel. Observations on Europe.
Legaré, Hugh S. Writings of.
Lewis, G. C. Observation, &c., in Politics.
MacNeil, Sir J. Progress, &c., of Russia.
Madden, D. O. Revelations of Ireland.
Mansfield, Edward D. Political Grammar.
Matthews, J. M. Bible and Civil Governm't.
Middleton, H. Government and Currency.
Miller, S. Retrospect of the 18th Century.
Navy of the United States. (See Emmons.)
Niles, H. Principles, &c., of the Revolution.
Niles, Hezekiah. Weekly Register.
Oliphant, L. Shores of the Black Sea.
Pigott, Charles. Political Dictionary.
Pitman, Sir G. Review of Great Britain.
Polson, A. Principles of National Law.
Register of Officers and Agents in the Service of the United States.
Report on Police of the Metropolis.
Report on the U. States Penitentiaries.
Ross, D. The Press on the Eastern Question.
Sarmiento, D. F. Civilization, &c.
Speeches of Chatham, Sheridan and Burke.
Statesman's Manual. Addresses & Messages.
Stryker's American Register.
Urquhardt, David. Progress of Russia.
Valentine, D. T. Corporation Manual.
Webster, Daniel. Works of.
Wilkes, John. Speeches of.

Political Science. II.

POLITICAL ECONOMY, COMMERCE, MANUFACTURES, CURRENCY, STATISTICS AND PUBLIC DOCUMENTS.

Aiken, Arthur. Arts and Manufactures.
Almanak Administrativo. Mercantil e Industrial.
Alms House. Reports of the Governors.
American Almanac.
Andrews, I. D. Trade and Commerce of the British North American Colonies.

Art-Journal Illustrated Catalogue of the Great Exhibition.
Auxiliador da Industria Nacional.
Bache, A. D. United States Coast Survey.
Bankers' Magazine and Register.
Barlow, P. Manufactures and Machinery.
Beames, Thomas. Rookeries of London.
Bulletin de la Société d'Encouragement pour l'Industrie Nationale.
Canada at the Universal Exhibition of 1855.
Catalogue of the Great Exhibition, 1851.
Catalogue of the World's Fair, 1851.
Census of the United States, 1850.
Census. Abstract of the Census, 1850.
Census. Compendium of the Census, 1850.
Cist, C. Sketches and Statistics.
Commerce and Navigation of the United States.
De Bow, J. D. B. Statistical View.
Dissertation on the Numbers of Mankind in Ancient and Modern Times.
Documents of the Assembly.
Documents of the Senate.
Dodd, G. Manufactures of Great Britain.
Eckfeldt, Jacob R. Gold and Silver Coins.
Exhibition of 1851. First Report of the Commissioners.
Exposition de l'Industrie Belge.
Exposition Nationale des Produits de l'Industrie, Agricole, et Manufacturiere, 1849.
Gallatin, A. Sketch of the Finances.
General Report of the British Commissioners upon the New York Exhibition.
Gilbart, J. W. Ancient Commerce.
Gilbart, J. W. Elements of Banking.
Goddard, F. H. Banking Institutions.
History of the Imperial and Government Printing Establishment at Vienna.
Hunt's Merchants' Magazine.
Hunt's Universal Yacht List for 1850.
Journal of Design and Manufactures.
Journal of the Franklin Institute.
Kellogg, Edw'd. Labor and other Capital.
Kelly, P. The Universal Cambist.
Knight, Charles. Cyclopædia of Industry.
London Journal. By Wm. Newton.
Messages of the Presidents of the U. States.
Middleton, H. Government and Currency.
Newman, F. W. Political Economy.
Official Catalogue of the Articles from the German Zoll-Verein and Nor. Germany.
Official Descriptive and Illustrated Catalogue of the Great Exhibition, 1851.
Olmsted, F. L. Sea-Board Slave States.
Parliamentary Reports. Catalogue of.
Patents. Commissioners' Reports.
Peyton, George. How to Detect Counterfeit Bank Notes.
Phillips, W. Protection and Free Trade.
Pitman, Sir G. Review of Great Britain.
Register of Officers and Agents in the Service of the United States.
Repertory of Patent Inventions.
Reports Concerning the N. Y. Volunteers.
Reports of the Commissioner of Patents.
Reports of the Comptroller of New York.
Report on Import Duties.
Reports by Juries of the World's Fair, 1851.
Reports upon Hand-Loom Weavers; Joint Stock Banks; and the Commerce and Manufactures of Switzerland.
Report of the Light-House Board.
Reports on the State of the Finances.
Results of the Great Exhibition of 1851.
Rordansz, C. W. European Commerce.
Sabine, Lorenzo. Principal Fisheries.
Senior, Nassau W. Political Economy.
Situation Economique et Agricole de l'Angleterre.
Smith, Adam. Wealth of Nations.
Southey, Thomas. Colonial Wools.
Tableau Général du Commerce.
Tables of the Revenue, Population, Commerce, &c., of the United Kingdom and its Dependencies.
Taylor, James N. Political Economy.
Teflen zur Statistik der Osterreischischen Monarchée, 1845–46.
Trade and Navigation of Canada.
United States Commercial Register.
United States Economist.
Valentine, D. T. Corporation Manual.
Walker, B. J. Code of Signals.
Waterston, George. Statistical View.
White, George. Statistics of Georgia, &c.
With, Emile. Railroad Accidents.

Exact Science.

ARITHMETIC, MATHEMATICS AND ASTRONOMY.

Annual of Scientific Discovery.
Astronomical Expedition. (See Gilliss, J. M.)
Bagay, V. Tables Astronomiques, &c.
Brewster, Sir D. More Worlds than One.
Byrne, O. Practical Model Calculator.
Crabb, George. Technical Dictionary.
Directions for Taking Observations.
Espy, James P. Report on Meteorology.
Ferguson, James. Scientific Lectures.
Grant, Robert. Physical Astronomy.
Grove, W. R. Correlation of Forces.
Hackley, C. W. Treatise on Algebra.
Herschel, Sir J. F. W. Admiralty Manual.
Herschel, Sir J. F. W. Outlines of Astronomy.
Holtzapffel, C. Scales of Equal Parts.
Hutton, C. Course of Mathematics.
Muller, J. Physics and Meteorology.
Nichols, J. P. Architecture of the Heavens.
Peirce, Charles. Meteorological Account.
Schoedler, F. The Book of Nature.
United States Astronomical Expedition.
Stoddart, Richard. Tables for Computing.
Year-Book of Facts.
Young, J. R. Integral Calculus.

Natural Science. I.

NATURAL PHILOSOPHY AND CHEMISTRY.

Alban, E. High Pressure Steam Engine.
Allen, Zachariah. Mechanics of Nature.
Allen, Zachariah. Science of Mechanics.
American Polytechnic Journal.
Annual of Scientific Discovery.
Arnott, Neil. Smokeless Fire-Places, &c.
Ashburner, John. Dynamics of Magnetism.
Bartol, B. H. Marine Boilers.
Bourne, J. Catechism of Steam Engine.
Brande, Wm. Thos. Manual of Chemistry.
Brewster, Sir D. Treatise on Magnetism.
Coues, S. E. Mechanical Philosophy.
Crabb, George. Technical Dictionary.
D'Aubuisson, J. F. Treatise on Hydraulics.
Directions for Taking Observations.
Esdaile, James. Clairvoyance.
Dutens, Louis. Origin of Discoveries.
Espy, James P. Report on Meteorology.
Faraday, M. P. Non-Metallic Elements.
Ferguson, James. Scientific Lectures.
Francis, J. B. Hydraulic Experiments.
Garvey, M. A. Future Effects of Steam, &c.
Glynn, Joseph. Power of Water.
Graham, Thomas. Elements of Chemistry.
Griffin, Wm. N. Motion of a Rigid Body.
Grove, W. R. Physical Forces.
Gwilt, Joseph. Equilibrium of Arches.
Hazen, Edward. Popular Technology.
Hedley, John. Working, &c., of Coal Mines.
Herschel, Sir J. F. W. Admiralty Manual.
Hoblyn, Richard D. Scientific Terms.
Hodge, P. R. Expansive Steam Engine.
Hunt, Robert. Solar Radiation.
Johnston, J. F. Chemistry of Common Life.
Jones, Alexander. Electric Telegraph.
Knapp, F. Chemistry Applied, &c.
Lardner, Dionysius. The Steam Engine, &c,
Lawrence, R. M. Electricity and Galvanism.
Lieber, Oscar M. The Assayer's Guide.
Liebig, Justus. Agricultural Chemistry.
Liebig, Justus. Letters on Chemistry.
Liebig, Justus. Progress of Chemistry.
Lloyd, H. The Wave Theory of Light.
Machinery. Collection of Drawings of.
Magazine of Science. (London.)
Mechanic's Magazine. (London.)
Mortimer, G. W. Pyrotechny.
Muller, J. Physics and Meteorology.
Murphy, John G. Review of Chemistry.
Newth, Samuel. Statics, Dynamics, &c.
Noad, Henry M. Lectures on Electricity.
Normandy, A. Agricultural Chemistry.
Normandy, A. Chemical Analyses.
Overman, F. Mechanics for Machinists, &c.
Overman, F. Treatise on Metallurgy.
Parnell, Edward A. Chemical Analyses.
Phillips, J. A. Metallurgy.
Philosophical Magazine and Journal.
Pierce, Charles. Meteorological Account.
Positive Medical Agents; the New Alkaloid Resinoid.
Powell, Baden. Undulatory Theory.
Practical Mechanic's Journal.
Practical Mechanic and Engineers' Mag.
Quekett, John. Use of the Microscope.
Report on the Application of Iron to Railway Structures.
Russell, J. S. Steam and Steam Navigation.
Ryland, A. The Assay of Gold and Silver.
Silliman's Journal of Science.
Smee, Alfred. Electro-Metallurgy.
Smith, George. School of Arts.
Smith, Thomas. Scientific Library.
Smithsonian Institution. Contributions.
Steam Engine Indicator.
Stockhardt, J. A. Chemical Lectures.
Sturgeon, William. Scientific Researches.
Swedenborg, E. Principles of Chemistry.
Thomson, Thomas. History of Chemistry.
Tredgold, Thomas. Steam Machinery.
Turnbull, Wm. Cast Iron Beams.
Vicat, L. J. Mortars and Cements.
Weisbach, J. Principles of Mechanics.
Woehler, Frederick. Chemist's Assistant.
Woodward, Charles. Polarized Light.
Year-Book of Facts.

Natural Science. II.

NATURAL HISTORY.

Animal Biography.
Annals of the Lyceum of Nat. Hist., 1824.
Annual of Scientific Discovery.
Audubon and Bachman. Quadrupeds of America.
Balfour, J. H. Class Book of Botany.
Balfour, J. H. Manual of Botany.
Barrington, A. Physical Geography.
Beecher, H. W. Nature and Art.
Brown, Thos. Illustrations of Conchology.
Comstock, J. L. The Precious Metals.
Coste, M. Pisciculture.
Crabb, George. Technical Dictionary.
Curtis, Wm. Observations on Grasses, &c.
Dana, J. D. Structure, &c., of Zoophytes.
Darlington, William. Agricultural Botany.
Darwin, Charles. Coral Reefs, &c.
Darwin, C. Geological Observations.
Darwin, C. Structure, &c., of Coral Reefs.
De la Bache, Sir H. T. Geological Observer.
Directions for Taking Observations.
Eaton, Amos. Geological Text Book.
Entertaining Naturalist.
Espy, James P. Report on Meteorology.
Foster, J. W. Report on Geology.
Foster, J. W. Report on Lake Superior.
Geological Survey of Great Britain.
Gervais, Paul. Atlas de Zoologie.
Green, Frances H. Class Book of Botany.
Guide to Knowledge. By R. Sears.
Harcourt, L. V. Doctrine of the Deluge.

Harris, Thaddeus W. Treatise on Insects.
Henfrey, A. The Vegetation of Europe.
Hoblyn, Richard D. Scientific Terms.
Hovey, C. M. Fruits of America.
Jameson, Robert. Mineralogy.
Journal of the Geological Society.
Lectures on Gold.
Lewis, Taylor. The Six Days of Creation.
Lindley, John. The Vegetable Kingdom.
Low, David. Domesticated Animals.
Lyell, Sir Charles. Principles of Geology.
Macgillivray, Wm. Molluscous Animals.
Mantell, Gideon A. Geology.
Mantell, Gideon A. The Medals of Creation.
Marcou, Jules. Geological Map.
Maury, M. F. Geography of the Sea.
Michaux, F. A. North American Sylva.
Natural History of New York. Palæontology and Agriculture.
Owen, David Dale. Geological Survey, 1852.
Peirce, Charles. Account of the Weather.
Records of the School of Mines.
Report of the British Association for the Advancement of Science.
Robinson, Samuel. American Minerals.
Rural Cyclopædia. By J. M. Wilson.
Schleiden, M. J. The Plant, a Biography.
Schoedler, F. The Book of Nature.
Schouw, J. F. The Earth, Plants and Man.
Seringe, N. C. Elements de Botanique.
Silliman's Journal of Science.
Smith, William. Organized Fossils.
Smithsonian Institution. Contributions.
St. John, Samuel. Elements of Geology.
Thorpe, Charles. British Conchology.
Torrey, John. A Flora of the United States.
Vasey, G. Delineations of the Ox Tribe.
Williams, J. J. Isthmus of Tehuantepec.
Wonders of the World. By R. Sears.
Wyatt, Thomas. Natural History.
Year-Book of Facts.

Natural Science. III.

ANATOMY, PHYSIOLOGY, MEDICINE AND SURGERY.

Anderson, William. Surgical Anatomy.
Ashburner, John. Physico-Physiological Researches.
Beaumont, W. Physiology of Digestion.
Beach, W. Practice of Medicine.
Beck, T. R. Medical Jurisprudence.
Brewster, Sir David. Magnetism.
Bushman, J. S. Cholera and its Cures.
Combe, George. Constitution of Man.
Crabb, George. Technical Dictionary.
Cragie, David. Elements of Anatomy.
Donaldson, P. Medicine and Chirurgery.
Fowler, O. S. Physiology.
Hooker, Worthington. Medical Delusions.
Knox, R. Great Anatomists, &c.
Lawrence, R. M. Medical Electricity, &c.
Lobstein, J. F. D. Semeiology of the Eye.
Meryon, Edward. Constitution of Man.
Mitchell, John. Falsification of Food.
Monthly Journal of Foreign Medicine.
New York Medical Gazette.
New York Medical Journal.
Noad, H. M. Lectures on Electricity.
Paine, Martyn. Institutes of Medicine.
Paine, Martyn. Materia Medica, &c.
Paine, Martyn. Medical Commentaries.
Parnell, Edward A. Chemical Analyses.
Positive Medical Agents.
Report on the Epidemic Yellow Fever.
Sinclair, Sir J. Health and Longevity.
Shew, Joel. Tobacco; its Effects, &c.
Stewart, F. C. Hospitals and Surgeons.
Sturgeon, W. Electricity, Magnetism, &c.
Trall, R. T. Hydropathic Encyclopædia.
Truman, M. Food and its Influence.
Willan, Robert. Vaccine Inoculation.
Williams, W. S. Medical Biography.
Wood, George B. Practice of Medicine.
Year-Book of Facts.

ARTS.

Mathematical Arts.

ENGINEERING, ART OF WAR AND NAVIGATION.

Alban, E. High Pressure Steam Engine.
American Railroad Journal.
Annual Report of the State Engineer.
Bache, A. D. United States Coast Survey.
Bartol, B. H. Marine Boilers.
Belcher, Edward. Nautical Surveying.
Bourne, J. Catechism of the Steam Engine.
Bourne, John. Screw Propeller.
Brees, S. C. Second Series of Railway Practice.
Brees, S. C. Fourth Series of Railway Practice.
Byrne, O. Practical Model Calculator.
Chapman, J. R. Improved American Rifle.
Daniel, James. Shipmasters' Directory.
D'Aubuisson, J. F. Treatise on Hydraulics.
Directions for Taking Observations.
Emmons, G. F. Navy of the United States.
Emory, W. H. Military Reconnoisance.
Gillespie, W. M. Manual of Road Making.
Glynn, Joseph. Power of Water.
Griffiths, John W. Marine Architecture.
Hedley, John. Working, &c., of Coal Mines.
Herschel, Sir J. F. W. Admiralty Manual.
Hodge, P. R. Expansive Steam Engine.
Hoste, P. Paul. Naval Tactics.
Hunt's Universal Yacht List for 1850.
James, Charles. Military Dictionary.
Lardner, Dionysius. Railway Economy.
Lardner, Dionysius. The Steam Engine, Steam Navigation, Roads and Railways.
Machinery. Collection of Drawings.
Maury, M. F. Geography of the Sea.

Norris, S. Handbook for Engineers.
Overman, F. Mechanics for Engineers, &c.
Owen, David Dale. Geological Survey.
Papers of the Corps of Royal Engineers.
Practical Mechanic and Engineers' Mag.
Records of the School of Mines, &c.
Report on the Application of Iron to Railway Structures.
Report of the Aqueduct Department.
Reports of Explorations and Surveys.
Robson, Thomas C. Marine Surveying.
Russell, John S. Steam Navigation.
Sganzin, M. J. Civil Engineering.
Shipmasters' Guide to the Baltic.
Simpson, J. H. Military Reconnoisance.
Stansbury, H. Explorations and Surveys.
Steam Engine Indicator.
Steel's Shipmasters' Assistant.
Stocqueler, J. H. Military Encyclopædia.
Ter Reehorst, K. P. Marine Dictionary.
Tredgold, T. Steam Machinery.
Turnbull, W. Cast Iron Beams.
United States Nautical Magazine.
Walker, B. J. Code of Signals.
Washington, G. Revolutionary Orders of.
Weale, John. Papers on Engineering.
Weisbach, J. Principles of Engineering.
Williams, J. J. Isthmus of Tehuantepec.
With, Emile. Railroad Accidents.

Natural Arts.

AGRICULTURE AND VETERINARY.

Agriculture Française.
Agriculture and Palæontology.
Agriculture of Massachusetts.
Allen, L. F. Farm Houses, Cottages, &c.
American Agriculturist.
American Rose Culturist.
Anales de Agricultura, &c.
Annals of Horticulture.
Baucher, F. Training of Horses.
Blake, John L. Agriculture for Schools.
Blake, John L. Farmers' Cyclopædia.
Blake, John L. Farmers' Day-Book.
Bon Jardinier Almanach.
Browne, D. J. American Muck Book.
Buchanan, R. Culture of the Grape.
Burnham, George P. The Hen Fever.
Chorlton, William. The Cold Grapery.
Concours d'Animaux de Boucherie en 1853.
Coste, M. Pisciculture.
Country House, Poultry Yard, Piggery, &c.
Curtis, William British Grasses, &c.
Darlington, Wm. Agricultural Botany.
Davy, J. T. Devon Herd-Book.
Donaldson, John. Treatise on Manures.
Drainage. Lois et Documents.
Etudes sur les Colonies Agricoles.
Farmers' Dictionary.
Farmers' Friend; or, Recent Discoveries.
Farmers' Magazine. (London.)
Fessenden, Thomas G. Complete Farmer.
Flint, C. L. Agriculture of Massachusetts.
Fortune, R. Agricole et Horticole.
Fowler, O. S. Home for All.
France. Statisque de Agricole.
Gasparin, M. de. Cours d'Agriculture.
Genesee Farmer: a Monthly Journal.
Glenny, George. Practical Gardening.
Harris, T. W. Insects inj. to Vegetation.
Henfry, A. Vegetation of Europe.
Hovey, C. M. Fruits of America.
Hovey's Magazine of Horticulture.
Journal of Agriculture. By J. S. Skinner.
Journal of Agriculture. (Edinburgh.)
Journal of the Royal Agricultural Society.
Knight, T. A. The Apple and Pear.
Lefebvre-St. Marie, M. G. Race Bovine.
Leuchars, Robert B. Hot Houses.
Liebig, Justus. Agricultural Chemistry.
Low, David. Domesticated Animals.
Mann, J. Bird Keepers' Manual.
McMullen, Thomas. Book of Wines.
Michaux, F. A. American Sylva.
Munn, B. Practical Land Drainer.
Normandy, A. Agricultural Chemistry.
Ohio State Board of Agriculture.
Pardee, R. G. The Strawberry.
Patent Office Reports. Agricultural.
Phillips, H. Companion for the Orchard.
Plough, Loom and Anvil.
Poiteau, A. Cours d'Horticulture.
Pratt, A. The Field, the Garden, &c.
Quimby, M. Bee-Keeping.
Rendu, Compte. Concours d'Animaux.
Rendu, V. Maladie de la Vigne.
Rennie, J. Alphabet of Gardening.
Reports of the Ohio State Board.
Rham, W. L. Dictionary of the Farm.
Royer, M. L'Agriculture Allemande.
Rural Cyclopædia.
Schleiden, M. J. The Plant.
Seringe, N. C. Petit Agriculteur.
Sheep; their Breeds, Management, &c.
Situation Economique et Agricole.
Skinner, J. S. (See Monthly Journal.)
Smith, Charles H. J. Pleasure Grounds, &c.
Smith, John. Cucumbers, Melons, &c.
Spooner, Alden. Grape Vines, &c.
Spooner, W. C. Veterinary Art.
Stephens, Henry. The Book of the Farm.
Stockhardt, J. A. Field Lectures.
Summary of the Principal Chinese Treatises upon the Culture of the Mulberry, &c.
Thaër, Alvert D. Principles of Agriculture.
Traité de la Taille et de la Culture des Arbres Fruitiers.
Vasey, George. The Ox Tribe.
Veterinarian: a Monthly Journal.
Waistell, Charles. Agricultural Buildings.
Wells, D. A. Year-Book of Agriculture.
Wilson, John M. The Potato.
Working Farmer, The. By J. J. Mapes.
Year-Book of Facts.
Youatt, W. The Horse, Ass and the Mule.
Youatt, W. and W. C. L. Martin. Cattle.

Fine Arts.

DRAWING, PAINTING, ENGRAVING, SCULPTURE, ARCHITECTURE AND MUSIC.

Allen, Lewis F. Farm Houses, Cottages, &c.
Antiquarian and Architectural Year-Book for 1844.
Arnot, D. H. Gothic Architecture.
Art-Journal, The. (London.)
Art-Union, The. (London.)
Beecher, H. W. Star Papers.
Brandon, R. and J. A. Open Timber Roofs.
Britton, John. Architecture, Sculpture and Painting.
Brooks, S. H. Architecture.
Bryan, Michael. Painters and Engravers.
Bullock, J. Art of Building.
Bullock, J. Rudiments of Architecture.
Burnet, John. Discourses of Reynolds.
Burnet, John. Education of the Eye.
Burnet, John. Essays on the Fine Arts.
Burnet, John. Landscape Painting.
Bury, T. T. Rudimentary Architecture.
Crayon, The. A Journal of Art, &c.
D'Agincourt, Seroux. History of Art.
Die entdeckung des Naturselbstdruckes oder die erfindung.
Downing, A. J. Country Houses.
Essays upon Art: the Old Masters and Modern Artists.
Fergusson, James. Beauty in Art.
Fowler, O. S. Octagonal Building.
Freeman, E. A. History of Architecture.
Fulton, R. Paintings. (See Reigart, J. F.)
Gwilt, J. Equilibrium of Arches.
Gwilt, J. Encyclopædia of Architecture.
Haskoll, W. D. Young Architects' Guide.
History of the Imperial and Government Printing Establishment at Vienna.
Hunt, T. F. Tudor Architecture.
Hosking, Wm. Treatise on Architecture.
Hunt, Robert. Photography.
Inkersley, T. Architecture in France.
Inquiry into the Difference of Style in Ancient Glass Paintings.
Jones, M. Views of the Seats, Castles, &c.
Journal of Design, &c.
Knox, R. Great Artists, &c.
Malton, T. Treatise on Perspective.
Merrifield, M. P. Art of Fresco Painting.
Overman, F. Mechanics for Architects, &c.
Owen, Robt. Dale. Public Architecture.
Peyton, George. How to Detect Counterfeit Bank Notes.
Pickett, W. V. System of Architecture.
Potter, Joseph. English Architecture.
Pugin, M. Designs for Goldsmiths, &c.
Ranlett, W. H. The Architect.
Ráz, Ram. Architecture of the Hindus.
Ricauti, T. J. Sketches for Rustic Work.
Robinson, P. F. Ornamental Villas.
Shaw, Henry. Draughts for Glaziers.
Smith, Chas. H. J. Parks and Pleasure Grounds.
*Stuart, Robt. Dictionary of Architecture.
Taylor, W. B. S. Manual of Painting.
Vaux, C. Designs for Villas and Cottages.
Village and Farm Cottages. By Backus.
Waistell, C. Designs for Buildings.
Wightwick, G. Palace of Architecture.
Wood, Henry. Designs for Furniture.

Miscellaneous Arts.

MECHANICAL, CHEMICAL, DOMESTIC, &C.

Aiken, Arthur. Arts and Manufactures.
Allen, Lewis F. Out-Buildings.
Annual of Scientific Discovery.
Arnott, Neil. Smokeless Fire Places.
Artisan, The. A Journal of the Arts.
Baird, Robert H. Cotton Spinner.
Baucher, F. Horsemanship.
Black, William. Treatise on Brewing.
Buchanan, Robert. Wine Making.
Bullock, John. Art of Building.
Byrne, O. Spinner and Manufacturer.
Carpentry and Joinery; a Guide-Book.
Comstock, J. L. Precious Metals.
Crabb, George. Technical Dictionary.
Dictionnaire des Arts et Metiers.
Dutens, Louis. Origin of Discoveries.
Dyer and Color Makers' Companion.
Egan, Pierce. Boxiana.
Encyclopædia of Domestic Economy.
Fowler, O. S. The Gravel Wall.
Guide to Knowledge. By R. Sears.
Haskoll, W. D. The Clerk of Works.
Hazen, Edward. Popular Technology.
History of the Imperial and Government Printing Establishment at Vienna.
Hoblyn, Richard D. Dictionary of Terms.
Hosking, William. Building, Masonry, Joinery and Carpentry.
Hunt, Robert. Photography.
Johnston, J. F. Chemistry of Common Life.
Jones, Alexander. Electric Telegraph.
Knight, Charles. Cyclopædia of Industry.
Knight, T. A. Cider and Perry.
Lectures on Gold.
Leuchars, R. B. Hot Houses.
Lieber, Oscar M. The Assayer's Guide.
Mann, James. Bird-Keeper's Manual.
McMullen, Thomas. Hand-Book of Wines.
Mitchell, John. Falsification of Food.
Mortimer, G. W. Pyrotechny.
Munn, B. Practical Land Drainer.
Napier, James. Art of Dyeing.
Overman, F. Mechanics for Millwrights.
Overman, F. Treatise on Metallurgy.
Pain, W. Carpenters' Repository.
Pardee, R. G. The Strawberry.
Practical Mechanics' Journal.
Peyton, George. How to Detect Counterfeit Bank Notes.

Phillips, J. A. Metallurgy.
Pugin, M. Designs for Goldsmiths.
Queckett, John. Lectures on Histology.
Queckett, John. Use of the Microscope.
Quimby, M. Bee-Keeping.
Report on Hand-Loom Weavers.
Ryland, Arthur. Assay of Gold, &c.
Shaw, Henry. Book of Draughts.
Smeaton, A. C. Builders' Companion.
Smee, Alfred. Electro-Metallurgy.
Smith, George. School of Arts.
Spooner, A. Making of Wine.
Symons, J. C. Arts and Artisans.
Timbs, John. Year-Book of Facts.
Tizard, W. L. Theory, &c., of Brewing.
Tredgold, Thos. Principles of Carpentry.
Turnbull, W. Cast Iron Beams.
Vicat, L. J. Mortars and Cements.
Villeroy, F. L'Eleveur de Bêtes a Cornes.
Wood, Henry. Designs for Furniture.
Year-Book of Facts.

BELLES LETTRES.

Elementary.

DICTIONARIES.

Barclay, James. Complete and Universal English Dictionary.
Donnegan, J. Greek and English Lexicon.
Dycke's Dictionary of English Language.
Holmboe, C. A. Det norske Sprogs væsentligste Ordforraad sammenlignet med Sanskrit og andre Sprog af samme Æt.
Kaerle, Joseph. Lexicon Chrestomathiæ Targumico-Chaldaicæ.
Roget, Peter M. Thesaurus of English Words and Phrases.
Spier's and Surenne's French and English Pronouncing Dictionary.

Belles Lettres Proper. I.

POETRY AND THE DRAMA.

Æschylus. The Tragedies of.
Apuleius. The Works of.
Bryant, William C. Poems.
Chaucer, Geoffrey. Poetical Works.
Collier, J. Paine. Notes and Emendations.
Gay, John. Poems on Several Occasions.
Homer. The Iliad.
Johnson, Samuel. English Poets.
Kirkland, C. M. Walks with the Poets.
Longfellow, H. W. The Song of Hiawatha.
Lystrus, Alexander. The Poetic Rambler.
Odd Fellows' Offering for 1853.
Plautus. Comedies of.
Sophocles. Tragedies in English Prose.
Virgil. The Æneïd of.
Virgilii Maronis Carmina.

Belles Lettres Proper. II.

LETTERS, ESSAYS AND ORATIONS.

Addison, Joseph. Dramatic Works.
Addison, Joseph. Works of.
Aiken, J. Letters on Various Topics.
Apuleius. The Works of.
Athenæum, The.
Bailey, Samuel. Discourses.
Becket, Andrew. Prose Miscellanies.
Beecher, Henry Ward. Star Papers.
Berkeley, George. The Works of.
Berrington, Joseph. Literary History.
Boyd, Sir Wm. History of Literature.
Burr, Aaron. Correspondence of.
Campan, Madame. Journal Anecdotique de.
Campbell, Thomas. Letters, &c., of.
Channing, William E. Extracts from.
Clinton, De Witt. Discourse before the N. Y. Historical Society.
Correspondence between John Adams and William Cunningham.
Craik, George L. The English Language.
De Quincey, T. Memorials and Papers.
Dickens, Charles. The Works of.
Didier, Franklin J. Letters from Paris.
Fox, Charles J. Speeches in the House of Commons.
Genin, S. Selections from his Works.
Hamilton, Alexander. Works of.
Hobhouse, M. Substance of Letters.
Hood, Edwin P. The Literature of Labor.
Importance of Literature to Men of Business.
Jefferson, Thomas. The Writings of.
Johnson, Samuel. The English Poets.
King, William R. Obituary Addresses on.
Kossuth in New England.
Lawrence, Sir Thos. Correspondence of.
Legare, Hugh S. Writings of.
Macauley, M. Tales of the Drama.
Malcolm, J. P. Miscellaneous Anecdotes.
Niebuhr, B. G. Letters, &c., of.
Oxberry's Dramatic Anecdotes.
Paine, Robert T. Writings, &c., of.
Sidmouth, Lord. Correspondence of.
Smith, Sidney. Wit and Wisdom.
Speeches of Chatham, Sheridan, Erskine and Burke.
St. Fargeau, G. de. Histoire Litteraire.
Thorburn, Grant. Writings of.
Webster, Daniel. Obituary Addresses.
Webster, Daniel. Works of.
Wellington, Duke of. Maxims and Opinions.
Wilkes, John. Speeches in the House of Commons.
Wilkes, John. Correspondence of.
Wilson, James. Works of.

GEOGRAPHY, VOYAGES AND TRAVELS.

Geography, Voyages, Travels, &c. I.

ASIA, AFRICA AND UNIVERSAL.

Bonomi, Joseph. Nineveh and its Palaces.
Browne, J. Ross. Journey of the Frangi.
Browne, J. Ross. Yusef.
Burton, Richard F. Sindh.
Burton, Richard F. Valley of the Indus.
Cabot, S. Maritime Discovery.
China, with some Account of Ava.
Coxe, William. Russian Discoveries.
Fisher, Richard S. Book of the World.
Fortune, Robert. Voyage en Chine.
Grover, Capt. The Bokhara Victims.
Huc, M. Tartary, Thibet and China.
Kane, Elisha K. Arctic Explorations.
Layard, Austen H. Nineveh and Babylon.
Lepsius, Richard. Egypt, Ethiopia, &c.
MacFarlane, Charles. Account of Japan.
Mangles, James. Arctic Expeditions.
Martin, R. M. Australasia.
McCormick, Jr., R. C. Visit to Sevastopol.
Mitchell's New Universal Atlas.
Modern Geography and General Gazetteer.
Moses, Henry. Sketches of India.
Neale, F. A. Kingdom of Siam.
Notes on the Roman Provinces.
Peck, George W. Melbourne and Chincha Islands.
Perry, Matthew C. Japan Expedition.
Pfeiffer, Ida. Journey round the World.
Pfeiffer, Ida. Second Journey.
Pfeiffer, Ida. The Holy Land and Egypt.
Postans, T. Observations on Sinah.
Richardson, Sir John. Arctic Expedition.
Selkirk, James. Recollections of Ceylon.
Sidney, S. The Colonies of Australia.
Sketches and Tales of Barbados.
Stephens, John L. Egypt and Arabia-Petrea.
Stephens, John L. Greece, Turkey, Russia and Poland.
Stocqueler, J. H. India.
Strabo. The Geography of.
Taylor, Bayard. Central Africa.
Taylor, Bayard. Cyclopædia of Travel.
Taylor, Bayard. Lands of the Saracen.
Thompson, T. Western Himalaya and Thibet.
Wait, B. Letters from Van Diemans' Land.
Wilkes, C. Voyage round the World.

Geography, Voyages, Travels, &c. II.

EUROPE.

Beames, Thomas. Rookeries of London.
British Gazetteer and Road-Book.
Chauchard, M. Description of Germany, Holland, the Netherlands, Switzerland, Prussia, Italy, Sicily, Corsica and Sardinia.
Constantinople and its Environs.
Foster, Thomas C. Condition of Ireland.
Hall, S. C. Ireland; its Scenery, &c.
Henderson, E. The Vaudois.
Holland, Lord. Foreign Reminiscences.
Jarves, James J. Italian Sights.
Jones' Views of Seats, Castles, &c.
MacFarland, Charles. South of Italy.
Oliphant, L. Shores of the Black Sea.
Pfeiffer, Ida. Iceland and the Scandinavian North.
Pinkerton, J. Recollections of Paris.
Russell, John. Tour in Germany.
Silliman, Benj. England and Holland.
Silliman, Benj. Visit to Europe.
Sprague, W. B. European Celebrities.
Symons, J. C. Arts and Artisans.
Taylor, J. N. Geography of France.
Trolloppe, T. A. Summer in Brittany.
Tyng, Steph. H. Recollections of England.
Whitlock, N. Picture of London.

Geography, Voyages, Travels, &c. III.

AMERICA.

Beltrami, J. C. Le Mexique.
Bonelli, L. H. de. Travels in Bolivia, &c.
Bremer, F. Homes of the New World.
Herndon, W. L. Valley of the Amazon.
Kane, Elisha K. The United States Grinnell Expedition.
Kane, Elisha K. Arctic Explorations, The Second Grinnell Expedition.
Kip, W. J. Early Jesuit Missions.
Lee, S. P. Cruise of the Dolphin.
Mangles, James. Arctic Expeditions.
Maps of the British Colonies.
Maps of the District of Columbia and City of Washington.
Mather, J. H. Geography of New York.
Maury, S. M. English Woman in America.
Miles, H. A. Lowell.
Murray, Amelia M. The United States, Cuba and Canada.
Olmsted, F. L. The Sea-Board Slave States.
Palmer, John. The United States and Canada.
Rachel and the New World.
Richardson, Sir John. Arctic Expedition.
Rivero, M. E. Peruvian Antiquities.
Robinson, Conway. Account of Discoveries.
Ross, Joel H. What I Saw in New York.
Semmes, Raphael. Afloat and Ashore.
Simpson, J. H. Santa Fé and the Navajo Country.
Sitgreaves, L. Expedition down the Zuni and Colorado Rivers.

Spalding, M. J. Missions in Kentucky.
Squier, E. G. Nicaragua.
Stansbury, Howard. Valley of the Great Salt Lake of Utah.
Stephens, John L. Central America, Chiapas and Yucatan.
Strain, Isaac G. Chili and the Argentine Provinces in 1849.
Taylor, Bayard. Eldorado.
Topographical Map of the City and County of New York.
United States Naval Astronomical Expedition.
Williams, J. J. Isthmus of Tehuantepec.
Wortley, Emmeline S. The United States.

HISTORY.

History. I.

ANCIENT, UNIVERSAL, ANTIQUITIES, ETHNOLOGY, &c.

Anquetil, M. Universal History.
Bayle, Peter. Critical Dictionary.
Bonomi, Joseph. Nineveh and its Palaces.
Boyle, Henry. Universal Chronologist.
Davis, J. F. History of China.
Dew, T. Ancient and Modern Nations.
Dutens, L. Origin of Discoveries.
Eadie, John. Oriental History.
Ellis, George. Irish Ethnology.
Gillies, John. History of the World.
Gutzlaff, Charles. Chinese History.
Kenrick, John. Ancient Egypt.
Knox, Robt. The Races of Men.
Latham, R. G. Ethnology of the British Colonies and Dependencies.
Latham, R. G. Ethnology of the British Islands.
Latham, R. G. Ethnology of Europe.
Layard, A. H. Nineveh and Babylon.
Lepsius, Richard. Egypt, Ethiopia, &c.
MacFarlane, Charles. Account of Japan.
Miller, Thomas. The Anglo-Saxons.
Pickering, Charles. The Races of Man.
Prichard, J. C. Ethnographical Maps.
Rendell, E. D. Antedeluvian History.
Schlegel, F. von. Philosophy of History.
Stockqueler, J. H. India; its History, &c.
Sullivan, Wm. Hist., Causes and Effects.
Thucydides. The Peloponnesian War.
Vericour, M. de. Historical Analysis.
Worsaae, J. J. A. Danes and Norwegians.
Wright, Thomas. The Celt, the Roman and the Saxon.

History. II.

EUROPE.

Arnault, M. F. Memoirs of Napoleon.
Baker, Richard. Kings of England.
Bensley, B. Henry the Eighth.
Berrington, Joseph. The Middle Ages.
Bodin, Felix. History of France.
Cormenin, L. M. de. History of the Popes.
Davies, C. M. History of Holland.
Dew, T. Ancient and Modern Nations.
Dunlap, Thomas. New Netherlands.
Elizabeth, Charlotte. The Siege of Derby.
England. Pictorial History of.
Geijer, Eric G. History of the Swedes.
Gurowski, Count. Russia as it Is.
Hallez, Theophile. L'Histoire de la Cours de Russie.
Henry the Eighth. (See Herbert, Lord.)
Keating, Jeoffry. History of Ireland.
Lamartine, A. de. Hist. of the Restoration.
Long, G. France and its Revolutions.
Macaulay, Thomas B. History of England.
MacFarlane, Charles. Account of Japan.
MacNeil, Sir John. Position of Russia.
Malcolm, James P. History of Europe.
Mignet, M. Notices Historiques.
Miller, Samuel. The Eighteenth Century.
Miller, Thomas. The Anglo-Saxons.
Napoleon Dynasty; or, Bonaparte Family.
Notes on the Roman Provinces, 1552.
O'Meara, Barry. Napoleon in Exile.
Pictorial History of England.
Pitman, Sir G. Great Britain.
Prescott, W. H. Charles the Fifth.
Prescott, W. H. Phillip the Second.
Roy, General. Military Antiquities.
Siborne, W. The War in France and Belgium.
Smollett, Tobias. History of England.
Speed, John. History of Great Britain.
Tennent, Sir James E. Modern Greece.
Thou, M. de. History of his own Time.
Wellington, Duke of. Campaigns of.

History. III.

AMERICA.

American Archives. By Peter Force.
Arthur, T. S. History of Georgia.
Arthur, T. S. History of Kentucky.
Arthur, T. S. History of Virginia.
Bancroft, G. History of the U. States.
Beltrami, J. C. Le Mexique.
Benton, Thomas H. Thirty Years' View.
Brown, Henry. History of Illinois.
Cist, Charles. Cincinnati.
Collections of the Georgia Historical Society.

Collections of the New York Historical Society.
Collins, L. Sketches of Kentucky.
Colton, Calvin. Life and Times of H. Clay.
Emmons, George F. History of the Navy.
French, B. F. Collections of Louisiana.
Gordon, William. History of the Independence of the United States.
Gordon, T. F. History of New Jersey.
Hammond, J. D. Life and Times of Silas Wright.
Hammond, J. D. Political Parties.
Hildreth, S. P. Pioneer History.
Hotchkin, James H. Western New York.
Howe, Henry. Collections of Virginia.
Howison, R. R. History of Virginia.
Ingersoll, C. J. History of the Second War.
Lamb, General. Life and Times of.
Lossing, B. J. Pictorial Field-Book.
Maryland Historical Society. Discourses and Addresses.
McSherry, James. History of Maryland.
Miner, Charles. History of Wyoming.
Morgan, L. H. League of the Iroquois.
Niles, Hezekiah. Principles and Acts.
O'Callaghan, E. B. History of New York.
Pickett, Albert J. History of Alabama.
Ramsay, J. G. M. Annals of Tennessee.
Rivero, M. E. Peruvian Antiquities.
Schoolcraft, H. R. History, &c., of the Indians.
Squier, E. G. Antiquities of New York.
Thompson, Zadoc. History of Vermont.
Washington, G. Revolutionary Orders.
White, George. Collections of Georgia.
Williamson, W. D. History of Maine.

BIOGRAPHY.

Biography. I.

EUROPEAN.

Abernethy, John. Memoirs of.
Arnault, M. F. Napoleon Bonaparte.
Bayle, Peter. Critical Dictionary.
Beattie, W. Life, &c., of Thomas Campbell.
Bensley, Benjamin. Henry the Eighth.
Biographical Dictionary.
Bruce, Robert. Life of. By G. Grant.
Bryan, Michael. Painters and Engravers.
Butler, Charles. Life of D'Aguesseau.
Butler, Charles. Life of Hugo Grotius.
Butler, Charles. Reminiscences of.
Cabot, Sebastian. Memoir of.
Campan, Madame. Journal Anecdotique de.
Cavendish, Henry. Life of.
Campbell, Thomas. Life and Letters of.
Clarkson, T. Sketch of Thomas Taylor.
Cockburn, Henry. Memorials of his Time.
Cormenin, L. M. de. The Popes.
Corneille and his Times. By M. Guizot.
D'Aguesseau, H. F. Memoirs of. (See Butler, C.)
Dumas, Count. Memoirs of his own Time.
Grant, George. Life of Robert Bruce.
Grotius, Hugo. Life of. (See Butler, C.)
Guizot, M. Corneille and his Times.
Hardwick, Lord. Life of. (See Harris, G.)
Harris, G. Life of Lord Hardwick.
Herbert, Lord. Henry the Eighth.
Hobart, N. Life of Swedenborg.
Hoby, J. Memoir of William Yates.
Houssaye, Arsene. Men and Women.
Johnson, Samuel. Lives of the Poets.
Klencke, Prof. Lives of Alexander and William Von Humboldt.
Knox, R. A Biographical Study.
Lawrence, Sir Thomas. Life, &c., of.
Marshall, John. Naval Biography.
Merriweather, F. Lives, &c., of Misers.
Napoleon Dynasty; or, the History of the Bonaparte Family.
Napoleon in Exile. By Barry O'Meara.
Napoleon. Memoirs of. (See Arnault, M. F.)
Niebuhr, B. G. Life and Letters of.
O'Meara, Barry. Napoleon in Exile.
Oxberry's Biographical Anecdotes.
Pellew, G. Life of Viscount Sidmouth.
Prescott, W. H. Phillip the Second.
Prescott, W. H. Robertson's Charles V.
Sidmouth, Viscount. Life. (See Pellew, G.)
Smith, Sidney. Wit and Wisdom of.
Sprague, W. B. European Celebrities.
Swedenborg, E. Life of. By N. Hobart.
Taylor, T. Biographical Sketch of.
Wellington, Duke of. Maxims and Opinions.
Wilkes, John. Memoirs of. By John Almon.
Wright, G. N. Life of Wellington.
Yates, Wm. Memoir of. By Jas. Hoby.

Biography. II.

AMERICAN.

Bainbridge, Wm. Life of. By T. Harris.
Baldwin, J. G. Party Leaders.
Bernard, H. Life of Rev. T. Gallaudet.
Burr, Aaron. Life of. (See Davis, M. L.)
Chalmers, T. Memoirs of. (See Hanna, W.)
Channing, William E. Memoir of.
Clay, H. Life and Times. (See Colton, C.)
Clinton, Dewitt. Life of. By J. Renwick.
Colton, Calvin. Life of Henry Clay.
Cooke, G. F. Memoirs of. By W. Dunlap.
Darlington, William. Memorials of John Bertram and Humphrey Marshall.
Davis, M. L. Memoirs of Aaron Burr.
Dunlap, Wm. Memoirs of Geo. F. Cooke.

Fulton, Robert. (See Reigart, J. F.)
Gallaudet, Thos. Life, &c., of. (See Bernard, Henry.)
Hammond, Jabez D. Life of Silas Wright.
Hanna, W. Memoirs of Thos. Chalmers.
Harris, Thos. Life, &c., of Bainbridge.
Headley, J. T. The Lives of Winfield Scott and Andrew Jackson.
Irving, W. Life of Washington.
Jackson, Andrew. Life of. By Joel T. Headley.
Johnson, J. Discourse on the Life of.
Lamb, John. The Life and Times of.
Lincoln, R. W. Lives of the Presidents.
Milnor, James. The Life of.
Mowatt, A. C. Biography of an Actress.
Reed, Joseph. Life of. By Wm. B. Reed.
Reigart, J. F. Life of Fulton.
Scott, Winfield. Life of. By J. T. Headley.
Sparks, Jared. Replies to Lord Mahon.
Stone, John S. Life of James Milnor.
Sullivan, Wm. Men of the Revolution.
Thorburn, Grant. Life of.
Van Santvoord, Geo. Lives of the Chief Justices.
Washington, Geo. Life of. By W. Irving.
Williams, W. S. American Biography.
Wright, Silas. Life of. By J. D. Hammond.

TRANSACTIONS, ETC.

Reports, &c., of Societies and Catalogues of Libraries.

American Bible Society. Reports of.
American Board of Commissioners for Foreign Missions. Reports of.
American Home Missionary Society. Reports of.
American Institute. Transactions of.
American Tract Society. Reports of.
Annals of the Lyceum of Natural History.
Annals of the Massachusetts Charitable Mechanics' Association.
Astor Library. Alphabetical and Analytical Index, or Catalogue of the Books collected and of the proposed Additions.
Catalogue of the Apprentices' and the Demilt Libraries.
Catalogue of the Library Company of Philadelphia.
Catalogue of the Library of Harvard University.
Catalogue of the Library of the Salfour Borough Royal Museum.
Catalogue of the Mercantile Library Company of Philadelphia.
Collections of the Georgia Historical Society.
Collections of the New York Historical Society.
Franklin Institute. Journal of.
Institution for the Instruction of the Deaf and Dumb. Annual Reports, &c., of.
Journal of the Franklin Institute.
Journal of the Royal Agricultural Society of England.
Maryland Historical Society. Discourses and Addresses.
Meigs, Henry. List of Members of the National Institute of France, and also of the American Institute.
New York Hospital. An Account of, and of the Bloomingdale Asylum for the Insane.
Ohio State Board of Agriculture. Reports.
Quarterly Journal of the Geological Society of London.
Report of the British Association for the Advancement of Science.
Smithsonian Institution. Contributions to Knowledge.
Smithsonian Institution. Annual Reports.
Transactions of the Agricultural Societies of Massachusetts.
Transactions of the American Institute.
Transactions of the Central Agricultural Society of Bavaria.
Transactions of the Highland Agricultural Society of Scotland.
Transactions of the Manchester Geological Society.
Transactions of the Massachusetts Charitable Mechanics' Association.
Transactions of the Michigan Agricultural Society.
Transactions of the New York State Agricultural Society.
Transactions of the Ohio State Board of Agriculture.
Transactions of the Pennsylvania State Agricultural Society.
Transactions of the Wisconsin State Agricultural Society.
Veterinary Record and Transactions of the Veterinary Medical Association.

PERIODICAL WORKS.

Periodical Works.

REVIEWS, JOURNALS AND MAGAZINES.

Abeja Argentina.
American Agriculturist.
American Magazine and Critical Review.
American Polytechnic Journal.
American Railroad Journal. H. V. Poor.
American Review; a Whig Journal.
Anales de Ciencias, Agricultura, etc.
Annals of Horticulture.
Annuaire des Deux Mondes.
Artisan, The. A Journal of the Arts.
Art-Journal, The. (London.)
Art-Union, The. (London.)
Athenæum, The. (London.)
Auxiliador da Industria Nacional.
Bankers' Magazine and Register.
Blackwood's Edinburgh Magazine.
Congressional Globe. Ed. by J. C. Rives.
Crayon, The. A Journal of Art, &c.
Edinburgh New Philosophical Journal.
Edinburgh Review.
Farmers' Magazine. (London.)
Farriers' Magazine. Edited by J. Carver.
Franklin Institute Journal.
Genesee Farmer; a Monthly Magazine.
Harper's New Monthly Magazine.
Hunt's Merchants' Magazine.
Illustrated London News.
International Monthly Magazine.
Journal of Agriculture. (Edinburgh.)
Journal of Agriculture. By J. S. Skinner.
Journal of Design and Manufactures.
Journal of the Franklin Institute.
Journal of the Royal Agricultural Society of England.
Knickerbocker Magazine. By L. G. Clark.
London Journal. Edited by Wm. Newton.
London Quarterly Review.
Magazine of Horticulture. By C. M. Hovey.
Magazine of Science and School of Art.
Mechanics' Magazine. By J. C. Robertson.
Merchants' Magazine and Com. Review.
Monthly Journal of Agriculture.
Monthly Journal of Foreign Medicine.
National Magazine. Ed. by A. Stevens.
Nautical Magazine and Quarterly Review.
New York Ecclesiologist.
New York Medical Gazette.
New York Medical and Physical Journal.
New York Review and Quarterly Journal.
Niles, Hezekiah. Weekly Register.
North American Review. General Index.
North British Review.
Philosophical Magazine and Journal.
Plough, the Loom and the Anvil.
Practical Mechanics' Journal.
Practical Mechanics' and Engineers' Magazine.
Putnam's Monthly Magazine.
Repertory of Patent Inventions.
Scientific American, The. By Munn & Co.
Silliman, Benjamin. American Journal.
Stryker's American Register.
Tallis' Dramatic Magazine.
United States Commercial Register.
United States Economist.
United States Magazine and Dem. Review.
Universal Chronologist and Historical Register. By H. Boyle.
Veterinarian, The. By Youatt & Percival.
Westminster Review.
Working Farmer, The. By J. J. Mapes.

NOVELS AND TALES.

Barnaby Rudge. By Charles Dickens.
Beecher, H. W. Star Papers.
Bleak House. By Charles Dickens.
Burnham, G. P. History of the Hen Fever.
Cervantes, Miguel de. El Buscopeé.
Christmas Stories. By Charles Dickens.
Dana, Jr., R. H. Two Years before the Mast.
David Copperfield. By Charles Dickens.
De Quincey, Thomas. Memorials and other Papers.
Dickens, Charles. Barnaby Rudge.
Dickens, Charles. Bleak House.
Dickens, Charles. Christmas Stories.
Dickens, Charles. David Copperfield.
Dickens, Charles. Dombey and Son.
Dickens, Charles. Hard Times.
Dickens, Charles. Martin Chuzzlewit.
Dickens, Charles. Oliver Twist.
Dickens, Charles. Pickwick Papers.
Dickens, Charles. Sketches by Boz.
Dombey and Son. By Charles Dickens.
Dream Life. By D. G. Mitchell.
Ellis, Mrs. Guide to Social Happiness, Pictures of Private Life and a Voice from the Vintage.
Ellis, Mrs. Family Monitor; comprising the Women of England, the Daughters of England, the Wives of England and the Mothers of England.
Haliburton, Thomas C. Rule and Misrule of the English in America.
Hard Times. By Charles Dickens.

Head, Sir Francis. A Faggot of French Sticks; or, Paris in 1851.
History of an Irish Family.
Hypatia. By Charles Kingsley, Jr.
Irving, Washington. Wolfert's Roost and other Papers.
Kingsley, Jr., Charles. Hypatia, or New Foes with an Old Face.
Lascallier, Baron. Trône Enchante, Conte Indien traduit du Persan.
Martin Chuzzlewit. By Charles Dickens.
Maury, Sarah M. An English Woman in America.
Mitchell, Donald G. Dream Life.
Odd Fellows' Offering for 1853.
Oliver Twist. By Charles Dickens.
Pastor's Fireside. By Jane Porter.
Peter Schlemihl in America.
Philip, Robert. The Hannahs, or Maternal Influence on Sons.
Philip, Robert. The Lydias, or the Development of Female Character.
Philip, Robert. The Marthas, or the Varieties of Female Piety.
Pickwick Papers. By Charles Dickens.
Porter, Jane. The Pastor's Fireside.
Porter, Jane. Thaddeus of Warsaw.
Reade, Charles. Peg Woffington; a Novel.
Salad for the Solitary. By an Epicure.
Sketches. By Charles Dickens.
Sketches and Tales of Barbados.
Smith, Sidney. Wit and Wisdom.
Star Papers. By H. W. Beecher.
Thaddeus of Warsaw. By Jane Porter.
Trône Enchante. By Baron Lascallier.
Two Years before the Mast. By R. H. Dana, Jr.
Wolfert's Roost. By Washington Irving.
Wonders of the World. Compiled by Robert Sears.

PAMPHLETS.

Vol. 60. 1. Priestley's Appeal to Professors of Christianity, and an Account of the Trial of Mr. Elwall for Heresy, &c. Philadelphia, 1794.

2. Revivals of Religion in New England and Nova Scotia. Boston, 1799.

3. Watson's Apology for the Bible. New York, 1796.

4. Theological Repository. July, 1808.

5. History of the Bible; its Happy Influence, &c. Boston, 1809.

6. An Important Case Argued, in Four Dialogues. Boston, 1810.

7. Essay on the Constitution of the Apostolic Churches. New York, 1817.

8. Plain Dealing with Calvinism. By Benjamin Gorton. Troy, 1811.

9. Westminster Catechism made Scriptural; and also the Apostolic or Christian Faith. By B. Gorton. Troy, 1812.

10. Late Revelations on the Doctrines of Election and Reprobation, &c., &c.

11. The End of Time; an Extract from Dr. Watts.

12. The Good Samaritan. By R. De Joncourt. Fishkill, 1815.

13. An Appeal occasioned by the Address of the Charitable Society. Hartford, 1815.

14. Reasons for Silent Waiting in order to the Solemn Worship of God. By Mary Brook. Philadelphia, 1816.

15. New York Pamphlet Society. New York, 1818.

" 61. 1. Solemn Review of the Custom of War. By Philo-Pacificus. Providence, 1818.

2. Defence of Universal Restoration from Sin, Death and Hell. Glasgow, 1819.

3. Two Letters on 1 John, v. 7, and on the Scriptural Argument for Unitarianism. By Henry Ware. Boston, 1820.

4. The Controversy upon Sunday Police. New York, 1820.

5. The Antitypical Essay, containing a Reply to G. Withy. New York, 1823.

6. What is Religion?

7. Third Report of the Missionary and Tract Society of the New Jerusalem Church. London, 1824.

8. Minutes of the 18th Conference of the Ministers of the New Church. London, 1825.

9. Third General Epistle of Peter. London.

10. True Object of Christian Worship Demonstrated, and the Doctrine of the Trinity Elucidated. London, 1824.

11. Letter from the Son of Man to Right Hon. John Adams. 1825.

12. Nature of Life after Death. London, 1825.

13. Second Letter to the Rev. C. B. M'Guire on his Defence of the Divinity of Christ. Pittsburgh, 1825.

14. A Mirror of Professing Christians. New York, 1825.

15. Letter to the King. By Thomas Thrush. New York, 1825.

16. Free Thoughts on Faith; or, the Religion of Nature. New York, 1825.

17. Three Persons in One God. Proved by B. Hibbard. New York, 1825.

18. The Road to Wealth. By John Clowes.

Vol. 61. 19. Doctrine of Pronouns applied to Christ's Testimony of Himself. By Noah Worcester. Boston, 1827.

20. Essay on the Lord's Supper. By F. W. P. Greenwood. Boston, 1827.

21. Right of Free Discussion. New York, 1829.

22. Considerations on the Foundation, Ends and Duties of the Christian Sabbath. Utica, 1829.

" 62. 1. Reformed Christian Guide. By John S. Thompson. New York, 1831.

2. Right of Conscience and of Free Discussion.

3. Letter on the Christian Sabbath. By Lewis Tappan. New York, 1831.

4. Reformed Christian's Guide. By John S. Thompson. New York, 1831.

5. Brief Illustration of the Principles of War and Peace. By Philanthropos. Albany, 1831.

6. Extracts from the Minutes of the Presbytery of Carlisle. Philadelphia, 1832.

7. Key to Accompany the Rev. R. C. Shimeall's Ecclesiastical Chart. New York, 1833.

8. Systematic Charity upon the Apostolic Model. Burlington, 1835.

9. Putnam and the Wolf; or, the Monster Destroyed. By John Marsh.

10. Female Wages.

11. Perfection of the Scriptures as a Rule of Faith. By James Lillie. New York, 1835.

12. Practical Pastorship. New York, 1835.

" 63. 1. Osgood's Letter upon Episcopacy. New York, 1807.

2. Rise of the Reformation. By William Robertson. London, 1813.

3. Plea against War. By Erasmus. New York, 1813.

4. Case of Rachel Baker. By Charles Mais. New York, 1814.

5. Right to Church Property Secured. By Robert Gourlay. London, 1815.

6. Memoir on the Progress of the Translations of the Sacred Scriptures. Serampore, 1816.

7. Directory to the Holy Scriptures. By John Stanford, M. A.

8. Plain Questions to Calvinists. By an Anti-Predestinarian. 1819.

9. "Short and Easy Method." By an Aged Clergyman. Boston, 1815.

10. Fourth Report of the Society for the Support of the Gospel. New York, 1817.

11. Christianity Unveiled. From the French of Boulanger. By W. M. Johnson. London, 1819.

12. Reply to Rev. H. J. Feltus on the Alliance of Unitarianism and Mahometanism. By H. D. Sewall. New York, 1820.

13. Memorial to the Legislature against the Enactment of Laws enforcing the Observance of the Sabbath.

14. Review of Swedenborgianism. Boston, 1820.

15. Doctrine of Salvation by Faith. By Adam Clark. New York, 1821.

16. Magic Harmonies exemplifying the Second Advent Dispensation. By Edward P. Page. New York, 1821.

17. Address before the American Bible Society. By the Rev. Dr. Milnor.

18. Remarks on Dr. Griffin's Requisition for 700,000 Ministers. New Haven, 1824.

19. Nature's Oracle the Word of God. By Edward P. Page. New York.

20. Later from Hell; or, Ely's Dream. Philadelphia, 1825.

Vol. 64. 1. A Peep into Hell.
2. Ecclesiastical Establishments. London, 1826.
3. Metaphorical Baptism Disproved. London, 1826.
4. Thoughts on Religion. New York, 1826.
5. Review of the Answer to the Remonstrance sent to the Bishops of the Protestant Episcopal Church. Philadelphia, 1827.
6. Candid Appeal to the Professors of Religion, upon the Subject of Free Masonry. By J. N. Hotchkin. New York, 1828.
7. Proceedings of the General Assembly of the General Baptist Church. Hackney, 1828.
8. Considerations on the Foundation, &c., of the Sabbath. Utica, 1829.
9. Account of the State of Unitarianism in Boston, in 1812. By Francis Parkman and others. 1829.
10. Exposition of Modern Scepticism. By William Gibbons, M. D. Wilmington, 1829.
11. Review of the Evidence of the Pretended General Conspiracy of the Roman Catholics of Ireland to Massacre the Protestants. By M. Carey. Philadelphia, 1830.
12. Letter on Religious Liberty. By Moses Stuart. Boston, 1830.
13. The Ferret, No. 1. By Wm. M'Gowin. Pittsburgh, 1831.
14. Address of the Trustees of St. Mary's Church to the Congregation. 1831.
15. Ministry at Large for the Poor of Cities.
16. Charter of Christ's Church and St. Peter's Church. Philadelphia, 1832.
17. A Mirror intended to be held to the Face of Mystic Babylon. By a Minister of the Gospel. New York, 1833.
18. Remonstrance against Stopping the Mail on the Sabbath.
19. Summary Statement of Facts, in reply to the Bill against Friends, &c., &c.
20. Review of the Evidence, &c. By M. Carey. Philadelphia, 1833.
21. Origin and Progress of the First Free Congregational Church. By J. H. Martyn. Buffalo, 1834.
22. Sherlock's Letter to Thomas Herttell. Albany, 1834.
23. Remarks on the Relation between Education and Crime. By Francis Lieber. Philadelphia, 1835.
24. Minutes of the General Assembly of the Presbyterian Church. Philadelphia, 1845.

" 65. 1. The Originality and Superior Excellence of the Mosaic Institutions Demonstrated. By Joseph Priestley. Northumberland, 1803.
2. Mr. Bogart's Thanksgiving Discourse. 1804.
3. Discourse delivered by the Rev. Jonathan French, in Portsmouth. 1805.
3½. Discourse delivered by Timothy Alden, Jr. Portsmouth, 1805.
4. Sermon on Duelling. By Timothy Dwight. New York, 1805.
5. Sermon. By Dr. Eliphalet Nott. Philadelphia, 1806.
6. Sermon delivered by Samuel Miller, D. D. New York, 1812.
7. Discourse on the Utility of Learning. By John Stanford. New York, 1814.
8. Discourse on the Death of an Unfortunate Youth. By John Stanford. New York, 1815.
9. The Life of Man Inviolable. By Aaron Cleveland. Colchester, 1815.
10. Thanksgiving Sermon. By Samuel F. Jarvis. New York, 1815.

Vol. 65. 11. Discourse by John Stanford, on Divine Benevolence to the Poor. New York, 1816.

12. Sermon on True Liberality. By Samuel Worcester. Andover, 1816.

13. Sermon on the Death of Elijah Hunter, with a Memoir. By John Stanford. New York, 1817.

14. Sermon on the Doctrine of Election. By Gardiner Spring. New York, 1817.

15. Review of a Sermon by G. Spring, on the Doctrine of Election. By Hosea Dodge. New York, 1817.

16. Discourse on Unlimited Submission and Non-Resistance to the Higher Powers. By Jonathan Mayhew. Boston, 1750.

17. Remarks upon the Carnal and Spiritual State of Man. By William Allen. New York, 1818.

18. Sermon by the Rev. Robert Daly. Dublin, 1819.

19. Discourse by the Rev. James Barnaby. New Bedford, 1819.

" 66. 1. Discourse on Robbery, Piracy, Murder, Duelling and Suicide. By Thomas Baldwin. Boston.

2. Discourse on the Duty and Advantages of Improving our Baptism. By John Stanford. New York, 1819.

3. Sermon by James R. Wilson, on the Subjection of Kings and Nations to Messiah. New York, 1820.

4. Sermon by Lyman Beecher, on the Means of National Prosperity. New York, 1820.

5. Discourse on the Urim and the Thummim. By J. Stanford. New York, 1820.

6. Discourse delivered at the Funeral of Mrs. Rachel Roome. By John Stanford. New York, 1820.

7. Discourse delivered at the Funeral of Mrs. Rachel Lewis. By John Stanford. New York, 1820.

8. Discourse on the Death of George Vanderpool. By John Stanford. New York, 1821.

9. An Act to Provide for the Instruction of the Indigent Deaf and Dumb. New York, 1822.

10. Sermon in behalf of the Deaf and Dumb Institution. By John Summerfield. New York, 1822.

11. Discourse delivered at the Hospital. By John Stanford. New York, 1824.

12. Sermon on Pestilence. By Paschal N. Strong. New York, 1822.

13. The Oracles of God; four Orations. By Edward Irving. New York, 1825.

" 67. 1. Lecture on Human Happiness. By John Gray. Philadelphia, 1825.

2. Three Sermons on Christian Theology. By Abner Kneeland. New York, 1826.

3. Discourse delivered at the House of Refuge. By John Stanford. New York, 1826.

4. Sermon, by Lyman Beecher, on the Resources of the Adversary, and Means of their Destruction. New York, 1827.

5. Sermon on Universal Charity. By William Sinclair. Baltimore, 1827.

6. Introductory Lecture delivered in the Theological Seminary. By Charles Hodge. 1829.

7. Sermon, by Charles Lowell, on the Source of Division in the Christian Church. Boston, 1829.

Vol. 67. 8. Sermon. By Hosea Ballou. 1829.

9. Sermon. By T. Fisk. 1829.

10. Sermon delivered at the Dedication of the Universalist Church in Grand-street. By T. Fisk. 1829.

11. Sermon, by Abel C. Thomas, on the Troubles of Israel. New York, 1829.

12. Sermon, by Rev. John A. Clark, on the Denial of Christ. 1832.

13. Sermon on the Cholera. By John Grigg. Hudson, 1832.

14. Thanksgiving Sermon. By Rodney A. Miller. Worcester, 1833.

15. Sermon on the Relation of Christianity to Civil Government in the United States. By J. Adams. Charleston, 1833.

16. Sermon, by John G. Morris, on the Glorious Reformation. Winchester, 1834.

17. Sermon, by John M. Krebs, on the Purpose and Success of the Gospel. Pittsburgh, 1834.

18. Address before the People of Color. By Daniel C. Colesworthy. Portland, 1835.

19. Sermon on Religious Ultraism. By William R. Sprague. Albany, 1835.

20. Sermon, by John M. Krebs, on National Prosperity. New York, 1835.

21. Sermon on the Great Fire. By William Ware. New York, 1835.

22. Sermon, by Samuel Miller, on Domestic Happiness. 1835.

23. Sermon, by Baxter Dickinson, on the Importance and Means of an able Ministry. 1836.

24. Rule of Faith. By Henry U. Onderdonk. Philadelphia, 1833.

" 68. 1. Sermon, by James Yates, on the Duty and Manner of Deciding the more important Religious Controversies. Glasgow, 1815.

2. Discourse. By Edward Payson. The Bible above all Price.

3. Discourse. By William Ellery Channing. New York, 1827.

4. Two Discourses. By William Turner. Newcastle-upon-Tyne, 1818.

5. Discourse. By William Kilpatrick. Glasgow, 1818.

6. Discourse. By Jacob de la Motta. Savannah, 1820.

7. Sermon. By Robert Cree. Liverpool, 1825.

8. Digest on Human Depravity. By Edmund Q. Sewall. Boston, 1826.

9. Fourth Epistle of Peter, translated from the Original. By Abner Kneeland. New York, 1829.

10. Sermon on the Influence of the Gospel on the Intellectual Powers. By George W. Blagden. Philadelphia, 1835.

11. Sermon, by James B. Taylor, on the Exigencies and Responsibilities of the Present Age. Philadelphia, 1836.

12. Address by E. L. Finley, before the Sunday School Union. Baltimore, 1831.

13. Address before the Humane Impartial Society. By E. L. Finley. Baltimore, 1831.

" 69. 1. The Antitypical Essay concerning the Divinity of Christ and the Doctrine of Satisfaction. New York, 1823.

2. Cabinet, or Works of Darkness brought to Light; a Retrospect of the Conduct towards Elias Hicks. Philadelphia, 1825.

3. Letter on the Dispute of the Statements of Anna Braithwaite and Elias Hicks, &c. Philadelphia, 1824.

Vol. 69. 4. Errors of Anna Braithwaite concerning the Doctrines of Elias Hicks, &c. New York, 1824.

5. Misrepresentations of Anna Braithwaite, and a Refutation of the same. By Elias Hicks. Philadelphia, 1824.

6. Sandy Foundation Shaken, &c. By William Penn. Philadelphia, 1825.

7. Declaration of the Yearly Meeting of Friends. Philadelphia, 1828.

8. Extracts, &c., from the Minutes of the Indiana Yearly Meeting. New York, 1827.

9. Review of a Pamphlet called "A Testimony, and Epistle of Advice." Philadelphia, 1828.

10. The Berean. Wilmington, Delaware, 1828.

11. Epistle and Testimony from the Yearly Meeting of Friends. New York, 1828.

12. Last Letter of Elias Hicks. 1830.

13. Orthodoxy Unmasked. By George W. Banks. Philadelphia, 1829.

14. Proceedings of the Friends of Liberal Christianity, with an Address by B. Bates. New York, 1829.

15. Sermon by Elias Hicks. 1829.

16. The Friend or Advocate of Truth. 1828.

17. Sermon by Stephen Crisp, preached at Devonshire-House, 1688.

18. Review of the Testimony against Elias Hicks. By Evan Lewis. New York, 1829.

19. Sermon delivered at the Friends' Meeting. By Elias Hicks. New York, 1830.

20. Six Queries proposed to Elias Hicks, with his Answers. New York, 1830.

21. Two Sermons and a Prayer delivered by Elias Hicks. New York, 1831.

22. The Answers, by Elias Hicks, to the Six Queries. New York, 1831.

23. Charge to the Grand Jury. By Charles G. Ferris.

" 70. 1. Funeral Sermon, by Alexander Macwhorter, on the Death of General Washington. Newark, 1800.

2. Funeral Eulogy, by William Linn, upon General Washington. New York, 1800.

3. Discourse delivered by Eliphalet Nott, occasioned by the Death of General Hamilton.

4. Letters on the Character and Conduct of Dewitt Clinton. By Milo. New York, 1812.

5. Eulogium on Dewitt Clinton. By James R. Manley. New York, 1828.

6. Discourse on the Character, &c., of Dewitt Clinton. By Samuel L. Mitchill. New York, 1828.

7. Discourse delivered by Alfred Conkling, on Dewitt Clinton. Albany, 1828.

8. Sermon, by Rev. James Milnor, occasioned by the Death of Dewitt Clinton. New York, 1828.

9. Discourse, by John F. Schroeder, on the Character, &c., of John Henry Hobart. New York, 1830.

10. Recollections of Dr. Rush. By Dr. Lettsom. London, 1815.

11. Sketch of the Character of Alexander Baron, M. D. By Samuel Wilson. Charleston, 1819.

12. Memoir of Edward Jenner. By Dr. Lettsom. 1804.

Vol. 70. 13. Notice Biographique sur le Docteur Jenner. Par Louis Valentin.
14. Memoirs of John Roberts. By Daniel Roberts. New-York, 1802.
15. Discourse on the Character of Wilbur Fisk. By J. Holdich. Middletown, 1839.
16. Life of John Tyler. New York, 1843.
17. Sketch of the Life, &c., of General Zachary Taylor. 1848.

" 71. 1. Discourse, by John Stanford, on the Death of an Unfortunate Youth. New York, 1815.
1½. Sketch of the Life, &c., of Dr. Pædagogus, the Reformer. By Correcter. New York, 1817.
2. Eulogium on Wright Post, M. D. By John A. Smith. New York, 1828.
3. Discourse on the Life, &c., of Thomas Addis Emmet. By Samuel L. Mitchill. New York, 1828.
4. Éloge de Thomas Jefferson. Par M. Charles Lemesle. Paris, 1827.
5. Memoir of the Life, &c., of Thomas Jefferson. By Samuel H. Smith. Washington, 1827.
6. Memoir of the Life, &c., of John Adams. By William Cranch. Washington, 1827.
7. Discourse on the Character, &c., of Thomas Jefferson. By Samuel L. Mitchill. New York, 1826.
8. Discourse, by Daniel Webster, in Commemoration of the Lives, &c., of John Adams and Thomas Jefferson. Boston, 1826.
9. Discourse on the Deaths of Thomas Jefferson and John Adams. By John Stanford. New York, 1826.
10. Discourse in Commemoration of the Lives, &c., of John Adams and Thomas Jefferson. By Daniel Webster. Boston, 1826.
11. Vindication of the Conduct and Character of Henry D. Sedgwick. New York, 1826.
12. Memoir of John Brooks, M. D., LL. D. By John Dixwell.
13. Discourse by Rev. Horace Holley, occasioned by the Death of Col. James Morrison. Lexington, 1823.
14. Remarks upon the Public Conduct, &c., of John C. Calhoun. New York, 1823.
15. Memoir of Thomas Bateman, M. D. New York, 1822.
16. Tribute to the Memory of Jacob Dyckeman, M. D. By Henry W. Ducatchet. New York, 1823.
17. Memoir of Samuel Bard, M. D., LL. D. By Henry W. Ducachet. Philadelphia, 1831.
18. Doubts of the Authenticity of the Memoirs attributed to Napoleon. By Comte de Grouchy. Philadelphia, 1820.

" 72. 1. Memoir of John Murray, Jun. By Thomas Eddy. New York, 1819.
2. Tribute to the late Caspar Wistar. By David Hosack. New York, 1818.
3. Funeral Address at the Interment of Dr. James Tillary. By David Hosack. New York, 1818.
4. Letter to General Brown. By Samuel A. Storrow. 1817.
5. Discourse on the Life, &c., of Thomas Addis Emmet. By Samuel L. Mitchill. New York, 1828.
6. Sketch of the Olden Time. By an Antiquary. New York, 1829.

Vol. 72. 7. Discourse delivered at the Interment of Edward Augustus Holyoke. By John Brazer. Salem, 1829.

8. Address, by William Allen, occasioned by the Death of Nathan Smith, M. D. Brunswick, 1829.

9. Discourse on the Advantages of Classical Learning, with a Sketch of the Character of William Samuel Johnson. By John T. Irving. New York, 1830.

10. Eulogy on Dr. Godman. By Thomas Sewall. Washington, 1830.

11. Memoir of John Watts, M. D. By Samuel W. Moore. New York, 1831.

12. Remarks on the Character of Napoleon Bonaparte. Ascribed to Dr. Channing. New York, 1831.

13. Eulogy on the Life, &c., of Samuel Latham Mitchill, M. D. By Felix Pascalis. New York, 1831.

14. Oration in Commemoration of the Birth-Day of Thomas Paine. New York, 1832.

15. Eulogy on James M. Pendleton, M. D. By Gunning S. Bedford. New York, 1832.

16. Conduct and Character of Lieut. Edward W. Carpender. 1834.

17. Documents in relation to Differences between Commodore Perry and Captain Elliott. Washington, 1831.

18. Reflections on Col. Humphrey's Life of General Putnam. By John Fellows.

19. Eulogy on Lafayette. By Francis Baylies. Boston, 1834.

20. Memoir of the Life of Daniel Webster. By Samuel L. Knapp. New York, 1835.

" 73. 1. Debate on a Memorial to Congress respecting the Illegal Conduct of General Wilkinson. New Orleans, 1807.

2. Memoirs of General Wilkinson. Washington, 1810.

" 74. 1. Report of the Committee appointed to inquire into the Conduct of General Wilkinson. Washington, 1811.

" 75. 1. Account of Miranda's Expedition. New York, 1808.

2. Narrative of the Occurrences in the Indian Countries of North America. London, 1817.

3. Letters from the South and West. By Arthur Singleton. Boston, 1824.

4. Captain Hall in America. By an American. Philadelphia, 1830.

" 76. 1. Mèmoires publiès par l'Acadèmie de Marseille. Marseille, 1807.

2. Ètats-Unis et l'Angleterre ou Souvenirs et Rèflections d'un Citoyen Americain. Bordeaux, 1814.

" 77. 1. Proposals for Publishing the Olive Branch. By M. Carey.

2. Appendix to the Eighth Edition of the Olive Branch. By M. Carey. Philadelphia, 1817.

3. Appeal to Common Sense and Common Justice. By M. Carey. Philadelphia, 1822.

4. Situation and Future Prospects of the United States. By a Pennsylvanian. Philadelphia, 1822.

5. Thirty Years' Facts against One Reviewer's Opinion. Philadelphia, 1825.

6. Colbert. Nos. 1, 2, 3 and 4.

7. Political Economy. Nos. 1, 2 and 3.

Vol. 77. 8. Hamilton. Eleventh Series. No. 6.
9. Examination of the Charleston Memorial.
10. Reflections on the Renewal of the Charter of the Bank of Pennsylvania. By M. Carey. Philadelphia, 1829.
11. Common Sense Address to the Citizens of the Southern States. By a Citizen of Philadelphia. Philadelphia, 1829.
12. Annals of Liberality, Generosity, Public Spirit, &c.
13. Essays on the Policy of Manufacturing in this Country. Philadelphia, 1830.
14. Review of Mr. Cambreleng's Report. By Mephistophiles. Baltimore, 1830.
15. Politics for Farmers. 1830.
16. Address of the Committee and Council of the Cherokee Nation. 1830.
17. Letter of J. S. Johnston on Reducing the Duty on Sugar. Washington, 1831.
18. Thoughts on Penitentiaries and Prison Discipline. By M. Carey. Philadelphia, 1831.

" 78. 1. Address to the Wealthy. By M. Carey. Philadelphia, 1831.
2. Defence of a Liberal Construction of the Powers of Congress as regards Internal Improvements, &c. By George McDuffie. Philadelphia, 1831.
3. Import Duties. By a Friend of the Administration. Philadelphia, 1832.
4. The Olive Branch. By M. Carey. Philadelphia, 1832.
5. The Olive Branch Once More.
6. Appeal to the Good Sense of the Nation against the Spirit of Resistance and Dissolution of the Union. Philadelphia, 1832.
7. Address of the Jackson Party. 1832.
8. Dissolution of the Union; a Sober Address. By a Citizen of Pennsylvania. Philadelphia, 1832.
9. Essay on the Dissolution of the Union. Philadelphia, 1832.
10. Prospects on the Rubicon. By M. Carey. Philadelphia, 1832.
11. Prospects beyond the Rubicon. By M. Carey. Philadelphia, 1833.
12. Review of the Veto. By Judge Johnston. Philadelphia, 1832.
13. Rise and Progress of the Tariff System of the United States. By M. Carey. Philadelphia, 1833.
14. Review, &c. By M. Carey. Philadelphia, 1833.
15. Prospects beyond the Rubicon.
16. Review of the Situation and Prospects of the Poor. By M. Carey. Philadelphia, 1833.
17. Appeal to the Wealthy on behalf of the Poor. By M. Carey. Philadelphia, 1833.
18. Proofs that Credit is Preferable to Coin. By Robert Hare. Philadelphia, 1834.
19. Addresses to the Citizens of the Southern States. By M. Carey. Philadelphia, 1835.

" 79. 1. Reflections on the Formation and Distribution of Wealth. By M. Turgot. London, 1793.
2. Address to the Laboring Poor of Wily Parish. By Robert Gourlay.
3. Wealth of Society. Newburgh, 1820.
4. Observations on the Report of the Committee of Ways and Means. Philadelphia, 1828.

Vol 79. 5. Letters of Algernon Sydney in Defence of Civil Liberty. Richmond, 1830.
6. Answer to the Charge of Immorality against the Inhabitants of Barbadoes. By Joseph D. Husbands. Cooperstown, 1831.
7. First and Second Annual Reports of the Penitentiary of Pennsylvania. Philadelphia, 1831.
8. Voice from Sing Sing; giving a General Description of the State Prison. By Col. Levi S. Burr. Albany, 1833.
9. Report of the State Treasurer upon the Subject of the Finances. Harrisburg, 1833.
10. Letters to John Quincy Adams. By B. Hazard. Providence, 1834.
11. Report of the State Treasurer on Finances. Harrisburg, 1833–34.
12. Apology for the United States. Liverpool, 1829.
13. Strictures on Mr. Lee's Exposition of Evidence on the Sugar Duty.
14. Report of the "Union Committee." New York, 1834.
15. Memorial to the Legislature of Maryland. By John Bellorris. Baltimore, 1836.
16. Petition for a General Bankrupt Law.
17. Manual of the State of New York. New York, 1822.

" 80. 1. Aristides' Letter to William H. Crawford, Secretary of the Treasury.
2. Paradox Solved; or, a Financial Secret Worth Knowing. By the Author of Statisticus. Baltimore, 1820.
3. Proceedings of a Meeting of Mechanics and others, held December 29, 1829. New York, 1830.
4. Examination of the Controversy between the Greek Deputies. By John Duer and Robert Sedgwick. New York, 1826.
5. Essay on the Interest of Money. By Thomas R. Dew. Shellbanks, Va., 1834.
6. What is a Monopoly? or, Considerations upon Corporations and Currency. By a Citizen of New York. 1835.
7. Memorial of the Philadelphia Chamber of Commerce. Philadelphia, 1834.
8. System of Finance. New York, 1836.
9. New Financial Project; with some Remarks upon the Currency and Credit System. New York, 1837.
10. Considerations on the Project, &c., of a Guarantee Company, with some Views on Credit, Confidence and Currency. By William L. Haskins. New York, 1837.
11. Brief Observations, &c., on the Militia System.
12. Defence of Nations. Edinburgh, 1806.
13. Memoir on the Principles, &c., of Organizing the General Staff of the United States Military Power. 1812.
14. Essay on the Necessity of Improving our National Forces. By William Theobald Wolfe Tone. New York, 1819.
15. Captain Partridge's Lecture on National Defence.
16. Documents and Facts relative to Military Events during the late War.

" 81. 1. The English Practice. By a Lover of Improvement. New York, 1822.
2. Letter on the Affairs of Portugal and Spain. By William Walton. London, 1827.
3. Who is the Legitimate King of Portugal? By a Portuguese. London, 1828.

Vol. 81. 4. Second Letter to Lord Palmerston on his Policy respecting Portugal. By William Walton. London, 1833.

5. Treatise on the Principles, Practice and History of Commerce. By J. R. McCulloch. London, 1833.

6. Letter to the Marquis Camden on the Disputes between Holland and Belgium. By Veritas. London, 1832.

7. Letter on Parliamentary Reform. By the Earl of Selkirk. London, 1809.

8. Observations on the General Orders of Wellington in Portugal, Spain and France. London, 1834.

" 82. 1. Circular Letter in Vindication of the Measures of the General Government. New York, 1809.

2. Appeal to the People on the Expediency of Abolishing the Council of Appointment. New York, 1819.

3. Address of Epaminondas to the Citizens of New-York. Albany, 1819.

4. Republican Address to the Electors of Seneca County. Waterloo, 1820.

5. Address by Edmund Charles Genet on the Means of Opening New Sources of Wealth for the Northern States. Troy, 1821.

6. Presidential Election. By Philo Jackson. Frankfort, 1824.

7. Address adopted by the Virginia Anti-Jackson Convention. New York, 1827.

8. Considerations which demand the attention of Farmers, Mechanics, &c. By a Citizen of New York. New York, 1828.

9. Considerations which demand the attention of the Friends of the American System. New York, 1828.

10. Address to the Citizens of Connecticut by the Friends of Andrew Jackson. Norwich, 1828.

11. Investigation of the Controversy on the Election of Mayor. By a Democratic Member of the Common Council. New York, 1830.

12. Preamble and Resolutions adopted on Choosing Delegates to the Anti-Tariff Convention. Boston, 1831.

13. Journal of the Baltimore Convention. Washington, 1831.

14. Facts, &c., in relation to the Rejection of Martin Van Buren by the Senate. New York, 1832.

15. Address to the People of Maryland. Baltimore, 1832.

16. Circular Address of James Clark to his Constituents. Washington, 1831.

17. Proceedings of a Meeting, and the Address of the General Committee of Whig Young Men of New York. 1834.

18. Report of a Committee of the New York Whig Convention. New York, 1834.

19. Address to the People of Pennsylvania by the Society for the Suppression of Lotteries. Philadelphia, 1834.

20. Address to the American People. By R. J. Breckenridge. Baltimore, 1836.

21. Address to the Mechanic and Laboring Classes. By a Mechanic. New York, 1840.

22. Anti-Jackson Essays on the Presidency. By an Old Man. Baltimore.

Vol. 83. 1. Propositions for Amending the Constitution of the United States, submitted by Mr. Hillhouse to the Senate, 1808.
2. Considerations on the Executive Government. By Augustus R. Woodward. Flatbush, 1809.
3. Constitution of the United States. Washington, 1806.
4. Proposals for Colonizing in the Republic of Mexico. Bath, 1831.
5. Constitution of the Republic of Mexico, and of the State of Coahuila, and Texas, &c., &c. New York, 1832.
6. Constitution of the United States and of New York. Boston, 1835.
7. Constitution of the Republic of Texas, and Declaration of Independence. Washington, 1836.
8. Examination of the Title of the United States to the Land called the Batture.
9. Remarks on John Jay's Letter to Cave Jones. New York, 1812.
10. Remarks and Criticisms on John Quincy Adams' Letter. Boston, 1808.

" 84. 1. Report against the Further Increase of Duties on Importations. New York, 1828.
2. Protection and Free Trade. The Question Stated and Considered. By Horace Greeley.
3. Proposed Alteration in the Tariff. By Thomas Cooper. New York, 1834.
4. Tariff or Rates of Duties on Merchandise. Compiled, &c., by J. K. Law. Baltimore, 1833.
5. Tariff or Rates of Duties on Merchandise. Revised, &c., by James Campbell. New York, 1832.
6. War without Disguise, or the Frauds of Neutral Commerce, &c. 1807.

" 85. 1. Considerations on the French War. By a British Merchant. London, 1794.
2. The Recantation; being an Anticipated Valedictory Address of Thomas Paine. New York, 1799.
2½. Political Essays. By Thomas Cooper. Philadelphia, 1800.
3. Letters on our Affairs with Spain. By James Cheetham. New York, 1804.
3½. The Opportunity; or, Reasons for an Immediate Alliance with St. Domingo. London, 1804.
4. The Go-Between; or, Two-Edged Sword. By a Gentleman from South Carolina. New York, 1807.
5. The Principal Cause that Disturbs the Tranquillity of a Republican Government. New York, 1807.
6. Letters to the Electors. By a Citizen of New York. New York, 1808.
7. Sketch of our Political Condition. By a Citizen of New York. New York, 1813.
8. The Reviewers Reviewed; or, British Falsehood detected by American Truths. New York, 1815.
9. The Second Crisis of America. By a Citizen of Philadelphia. 1815.

" 86. 1. Address to the Government of the United States on the Cession of Louisiana to the French. 1803.
2. Letter from the Secretary of the Navy, transmitting Documents relating to the City and Harbor of New York. Washington, 1811.

Vol. 86. 3. Remarks on the Law of Imprisonment for Debt. By Thomas Herttell. New York, 1823.

4. Second Letter on the Mischiefs incidental to Tread-Wheels, &c. By John Mason Good. London, 1824.

5. Letter on the Nature and Effects of the Tread-Wheel. By a Magistrate. London, 1824.

6. Review of the Administration and Civil Police of the State of New York. By Ferris Pell. New York, 1819.

" 87. 1. Review of the Political State of Lower Canada. By Robert Christie. New York, 1818.

2. Memoirs of Lower Canada, by Sir James Henry Craig and Sir George Provost. By Robert Christie. Quebec, 1818.

3. Fourteenth Annual Report of the American Education Society. New York, 1830.

" 88. 1. Medical Statistics. By Nathaniel Niles and John D. Russ. New York, 1827.

2. Account of Memorials against Sabbath Mails. New York, 1829.

3. Let not the Faith nor the Laws of the Commonwealth be Violated.

4. Correspondence between Andrew Jackson and John C. Calhoun, relating to the Seminole War. Washington, 1831.

5. Strictures on Mr. Lacock's Report on the Seminole War.

6. Discourse by H. W. Warner, on Legal Science. New York, 1833.

7. Speech of Mr. Johnston relative to the Public Lands. Washington, 1830.

7½. Reply of Mr. Davis to the Charge of Mr. Buchanan. Washington, 1840.

8. Speech of Mr. Webster in reply to Mr. Calhoun. Washington, 1833.

9. Political Register. Washington, 1833.

10. Brief Survey of the Great Extent and Evil Tendencies of the Lottery System. Philadelphia, 1833.

11. Voyage of the Potomac. By J. N. Reynolds. New York, 1834.

12. Proceedings of the Overseers of Harvard University. Boston, 1834.

13. Plan for the Organization of a Law Faculty. By Benj. F. Butler. New York, 1835.

14. Answer and Report in the Matter of the New York Life Insurance and Trust Company. New York, 1837.

15. Common Sense Addresses to the Citizens of the Southern States. By M. Carey. Philadelphia, 1829.

" 89. 1. A Word to Federalists.

2. Introduction to the Science of Government. 1822.

3. Speech of Daniel Webster in reply to Mr. Hayne, relative to Public Lands. New York, 1830.

4. Machiavelian. Tragi-Comedy. 1831.

5. Proceedings of the Officers of the Late War, in reference to an Application to Congress for Remuneration. New York, 1826.

6. Documents relating to Grants of Lands in Texas. New York, 1831.

7. Statement of the Indian Relations. New York, 1830.

8. Thoughts on Emigration and on the Canadas. Quebec, 1831.

9. Voice of the West Indies, and the Cry of England. London, 1832.

10. Memorial of the Friends of Domestic Industry. 1833.

Vol. 89. 11. Report of the Special Committee on Lotteries. 1833.
12. Brief Survey of the Lottery System. Philadelphia, 1833.
13. Letter on the President's Message; supposed to be written to La Fayette. New York, 1833.
14. Lecture on Money and Currency. By William Reid. New York, 1834.
15. Letters to John Quincy Adams. By B. Hazard. Providence, 1834.
16. Fatal Mistake; showing the Nature, &c., of Popery. By a Native American. Rochester, 1835.
17. What is a Monopoly? or, some Considerations on Corporations and Currency. By a Citizen of New York. New York, 1835.
18. Parochial Settlements an Obstruction to Poor Law Reform. By John Meadows White. London, 1835.
19. Questions upon Various Subjects connected with Architecture. London, 1835.
20. Speech of Daniel Webster on the Currency. New York, 1840.
21. Correspondence of John A. Graham. New York, 1835.

" 90. 1. Anniversary Oration on Quarantines. By Charles Caldwell. Philadelphia, 1807.
2. An Act for the Effectual Performance of Quarantine. New York, 1809.
3. Documents and Facts showing the Fatal Effects of Interments in Populous Cities. New York, 1822.
4. Considerations on the Principal Events of the French Revolution. By Madame de Staël. New York, 1818.
5. Dissertatio Inauguralis Medica. By Francisci Xaverii Koller. 1778.
6. De la Tievre en Général. Par M. Reich. 1800.
7. Recueil de Préceptes. Par Laurent Bodin. Paris.

" 91. 1. Address of the Society of Tammany, or Columbian Order. New York, 1819.
2. Plain Sense or National Industry. New York, 1820.
3. Address before the New England Society of Philadelphia. By Joseph G. Nancrede. Philadelphia, 1820.
4. Address of the Friends of Domestic Industry. Baltimore, 1831.
5. Facts for the Laboring Man. By a Laboring Man. Newport, 1840.
6. Rights of Labor. By Calvin Colton. New York, 1847.
7. Cheap Postage. Remarks on the Subject. By Joshua Leavitt. Boston, 1848.
8. Letter to John M. Clayton, submitting a Plan for Opening, &c., &c., American Commerce in the East. By Aaron H. Palmer. Washington, 1849.

" 92. 1. Speech of John C. Spencer on the Repeal of the Laws prohibiting Private Banking. Albany, 1825.
2. List of Officers and Members of the New York Convention. 1831.
3. Speech of John Hume, M. P., on the Bank of England. London, 1839.
4. Failure of the Franklin Bank, &c. By Robert Bartow. New York, 1831.
5. Explanation and Vindication of Samuel Leggett. New York, 1831.
6. Thirteenth Report of the Bank for Savings. New York, 1832.
7. Credit, Currency and Banking. By Eleazer Lord. New York, 1834.
8. Charter of the State Bank of Illinois. Springfield, 1835.

Vol. 92. 9. Short History of Paper Money and Banking. By William M. Gouge. New York, 1835.

10. Collection of Acts relative to the Bank of New York. 1811.

11. Letter to Albert Gallatin on the Doctrine of Gold and Silver. By Publicola. New York, 1815.

12. Appeal to the Public on the Conduct of the Banks of New York City. By Isaac Brunson. New York, 1815.

13. Bank for Savings. An Address to the Public. New York, 1819.

14. First Report of the Bank for Savings. New York, 1820.

15. Disclosure of the Real Parties to the Purchase and Sale of the Tradesmen's Bank in 1826.

" 93. 1. Remarks upon Usury and its Effects. By Whitehook. New York, 1841.

2. Bank of the United States. Boston, 1831.

3. Webster's Speeches on the United States Bank. Washington, 1832.

4. President's Message on the Bank Bill; Extract from Clay's Speech; Clinton's Address; and a Sketch of Van Buren. New York, 1832.

5. Extracts from the Veto Message of General Jackson. New York, 1832.

6. Speech of W. H. Maynard on the United States Bank. Albany, 1832.

7. The War on the United States Bank. Philadelphia, 1834.

8. Considerations in favor of a National Bank. By Alexander Hamilton. New York, 1834.

9. Essay on the Spirit of Jacksonism. By Aristides. Philadelphia, 1835.

" 94. 1. Report on the proposed Canal from the Hudson to the Head Waters of the Lackawaxen River. Philadelphia, 1824.

2. Facts and Observations in relation to the Origin and Completion of the Erie Canal. New York, 1825.

3. Monograph of the Doubtful Reptiles. By Daniel H. Barnes.

4. Report of the Engineers of the Lehigh Coal and Navigation Company. 1826.

5. Report of the Commissioners appointed to Explore the Route of a Canal to unite the River Delaware with the Passaic. Morristown, 1823.

6. Report on the Practicability of Navigating with Steamboats on the Southern Waters. By Robert Fulton. Philadelphia, 1828.

7. Report of the Board of Managers of the Lehigh Coal and Navigation Company. Philadelphia, 1830.

8. Annual Report of the Managers of the Union Canal Company. Philadelphia, 1830.

9. Letter to John Wurtz, in relation to the Delaware and Hudson Canal. By Fair Play & Co. Philadelphia, 1831.

10. Rules and Regulations of the Morris Canal. Jersey City, 1831.

11. Report of the Committee on Internal Improvement and Inland Navigation. By Charles J. Ingersoll. Harrisburgh, 1831.

12. Remarks on the Sodus Canal. New York, 1832.

13. Address on the Subject of a Railroad. Pittsburgh, 1832.

14. Annual Report of the Union Canal Company. Philadelphia, 1832.

15. Report of the Canal Commissioners of Pennsylvania. Harrisburgh, 1832.

16. Appeal in favor of Constructing the Genesee and Allegany Canal. New York, 1833.

Vol. 94. 17. Bericht der Canal Commissioners von Pennsylvanien. Harrisburgh, 1833.

18. Charter and Reports of the Sandy and Beaver Canal Company. New Lisbon, O., 1834.

19. Report of the Probable Revenue of the Chesapeake and Ohio Canal. 1834.

" 95. 1. Report of Engineers on the Practicability of the Long Island Railroad Company. New York, 1834.

2. Report on the Survey of a Route for the Susquehanna and Delaware Railroad. By Ephraim Beach. New York, 1832.

3. First Annual Report of the Phillipsburg and Juniata Railroad Company. New York, 1833.

4. Circular to Capitalists, relative to Milwaukie City Loans. Milwaukie, 1850.

5. Sixth Annual Report of the Baltimore and Ohio Railroad Company. Baltimore, 1832.

6. First Annual Report of the Hartford and New Haven Railroad Company. New Haven, 1836.

7. Address of the New York and Erie Railroad Company. Auburn, 1837.

8. Third Annual Report of the Hartford and New Haven Railroad Company. 1838.

9. First Annual Report of the Housatonic Railroad Company. New Haven, 1838.

10. Papers and Documents relative to the Mohawk and St. Lawrence Railroad and Navigation Company. Albany, 1838.

11. Philosophy of Railroads. By Thomas C. Keefer. Montreal, 1850.

12. Report of the Committee on the Delaware and Raritan Canal. Princeton, 1836.

13. Report on a Railroad from Watertown to Rome. By William Dewey. Watertown, 1836.

14. Letter on the Advantages of Railroads. By John L. Sullivan. New Haven, 1836.

15. Proceedings of a Railroad Convention. Windsor, 1836.

16. Report Relative to the Termination of the Columbia and Philadelphia Railroad. Philadelphia, 1830.

17. Proceedings of a Railroad Convention. Windsor, 1836.

18. Facts and Suggestions relative to the New York and Albany Railroad. Albany, 1835.

" 96. 1. Report against the Direct Route for the Eastern Termination of the Erie Canal, and answer to the Report of Allen Campbell. Troy, 1836.

2. Report of the Committee on Roads and Canals on the Petition of the Harlem River Canal Company. New York, 1839.

3. Prize Essay; The Canals of Canada, their Prospects and Influence. Toronto, 1850.

4. Correspondence on the Importance and Practicability of a Railroad from New York to New Orleans. By Dewitt Clinton. New York, 1830.

5. Sketch of the Geographical Route of a Great Railway proposed to Connect the Atlantic States and the Valley of the Mississippi. New York, 1830.

Vol. 96. 6. Report of Examinations and Surveys of a Route for a Railroad from Canajoharie to Catskill. By John Pickell. Catskill, 1831.
7. Remarks, &c., of Capt. E. Bech, on the Canajoharie and Catskill Railroad. New York, 1831.
8. Prospectus of a Route of the Hudson and Delaware Railroad. Newburgh, 1831.
9. Report of the Boston and Providence Railroad Company. Boston, 1832.
10. The Same.
11. Annual Report of the Canal Commissioners. Harrisburgh, 1831.
12. Report relative to the Use of the Water of the River Delaware. Harrisburgh, 1834.
13. Genesee and Alleghany Canal Meeting.
14. Documents relative to the Susquehanna Canal Company. Baltimore, 1835.
15. Report on the Bill to Expedite the Construction of a Railroad from New York to Lake Erie. Albany, 1836.
16. Appeal in relation to the Proposed Enlargement of the Erie Canal. 1836.

" 97. 1. Impartial Inquiry into the Conduct of Governor Lewis. By Politicus. New York, 1806.
2. Impartial Examination of the Case of Capt. Isaac Phillips. Baltimore, 1825.
3. Speeches of Jacob Barker. New York, 1826.
4. Report of the Evidence in the Conspiracy Case. New York, 1832.
5. Charge to the Grand Jury. By Charles G. Ferris.
6. Court for the Trial of Impeachment and the Correction of Errors. The Case of Bogardus against Trinity Church. New York, 1835.
7. Cow Pox Epistle to Rev. Rowland Hill. By Benjamin Moseley. London, 1807.

" 98. 1. Opinion of the Court on a Motion for a New Trial on behalf of Col. Lehre. By a Member of the Bar.
2. Report of the Proceedings in the Case of Surgeon Jacques, and in the Case of Lieut. Col. De la Montagnie. By John Anthon. New York, 1812.
3. Trial of Capt. Henry Whitby, and the Trial of Capt. George Crimp. New York, 1812.
4. Report of the Trial of Charles N. Baldwin. By H. W. Warner. New York, 1818.
5. Vindication of Col. J. A. Coles from the charges of Dr. Bronaugh. Washington, 1814.
6. Report of the Trial of John Quay. By Daniel Rodgers. New York, 1817.
7. Report of the Trial of Henry R. Hagerman. By David Bacon. New York, 1818.
8. Report of the Case of James Maurice against Samuel Judd. By William Sampson. New York, 1819.
9. Exposé of Facts relating to the Conduct of Winslow Lewis. By David Melville. Providence, 1819.
10. Case of George W. Nevin. By William Sampson. New York, 1822.
11. Trial of the Case of the Commonwealth *vs.* J. T. Buckingham. Boston, 1822.

Vol. 98. 12. Documentary Evidence in the Controversy of the Regents of the University and the Trustees of Union College. 1823.

" 99. 1. Case of Gibbons against Ogden. By Henry Wheaton. New York, 1824.

2. Exhibit of Injustice suffered by John Randel, Jr. Philadelphia, 1825.

3. Examination of the Case of Capt. Isaac Phillips. Baltimore, 1825.

4. The Demurrer or Proofs of Error in the Decision of the Supreme Court. By Thomas Herttell. New York, 1828.

5. Reply to the Criticisms of J. N. Barker. By James Mease. Philadelphia, 1828.

6. Verdict of Condemnation on the Appeal of H. G. Otis & Co., with the Decision of John Q. Adams. New York, 1829.

7. Reports of the Trials of David T. Chase, John W. Fellows and Jired Bull. By J. S. Carpenter. New York, 1829.

8. Opinion of Chief Justice Marshall, and the Opinion of Justice McLean, in the Case of Samuel A. Worcester against the State of Georgia. Washington, 1832.

9. Trial of Reuben Crandall, M. D. New York, 1836.

10. Report of the Trial of Dr. J. G. Vought for Libel. New York, 1831.

11. Report of the Case in Chancery of Thomas R. Walker against N. Devereux and others. By Benjamin F. Cooper. Utica, 1834.

" 100. 1. Inquiry into the Effects of Ardent Spirits. By Benjamin Rush. Boston, 1812.

2. Extracts from Dr. Rush's Inquiry into the Effects of Ardent Spirits. Philadelphia, 1816.

3. Exposé of the Causes of Intemperance and the Remedy. By Thomas Herttell. New York, 1819.

4. Discourse on Intemperance. By Beman.

5. Report of the Providence Association for the Promotion of Temperance. Providence, 1830.

6. Constitution of the Providence Association for the Promotion of Temperance. 1830.

7. Address delivered by H. Lyman on Temperance. 1830.

8. Report of the New York City Temperance Society. New York, 1830.

9. Oration, by Daniel Drake, on the Intemperance of Cities, Gambling, Idleness, Fashion and Sabbath Breaking. Philadelphia, 1831.

10. Essay on the Sins of the Temperate. By Ephraim Peabody. Meadeville, 1831.

11. Address, by Hon. W. Cranch, for the Promotion of Temperance. Alexandria, 1831.

12. Report of the New York State Society for the Promotion of Temperance. Albany, 1831.

13. Report of the American Temperance Society. Boston, 1832.

" 101. 1. Oration, by Charles Caldwell, Commemorative of American Independence. Philadelphia, 1810.

2. Oration, by Richard Rush, on the Anniversary of American Independence. Washington, 1812.

3. Oration, by Samuel H. Smith, on the Fifth of July, 1813. Washington.

4. Fourth of July Oration. By Samuel Berrian. New York, 1815.

Vol. 101. 5. Fourth of July Oration. By Samuel Jackson. Philadelphia, 1818.
6. Fourth of July Oration. By Hooper Cummings. New York, 1824.
7. Fourth of July Oration. By Alexander B. Johnson. Utica, 1824.
8. Oration on Washington's Birthday. By Thomas H. Genin.
9. Fourth of July Oration. By Henry V. S. Vanderbergh. Albany, 1824.
10. Public Oration before the Phi Alpha Theta Society, July 4, 1826. By Benjamin Drake. Cincinnati, 1826.
11. Fourth of July Oration. By Oliver Smith. Burlington, 1826.
12. Fourth of July Address delivered at West Point. By Cadet Joseph Ritner. Newburgh, 1829.
13. Address by General Harrison, delivered on the Fourth of July. Cincinnati, 1833.
14. Fourth of July Oration. By John B. Scoles. Rahway, 1835.
15. Oration on the Power and Extent of Political Delusion. By Abraham Bishop. Philadelphia, 1800.
16. Oration on the Cession of Louisiana. By David Ramsay. Charleston, 1804.
17. Oration delivered on the Anniversary of the Sortie from Fort Erie. By James T. B. Romayne. New York, 1816.
18. Discourse by Daniel Sharp. Boston, 1824.
19. Address delivered by Robert Owen. Cincinnati, 1825.
20. Lecture on the Working Men's Party. By Edward Everett. Boston, 1830.
21. Speech of the Hon. Tristam Burges. New York, 1831.
22. Baccalaureate Address. By Philip Lindsley. Nashville, 1832.
23. The same.
24. Address on the Principles of Peace. By Thos. S. Grimke. Hartford, 1832.
25. Centennial Address. By Samuel L. Southard. Trenton, 1832.

" 102. 1. Observations on Slavery. By James Anderson. Manchester, 1789.
2. Negro Slavery Unjustifiable; a Sermon by Alexander McLeod. New York, 1802.
3. Minutes of the Convention for the Abolition of Slavery. Philadelphia, 1806.
4. Remarks on Slavery. By John Parish. Philadelphia, 1806.
5. Observations on Slavery. By Elias Hicks. New York, 1814.
6. Laws relative to Slaves and Servants. New York, 1817.
7. Examination of the Constitutionality, &c., of Prohibiting Slavery. By Mr. Blunt. New York, 1819.
8. Minutes of the Abolition Convention. Philadelphia, 1819.
9. Substance of Two Speeches on the Missouri Bill by Rufus King. New York, 1819.
10. Minutes of the Abolition Convention. Philadelphia, 1818.
11. Speech of James Tallmadge, Jr., on Slavery. New York 1819.
12. Speeches of Messrs. King, Taylor and Tallmadge. Philadelphia, 1819.
13. Report of the New York Colonization Society. New York, 1823.
14. Thoughts on Improving the Condition of the Slaves. By T. Clarkson. New York, 1823.

" 103. 1. Immediate, not Gradual Abolition. New York, 1825.

Vol. 103. 2. Address on the Progress of Manufactures, &c. By Thomas P. Jones. Philadelphia, 1827.

3. Letters, &c., of Distinguished Citizens. New York, 1828.

4. Treatise on the Patriarchal or Co-operative System of Society. 1828.

5. Addresses, &c. By Rev. T. Gallaudet, Captain Stockton, Francis S. Kiy, and Letters by Captain Nicholson. New York, 1829.

6. Laws relative to Slaves. New York, 1830.

7. Address on Slavery. By Robert J. Breckenridge. Frankfort, 1831.

8. Practicability of the Abolition of Slavery. New York, 1831.

9. Excessive Cruelty to Slaves. By Henry Whiteley. 1832.

10. Discourse on the Condition of the Colored Population. By J. K. Converse. Burlington, 1832.

11. Address of the American Colonization Society. Washington, 1832.

12. Review of Pamphlets on Slavery and Colonization. New Haven, 1833.

13. Immediate Emancipation. By Charles Stuart. New Haven, 1833.

14. Dissolution of the Union. By M. Carey. Philadelphia, 1832.

15. Common Sense Addresses. By M. Carey. Philadelphia, 1829.

16. Appeal to Common Sense and Common Justice. By M. Carey. Philadelphia, 1822.

17. Appeal to the Wealthy. By M. Carey. Philadelphia, 1833.

18. Annals of Liberality, Generosity, Public Spirit, &c.

" 104. 1. Review of the Report of the American Anti-Slavery Society. By David M. Reese. New York, 1834.

2. Appeal to the Churches in behalf of Africa. New York, 1834.

3. Address against Immediate Emancipation. By Heman Howlett. New York, 1834.

4. Address of the Colonization Society to the Public. New York, 1834.

5. The "Extinguisher" Extinguished; or, David M. Reese "used up." By David Ruggles. New York, 1834.

6. The Liberian Colony, and Letters on the Colonization Society. By M. Carey. Philadelphia, 1834.

7. Amenability of Northern Incendiaries, and an Inquiry into the Lawfulness of Slavery. By Richard Yeadon, Jr. Charleston, 1835.

8. Remarks upon Slavery. By a Citizen of Georgia. Augusta, 1835.

9. The Abolitionist. February, 1835.

10. Letter to Lord Brougham on American Slavery. By an American. London, 1835.

11. Remarks upon Slavery. By a Citizen of Georgia. Philadelphia, 1835.

12. Report of the Executive Committee of the American Union. Boston, 1836.

13. The same.

14. The Bible against Slavery. New York, 1838.

15. Correspondence between Hon. F. H. Elmore and James G. Birney. New York, 1838.

16. Anti-Slavery Magazine. January, 1836.

" 105. 1. Proceedings, &c., of a Temperance Meeting. Washington, 1833.

2. Address on the Traffic in Ardent Spirits. By Worthington Smith. St. Albans, 1833.

I. 105. 3. National Temperance Circular.
4. Address on Temperance. By A. D. Eddy.
5. Report of the Pennsylvanian Society for Discouraging the Use of Ardent Spirits. 1830.
6. Temperance Address. By Joel G. Seaver. New York, 1835.
7. Report of the New York City Temperance Society. New York, 1837.
8. Report of the Royal Humane Society. London, 1814.
9. Report on the General Character and Forms of the Language of the American Indians. Philadelphia, 1819.
10. Report of the Society for Promoting Manual Labor in Literary Institutions. New York, 1833.
11. Thirty-Seventh Annual Report of the Trustees of the Public School Society of New York. 1842.
12. Fourth Annual Report of the Trustees of the High School. New York, 1828.
13. Address of the Trustees of the Public School Society. New York, 1828.
14. Fifth Annual Report of the Trustees of the High School. New York, 1829.
15. Twenty-Ninth Annual Report of the Trustees of the Public School Society. New York, 1834.

" 106. 1. Mode of Instruction pursued by the Rev. John M. Mason. New York, 1828.
2. Annual Report of the Superintendent of Common Schools. Albany, 1829.
3. Report of the Committee on Education. Lexington, 1830.
4. Report on the State of Education in Pennsylvania; also an Address by M. M. Carll. Philadelphia, 1830.
5. Considerations upon the Expediency and the Means of Establishing a University in New York. 1830.
6. Address of the State Convention of Teachers and Friends of Education. Utica, 1831.
7. Annual Report of the Regents of the University of the State of New York. Albany, 1831.
8. Report on the Objects and Modes of Sunday School Instruction. By James W. Weir. Philadelphia, 1833.
9. Report on the Subject of a System of General Education. By Samuel Beck. Harrisburgh, 1834.
10. Remarks on the Relation between Education and Crime, by Francis Lieber; with some Observations by N. H. Julius. Philadelphia, 1835
11. The Schoolmaster and Advocate of Education. March, 1836.
12. Thoughts on Popular Education. By a Citizen of Pennsylvania. 1836
13. Method of Spiritual Culture. Boston, 1836.
14. Remarks on Education. By Mr. Rantoul.
15. Address upon Education and Common Schools. By James Henry, Jr. New York, 1846.

" 107. 1. Address to the Benefactors, &c., of the Free School Society. By De Witt Clinton. New York, 1810.
2. Hints relative to Native Schools. Serampore, 1816.

Vol. 107. 3. Seventh Report of the Society for Promoting the Education of the Poor of Ireland. Dublin, 1819.

4. First Annual Report of the Controllers of the Public Schools. Philadelphia, 1819.

5. Letters on National Subjects auxiliary to Universal Education. By Joseph Lancaster. Washington, 1820.

6. Memorials concerning the Law granting Peculiar Privileges to the Bethel Baptist Church. 1823.

7. Report of the High School Committee on a Plan of Instruction. New York, 1824.

8. An Act relating to Common Schools. New York, 1825.

9. Report on the Distribution of the Common School Fund. New York, 1825.

10. Law regulating the Distribution of the Common School Fund.

11. Report of the Free School Society. New York, 1825.

12. Report of the Committee on Laws. New York, 1825.

13. Outline of a System of Education. By Robert Dale Owen. Glasgow, 1824.

14. Report of the Controllers of the Public Schools. Philadelphia, 1825.

15. Report of the High School Society. New York, 1826.

16. Proposal for a Plan of a French School. By John Manesca. New York, 1826.

17. By-Laws of the Public School Society. New York, 1826.

18. Acts providing for the Education of Children. Philadelphia, 1827.

19. Report of the Trustees of the Public School Society. New York, 1827.

" 108. 1. Report of the New Church Free School Society. London, 1826.

2. Report of the Protestant Episcopal Sunday School Society. N. Y., 1833.

3. The same. 1832.

4. Report of the Female Union Society. New York, 1823.

5. Report of the American Sunday School Union. Philadelphia, 1832.

6. Report of the Sunday School Society for Ireland. Dublin, 1828.

7. Appeal in behalf of the Illinois College. New York, 1831.

8. Facts and Documents in relation to Harvard College. By Hollis and others. Boston, 1829.

9. Address to the Patrons and Friends of Harvard College. By Alumnus.

10. Letter to Governor Lincoln in relation to Harvard University. By F. C. Gray. Boston, 1831.

" 109. 1. Address delivered by the Rev. John Rudd. Preston, 1811.

2. Substance of an Address to the Lord Mayor of London. By R. H. Marten. London, 1812.

3. Address to the Officers composing the Medical Staff. By Samuel L. Mitchill. New York, 1820.

3½. Address before the Apprentices' Library. By Solomon Southwick. Albany, 1821.

4. Discourse delivered by John Stanford to the Lunatics. New York, 1821.

5. Discourse. By De Witt Clinton. Albany, 1823.

Vol. 109. 6. Discourse, by De Witt Clinton, before the New York Alpha of the Phi Beta Kappa. New York, 1823.

7. Discourse delivered by Rev. Gregory T. Bedell, at the request of the Committee for the Relief of the Greeks. Philadelphia, 1827.

8. A Voice from Greece. From Dr. Howe's Remarks.

9. Oration. By Edward Everett. New York, 1824.

10. The same.

11. Address. By A. R. Johnson. Utica, 1824.

12. Lecture. By Thomas Henderson. Washington, 1825.

13. Oration. By Hon. Archibald D. Murphy. Raleigh, 1827.

14. Discourse, by Thomas Whittemore, before the Female Samaritan Society. Boston, 1828.

15. Speech of Henry Clay, with Remarks by a Citizen of Virginia. Richmond, 1829.

16. Address, by William Wirt, at Rutger's College. 1830.

17. Oration, delivered by Samuel L. Gouverneur, in Commemoration of the Revolution in France. New York, 1830.

18. Discourse, by Lewis Cass, before the Historical Society of Michigan. Detroit, 1830.

19. Address, by Barnabas Bates, at Tammany Hall. New York, 1830.

20. Address. By William Wirt. 1830.

21. Address, by William Price, at Dickinson College. Carlisle, 1830.

22. Discourse, by Job R. Tyson, before the Historical Society. Philadelphia, 1831.

23. Address, by John W. Francis, before the Philolexian Society. New York, 1831.

24. Address before the Working Men's Society. By Samuel Whitcomb, Jr. Dedham, 1831.

" 110. 1. Address delivered at Nashville. By William G. Hunt. Nashville, 1831.

2. Address, by George M. Dallas, at the Commencement of the College of New Jersey. Princeton, 1831.

3. Indian Rights and Our Duty. An Address by Heman Humphrey. Hartford, 1831.

4. Address, by Theron Metcalf, at Brown University. Boston, 1833.

5. Lecture on the Parotid Gland. By Granville S. Pattison. Philadelphia, 1833.

6. Discourse, by R. Bunner, on the Genius and Spirit of the People. New York, 1834.

7. Address before the Peithologian Society. By William B. Maclay. New York, 1835.

8. Despotism of Freedom. By David L. Child. Boston, 1833.

9. Discourse by R. Bunner. New York, 1834.

10. Oration on the History of the first Discovery and Settlement of the New World. By James F. Conover. Cincinnati, 1835.

11. Address on Education. By John Rennie. Columbia, 1835.

12. Address by Henry Vethake. Lexington, 1835.

13. Inaugural Address by Thomas J. Conant. Utica, 1835.

Vol. 110. 14. Address by Gunning S. Bedford. New York, 1836.

15. Address, by James L. Homer, delivered before the Massachusetts Association. Boston, 1836.

16. Oration before the Literary Association. By William B. Maclay. New York, 1836.

17. Address before the Boston Phrenological Society. By S. G. Howe. Boston, 1836.

18. Considerations in Favor of Classical Studies. By Charles H. Lyon. New York, 1839.

19. Address on Patent Laws.

20. Discourse before the New England Society. By J. Prescott Hall. New York, 1848.

21. Anniversary Oration before the Academy of Medicine. By Alfred C. Post. New York, 1849.

22. Address delivered at the Provincial Industrial Exhibition. By Charles D. Day. Montreal, 1850.

" 111. 1. Considerations upon the Expediency, &c., of Establishing a University. New York, 1830.

2. Exposition of the Reasons for the Resignation of some of the Professors in the University. New York, 1833.

3. Annual Report of the Regents of the University. Albany, 1847.

" 112. 1. Observations on the Hurricanes and Storms of the West Indies, &c. By William C. Redfield.

2. Report upon an Examination of some of the Gas Manufactories in Europe. By S. V. Merrick. Philadelphia, 1834.

3. Examination of the Theory of a Resisting Medium. By R. W. Haskins.

4. Physiological Explanation of the Beauty of Form. By Benjamin F. Joslyn. Albany, 1837.

5. Phrenology Vindicated. By Charles Caldwell. Lexington, 1835.

6. Gales and Hurricanes of the Western Atlantic. By William C. Redfield.

7. Electro-Magnetism; the History of Davenport's Invention. By Professor Silliman and Mrs. Somerville. New York, 1837.

8. Advantages of Ralston for the Manufacture of Iron. New York, 1843.

9. Democracy in Modern Communities. From the French of M. Guizot. London, 1838.

10. Exposition of Hazlitt's Translation of Guizot's History of Civilization. By R. W. Haskins. Buffalo, 1846.

11. Great Astronomical Discoveries by Sir John Herschel; also, Observations on Ewbank's Patent Office Report.

12. Statistics of Onondaga Salt Springs. By Thos. Spencer. Syracuse, 1850.

13. The same.

14. Reports and other Documents on Ventilation. Boston, 1848.

15. Report on the History of the Discovery of Neptune. By Benjamin A. Gould, Jr. Washington, 1850.

16. Essay on Alcoholic and Narcotic Substances. By Edward Hitchcock. Amherst, 1830.

17. Mechanic's Assistant in the Sciences and Arts. 1833.

18. Account of the Discovery, &c., of Gutta Percha.

Vol. 113. 1. Catalogue of Organic Remains. By Samuel L. Mitchill. New York, 1826.

2. Natural History of the Fishes inhabiting the River Ohio. By C. S. Rafinesque. Lexington, 1820.

3. Essai d'une Description Minéralogique. Par Léopold de Buck. Paris. 1805.

4. Prospectus of Audubon's Birds of America.

5. Description of New Species of Fossil Shells. By J. G. Morton. 1828.

6. Catalogue of Organic Remains. By Samuel L. Mitchill. New York, 1826.

7. Charter, &c., of the Lyceum of Natural History. New York, 1826.

8. Report on Shells from Delaware. By J. E. De Kay. 1827.

9. Supplement to the Genera of North American Birds, &c. By Charles Lucien Bonaparte.

10. Essay on a New Species of Duck. By Charles Bonaparte. 1824.

11. Description of a New Species of South American Fringilla. By Charles Bonaparte. 1825.

12. Introductory Lecture. By Prof. Silliman. New Haven, 1828.

13. Anniversary Discourse, by Peter S. Townsend, before the Lyceum of Natural History. New York, 1820.

14. Catalogue of Plants indigenous to the State of New York. 1840.

15. Report relative to a large Marine Animal, supposed to be a Serpent. Boston, 1817.

16. Natural History of the Fishes of the Ohio. By C. S. Rafinesque.

" 114. 1. Report on Steam Carriages. Washington, 1832.

2. Report on the Survey and Examination of the Neversink River. New York, 1838.

3. Substitute for Railroads and Canals; embracing a New Plan of Road-way. By Robert Mills. Washington, 1834.

4. Memorial in favor of Relieving Broadway by making a New Thoroughfare.

5. Considerations on Communication between the Atlantic and Pacific. By a Citizen of New York. Georgetown, 1836.

6. Report of Samuel B. Cushing, respecting the Harbor of Van Buren. New York, 1836.

7. Sketch of a Railway. New York, 1841.

8. Report on the Project of uniting the Great Bays of Long Island by Canals. Brooklyn, 1848.

9. Essay on the Propulsion of Navigable Bodies. By C. A. Busby. New York, 1818.

10. Description of a Plan for Navigating the Rapids in Rivers. By Edward Clark. Philadelphia, 1823.

11. Circular in favor of Improving the Navigation of the Delaware.

12. Remarks on the Proposed Breakwater at Cape Henlopen. By William Jones. Philadelphia, 1826.

13. Account of the Ship Life-Boat. By James Mather. Edinburgh, 1830.

" 115. 1. The Hydraulic Railway. By J. G. Shuttleworth. London, 1842.

Vol. 115. 2. The Nature of Electricity. By Robert S. Wood. Philadelphia, 1844.
3. Cosmos. By Humboldt.
4. Hurricanes of the Atlantic. By W. C. Redfield. New Haven, 1846.
5. Mysteries of Nature Revealed. By James Glenn. New York, 1846.
6. Polygonal Equation and Progression, &c. By Augustus Young.
7. Hints to Inventors and others. By J. P. Pirsson. New York, 1849.
8. Isometrical Drawing. By Professor Farish. New York, 1849.
9. Teeth of Gear Wheels. By Professor R. Willis. New York, 1849.
10. Quadrature of the Circle, &c. By Augustus Young.
11. Astronomy for Schools. By R. W. Haskins. New York, 1841.
12. Address, &c., of the Astronomical Society of London. 1821.
13. Water Power at the Potomac. By M. C. Ewing.
14. Gales and Hurricanes of the Western Atlantic. By W. C. Redfield.

" 116. 1. Geological Survey of the County of Albany.
2. Experimental Inquiry into the Spirœa Tomentosa of Linnæus. By Elijah Mead. New York, 1821.
3. Geological and Agricultural Survey of Rensselaer County. Albany, 1822.
4. Essay on Salt. By Jeremiah Van Rensselaer. New York, 1823.
5. Report on the Geology of North Carolina. By Denison Olmsted. 1824.
6. Remarks on the Cut-Worm.
7. Remarks on the Preparation of Mortar. By Denison Olmsted. 1825.
8. Memoir on the Culture of Cotton. By George W. Jeffreys.
9. Geological Text-Book. By Amos Eaton. 1832.
10. First Annual Report of the Natural History Society of Montreal. 1828.
11. Constitution and By-Laws of the Natural History Society of Montreal. 1828.
12. Lecture on Natural History. By Samuel L. Mitchill. New York, 1828.

" 117. 1. Immobility of the Earth. By M. De la Jonchere. London, 1728.
2. Pettibone's Economy of Fuel. Philadelphia, 1812.
3. Essay on the Central Influence of Magnetism. By Joel Abbot. Philadelphia, 1814.
4. Mobility and Motion in Animal Bodies. By Charles W. Windship. Boston, 1818.
5. Observations on the Influence of the Moon. Philadelphia, 1798.
6. Essays on the General Phenomena of the Universe. By Sir Richard Phillips. London, 1818.
7. Exposition of the Atomic Theory, &c. By William James Macneven. New York, 1819.
8. Chemical Exercises. By William James Macneven. New York, 1819.
9. Annals of Nature. By C. S. Rafinesque. 1820.
10. Philosophical Essays on the Conformation of Matter and the Earth. By James Sims. Cincinnati, 1823.
11. Some further Facts in Vision. By Edward C. Cooper. New York, 1824.
12. Essay on Electrical Fluids. By Robert Hare.
13. Theory of Thunder Showers, &c. By Hortensius. New York, 1823.
14. Observations on Electricity. By George F. Hopkins. New York, 1825.
15. Vindication of Mr. Genet's Memorial on the Upward Forces of Fluids. New Haven, 1827.

Vol. 117. 16. Answer to one of the Committee of the American Academy. By Marcus Bull. Philadelphia, 1828.

17. Statement of a Theory of Life. By David Porter. 1820.

" 118. 1. Caratteri di Alcuni Nuovi Generi e Nuove Specie di Animali. By C. S. Rafinesque Schmaltz. Palermo, 1810.

2. Principios Fundamentales para Servir de Introduccion a la Escuela Botanica-Agricola. By Ramon de la Sagra.

" 119. 1. Le Livre de Tous des Ménages ou l'Art de Conserver.

2. Compte Rendu des Travaux de la Société Linnéenne de Paris. By Thiebaut de Berneaud. Paris, 1822.

3. The same. 1823.

4. Eloge Historique de A. M. F. J. Palisot de Beauvois. By Thiebaut de Berneaud. Paris, 1821.

5. Exposition de la Doctrine Botanique. By Thiebaut de Berneaud. Paris, 1822.

" 120. 1. Fragmens sur la Theorie des Sources. Lausanne, 1804.

2. Disertaciones Médico-Quirurgicas, sober varios Puntos Importantes. By José Manuel Valdes. Madrid, 1815.

3. Sul Gesso considerato Come Ingrasso Memoria del Dottor Filippo Gallizioli. Firenze, 1816.

4. Catalogo dei Generi Vendibili presso Giacinto Micali e Figlio. 1793.

" 121. 1. Method for Draining Lands Overflowed by the Tides. By Lescallier Roseau. 1802.

2. Statement of Facts relative to the Establishment and Progress of the Elgin Botanic Garden. By David Hosack. New York, 1811.

3. Discours sur l'état Ancien et Moderne de l'Agriculture et de la Botanique. By Charles Van Hulthem. Gand, 1817.

4. Memorias para Servir de Introduccion, a la Horticultura Cabana. By Ramon de la Sagra. New York, 1827.

5. Description, Cultivation and Management of Honey Bees. By Francis Kelsey. New York, 1835.

6. Report on the Culture of the Beet Root, &c. By James Pedder. Philadelphia, 1836.

7. Tables and Notes on the Cultivation, Manufacture and Foreign Trade of Cotton. Washington, 1836.

8. Treatise on Peruvian and Ichaboe African Guano. By J. H. Sheppard. Liverpool, 1844.

9. Proceedings of the Agricultural Chemistry Association of Scotland. Edinburgh, 1845.

10. Report of the Committee of Management. Edinburgh, 1846.

11. The Potato Disease in Scotland. Edited by Professor Johnston. Edinburgh, 1845.

" 122. 1. Considerations on the Necessity of Establishing an Agricultural College. Albany, 1819.

2. Address of the General Committee of the Board of Agriculture of the State of New York. Albany, 1820.

3. Address of Jonathan Allen before the Berkshire Association. Pittsfield, 1821.

Vol. 122. 4. Address of Thos. Gold before the Berkshire Association. Pittsfield, 1811.

5. Address on the Botany of the United States. By Jacob Green. Albany, 1814.

6. Discourse on Agriculture. By Richard Peters. Philiadelphia, 1815.

7. Addresses of Gen. Jacob Morris and Elkanah Watson, before the Otsego County Agricultural Association. Cooperstown, 1817.

8. Examination into the Expediency of Establishing a Board of Agriculture. Brooklyn, 1819.

9. History of the Berkshire Agricultural Society. By Elkanah Watson. Albany, 1819.

10. Address before the Philadelphia Society for Promoting Agriculture. By William Tilghman. Philadelphia, 1820.

11. Address on the Disorder which prevailed among Horned Cattle. By David R. Arnell. Goshen, 1821.

12. Address before the Philadelphia Society for Promoting Agriculture. By James M. Broom. Philadelphia, 1821.

13. Address before the Philadelphia Society for Promoting Agriculture. By Nicholas Biddle. Philadelphia, 1822.

14. Address before the Agricultural Society of North Carolina. By R. H. Helme. Raleigh, 1822.

15. Address before the Philadelphia Society for Promoting Agriculture. By Mathew Carey. Philadelphia, 1824.

16. Address before the Philadelphia Society for Promoting Agriculture. By Robert Vaux. Philadelphia, 1825.

17. Address before the Agricultural Society. By Noah Webster. Northampton, 1818.

18. Address before the Philadelphia Society for Promoting Agriculture. By William Rawle. Philadelphia, 1819.

" 123. 1. Address, by Zebedee Cook, Jr., before the Massachusetts Horticultural Society. Boston, 1830.

2. Statistical Report of the County of Albany. Albany, 1824.

3. Horticultural Register and Gardener's Magazine. January, 1835.

4. Address, by V. Le Ray de Chaumont, before the Jefferson County Agricultural Society. 1830.

5. Address by Josiah T. Marshall, before the Agricultural Meeting of Jefferson County. Watertown, 1838.

6. Address at the Cattle Shows, on Labor. By Henry Coleman. Boston, 1839.

7. Address, by Thaddeus Burr Wakeman, before the New Jersey State Agricultural Society. Princeton, 1840.

8. Address, by J. B. Nott, before the New York State Agricultural Society. Albany, 1842.

9. Address, by William T. McCoun, before the Queen's County Agricultural Society. New York, 1843.

10. Second Annual Report of the Monroe County Agricultural Society, and Address by Daniel Lee. Rochester, 1845.

11. Address, by Hon. I. W. Stuart, before the Hartford County Agricultural Society. Hartford, 1845.

Vol. 123. 12. Address, by John S. Skinner, before the Queen's County Agricultural Society. Jamaica, 1846.

13. Address, by Charles M. Shepard, before the Agricultural Societies of Hampshire, &c. Northampton, 1847.

14. Address, by Phineas Taylor Barnum, before the Fairfield County Agricultural Society. New York, 1849.

15. Report of the Horticultural Exhibition at Salem, Massachusetts. 1850.

16. Proceedings of the Associated Agricultural Convention. Boston, 1851.

" 124. 1. Quarterly Journal of Agriculture, &c., Vol. 2, No. 2.

2. The Wool Grower and Magazine of Agriculture and Horticulture. By T. C. Peters. Buffalo, 1850.

" 125. 1. Text Book on Agricultural Chemistry. By Asahel K. Eaton. Utica, 1847.

2. Sheep; their Breeds, Management and Diseases. By WIlliam Youatt. New York, 1848.

3. Practical Instructions and Directions for Silk-Worm Nurseries, and for the Culture of the Mulberry Tree. By Felix Pascalis. New York, 1829.

" 126. 1. Proceedings of the Massachusetts Horticultural Society. Boston, 1847.

2. The Same.

3. Materia Medica Botanica. Numbers 1, 2, 3 and 4.

4. Zeitschrift des Niederösterreichischen Gewerb-Bereins. Vienna, 1856.

" 127. 1. Address of the Advocate of the Patentees in Defence of Mental Property. Washington, 1806.

2. Report, in part, on the State and Condition of the Patent Office. Washington, 1812.

3. Annual Address before the Society for the Promotion of Useful Arts. By T. C. Beck. Albany, 1813.

4. Report on the State of Manufactures in Pittsburgh and vicinity. Pittsburgh, 1816.

5. Report of the Library Committee of the Pennsylvania Society for the Promotion of Public Economy. Philadelphia, 1817.

6. Address of the Connecticut Society for the Encouragement of American Manufactures. Middletown, 1817.

7. Address, by Edward Cutbush, before the Columbian Institute. Washington, 1817.

8. Addresses of the Philadelphia Society for the Promotion of National Industry. Philadelphia, 1819.

9. Address, by George B. Emerson, before the Boston Mechanics' Institution. Boston, 1827.

10. Observations, by Stephen Allen, on the Duties on Foreign Manufactured Articles. New York, 1827.

11. Anniversary Address before the Columbian Institute. By Samuel L. Southard. Washington, 1828.

12. Report of a Special Committee of the American Institute on Cash Duties, the Auction System, &c. New York, 1829.

13. Address of the Friends of Domestic Industry. New York, 1831.

Vol. 127. 14. Report of John Quincey Adams and Lewis Condict on Domestic Manufactures. Boston, 1833.

15. Plain Statement addressed to the Proprietors of Real Estate in New York. 1818.

" 128. 1. First Report of the Directors of the Mechanics' Institute. New York, 1831.

2. Circular of the Mechanics' Institute, with an Address to Mechanics and Manufacturers. New York, 1835.

3. Circular of the Mechanics' Institute, with an Address to Mechanics and Manufacturers. New York, 1836.

4. Charter, Constitution and By-Laws of the Franklin Institute. Philadelphia, 1824.

5. Sixteenth Exhibition of American Manufactures of the Franklin Institute. Philadelphia, 1846.

6. Address, by Joseph R. Chandler, at the Seventeenth Exhibition of the Franklin Institute. Philadelphia, 1847.

7. Seventeenth Exhibition of American Manufactures of the Franklin Institute. Philadelphia, 1847.

8. Reports of the First Exhibition of the Salem Charitable Mechanic Association. Salem, 1849.

9. Constitution and By-Laws of the Polytechnic Institute of New Jersey. New York, 1829.

9½. Catalogue of the Gallery of the Society for the Promotion of Practical Science. London, 1836.

10. Catalogue of the Polytechnic Institution. London, 1840.

11. Catalogue of the Royal Polytechnic Institution. London, 1842.

12. Transactions of the Rhode Island Society for the Encouragement of Domestic Industry. Providence, 1851.

13. Report of the Eighth Annual Fair of Utica Mechanics' Association. 1851.

" 129. 1. Constitution and By-Laws of the Society of Arts. London, 1851.

2. Elementary Drawing and Modelling Schools of the Society of Arts. London, 1851.

3. Inaugural Lecture, by William Whewell, on the General Bearing of the Great Exhibition on the Progress of Art and Science. London, 1851.

4. Lecture, by Sir Henry T. De la Beche, on Mining, Quarrying and Metallurgical Processes and Products. London, 1851.

5. Lecture, by Richard Owen, on the Raw Materials from the Animal Kingdom displayed in the Great Exhibition. London, 1851.

6. Lecture, by Jacob Bell, on Chemical and Pharmaceutical Processes and Products. London, 1851.

7. Lecture, by Lyon Playfair, on the Chemical Principles involved in the Manufactures of the Great Exhibition, as Exhibiting the Necessity of Industrial Instruction. London, 1852.

8. Catalogue of Agricultural Implements at the Great Exhibition, exhibited by Barrett, Exall & Andrewes. London, 1851.

9. Catalogue of Agricultural Implements at the Great Exhibition, exhibited by Smith & Co. London, 1851.

10. New Catalogue of Richmond & Chandler's Agricultural Implements. London, 1851.

Vol. 129. 11. Hussey's American Reaping Machine—its Demonstrations of Superiority over all other Reapers. London, 1851.

12. Farmers' Account Books. London, 1851.

13. Williams' List of Agricultural Implements. London, 1851.

14. Howard's Catalogue of Agricultural Implements and Machines. London, 1851.

15. Improved Agricultural Implements and Machines, manufactured by J. Holmes & Sons. London, 1851.

16. Agricultural Implements and Machines, manufactured by William Smith. London, 1851.

17. Agricultural Implements and Machines, manufactured by Clayton, Shuttleworth & Co. Lincoln, 1851.

18. Patent Corn, Seed and Manure Drills, manufactured by James Smyth & Son. Essex, 1852.

19. Descriptive Illustrated Guide to the Ware-houses, Show-rooms and Manufactories of Deane, Dray & Co. London, 1851.

20. Agricultural Implements and Machines, manufactured by E. H. Bentall. London, 1851.

" 130. 1. Report of the Committee of Management of the Royal Association for the Promotion of the Fine Arts. Edinburgh, 1848.

2. Twelfth Annual Report of the Council of the Art-Union of London. 1848.

3. Transactions of the Art-Union of Philadelphia. Philadelphia, 1849.

4. Report on the State of Agriculture in Lower Canada. Toronto, 1850.

5. Third Report of Drummond's Agricultural Museum. Stirling, 1835.

" 131. 1. List of Works on Agriculture, &c., published by James Ridgway. London, 1851.

2. List of Iron and Wire Manufactures, for Gardens, Ornamental Grounds, &c., made by Charles D. Young & Co. London, 1851.

3. List of Watches and Jewelry, manufactured by S. S. & J. W. Benson. London, 1851.

4. Emigration to Ireland. From the Dunfries Standard.

5. International Depot for Patented and other New and Useful Inventions. London, 1851.

6. Compendium of Charles D. Young & Co.'s larger Catalogue of Iron and Wire Work. Edinburgh, 1850.

7. Account of Zinc Ship Sheathing, manufactured by Vieille Montagne Zinc Mining Company. London, 1851.

8. Circular of Benjamin Edgington, Marquee Tent and Rick Cloth Manufacturer. London, 1851.

9. Meches a Lampes, Veillenses, etc., des Fabriques d'Adrien Grison. Paris, 1851.

10. Manuel Theorique et Pratique des Lois Anglaises sur les Brevets d'Invention et de Perfectionnement. Paris, 1851.

11. Catalogue des Bronzes de Tratin.

12. The History of a Year and the Life of Man. By George T. Thomason.

13. Catalogue of Stock and Award of Prizes of the Smithfield Club Cattle Show, 1851.

Vol. 131. 14. Catalogue of the Birmingham and Midland Counties Exhibition of Fat Cattle, Sheep, &c. Birmingham, 1851.

15. Illustrated Catalogue of Agricultural Implements, made by John Smith. London, 1851.

16. Catalogue of Improved Agricultural Machinery, manufactured by R. Hornsby & Son. London, 1851.

16½. Catalogue of Agricultural Implements and Machines, manufactured by William Hensman & Son. Bedfordshire. 1851.

17. Address to Landed Proprietors, Agriculturists, &c. By Charles D. Young & Co. Edinburgh, 1851.

" 132. 1. Charter and By-Laws of the American Institute. New York, 1830.

2. Report of the Third Annual Fair of the American Institute, at Masonic Hall. New York, 1830.

3. Address of James Tallmadge, before the American Institute. New York, 1831.

4. Charter and By-Laws of the American Institute. New York, 1832.

4½. Remonstrance of the American Institute against the Bill for Reducing the Revenue. New York, 1833.

5. Report of the Superintending Agent of the American Institute. New York, 1840.

6. Report of the Committee on Manufactures, of the Senate, on the Petition of the American Institute for Aid from the State. Albany, 1840.

7. Act Incorporating the Repository of the American Institute. New York, 1836.

8. Charter of the American Institute, &c., &c. New York, 1839.

9. Report of the Committee of the American Institute appointed to Investigate all Charges of Improper Conduct against all Officers and Members of the Institute. New York, 1840.

10. Report of the Special Committee of the American Institute on the Minutes of Evidence received from Joseph Hume, M. P.

11. Agriculture of the United States; an Address. By Henry Colman. New York, 1841.

12. Annual Report of the Central Committee of the Home League. New York, 1843.

13. Report of the Royal Jennerian Society for the Extermination of the Small Pox by Extension of Vaccination. London, 1820.

14. The same. 1821.

15. The same. 1823.

16. Whitlaw's Vegetable Medicated Vapor Bath. London, 1846.

17. Opinions and New Discoveries in Agriculture, Medicine, &c., &c. By Charles Whitlaw. London, 1847.

" 133. 1. Heads of Lectures on the Theory and Practice of Medicine. By Andrew Duncan. Edinburgh, 1776.

2. Lectures upon Animal Life. By Benjamin Rush. Philadelphia, 1799.

3. Notes on the Stomach and Secretion. By Thomas Ewell. Philadelphia, 1805.

4. Concise Treatise on Leeches. By George Horne. New York, 1805.

Vol. 133. 5. Essay on Difficult Parturition. By William P. Dewees. Philadelphia, 1806.

6. Hydrophobia; its Prevention and Cure; with a Dissertation on Canine Madness. By Benjamin Moseley. London, 1808.

7. Essay on the Lungs. By John C. Stroebel. New York, 1810.

8. Dissertation on the Approximate Cause of Inflammation. By Alexander H. Stevens. Philadelphia, 1811.

9. Introductory Lecture on the Cause, Seat and Cure of Diseases. By John Crawford. Baltimore, 1811.

10. Observations on Croup or Hives. By David Hosack. New York, 1811.

" 134. 1. Collection of Papers on Bilious Fevers. Compiled by Noah Webster, Jr. New York, 1796.

2. Account of the Epidemic Yellow Fever. By Valentine Seaman. New York, 1796.

3. History of the Proceedings of the Board of Health, and an Account of the Yellow Fever. New York, 1823.

" 135. 1. Account of the Epidemical Fever. By M. L. Davis. New York, 1795.

2. Account of the Contagious Epidemic Yellow Fever of 1797. By Felix Pascalis Ouviere. Philadelphia, 1798.

3. Inaugural Dissertation on the Yellow Fever. By James R. Manley. New York, 1803.

4. Strictures on Dr. Grant's Latin edition of his Essay on Yellow Fever. Jamaica, 1806.

5. Inaugural Dissertation on the Origin and Propagation of the Yellow Fever. By Joseph Bayley. New York, 1802.

6. Inaugural Dissertation on the Yellow Fever. By James R. Manley. New York, 1803.

6½. Popular Treatise on Yellow Fever. By Jacob Vredenburgh Brower. New York, 1805.

7. Essay on Yellow Fever. 1817.

8. Statement of Occurrences during the Malignant Yellow Fever. New York, 1819.

9. Rapport fait a la Société Médicale sur la Fièvre Jaune. By Gros and Gerardin. New Orleans, 1818.

" 136. 1. Account of the Malignant Fever. By James Hardie. New York, 1805.

2. Quaedam Observations in Scarlatinam. By A. O. H. Tellegen. Groningal, 1808.

3. Essay on the Bilious Epidemic Fever, by Dr. James Mann; and a Dissertation by Dr. John Stearns; with Notes, &c., by C. C. Yates. Albany, 1813.

4. Review of an Essay on the Bilious Epidemic Fever. By Christopher C. Yates. Albany, 1813.

5. Act to provide against Infectious and Pestilential Diseases. Albany, 1813.

6. Letter on Febrile Contagion. By John W. Francis. New York, 1816.

7. An Inquiry into the Nature and Treatment of the Spotted Fever. By Job Wilson. Boston, 1815.

" 137. 1. Essay on Contagions and Infections. By J. L. E. W. Shecut. Charleston, 1818.

Vol. 137. 2. Dissertation on the Nature and Treatment of the Typhus or Nervous Fever. By J. Gorman. Milledgeville, 1819.
3. Report on the Epidemic of 1820. New Orleans, 1821.
4. Treatise on Fever. By Frederick Buckelow. New York, 1821.
5. Thesès pro Gradu Baccalaureatus. Lima.
6. Examination of the Strictures on Essays on Fevers. By Thomas Miner and William Tulley. Middletown, 1823.
7. Letter on the Yellow Fever of the West Indies. By Daniel Osgood. New York, 1820.
8. Memoires sur la Fièvre Jaune. By N. V. A. Gerardin. Paris, 1820.
9. Observations on the Lake Fevers and other Diseases of the Genesee County. By Edward G. Ludlow. New York, 1823.
10. Index to the Library of the Lyceum of Natural History. New York, 1830.
11. Oregon; a Journey from the Atlantic to the Pacific. By John B. Wyeth. Cambridge, 1833.
12. Natural History of Water. By C. T. Jackson.
13. Abstract of a New Theory of the Formation of the Earth. By Ira Hill. Baltimore, 1823.

" 138. 1. Reflections on Yellow Fever Periods. By Lyman Spalding. New York, 1819.
2. Reflextions sur le Rapport Concernant la Fièvre Jaune. By Louis Valentin.
3. New Theory of Yellow Fever. By James Tinsley. Charleston, 1819.
4. Opinion de M. Lefort sur la Non-Contagion et Non-Importation de la Fièvre Jaune. By J. Sedillot.
5. Letter on the Yellow Fever of the West Indies. By Daniel Osgood. New York, 1820.
6. Lettre de J. Sedillot a M. Audouard sur la Fièvre Jaune, &c.
7. Méthode de Traitement dans la Fièvre Jaune. By J. R. Raoul de Champmanoir. New Orleans, 1821.
8. Irvine's Treatise on the Yellow Fever.
9. Observations Preparatory to the Use of Dr. Myersbach's Medicines. By J. C. Lettsom. London, 1776.
10. Essay on the Partial and Concealed Inversion of the Uterus. By Charles Drayton, Jr. Philadelphia, 1809.
11. Report on the Malignant Disease. By Edward Miller. New York, 1805.
12. Inaugural Essay on the Bilious Typhus. By Richard Pennell. New York, 1821.

" 139. 1. Letter of Hon. Stephen Allen on Yellow Fever. New York, 1822.
2. The same.
3. Letters on the Yellow Fever. By Grant Thorburn. New York, 1824.
4. History of the Yellow Fever at Natchez. By Henry Tooley. Washington, 1823.
5. Importation and Specific Personal Contagion in Yellow Fever Disproved. By Benjamin Romaine. New York, 1823.

Vol. 139. 6. Extract of a Dissertation on the Source of Epidemic and Pestilential Diseases. By Charles Maclean.

7. Examination of a Work entitled Recherches Pratiques sur la Fièvre Jaune, par A. J. Dariste. By Felix Pascalis.

8. Vues sur la Fièvre Jaune. By Foureau de Beauregard. Paris, 1826.

9. Observations on Fevers. By Elijah Griffiths.

10. Hints to the People on the Prevention and Early Treatment of Spasmodic Cholera. By C. R. Gilman. New York, 1832.

11. Observations on a Letter from Dr. H. Chapman, on Cholera. Philadelphia, 1832.

12. Lecture on Epidemic Diseases generally, and particularly Spasmodic Cholera. By Sylvester Graham. New York, 1833.

13. Cases of Organic Disease of the Heart. By John C. Warren. Boston, 1809.

14. Reply to a Pamphlet on the College of Physicians. Boston, 1812.

15. Diuretic Properties of the Pyrola Umbellata. By W. Somerville. London, 1814.

16. Inaugural Dissertation on Infanticide. By John R. Beck. New York, 1817.

" 140. 1. Rèsultats de l'Inoculation de la Vaccine. By Louis Valentin. 1802.

2. Inaugural Dissertation on the Nature and Origin of Vaccina or Cow Pock. By Samuel Scofield. New York, 1803.

3. Address on Variolous and Vaccine Inoculations. By J. C. Lettsom. London, 1803.

4. Address on Cow Pox or Vaccine Inoculation. By Thomas A. Warren. London, 1803.

5. Manual of Inoculation. By George Lipscomb. London, 1806.

6. Report on the Necessity of Modifying the Law to Encourage Vaccination. 1822.

7. Value of Vaccinal Virus. By Felix Pascalis. 1825.

8. Letter on Coercive Vaccination. By F. S. Stuart. London, 1807.

9. Information on the Kine Pock Inoculation. By Benjamin Waterhouse. Cambridge, 1810.

10. Suggestions on the Prevention and Cure of the Small Pox and Varioloid. By Hunting Sherrill. New York, 1852.

11. Observations on the Absorbent Tubes of Animal Bodies. By Samuel L. Mitchill. New York, 1837.

12. Fourth Report of the Doctors of the American Society for Educating Pious Youth for the Gospel Ministry. Andover, 1819.

13. Eighth Annual Report of the American Education Society.

14. Ninth Annual Report of the American Education Society. Boston, 1824.

15. Eleventh Annual Report of the American Education Society. Andover, 1827.

16. Twelfth Annual Report of the American Education Society. Andover, 1828.

17. Thirteenth Annual Report of the American Education Society. Andover, 1829.

Vol. 141. 1. Answer to Gibson's Strictures on Pattison's Reply. By G. S. Pattison. Baltimore, 1820.
2. Essay on the Devastation of the Gums and the Alveolar Processes. By L. Koecker.
3. Treatment of Denuded Nerves of the Teeth. By L. Koecker.
4. Lecture on Dyspepsia and Chronic Diseases, showing the Evil Tendency of the Use of Tobacco upon Young Persons. By Benjamin Waterhouse. Cambridge, 1822.
5. System of Medical Ethics, &c.
6. Constitution, Medical Police, and Extracts from the By-Laws of the Medical Society. Augusta, 1823.
7. Treatise on Bowel Complaints. By John G. Vought. Rochester, 1823.
7½. Strictures on the Doctrine of a Modern French Writer on Syphilis. By Felix Pascalis.
8. Surgical Anatomy of the Groin. By Alexander F. Vaché. New York, 1825.
9. Case of Three Remarkable Tumors extirpated from the Nose. By P. S. Townsend. New York, 1825.
10. The Characteristic of Homöopathia. By H. B. Gram. New York, 1825.
11. Lecture introductory to the Course delivered by John D. Godman. Philadelphia, 1826.
12. Practical Elucidation of the Nature of Hernia. By A. G. Hull. New York, 1826.
13. Exposition of Facts concerning Coventry's Advertisement. By J. P. Batchelder. Utica, 1829.
14. Elements of Gymnastics. New York, 1830.

" 142. 1. Apology of J. C. Lettsom for Differing in Opinion from the Authors of the Monthly and Critical Reviews. London, 1803.
2. Programme d'un Prix relatif a la Trachéotomie dans le Traitement du Croup. By Ch. Fél. Caron.
3. Case of Hydrocephalus. By Joseph Glover. Charleston, 1818.
4. Pathological Reflections on General Diseased Action. By Joseph A. Gallup. Montpelier, 1819.
5. History of the Introduction and Use of Scutellaria Lateriflora as a Remedy for Hydrophobia. By Lyman Spalding. New York, 1819.
6. Abhandlung über das Delirium tremens. By Dr. Thomas Sutton. Bremen, 1820.
7. De Viis Clandestinis Urinae Dissertatio. By P. G. C. E. Barkhausen.
8. Introductory Lecture. By John D. Godman. New York, 1827.
9. Lecture on the Parotid Gland. By G. S. Pattison. Philadelphia, 1833.
10. Inaugural Dissertation on the Physiology and Diseases of the Teeth. By Shearjashubo Spooner. New York, 1835.
11. Thoughts on the Influence of Quackery. By a Citizen. New York, 1836.
12. Report upon the Effects of Poisonous Smoked Beef. By Drs. M. Post, Hosack and Chilton. New York, 1842.

Vol. 142. 13. Appeal to the Authors of the Critical Review. By J. C. Lettsom. London, 1803.

14. Medical Dissertations on Hemoptysis or the Spitting of Blood, and on Suppuration. By John Ware. Boston, 1820.

" 143. 1. Testamen Medicum de Cholera Spontanea. By William Robertson. Edinburgh, 1771.

2. Inaugural Dissertation on the Influenza. By Peter Irving. New York, 1794.

3. Dissertatio Medica Inauguralis de Physconia Splenica. By D. J. Ewing. Philadelphia, 1789.

4. Dissertatio Medica Inauguralis sistens Observationes ad Abscessum Bursalem. By Joseph Willard, Boston, 1804.

5. Inaugural Dissertation on Lumbar Abscess. By William Barrow. New York, 1804.

6. Oration, by John B. Davidge, before the Medical Faculty of Maryland. Baltimore, 1805.

7. Inaugural Dissertation on Respiration. By Thomas Cook. New York, 1805.

8. Inaugural Dissertation on Fistula in Ano. By Benjamin Kissam. New York, 1805.

9. Inaugural Dissertation for the Degree of Doctor of Medicine. 1806.

10. Dissertatio Medica Inauguralis de Tetano. By Jacob Low. Edinburgh, 1807.

11. Inaugural Dissertation on Pulmonary Consumption. By Alire R. Delile New York, 1807.

12. Dissertatio Medica Inauguralis de Morbo Coxario. By John Watts. Edinburgh, 1809.

13. Dissertation on the Progress of Medical Science. By Josiah Bartlett. Boston, 1810.

14. Inaugural Dissertation on the Use of the Digitalis Purpurea in the Cure of Certain Diseases. By Thomas E. Steell. New York, 1811.

" 144. 1. Dissertatio Medica Inauguralis de Synocha. By Alexander Manson. Edinburgh, 1811.

2. Inaugural Dissertation on Mercury. By John W. Francis. New York, 1811.

3. Investigation of the Properties and Effects of the Spiraea Trifoliata of Linnæus, or Indian Physic. By Jacob De la Motta. Philadelphia, 1810.

4. Inaugural Dissertation on Insanity. By Theodric R. Beck. New York, 1811.

5. Inaugural Dissertation on the Medical Properties of Gold. By John C. Cheeseman. New York, 1812.

6. Inaugural Dissertation on the Eupatorium Perfoliatum of Linnæus. By Andrew Anderson. New York, 1813.

7. Experiments on the Production of Animal Heat by Respiration. By Enoch Hale. Boston, 1813.

8. Inaugural Dissertation on Angina Pectoris. By Henry Bogart. New York, 1813.

Vol. 144. 9. Inaugural Dissertation on the Eupatorium Perfoliatum of Linnæus. New York, 1813.
10. The same.

" 145. 1. Address at the Inauguration of the Officers of the College of Physicians and Surgeons. By Lyman Spalding. New York, 1814.
2. The same.
3. Conjectural Inquiry into the Relative Influence of the Stomach and Mind. By Elias Marks. New York, 1815.
4. Dissertatio Inauguralis de Sanguine Misso. By Thomas Seeds. Edinburgh, 1815.
5. Inaugural Dissertation on the Diseases of Old Age. By John Scudder. New York, 1815.
6. Inaugural Dissertation on Permanent Strictures of the Urethra. By James C. Bliss. Troy, 1815.
7. Report of the Proceedings of the Medico-Chirurgical Society. New York, 1815.
8. Charge to the Graduating Class of the Columbian College. By Thomas Sewall. Washington, 1828.
9. Introductory Discourse before the Medico-Chirurgical Society. By John B. Beck. New York, 1816.
10. Dissertation on the Human Stomach. By Selah Gridley. Montpelier, 1816.
11. Experimental Inquiry into the Function of the Liver. By Luke Douglass. New York, 1816.
12. Inaugural Essay on Genius and its Diseases. By Thomas M. Stuart. New York, 1819.
13. Oration on the Causes of the Mortality among Strangers. By Jacob De la Motta. Savannah, 1820.
14. Essay on the Chemistry of Animated Matter. By John P. Emmet. New York, 1822.
15. Inaugural Dissertation on the Medical Topography of Shepherdsville and its vicinity. By William Jewell. Danville, 1820.

" 146. 1. An Act to Incorporate Medical Societies, and By-Laws of the Medical Society of New York. New York, 1806.
2. Report of the Medical Society of the County of New York, and Charter of the College of Physicians and Surgeons. New York, 1807.
3. By-Laws of the Medical Society of the County of New York, 1808.
4. An Act to Incorporate Medical Societies, &c. New York, 1813.
5. Report of the Epidemic Small Pox and Chicken Pox. New York, 1816.
6. Statutes regulating the Practice of Physic and Surgery. New York, 1819.
7. By-Laws of the Medical Society. New York, 1819.
8. Report explanatory of the Causes and Character of the Epidemic Fever. New York, 1820.
9. Remarks on the Epidemic Fever. By P. S. Townsend. New York, 1820.

Vol. 146. 10. Address, by Felix Pascalis, before the Medical Society. New York, 1822.

11. Statutes regulating the Practice of Physic and Surgery, &c. New York, 1823.

12. The same.

13. Inaugural Address, by David Hosack, before the Medical Society. New York, 1824.

14. Inaugural Address, by John Onderdonk, before the Medical Society. New York, 1825.

15. The same.

16. Reports of the Medical Society on Nostrums, or Secret Medicines. New York, 1827.

17. Report of the Medical Society on a Secret Medical Association. New York, 1831.

18. Address, by Stephen Elliott, at the Opening of the Medical College. Charleston, 1826.

" 147. 1. Transactions of the Medical Society of the State of New York, and Annual Address. By T. R. Beck. Albany, 1828, 1829, 1830.

2. Statutes regulating the Practice of Physic and Surgery, &c. New York, 1828.

3. Inaugural Address, by James R. Manley, before the Medical Society. New York, 1826.

3½. Transactions of the Medical Society of the State, and Annual Address. By Alexander Coventry. Albany, 1824.

4. System of Medical Ethics. New York, 1823.

5. Transactions of the Medical Society and Annual Address. By Joseph White. Cooperstown, 1817.

6. Transactions of the Medical Society and Annual Address. By John Stearns. Albany, 1818.

7. Transactions of the Medical Society and Annual Address. By John Stearns. Albany, 1819.

8. Transactions of the Medical Society and Annual Address. By John Stearns. Albany, 1820.

9. Transactions of the Medical Society and Annual Address. By John Stearns. Albany, 1821.

10. Transactions of the Medical Society. Albany, 1822.

11. Address before the New York County Medical Society. By Felix Pascalis. 1822.

" 148. 1. Address, by Nicholas Romayne, in the College of Physicians and Surgeons. New York, 1808.

2. By-Laws of the College of Physicians and Surgeons.

3. Report of the College of Physicians and Surgeons. New York, 1808.

4. Charter of the College of Physicians and Surgeons.

5. Supplementary Charter.

6. Observations on the Establishment of the College of Physicians and Surgeons. By David Hosack. New York, 1811.

7. Memorial of the College of Physicians and Surgeons. New York, 1814.

Vol. 148. 8. Memorial of the College of Physicians and Surgeons. New York, 1816

9. Discourse on Medical Education. By Samuel Bard. New York, 1819.

10. Catalogue of the Anatomical Museum of New York. By F. G. King New York, 1825.

11. Report of the Anatomical Museum of Pennsylvania. By W. E. Horner 1824.

12. Introductory Lecture, by David Hosack, in the College of Physicians and Surgeons. New York, 1825.

13. Report of a Committee of the University appointed to visit the College of Physicians, &c. Albany, 1826.

14. Communication from the Regents of the University on the College of Physicians, &c. Albany, 1826.

15. Observations on the Medical Character. By David Hosack. New York, 1826.

16. Introductory Lecture at the College of Physicians. By John B. Beck. New York, 1829.

17. Memorial of the Trustees of the College of Physicians, &c. New York, 1830.

" 149. 1. Thoughts on the Doctrines of Peace. New York, 1816.

2. Solemn Review of the Custom of War. By Philo Pacificus. Cambridge. 1816.

3. Extracts from the Writings of Erasmus on War. London, 1817.

4. Sketches of the Horrors of War. By Evan Rees. London, 1818.

5. Question of War Reviewed. New York, 1818.

6. Report of the New York Peace Society. New York, 1818.

7. Elegy, supposed to be written on a Field of Battle. London, 1818.

8. Substance of a Sermon. By James Hargreaves. London, 1818.

9. Proposed Memorial to Congress for the Abolition of Privateering. 1819.

10. National Dangers and Means of Escape.

11. Observations on the Applicability of the Pacific Principles of the New Testament to the Conduct of States. By Jonathan Dymond. London, 1825.

12. Wonderful Narrative of Two Families. By Telemachus.

13. Reflections on War. By a Layman.

14. Letter on the Condition of the Poor. By Matthew C. Carey. Philadelphia, 1835.

15. Address to the Massachusetts Peace Society. By Thomas Dawes.

16. Catalogue of the Officers, &c., of the Massachusetts Peace Society. Cambridge, 1819.

17. Constitution of the Massachusetts Peace Society.

18. Address, by Josiah Quincey, at the Massachusetts Peace Society. Cambridge, 1821.

19. Address, by Richard Sullivan, at the Massachusetts Peace Society. Cambridge, 1823.

20. The same.

21. Seventh Annual Report of the Massachusetts Peace Society.

22. Seventh Annual Report of the Society for the Promotion of Universal Peace. London, 1823.

Vol. 149. 23. Seventh Annual Report of the Peace Society. Providence, 1824.

24. Second Annual Report of the Society for the Promotion of Universal Peace. London, 1818.

25. Fourth Annual Report of the Society for the Promotion of Universal Peace. London, 1820.

" 150. 1. Proceedings of a Meeting of the Citizens of New York, in relation to the American Bible Society. New York, 1816.

1½. Report of the Bible Society. Providence, 1820.

2. Eighth Report of the Connecticut Bible Society. Hartford, 1818.

3. Third Annual Report of the Western Association of the New Jerusalem Church. 1820.

3½. Twenty-third Annual Report of the New York Protestant Episcopal Tract Society. New York, 1832.

4. Eighth Annual Report of the New York City Tract Society. New York, 1835.

5. Eighteenth Annual Report of the New York Marine Bible Society. New York, 1835.

6. Twentieth Annual Report of the New York Marine Bible Society. New York, 1836.

7. Report of the Governors of the New York Hospital. New York, 1830.

8. Charter and By-Laws of the New York Dispensary. New York, 1814.

9. Charter and Ordinances of the New York Dispensary. New York, 1797.

10. Report of the Physicians of the New York Lunatic Asylum. New York, 1818.

11. Second Annual Report of the New York Eye Infirmary. New York, 1823.

12. Report of the Surgeons of the New York Eye Infirmary.

13. Fourth Annual Report of the New York Asylum for Lying-in Women. New York, 1827.

14. Constitution and By-Laws of the Northern Dispensary. New York, 1827.

15. First Annual Report of the Northern Dispensary. New York, 1828.

16. Address, by John F. Schroeder, at the Opening of the New York Dispensary. New York, 1830.

17. Annual Report of the New York Dispensary. New York, 1831.

18. Annual Report of the New York Dispensary. New York, 1832.

19. Annual Report of the New York Dispensary. New York, 1833.

20. By-Laws of the Eastern Dispensary. New York, 1834.

21. Charter and By-Laws of the New York Dispensary. New York, 1834.

22. Annual Report of the New York Dispensary. New York, 1835.

22½. Rantoul's Remarks on Education.

23. Brief Outline of the Mode of Instruction pursued by Rev. John M. Mason. New York, 1828.

24. Remarks on the Relation between Education and Crime, by Francis Lieber; with Observations by N. H. Julius. Philadelphia, 1835.

" 151. 1. Fourth Annual Report of the Prison Discipline Society. Boston, 1829.

2. Seventh Annual Report of the Prison Discipline Society. Boston, 1832.

3. Proceedings of the State Convention of Mechanics. Utica, 1834.

4. Constitution of the American Seamen's Friend Society.

Vol. 151. 5. Fourth Annual Report of the House of Refuge. Philadelphia, 1832.
6. Sixth Annual Report of the House of Refuge. Philadelphia, 1834.
7. By-Laws, &c., of the New York Hospital and Bloomingdale Asylum. New York, 1833.
8. Annual Report of the New-York Dispensary. New York, 1833 and 1834.
9. Report of the Port Society. Boston, 1836.
10. Seventh Annual Report of the American Home Missionary Society. New York, 1833.
11. Nineteenth Annual Report of the Board of Missions. Philadelphia, 1835.

" 152. 1. Proceedings of the Baptist Convention for Missionary Purposes. Philadelphia, 1814.
2. First Annual Report of the Baptist Board of Foreign Missions. Philadelphia, 1815.
3. Fifteenth Report of the British and Foreign Bible Society. London, 1819.

" 153. 1. Account of the Benevolent Christian Society. New York, 1815.
2. Poems upon the Death of John Alden.
3. Second Annual Report of the American Society for Colonizing the Free People of Color. Washington, 1819.
4. Correspondence relative to the Emigration to Hayti of the Free People of Color. New York, 1824.
5. Fourteenth Annual Report of the American Society for Colonizing the Free People of Color. Washington, 1831.
6. Minutes and Proceedings of the Third Annual Convention for the Improvement of the Free People of Color. New York, 1823.
7. Second Annual Report of the Society for the Encouragement of Faithful Domestic Servants. New York, 1827.
8. The same. 1834.
9. Address in behalf of the New York Magdalen Asylum. New York, 1831.
10. Report of the Female Hospitable Society. Philadelphia, 1832.
11. First Annual Report of the Union Benevolent Association. Philadelphia, 1832.
12. Twenty-Sixth Annual Report of the Orphan Asylum. New York, 1832.
13. Third Annual Report of the Union Benevolent Association. Philadelphia, 1834.
14. Eleventh Annual Report of the New York Asylum for Lying-in Women. New York, 1834.
15. First Annual Report of the Female Benevolent Society. New York, 1834.
16. Second Annual Report of the Female Benevolent Society. New York, 1835.
17. Essays, by M. Carey, on the Public Charities of Philadelphia. 1830.

" 154. 1. First Annual Report of the Education and Missionary Society. New York, 1832.
2. First Report of the Young Ladies' Association of the Northampton Female Seminary. Concord, 1835.
3. Eighth Annual Report of the London City Mission. London, 1843.

Vol. 154. 4. Twenty-First Annual Report of the New York Missionary Society. New York, 1818.

5. Report of the Female Missionary Society for the Poor. By Ward Stafford. New York, 1817.

6. Second Annual Report of the New York Protestant Episcopal City Mission Society. New York, 1833.

7. The same.

8. Report of the Society for Promoting Christian Knowledge. London, 1831.

9. Fifth Report of the Missionary and Tract Society of the New Church. London, 1826.

10. Second Annual Report of the Baptist Board of Foreign Missions. Philadelphia, 1816.

11. Seventh Annual Report of the American Foreign Bible Society. New York, 1844.

" 155. 1. First Annual Report of the Society for the Prevention of Pauperism. New York, 1818.

2. Report of a Committee on the subject of Pauperism. New York, 1818.

3. Report of the Society for the Prevention of Pauperism. New York, 1819.

4. Documents relative to Savings Banks, Intemperance and Lotteries. New York, 1819.

5. Second Annual Report of the Society for the Prevention of Pauperism. New York, 1820.

6. Fourth Annual Report of the Society for the Prevention of Pauperism. New York, 1821.

7. Plain Directions on Domestic Economy. New York, 1821.

8. Report on the Expediency of Erecting an Institution for the Reformation of Juvenile Delinquents. New York, 1824.

9. Third Annual Report of the Society for the Reformation of Juvenile Delinquents. New York, 1828.

10. Fifth Annual Report of the same. New York, 1830.

11. Ninth Annual Report of the same. New York, 1834.

12. Tenth Annual Report of the same. New York, 1835.

13. Twenty-Seventh Annual Report of the same. New York, 1852.

" 156. 1. Catalogue of the Books, Pamphlets, &c., in the Massachusetts Historical Library. Boston, 1811.

2. Catalogus Bibliothecæ Collegii Alleghaniensis. 1823.

3. Address of the Trustees of the New York Society Library. New York, 1833.

4. Address to the Stockholders of the City Library, on the Management of that Institution. New York, 1833.

5. Proceedings of a Meeting in relation to International Literary Exchanges. Paris, 1843.

6. Report of the Joint Library Committee of the Legislature of New York on International Exchanges. Albany, 1847.

7. Report of the Committee on the Library of the City of Boston on International Exchanges. Boston, 1849.

Vol. 156. 8. Ninth Annual Report of the Mercantile Library Association. New York, 1850.

9. Catalogue of the Printers' Library. New York, 1850.

" 157. 1. Fourth Annual Report of the Regents of the Smithsonian Institute. Washington, 1850.

2. Notices of Public Libraries in the United States. By Charles C. Jewett. Washington, 1851.

3. Movement of the International Literary Exchanges. Paris, 1846.

4. Report on International Exchanges. Albany, 1847.

5. Letter to the President on the Enlargement of the Capitol. By C. F. Anderson. 1851.

6. Extracts by D. B. Reid, from "Illustrations of the Theory and Practice of Ventilation."

7. Thirty-First Annual Report of the Mercantile Library Association. New York, 1852.

8. Seventh Day Baptist Memorial. Vol. 1, No. 1. New York, 1852.

" 158. 1. Jachin and Boaz; or, an Authentic Key to the Door of Free Masonry. New York, 1796.

2. Address, by De Witt Clinton, to the Grand Lodge, at his Installation. New York, 1806.

3. Masonic Oration, by Jesse Bledsoe; and the Battle of Tippecanoe, an Ode. Albany, 1812.

4. Extract from the Minutes of the Grand Consistory.

5. Oration, by George H. Richards, before the Union Lodge. New York, 1819.

6. Address, by Rev. Cheever Felch, before the Mount Carmel Lodge. Boston, 1821.

7. Candid Appeal upon Speculative Free Masonry. By Jedediah N. Hotchkin. New York, 1818.

8. Proceedings of a Meeting of Free Masons. Washington, 1822.

9. Letter on Speculative Free Masonry. By Charles P. Sumner. Boston, 1829.

10. Proceedings of the Anti-Masonic Convention at Utica. 1830.

11. Masonic Penalties. Castleton, Vermont, 1830.

12. Report on the Abduction and Murder of William Morgan.

13. Address of the Committee of the Grand Lodge to the People of Rhode Island.

14. Address of the Grand Lodge of Rhode Island. Providence, 1831.

15. Anti-Masonic Republican Convention. Boston, 1832.

16. Resolutions of the Anti-Masonic Members of the Legislature of Massachusetts. Boston, 1836.

17. Address, delivered by Daniel Webster, on Laying the Corner Stone of the Bunker Hill Monument. Boston, 1825.

18. Narrative of the Material Facts in Relation to the Two Greek Frigates. By Alexander Contostavlos. New York, 1826.

19. Homes of the Poets.

" 159. 1. Catalogue of the Library of the New York Hospital. New York, 1829.

2. By-Laws and Regulations of the New York Hospital. New York, 1826.

Vol. 159. 3. Catalogue of the Library of the New York Hospital. New York, 1818.
4. An Ordinance of the New York Hospital. New York, 1821.
5. An Account of the New York Hospital. New York, 1811.
6. Catalogue of the Library of the New York Hospital.

" 160. 1. Annual Report of Deaths in New York, from 1817 to 1835.
2. Documents relating to the Board of Health for 1805. New York, 1806.
3. Extracts from the Records of the Health Office, for 1796, 1797 and 1798, and a Letter on the Pestilential Disease of 1798. By Richard Bayley. New York, 1798.

" 161. 1. Communication on the Source, Quality and Purity of the Water on Manhattan Island. New York, 1831.
2. Report on Supplying the City of New York with Pure and Wholesome Water. New York, 1831.
3. Address, by John L. Sullivan, on the Advantages of a Rock Water Company. New York, 1833.
4. Memorial and Address on Water. By John L. Sullivan and Levi Disbrow.
5. Report on Supplying the City of New York with Water. New York, 1833.
6. The same.
7. Memorial of John L. Sullivan on Water. New York, 1834.
8. Report in Relation to Supplying the City of New York with Water. New York, 1835.
9. De Witt Clinton's Report on a Supply of Water for the City of New York. 1832.
10. Semi-Annual Report of the Water Commissioners. New York, 1838.
11. Report of the Water Commissioners. New York, 1849.

" 162. 1. Report of the Committee of Ways and Means, on the President's Message relating to Foreign Importations, &c. Washington, 1812.
2. Case of the Merchants Considered. Washington, 1812.
3. Facts and Observations in relation to the Origin and Completion of the Erie Canal. New York, 1825.
4. Speech of Mr. Clayton on the Management of the Post Office Department. Washington, 1831.
5. Observations on the Report of the Committee of Ways and Means. Philadelphia, 1828.
6. Frauds on the Revenue.
7. Southern Excitement against the American System. Poughkeepsie, 1829.
8. Proceedings and Report at the Opening of Clinton Hall. New York, 1830.
9. Communication relative to the West Branch and Alleghany Canal. By Benjamin Aycrigg. Harrisburgh, 1839.
10. Report on a Public Cemetery in the City of Roxbury. Roxbury, 1847.
11. Jacob Barker's Second and Third Letters Developing the Conspiracy formed in 1826, for his Ruin.

Vol. 162. 12. Fourth and Fifth Letters of the same.
13. Eighth Letter of the same.
14. Herald of Peace.

" 163. 1. Letter on the Errors in Johnson's Dictionary. By Noah Webster. New Haven, 1807.
2. Short Sketch of Gillespie's Improvement on Distillation.
3. Cursory Observations on the construction of Wheel Carriages. By Horatio G. Spofford. Albany, 1815.
4. Improvement for Constructing Fire Places and Chimneys. By J. Jenkins. Warren, R. I. 1815.
5. Observations relative to the Mounting of Cannon. By James Jay. New York, 1785.
6. English Phonology. By Peter S. Duponceau. Philadelphia, 1817.
7. Veterinary Science. By J. Carver. 1817.
8. Short Vocabulary in the Language of the Seneca Nation and in English. London, 1818.
9. Remarks on the Pronunciation of the Greek Language. By N. F. Moore. New York, 1819.
10. Essay on the Propulsion of Navigable Bodies. By C. A. Busby. New York, 1818.
11. Description of Annesley's New System of Naval Architecture. London, 1818.
12. Description of a Printing Press.
13. History of the Tread-Mill. By James Hardie. New York, 1824.
14. Census of the New Buildings erected in 1824, and other Statistics. By James Hardie. New York, 1825.
15. Circular on Steam Mills and Distilleries. Cincinnati, 1828.

" 164. 1. Morality of Poverty. By W. J. Fox. Boston, 1836.
2. Second Advent Tracts, from No. 1 to No. 12.
3. The Brothers; or, Usefulness of Savings Banks. Boston, 1823.
4. Description of the Book presented to La Fayette. New York, 1825.
5. Freaks of Columbia. By Timothy Taste. Washington, 1808.
6. Supplement to Grimshaw's History of the United States. Philadelphia, 1831.
7. Empire of Reason; an Allegory. New York, 1829.

" 165. 1. Proceedings in Maintaining the Public Right to the Beach of the Mississippi. By Thomas Jefferson. New York, 1812.
2. Some Account of the White Mountains of New Hampshire. By Jacob Bigelow, 1816.
3. Discourse on the Early History of Pennsylvania. By P. S. Duponceau. Philadelphia, 1821.
4. Papers, &c., relative to the Iron Ore Veins, Water Power and Wood Land in Essex County, New York. New York, 1840.
5. Description of the Suspension Railway, invented by Maxwell Dick. Irvine, 1830.
6. View of the City of New Orange, (now New York.) By Joseph W. Moulton. New York, 1825.
7. Six Months in Central America. By J. Hale. New York, 1826.

Vol. 165. 8. Observations on the Best Means of Propelling Ships. By A. S. Byrne. New York, 1841.
9. Olive Branch. By M. Carey. Philadelphia, 1832.
10. Norcross' Planing Machine and Circular Saw Mill. Lowell, 1850.
11. Report of the Committee on Establishing a General Smelting and Refining Company. New York, 1851.
12. Steam Vessels for War Purposes and Ocean Navigation. By E. F. Aldrich. New York, 1847.

" 166. 1. History of the Towns of Haddam and East Haddam. By David D. Field. Middletown, 1814.
2. Jaw Bone of an Ass Examined. By Price Armstrong. New York, 1811.
3. Vieille Montagne Zinc Mining Company.
4. Memoirs on the Antiquities of the Western Parts of the State of New York. By De Witt Clinton. Albany, 1818.
5. Musical Reader; or, Practical Lessons for the Voice. By Thomas Hastings. Utica, 1819.
6. Procès Verbal of the Ceremony of Installation of President of the Historical Society. New York, 1820.
7. The Highway of all Nations. By Joseph Foos. Columbus, 1820.
8. Fanny; a Poem. New York, 1820.
9. Documents showing that Mecklenburg County, North Carolina, declared her Independence, 1755. Raleigh, 1822.
10. Unitarian Monitor. 1825.
11. Letters on Florida.
12. Sketch of the Olden Time; or, General Lee's Farewell Dinner. New York, 1829.
13. Songs, Duetts, &c., in the White Lady. New York, 1832.
14. Poem on the Meditation of Nature. By Park Benjamin. Hartford, 1832.
15. The Words of the Creation; an Oratorio. By Joseph Haydn. New York, 1833.
16. Poland; a Poem. New York, 1834.
17. Messiah; a Sacred Oratorio. By Handel. New York, 1834.
18. Romance and Reality; or, the Advantages and Disadvantages of Joining Independent Military Companies. Boston, 1835.
19. Grammatical Dissertation on the Italian Language. By Francois M. J. Surault. Boston, 1835.
20. Tale of a New-Yorker. New York, 1835.
21. Dancing Girl. By T. K. Hervey.

" 167. 1. West London Medicated Vapor Bath Institution. London, 1842.
2. Extracts from the Reports of the Asylum for the Cure of Scrofula, &c. London, 1841.
3. The same. London, 1822.
4. Opinions and New Discoveries in Agriculture, Medicine, &c. By Charles Whitlaw. London, 1847.
5. Vegetable Medicated Vapor Bath Establishment. Brighton, 1849.
6. La Tour de l'Europe. By J. R. Smith. London, 1851.
7. Museum of Mankind. London, 1852.

Vol. 167. 8. The Monthly Messenger.
9. The Infallible Guide.
10. Report of the Commissioners of School Moneys. 1841.
11. Report on the Petition of the Catholics, relative to the School Fund.
12. Address upon Education and Common Schools. By James Henry, Jr. New York, 1847.
13. Memoir of Samuel G. Morton. By Charles D. Meigs. Philadelphia, 1851.

" 168. 1. Dissertation on Chivalry, and History of the Chevalier Bayard.
2. Memoir on the Subject of Wheat and Flour. New York, 1820.
3. Tract on Wheat and Flour. Washington, 1820.
4. Controversy on the Sunday Police. New York, 1826.
5. Bread Laws Examined. By a Loaf-Bread Baker. New York, 1827.
6. Remarks upon the Auction System. New York, 1828.
7. Ruinous Tendency of Auctioneering. 1828.
8. Reasons why Auctions ought to be Abolished. New York, 1828.
9. Account of Memorials against Sabbath Mails, &c. New York, 1829.
10. The same.
11. Brief Survey of the Lottery System. By J. R. Tyson. Philadelphia, 1833.

" 169. 1. Report to the Corporation on Interment in the City. New York, 1825.
2. Report on Quack Medicines. Philadelphia, 1828.
3. Report of the Secretary of State in relation to a Geological Survey. Albany, 1836.
4. Abstract of the Proceedings of American Geologists and Naturalists. New Haven, 1845.
5. Discourse on the National Institution for the Promotion of Science. By Joel R. Poinsett. Washington, 1841.
6. Abstract of the Proceedings of the Association of Naturalists.
7. Address, by Henry D. Rogers, before the Association of American Naturalists. New York, 1844.
8. Medical Magazine, vol. 1. New York, 1815.

" 170. 1. Collections of the Rhode Island Historical Society, vol. 1. Providence, 1827.
2. The Academician. By Albert and John W. Picket. New York, 1820.
3. Literary Magazine and American Register. 1806.
4. Annals of the Lyceum of Natural History. 1827.

" 171. 1. The British Critic. 1817.
2. Magazine of Useful and Entertaining Knowledge. New York, 1830.
3. Magazine of Useful and Entertaining Knowledge. New York, 1831.
4. American Monthly Review. 1832.
5. The Guardian. 1833.
6. The Philomathesian.
7. American Historical Magazine. 1836.
8. Arcturus; a Journal of Books and Opinions. No. 1.
9. Arcturus; a Journal of Books and Opinions. No. 2.
10. Baptist Magazine. 1813.
11. The Missionary Herald and Irish Chronicle. 1843.

Vol. 172. 1. New York Medico-Chirurgical Bulletin. 1831.
2. Missionary Herald. 1832.

" 173. 1. United Brethren's Missionary Intelligencer and Religious Miscellany. 1822.
2. Farmers, Mechanics and Manufacturers' Magazine. New York, 1826.

" 174. 1. Columbian Almanack. New York, 1792.
2. Greenleaf's Almanack. New York, 1793.
3. Greenleaf's Almanack. New York, 1794.
4. Greenleaf's Almanack. New York, 1795.
5. Hutchins' Improved Almanack. New York, 1798.
6. Hutchins' Improved Almanack. New York, 1799.
7. Hutchins' Improved Almanack. New York, 1800.
8. Greenleaf's Almanack. Brooklyn, 1801.
9. Greenleaf's Almanack. Brooklyn, 1802.
10. Hutchins' Improved Almanack. New York, 1803.
11. Hutchins' Improved Almanack. New York, 1803.
12. Hutchins' Improved Almanack. New York, 1804.
13. Hutchins' Improved Almanack. New York, 1805.
14. Oram's New York Almanack. New York, 1807.

" 175. 1. Agricultural Almanack. By S. Southwick. Albany, 1821.
2. Wood's Almanack. By Joshua Sharp. New York, 1821.
3. Agricultural Almanack. Philadelphia, 1821.
4. Middlebrook's Almanack. Norwalk, Ct., 1822.
5. Wood's Almanack. By Joshua Sharp. New York, 1822.
6. Agricultural Almanack. By S. Southwick. Albany, 1822.
7. Agricultural Almanack. Philadelphia, 1823.
8. Wood's Almanack. By Joshua Sharp. New York, 1823.
9. New Hampshire Register. Concord, 1823.
10. Hutchins' (Revived) Almanack. By David Young. New York, 1827.
11. Agricultural Almanack. Philadelphia, 1827.

" 176. 1. Alegato que en la Oposicion a la Catedra de Metodo de Medicina. By D. Josef Manuel Dábalos. Cadiz, 1810.
2. Observations on Vision. By David Hosack. London, 1794.
3. Extracts from the Minutes of the United States Military Philosophical Society. New York, 1809.
4. Statement of the Arts and Manufactures of the United States. By Albert Gallatin. Washington, 1812.
5. Berhandlungen des Bereins.
6. Questions upon Subjects connected with Architecture. London, 1835.
7. Address and Regulations of the Institute of British Architects. London, 1835.
8. Charter, By-Laws and Report of the Royal Institute of British Architects. London, 1838.
9. Report, &c., of the Royal Institute of British Architects. London, 1839 and 1840.

" 177. 1. Journal of the Proceedings of the Episcopal Convention. New York, 1838.

Vol. 177. 2. Canons and Constitution of the Episcopal Church. New York, 1838.
3. Tracts for the Times. No. 90. Remarks on the Thirty-Nine Articles. Oxford, 1841.
4. Acts and Proceedings of the General Synod of the Reformed Dutch Church. New York, 1844.

" 178. 1. Address, by A. S. Monson, and the Transactions of the New Haven Horticultural Society. New Haven, 1843.
2. Proceedings of the New Castle County Agricultural Society and Institute. Wilmington, 1843.
3. Address before the Queens County Agricultural Society. By William T. McCoun. New York, 1843.
4. Address before the Rensselaer County Agricultural Society. By William P. Van Rensselaer. Troy, 1843.
5. Transactions of the Queens County Agricultural Society, with an Address. By D. S. Dickinson. 1843.
6. Transactions of the Agricultural Society and Institute of New Castle County; with an Address by John S. Skinner. Wilmington, 1844.
7. Transactions of the Hartford County Agricultural Society for 1843–44.
8. Transactions of the Essex Agricultural Society for 1845. Salem, 1846.
9. Transactions of the Agricultural Society and Mechanics' Institute of New Castle County, Del. 1846.
10. Charter, Constitution, &c., of the Cincinnati Horticultural Society. Cincinnati, 1846.
11. Letter of N. Longworth, on the Cultivation of the Grape and Manufacture of Wine; also, on the Strawberry. 1845.
12. Transactions of the Fruit Growers and Nursery-Men's Convention. Columbus, 1847.
13. Transactions of the Rensselaer County Agricultural Society. 1846.

" 179. 1. Report on the Agriculture of Massachusetts. By Henry Colman. 1839.
2. Report of the Agricultural Meeting held in Boston in 1840.
3. Address before the Monroe County Agricultural Society. By Henry Colman. Rochester, 1842.
4. Address before the Hartford County Agricultural Society. By S. H. Huntington. Hartford, 1842.
5. Letter to the Rensselaer County Agricultural Society. By George Tibbits. Troy, 1842.
6. Transactions of the Monroe County Agricultural Society for 1842.
7. Transactions of the Massachusetts Horticultural Society for 1842–3.
8. Address before the Massachusetts Horticultural Society. By J. E. Teschemacher. Boston, 1842.

" 180. 1. Charter, Constitution and By-Laws of the New York Mechanics and Scientific Institution. 1822.
2. Constitutions of Tammany Society or Columbian Order.
3. Address of the National Institution for the Promotion of Industry. New York, 1820.
4. Memorial of the National Institution for the Promotion of Industry. Washington, 1821.

Vol. 180. 5. Address before the Newark Mechanics' Association. By John Griscom. Newark, 1831.
6. Constitution and By-Laws of the Mechanics' Institute. New York, 1833.
7. Report of the First Annual Fair of the Mechanics' Institute. 1835.
8. First Report of the Directors of the Mechanics' Institute. 1831.
9. Journal of the American Association for the Promotion of Science, Literature and the Arts. 1831.
10. Report of the Third Annual Fair of the Ohio Mechanics' Institute. 1840.
11. Discourse on the National Institution for the Promotion of Science. By J. R. Poinsett. Washington, 1841.
12. Address at the Twelfth Exhibition of the Franklin Institute. By A. D. Bache. Philadelphia, 1842.
13. Sherman Institute for the Encouragement of Industry and Education.
14. Advantages of Ralston, Lycoming Co., for the Manufacture of Iron.
15. Valedictory Lecture before the Philosophical Society of Delaware. By John Vaughan. 1800.
16. Indenture, &c., of the United States Stone-Dressing Machine Company.
17. Considerations on a Guarantee Company. By William L. Haskins.
18. Plan of Cornell's Stave Machine Company.
19. Prospectus of the Missouri Iron Company.
20. Statutes and Regulations of the Philosophical Society of London. 1813.
21. List of Members of the Philosophical Society of London. 1816.
22. Address before the Silk Culturists. By Lewis Tinelli. 1840.
23. First Annual Report of the New England Silk Convention. 1842.

" 181. 1. The Correspondent; a Deistical Journal. New York, 1828.
2. Second Annual Report of the Society for the Reformation of Juvenile Delinquents. 1827.
3. First Annual Report of the New York City Temperance Society. 1830.
4. Tenth Annual Report of the Young Men's New York Bible Society. 1833.
5. Eleventh Annual Report of the American Sunday School Union. 1835.
6. First Annual Report of the United States Naval Lyceum. 1835.
6½. Thirteenth Annual Report of the Society for the Reformation of Juvenile Delinquents. 1838.
7. Anniversary Report of the Pennsylvania Temperance Society. 1833.
8. A Sermon. By William Toase. 1841.
9. Third Annual Report of the New York Lyceum. 1842.
10. Fourteenth Annual Report of the Colonization Society. 1846.
11. Forty-First Annual Report of the Public School Society. 1847.
12. Eighteenth Annual Report of the Hartford Retreat for the Insane. 1842.
13. Nineteenth Annual Report of the same. 1843.
14. Twentieth Annual Report of the same. 1844.
15. Philadelphia Lying-in Charity. 1832.
16. First Annual Report of the Peace Society. London, 1817.

Vol. 182. 1. First Annual Report of the Prison Discipline Society. Boston, 1826.
2. Second Annual Report of the same. 1827.
3. Fifth Annual Report of the same. 1830.
4. Important Disclosures.
5. Second Annual Report of the Prison Association. New York, 1846.

Vol. 182. 6. Fourth Report of the American Bible Society. New York, 1820.
7. Ninth Report of the same. 1825.

" 183. 1. Ninth Annual Report of the American Tract Society. Andover, 1823.
2. Second Annual Report of the same. New York, 1827.
3. Address of the United States Anti-Masonic Convention, held in Philadelphia, 1830.
4. Letter of C. D. Colden upon the Secret Order of Freemasonry. 1829.
5. Address of the Anti-Slavery Society. 1833.
6. Discourse before the Young Men's Colonization Society. By J. R. Tyson.
7. Tenth Report of the American Home Missionary Society. 1836.
8. Method of Spiritual Culture. 1836.
9. The Anti-Slavery Examiner. 1836.
10. Views of Slavery and Emancipation. By Harriet Martineau. 1837.
11. Constitution of the American Anti-Slavery Society. 1838.
12. Seventh Annual Report of the Colonization Society. 1839.

" 184. 1. Constitution and By-Laws of the New York Typographical Society.
2. An Oration before the New York Typographical Society. By Edward S. Bellamy. 1821.
3. Charter and By-Laws of the General Society of Mechanics and Tradesmen. New York, 1833.
4. Proceedings of the Meetings of the Printers relative to the Washington Institute. 1834.
5. Protest of the Columbia Typographical Society against the Washington Institute. 1834.
6. Communication of the President of the American Antiquarian Society. Worcester, 1814.
7. Memorial, &c., of the New York Historical Society. 1827.
8. Journal of the National Convention of Young Men's Societies. 1834.
9. Address on Mental Culture. By James Arbuckle.
10. Address before the Literary Societies of the New York University. By John Breckinridge. 1836.
11. Means of Perpetuating Civil Liberty. By Edward D. Mansfield.
12. Eighth Annual Report of the Young Men's Association. 1844.
13. Address to the Graduates of Rutger's College. By P. Milledoler. 1831.
14. Catalogus Universitatis Transylvaniensis. Lexington, 1822.
15. Catalogue of the Officers and Students of Dartmouth College. 1833.
16. Address, by Henry Vethaker, as President of Washington College, Virginia. 1835.
17. Catalogue of Rutger's College. New York, 1835.
18. Catalogue of the College of New Jersey. Princeton, 1834–5.
19. Catalogue of Harvard University. Boston, 1835–6.
20. Valedictory Letter to the Trustees of Dartmouth College. 1835.
21. Catalogue of the College of Physicians and Surgeons. 1835–6.
22. Edgehill School. Prospectus.

" 185. 1. Catalogue of Columbia College. New York, 1826.
2. Catalogue of the Fraternity of ΦBK, Alpha of Massachusetts. 1839.
3. Catalogus Collegii Yalensis. New Haven, 1835.

Vol. 185. 4. Catalogue of Yale College. New Haven, 1835–6.
5. Catalogus Collegii Yalensis. New Haven, 1841.
6. Catalogus Collegii Yalensis. New Haven, 1844.
7. Catalogue of Yale College. New Haven, 1848–9.
8. Catalogue of the New York University. 1842–3.
9. Catalogue of the same. 1844–5.

" 186. 1. Account of Abimelech Coody and other Celebrated Writers. 1815.
2. Proceedings of the Committee on the Official Conduct of W. W. Van Ness. New York, 1820.
3. Discourse on the Life, &c., of Thomas Addis Emmet. By Samuel L. Mitchill. 1828.
4. Proceedings of a Meeting of Mechanics and Workingmen. 1829.
5. Memoir upon Staphyloraphy. By Alexander E. Hosack. 1833.
6. Documents relating to the Differences between Commodore O. H. Perry and Captain J. D. Elliott. Washington, 1821.
7. Sermon on the Death of De Witt Clinton. By Rev. James Milnor. New York, 1828.
8. Eulogy on Lafayette. By Francis Baylies. Boston, 1834.
9. Sketch of the Life, &c., of William Henry Harrison. New York, 1835.
10. Life of Henry Clay. By Junius.
11. Papers in relation to the Attack upon the Brig General Armstrong. New York, 1814.
12. Biography of John Randolph. By Lemuel Sawyer. New York, 1844.

" 187. 1. John Finch's Temperance Tracts. No. 4. Teetotalism.
2. The Foolery of Drunkenness. Liverpool, 1836.
3. By-Laws, &c., of the National Teetotal Society. 1838.
4. Letters on the Best Means of Preventing Drunkenness. By John Finch.
5. The Foolery of Drinking Drunkard's Drink. By John Finch.
6. Memoir relative to the Progress of the Translations of the Sacred Scriptures. 1816.
7. Trial of Calvin and Hopkins versus The Bible and Common Sense. Boston, 1819.
8. Arguments on the Doctrine of the Trinity.
9. Letter to Mr. Channing in favor of the Doctrine of the Trinity.
10. Den Zegeprael van het Kruys van Jesus-Christus. 1821.
11. The New Jerusalem Missionary.
12. Arcana Celestia. By Emanuel Swedenborg.
13. Address on the Observance of the Christian Sabbath. 1828.
14. Exposition of Modern Scepticism. By William Gibbons.
15. Constitution, &c., of the Bible Association of Friends. Phila., 1829.
16. Sermon before the Philadelphia Young Men's Society. By Henry A. Boardman. 1834.
17. Inquiry into the Spirit of Truth. By Edward C. Cooper. 1837.

" 188. 1. Suggestion concerning the Search for Sir John Franklin. By A. Petermann. London, 1852.
2. Mehemet Ali, Lord Palmerston, Russia and France. By William Cargill. London, 1840.

Vol. 188. 3. Three Lectures before the University of Oxford. By G. K. Rickards. London, 1852.
4. Microscopic Examination of the Water of London. By A. H. Hassell. London, 1850.

" 189. 1. The Modern Hermes; or, Experiments in Combining Quicksilver with Acids. By Robert Scott. Dumfries, 1811.
2. Catalogue of the Organic Remains, &c., of the New York Lyceum of Natural History. By Samuel L. Mitchill. 1826.
3. Geological Nomenclature for North America. Albany, 1828.
4. Improvement in the Mariner's and Surveyor's Compass Needle. By M. Smith. New York, 1834.
5. Letter on Animal Magnetism. By William L. Stone. New York, 1837.
6. Animal Magnetism; Past Fictions—Present Science. By John Bell. Philadelphia, 1837.
7. Application of Electro-Magnetism as a Motive Power to Machinery.
8. Remarks on Thorough Draining and Deep Ploughing. By James Smith. Stirling, 1838.
9. Compendium of Seeds, Plants, Implements, &c. By W. Drummond.
10. Rise and Fall of the Lakes, and Theory of Magnetism. By Edward Giddins. Lockport, 1838.
11. Motive Power of the Human System. By H. H. Sherwood. 1840.
12. Memorial of the Paper Manufacturers. New York, 1842.
13. Advantages for the Manufacture of Iron. New York, 1843.
14. The Power of the Pressure of the Atmosphere. By Henry Pratt. 1843.
15. Opinions and New Discoveries in Agriculture, Medicine, &c. By Charles Whitlaw. London, 1847.

" 190. 1. Dissertatio Medica de Hydrope Anasarca. Edinburgh, 1808.
2. Anatomy and Diseases of Domestic Animals. By James Mease. 1814.
3. Essay on the Epidemics of 1813 and 1814. By Ennalls Martin. 1815.
4. Prospectus of Lectures. By Alexander Ramsay. New York, 1816.
5. Influence of the Passions. By Peter S. Townsend. New York, 1816.
6. Remarks on the Dislocation of the Hip Joint. By J. C. Warren. 1826.
7. Treatise on the Teeth. By James A. Pleasants. New York, 1832.
8. Malignant Cholera. New York, 1832.
9. Epidemic Cholera of Canada. 1832.
10. Motive Power of the Human System. 1840.
11. Correct Vaccination and Impediments Thereto.

" 191. 1. Chemical and Medical Properties of the Statice Limonium of Linnæus. By Valentine Mott. New York, 1806.
2. Essay on the Scotch and Irish Nations. By D. Fraser. New York, 1809.
3. Report on a Route for the proposed Erie Canal. New York, 1811.
4. Index to the Geology of the Northern States. By Amos Eaton. 1818.
5. Address of the American Society for the Encouragement of Domestic Manufactures. New York, 1817.
6. Address before the New Bedford Temperance Society. By William Willis. New Bedford, 1819.
7. Inaugural Address before the New York Historical Society. By David Hosack. 1820.

Vol. 191. 8. Inaugural Discourse. By James Renwick. New York, 1821.
9. Remarks on the Preparation of Mortar. By D. Olmsted. 1821.
10. Society for the Benefit of the Indians. Washington, 1822.
11. Description of a Land Tortoise, known as the Elephant Tortoise. By R. Harlan. 1826.
12. Catalogue of Plants in the Royal Botanic Garden of Glasgow. 1825.
13. Speech of John A. Graham at White Plains. 1828.
14. Address to Physicians. By the Temperance Society. New York, 1829.
15. Disquisition on Creation, Annihilation, the Future Existence and Final Happiness of all Sentient Beings. 1828.
16. Oration on "The Model Administration." By William B. Reed. Philadelphia, 1844.
17. Address to Sir John Soane, Architect. 1835.
18. Analysis of Book-keeping. By Thomas Jones.
19. Letters from the Hon. Abbott Lawrence to the Hon. W. C. Rives. Boston, 1846.

" 192. 1. Traité de Vinification. By H. Machard. 1845.
2. Recueil de Mémoires relatifs a l'Emploi du Sel Marin en Agriculture.
3. Recherches sur l'Action du Sel dans la Végétation.
4. Quantités de Sel (Chlorure de Sodium) contenues dans les Plantes des Terrains Salifères et Non Saliferes. By M. Becquerel.
5. Mémoire sur l'Etat de la Végétation dans les Terrains Saliféres, etc. By M. Ancelon and M. Parisot.
6. Musée des Thermes et de l'Hotel de Cluny. Paris, 1851.
7. Rapport. By Casimir Périer of the National Assembly. 1850.

" 193. 1. Dialogues to Facilitate the Acquisition of the English Language by the Polish Emigrants. 1834.
2. New System of Orthography. By Abner Kneeland. 1807.
3. Critical Review of the Orthography of Webster's Series of Books. By Lyman Cobb. 1831.
4. Principles and Advantages of Elocution. By J. F. Foot. 1833.
5. Prospectus, &c., of Wright's Grammar.
6. Emma Willard's Appeal against Wrong and Injury.
7. Emma Willard's Answer; or, Second Appeal.
8. Remarks on the Orthöepy and Orthography of the English Language.
9. Valley of the Upper Wabash. By H. W. Ellsworth. New York, 1838.
10. Discourse before the Literary and Philosophical Society. By Samuel Miller. Princeton, 1825.
11. Dissertations on the Croup. By William Sweetser. Boston, 1823.

" 194. 1. Speech of Mr. Archer on the Removal of the Deposits. Washington, 1834.
1½. Speech of Mr. Ellsworth on the same. Washington, 1834.
2. Speech of Mr. Binney on the same. Washington, 1834.
3. Remarks of Mr. Calhoun on the same. Washington, 1834.
4. Speech of Mr. Clay on the same. Washington, 1834.
5. Report of the Secretary of War. Washington, 1833.
6. Report of the Secretary of the Navy. Washington, 1833.
7. Letter of the Secretary of the Treasury. Washington, 1833.

Vol. 194. 8. Payment of Pensioners of the United States. Washington, 1834.
9. Report of Mr. Webster on the Removal of the Deposits. 1834.

" 195. 1. Remarks and Documents relative to the Preservation and Keeping of the Public Archives. By Richard Bartlett. 1837.
2. Statistical Tables of certain Branches of Industry of Massachusetts. By John P. Bigelow. 1838.
3. Memorial for the Agricultural Survey of Massachusetts. 1840.
4. Report of the Board of Public Works of Ohio. Columbus, 1842.
5. Report of the Bank Commissioners. Hartford, 1845.
6. New York Political Manual. Albany, 1843.
7. Report of the Board of Public Works of Ohio. Columbus, 1845.

" 196. 1. Reply to the Letter of the Hon. Langdon Cheves.
2. Common-Sense Address to the Citizens of the Southern States. No. 2.
3. The same. No. 3. Philadelphia, 1828.
4. Examination of the Charleston Memorial. Philadelphia, 1827.
5. Political Tract. By Hamilton. Philadelphia, 1826.
6. Matter of Fact versus Huskisson and Peel. Philadelphia, 1828.
7. Essays on Penitentiary Discipline. Philadelphia, 1829.
8. Plea for the Poor. Philadelphia, 1831.
9. The Tocsin; a Warning against Nullification. Philadelphia, 1832.
10. Review of the Address of the Free Trade Convention. 1831.
11. Payment of Pensioners of the United States. Washington, 1834.
12. Review of the Evidence of a Conspiracy of the Catholics to Massacre the Protestants in 1641. By M. Carey. Philadelphia, 1834.
13. Petition for a General Bankrupt Law.
14. Report on the Trade and Commerce of Upper Canada. 1835.
15. Resolutions of the Committee on Trade and Commerce.
16. Essays on the Spirit of Jacksonism. By Aristides. Philadelphia, 1835.
17. Opinion of Daniel B. Tallmadge in relation to the Powers of the Legislature. New York, 1835.
18. Tariff *versus* Distribution.
19. Dangerous Position of the Whig Party. Albany, 1838.
20. Expenses of the Past and Present Administrations Contrasted. 1840.
21. Strictures of Montgomery on the Cotton Manufactures of Great Britain and America; also, a Practical Comparison of the Cost of Steam and Water Power in America. Newburyport, 1841.
22. Report on the Territory of Oregon. Columbus, 1843.
23. Annual Report of the Home League. New York, 1843.
24. Plan for the Promotion of Art, Science and Literature. By Thomas L. Donaldson. London, 1838.
25. Letter on the Importance of the Corn and Flour Trade. 1842.
26. Farewell Address of George Thompson to the Anti-Corn-Law League.
27. Letter to Baron Ashburton on Introducing Maize into Great Britain.
28. Speech of James Wilson on the Cause of the Commercial Distress. London, 1843.
29. Condition of the Iron and Coal Trades, and the Advantages of Free Trade Principles. London, 1843.

Vol. 196. 30. Reasons in favor of Free Trade in Corn. By Edward Baines, Jr.
31. Repeal of the Corn Laws and Free Trade. By J. C. Fitzgerald. 1843.
32. Sir Robert Peel's Speech on the Corn Laws. London.

" 197. 1. Report on Interment within the City. New York, 1825.
2. Report on Regulating the Grounds between North and Fourteenth-streets, the Bowery and East River. New York, 1826.
3. Report of the Commissioners of School Money. New York, 1832.
4. Annual Report of Deaths in New York for 1833.
5. Report on the Application of the Village of Brooklyn to become a Chartered City. New York, 1833.
6. Report of the Commissioners of the Alms House. New York, 1834.
7. Exposition of Errors of the Board of Water Commissioners. By J. L. Sullivan. New York, 1835.
8. Report on the Re-organization of the Police Department. 1837.
9. Reports and Opinions on the Powers and Duties of the Water Commissioners. New York, 1840.
10. Semi-Annual Report of the Water Commissioners. New York, 1840.
11. Report on the Communication of the New York and Albany Railroad Company. New York, 1842.
12. Report on the Appropriation of School Money to Religious Societies for the Support of Schools. New York, 1840.
13. Report on the Opening of the New York and Albany Railroad. 1842.
14. Acts and Ordinances in relation to Introduction of Water into the City.
15. Semi-Annual Report of the Water Commissioners. New York, 1843.
16. Report of the Georgia Railroad and Banking Company. 1845.
17. Report of the Commissioners of the Alms House. New York, 1845.

" 198. 1. Constitution of the United States and the Declaration. London, 1794.
2. Plan de la Constitution Françoise. Paris, 1793.
3. Reply to Mr. Burke's Invective. By Thomas Cooper. London, 1792.
4. Englishman's Right; a Dialogue. By Sir John Hawles. London, 1793.
5. Constitutional Maxims. By Charles Lord Hawkesbury. London, 1794.
6. Constitution of the London Corresponding Society. London.
7. Revision and Abridgment of the same.
8. Speech of Earl Stanhope. London, 1794.
9. Account of the Seizure of Thomas Hardy, Secretary to the London Corresponding Society.
10. The Torch for the Nations of Europe. London, 1793.
11. Proceedings of a General Meeting of the Corresponding Society. 1795.
12. Extermination; or, an Appeal on the War with France. 1795.
13. Prophetic Conjectures on the French Revolution. London, 1793.
14. Transactions at Paris on the Tenth of August, and the Perfidy of Louis XVI. London, 1792.
15. Plain Truth; or, an Account of the Proceedings at Paris. By an Eye-witness. London, 1792.
16. An Extenuation of the Conduct of the French Revolutionists. By Charles James. London, 1792.
17. Narrative of the Suspension of the King of the French. By J. B. D'Aumont. London, 1792.

Vol. 199. 1. Geographical Route of a Great Railway. New York, 1830.
2. Report on the Saratoga and Schenectady Railroad. New York, 1833.
3. Act to incorporate the Worcester and Hartford Railroad Company.
4. Railroad from the Ohio to the Tide Waters of the Carolinas and Georgia. Cincinnati, 1835.
5. Report of the Wilmington and Susquehanna Railroad Company. 1836.
6. Observations, Act of Incorporation, &c., of the Kennebunk-Port Granite and Railroad Company. 1837.
7. Abstract of a Report on the Affairs of the New York and Erie Railroad Company. New York, 1841.
8. Report on the New York and Albany Railroad. New York, 1839.
9. Report on the Delaware and Hudson Canal Company. 1842.
10. Report of the Raleigh and Gaston Railroad Company. 1840.
11. Report relative to the New York and Albany Railroad. 1840.
12. Remarks of the President of the New York and Albany Railroad Company. New York, 1840.
13. Opinions of D. B. Ogden, C. McVean, J. Anthon and J. P. Hall on the Subject of the New York and Albany Railroad Company. 1840.
14. Essay on the Enlargement of the Erie Canal. By Jesse Hawley. 1840.
15. Report of the New York and Erie Railroad Company. 1841.
16. Bill for the Relief of the New York and Erie Railroad Company. 1842.
17. Truths in relation to the New York and Erie Railroad Company.
18. Plan of a Cast-Iron Rail and Superstructure for Railroads. 1842.
19. Railroad Communication between New York and Buffalo. 1842.
20. Policy and Prospects of the Reading Railroad Company. 1844.
20½. Annual Report of the Susquehanna and Tide-Water Canals. Baltimore, 1844.
21. Report of the Philadelphia and Reading Railroad Company. 1845.
22. Reading Railroad Company. By Charles Ellet, Jr. New York, 1845.
23. Prospects, &c., of the North Branch Canal Company. Phila., 1845.
24. Annual Report of the Delaware and Hudson Canal Company. 1845.
25. Report of the Chesapeake and Delaware Canal Company. Phila., 1845.
26. Act incorporating the Hudson River Railroad Company. 1846.
27. Report on the Location of Certain Portions of the New York and Erie Railroad. New York, 1847.

" 200. 1. Thermometrical Navigation. Philadelphia, 1799.
2. Catalogue of Plants in the Elgin Botanic Garden. By David Hosack. New York, 1811.
3. Vindication of the Steamboat Right. By C. D. Colden. 1819.
4. Steamboat Explosions and Means of Prevention. By W. C. Redfield.
5. Groening's Machine for Corking Bottles. Brooklyn, 1837.
6. Our Colleges, Academies and Common Schools. By Lorin D. Chapin.
7. Ærostation; or, Steam Aerial Navigation. By J. H. Pennington.
8. Stereotomic Wood Pavement, invented by Augustus, Count de Lisle. New York, 1840.
9. Astronomical Discoveries recently made by Sir John Herschel. 1834.
10. Reply to Dr. Hare on Whirlwind Storms. By W. C. Redfield. 1842.
11. Logs of the First Voyage of the Great Western. Bristol, 1838.

Vol. 200. 12. Observations on the Storm of December 15, 1839. By W. C. Redfield.
13. Remarks on the Tornado of June 19, 1835. By W. C. Redfield.
14. Redfield's Reply to Dr. Hare's Objections. New York, 1842.
15. Description of the Steamship Great Britain. By Captain Claxton.
16. Report on the Steam Frigate Princeton.
17. Lecture on Steam Navigation, Naval Warfare and Ericsson's Caloric Engine. By John O. Sargent. 1844.

" 201. 1. Report of Western Inland Lock Navigation Company. Albany, 1798.
2. Report on a Route for the Proposed Erie Canal. New York, 1811.
3. Message of the President on the Erie Canal. Washington, 1811.
4. Report on the Memorials of the Canal Companies. Washington, 1812.
5. Report on the Internal Navigation of the State. Albany, 1812.
6. Advantages of Railways and Steam Carriages. New York, 1812.
7. Serious Appeal for the Proposed Erie Canal. By Ferris Pell. 1816.
8. Memorial in favor of the Proposed Erie Canal. 1816.
9. Remarks on the Proposed Erie Canal. By Hugh Williamson. 1816.
10. Laws of the State respecting the Proposed Erie Canal. 1817.
11. Report of the Commissioners on the Erie Canal. Albany, 1817.
12. Report of the Joint Committee on the Erie Canal. Albany, 1817.
13. Memorial on the Obstructions in the Hudson River. By E. C. Genet. Albany, 1818.
14. Considerations on the Erie or Great Western Canal; its Expense, Advantages and Progress. 1818.
15. Letters on the Great Western Canal. 1822.
16. Sketch of the Great Northern or Champlain Canal. 1822.
17. Plans for Improving the Navigation of Hudson River. Albany, 1820.
18. Annual Report of the Canal Commissioners. Albany, 1819.
19. Annual Report of the Canal Commissioners. Albany, 1820.
20. Report on a Communication between Canandaigua Lake and the Erie Canal. 1820.

" 202. 1. Letter to Robert Troup on the Canal Policy of the State of N. Y. 1821.
2. Letter by Robert Troup on the Lake Canal Policy of the State of New York. Albany, 1822.
3. Memorial for the Survey of a Route for a Canal between Lakes Ontario and Champlain. 1824.
4. Address on the Proposed Canal by the Lackawaxen Coal Mine and Navigation Company. 1824.
5. Report of the Engineers upon the Route of the Proposed Canal. Philadelphia, 1824.
6. Address on Canals, &c. By Edmond C. Genet. Albany, 1825.
7. Documents relative to the Long Island Canal Company. 1826.
8. Report of the Morris Canal and Banking Company. 1827.
9. General Report of the Delaware and Hudson Canal Company. 1828.
10. Report relative to the Construction of a Railroad from Boston to New York. Albany, 1828.
11. Act to Incorporate the Black River Canal Company. Albany, 1828.
12. Report relative to the Crooked Lake Canal. Albany, 1829.
13. Report relative to the Construction of the Black River Canal. 1829.

Vol. 202. 14. Report relative to the Continuation of the Erie Canal to the Alleghany River. Albany, 1829.
15. Annual Report of the Canal Commissioners. Albany, 1829.
16. Finances of the Canal Fund. By George Tibbets. Albany, 1829.
17. Report relative to the Construction of the Owasco and Erie Canal Company. Albany, 1829.
18. Annual Report of the Commissioners of the Canal Fund. 1829.
19. Report on the Chemung and Crooked Lake Canal. Albany, 1830.
20. Report of the Canal Commissioners on the Chenango Canals. 1830.

" 203. 1. The Right of a State to Grant Exclusive Privileges in Roads, Bridges, Canals, &c. New York, 1811.
2. Chancellor's Opinion in the Case of R. R. Livingston and Robert Fulton *versus* J. Van Ingen, Lansing and others. Albany, 1812.
3. Examination of the Chancellor's Opinion in the Case of R. R. Livingston and R. Fulton *versus* J. Van Ingen, Lansing and others.
4. Charges of John White against Henry Cahoone. New York, 1825.
5. Address relating to the Galveston Bay and Texas Land Company. New York, 1831.
6. Outline of a System of National Currency. New York, 1834.
7. Twenty-Third Report of the Bank for Savings. New York, 1841.
8. Letter on Banks and the Currency. By Alexander Hamilton. New York, 1839.
9. Answer and Report in the Matter of the New York Life Insurance and Trust Company. 1838.
10. Bill of Complaint in the Case between Thomas Davenport and M. W. Nelson, complainants, and Edwin Williams, defendant. 1838.
11. Report of the Directors of the Bank of the United States. 1833.
12. Essays on the Spirit of Jacksonism. By Aristides. Philadelphia, 1835.
13. Annual Statements of the Banks of New Jersey. Trenton, 1845.

" 204. 1. Acts passed at the First Session of the Twelfth Congress. 1811.
2. Acts passed at the Second Session of the Twelfth Congress. 1812.

" 205. 1. Acts passed at the Second Session of the Thirteenth Congress. 1814.
2. Acts passed at the Third Session of the Thirteenth Congress. 1815.

" 206. 1. Message of the President, James Monroe, in relation to the Seminole War, &c. Washington, 1818.
2. Letter of the Secretary of the Treasury, in relation to the Bank of the United States. 1816.
3. Message of the President, James Monroe. Washington, 1818.
4. Memorial of Merchants and Ship-Owners of Baltimore. 1818.
5. Letter of the Secretary of the Treasury. Washington, 1817.
6. Letter of the Secretary of the Treasury, on the Tonnage of Vessels. 1818.
7. Message of the President, James Monroe, on Spanish Affairs. 1818.
8. Report of the Secretary of War, on Pensions. Washington, 1818.

" 207. 1. Message of the President, James Monroe. Washington, 1819.
2. Message of the President, James Monroe, on Spanish Affairs. 1818.
3. Report of the Secretary of the Treasury, on the Bank of the United States. Washington, 1820.

Vol. 208. 1. Letter of the Secretary of the Treasury, on the Bank of the United States. Washington, 1816.
2. Message of the President, James Monroe. Washington, 1818.

" 209. 1. Letter to C. D. Colden. By W. A. Duer. Albany, 1817.
2. Vindication of the Steamboat Right; Mr. Colden's Answer to Mr. Duer.
3. Reply of Mr. Duer to Mr. Colden's Vindication. Albany, 1819.

" 210. 1. Considerations on the Great Western Canal. Brooklyn, 1818.
2. Report on Canals. Albany, 1817.
3. Expediency of a Board of Agriculture in the State of New York. 1819.
4. Comparison of the Arguments in favor of the Western Section of the Grand Canal. Oswego, 1820.
5. Considerations against Continuing the Great Canal west of Seneca. By Peter Ploughshare. Utica, 1819.

" 210. 6. Annual Report of the Canal Commissioners. Albany, 1820.
7. Report of the Committee on Canals. Albany, 1820.
8. Report of the Canal Commissioners. Albany, 1820.
9. Report relative to Buffalo Harbor. Albany, 1820.
10. Documents relative to Savings Banks, Intemperance and Lotteries.

" 211. 1. Review of the Administration of the Civil Police. New York, 1819.
2. Address to the Electors of the State of New York. Albany, 1815.
3. Speech of Martin Van Buren, on Governor Tompkins' Accounts. 1820.
4. Speech of James Tallmadge, Jr., on Slavery. Washington, 1819.
5. Address of the Republican Members of the Senate and Assembly.
6. Reasons of Mr. Granger for Opposing the Grant to Governor Tompkins.
7. Address of Epaminondas to the Citizens of the State of New York.
8. Considerations in favor of Rufus King's Appointment to the Senate.
9. Republican Nominations for Governor and Lieutenant Governor, with an Address to Electors. New York, 1820.
10. Proceedings of the First Cattle Show and Fair of the Agricultural Society of Jefferson County. 1818.
11. Transactions of a Convention of Delegates from Moral Societies. 1819.
12. Transactions of the Medical Society, with an Address by John Stearns.
13. Review and Exposition of Falsehoods and Misrepresentations. By an Elector. Ballston Spa, 1816.
14. Trial of James Graham for Murder. Albany, 1814.

" 212. 1. Tribute to the Memory of Casper Wistar, M. D. By David Hosack.
2. Trial of Henry B. Hagerman for an Assault and Battery on William Coleman. New York, 1818.
3. Obstructions in the Hudson River. By Edmund C. Genet. 1818.
4. Memorial against the Removal of the Court House from Ogdensburgh.
5. Exposition of a most Villainous Attempt at Extortion. 1817.
6. Remarks on Private Banking. Albany, 1818.
7. Report of the Select Committee on Lotteries. Albany, 1819.

" 213. 1. Examination of the Charges against Aaron Burr. By Aristides. 1804.
2. Nine Letters on Aaron Burr's Political Defection. By James Cheetham. New York, 1803.

Vol. 213. 3. Letter to James Madison, Secretary of State. By Thomas Jefferson.

4. Motives of Aaron Burr for the Suppression of Wood's History of the Administration of John Adams. New York, 1802.

" 214. 1. Transactions of the Medical Society. New York, 1809.

2. Address of the Pennsylvania Insurance Company. Philadelphia, 1814.

3. The Address of the People of Great Britain to the Inhabitants of America. London, 1775.

4. Laws of Union College. Schenectady, 1807.

5. Essay on the Bilious Epidemic Fever. By C. C. Yates. Albany, 1813.

" 215. 1. Scriptural View of the Present War. By Alexander McLeod, D. D. New York, 1815.

2. Observations on Wheel Carriages. By H. G. Spafford. Albany, 1815.

3. Declaration of the Society of Shakers, refusing to Aid in the War. Albany, 1815.

4. Introductory Discourse. By David Hosack. New York, 1813.

5. Address before the Free School Society. By De Witt Clinton. 1810.

6. Charter and By-Laws of the Society for the Promotion of the Useful Arts. Albany, 1815.

7. Memorial of the New York Historical Society. 1814.

8. Serious Appeal for the Proposed Erie Canal. 1816.

9. Remarks on the Proposed Canal from Lake Erie to the Hudson River. By Atticus. New York, 1816.

" 216. 1. Discourse on the Duty of Union in a Just War. By John H. Stevens. Albany, 1814.

2. Address to the Electors of the State of New York. 1815.

3. Address to the Republican Citizens of New York. 1813.

4. Letter to Albert Gallatin, on the Doctrine of Gold and Silver, and the Evils of the Present Banking System. By Publicola. 1815.

5. Trial of Maturin Livingston against James Cheetham for Libel. New York, 1807.

6. Trial of Lambert and Perry, and also of William Cobbett, for Libelling George the Third and his Government. New York, 1810.

7. Ebenezer's Dream; or, the Trial of Louisa Williams for Assault and Battery. New York, 1808.

8. Proceedings of the Republican Meeting. Albany, 1810.

9. Murders. Report of the Trial of James Johnson, and also of John Sinclair. New York, 1811.

10. Oration delivered at Lansingburgh, by David Allen, July 4, 1809.

11. Letter of Timothy Pickering on the Danger of a War. 1808.

12. Circular Letter from the General Republican Committee. 1809.

13. Critical Review. 1795.

" 217. 1. The Stranger; a Literary Paper. Albany, 1814.

2. List of Lands to be Sold for Arrears of Taxes. Albany, 1819.

" 218. 1. Comparative Anatomy and Physiology of the African Negro. By Hermann Burmeister. New York, 1853.

2. Negroes and Negro Slavery. By J. H. Van Evrie. Washington, 1853.

3. Lecture on the North and the South. By John Forsyth. Mobile, 1854.

Vol. 218. 4. Rights of Labor. By Calvin Colton. New York, 1847.
5. Remarks on a Reprint of Original Letters. By J. Sparks. Boston, 1853.
6. Funeral Oration on the Death of Daniel Webster. By Amasa McCoy. Boston, 1853.
7. Exposition of the Causes, &c., of the late War. London, 1815.
8. Schuyler Frauds. Argument of William C. Noyes and Opinion of the Court of Appeals. New York, 1856.
9. Review of the Decision in the Case of Gabriel Furman and others, against the City of New York. New York, 1852.
10. Essay on the Breeds of Sheep in Great Britain and their Wool. By John Wilson. London, 1855.
11. Treatise on the Culture of Silk in Germany, and on the Rearing of Silk Worms. By Mr. De Hazzi. Washington, 1828.
12. Orchard Planting and the Culture of Fruits. By David W. Ray. Syracuse.
13. Letter on Temperance Organizations. By William J. Haskett. New York, 1853.
14. Report on Certain Mineral Lands in the Island of Jamaica. By Dr. Isaiah Deck. New York, 1854.
15. Peruvian Guano Trade. Statements and Documents. Washington, 1854.

" 219. 1. Holländisch Rindviehzucht und Milchwirthschaft. By J. J. Ellerbrock, Braunschweig, 1853.
2. Extraites des divers Journaux d'Agriculture Anglais. By Conrad De Gourcy. Paris, 1853.
3. Promenades Agricoles dans le Centre de la France. By Conrad De Gourcy. Paris, 1853.
4. Rapport sur la Situation de l'Algérie. By M. Vaillant. Paris, 1854.
5. Annales de la Tempérance. Montreal, 1854.
6. Geografia de la Isla de Cuba. By Jose M. De la Torre. Havana, 1854.

" 220. 1. Letter on the French Metrical and Decimal System of Weights, Measures and Currency. By William W. Mann. Paris, 1853.
2. Annual Report of the Central Board of Agriculture. Halifax, 1852.
3. Industrial Exhibition of Nova Scotia in 1853. Halifax, 1852.
4. Acte pour pourvoir à l'Establissement d'un Bureau d'Agriculture. Quebec, 1852.
5. Act to Regulate the Militia of Canada. Quebec, 1853.
6. Rapport Annuel de l'Ecole Normale des Ecole Modeles, etc., du Haut-Canada pour 1854. Quebec, 1855.
7. Rapport Annuel des Inspecteurs du Penitencier Provincial pour 1855. Toronto, 1856.
8. Rapport des Commissaires des Travaux Publics. Toronto, 1856.
9. Rapport des Travaux de Colonization. By T. Boutillier, Ecuyer.
10. Hopital Général de Toronto. 1856.
11. Exploration des Lacs Superieur et Huron. By Count Rottermund. Toronto, 1856.
12. Art Dentaire. By Fowler and Preterre. 1857.
13. Résponse de Secrétaire Provincial. Toronto, 1856.

Vol. 221. 1. Movement of the International Literary Exchanges. By Alexander Vattemare. Paris, 1846.
2. Reports in relation to the International Exchanges and the Vermont State Library. Montpelier, 1850.
3. Lecture before the Mercantile Library Association, on Algernon Sidney. By Robert C. Winthrop. Boston, 1853.
4. Thirty-sixth Annual Report of the Mercantile Library Association. Boston, 1856.
5. Annual Reports of the Cincinnati Mercantile Library Association for 1854 and 1855.
6. Annual Report of the Trustees of the State Library. Albany, 1856.
7. Catalogue of the Brooklyn Athenæum. New York, 1853.
8. Smithsonian Catalogue System. Washington, 1850.

" 222. 1. History of the Chamber of Commerce of New York. By Charles King. Also the Charter and By-Laws of the same. New York, 1849.
2. Communication of the Directors of the Panama Railroad Company to the Stockholders, and the Engineer's Report. New York, 1853.
3. Contract between the Republic of New Granada and the Panama Railroad Company. New York, 1856.
4. Letter of the Directors of the Panama Railroad Company to Congress. New York, 1856.
5. Report, Contract, &c., of the Costa Rica Railway. New York, 1854.
6. Report on the Acts and Doings of the Directors of the New York Central Railroad Company. Boston, 1855.
7. Philosophy of Railroads. By Thomas C. Keefer. Montreal, 1853.
8. How to make Railroads pay a Good Dividend. By J. La Mothe. New York, 1856.
9. Farmers' Railroad. By Lewis A. Hall. Trenton, 1856.
10. Reports of the Cumberland Coal and Iron Company for 1853, '54, '55 and '56.
11. Report of the New Jersey Franklinite Company. New York, 1855.
12. Third Report of the Chester County Mining Company. 1852.

" 223. 1. New York Universal Exhibition. Awards of Juries. New York, 1853.
2. Record of the First Exhibition of the Metropolitan Mechanics' Institute. Washington, 1853.
3. Book of the Exhibition of the Maryland Institute. Baltimore, 1852.
4. Report of the Exhibition Committee of the Kentucky Mechanics' Institute. Louisville, 1856.
5. Rensselaer Polytechnic Institute. Troy, 1855.
6. Report of the Twenty-fifth Exhibition of the Franklin Institute. Philadelphia, 1857.

" 224. 1. Book of the Exhibition of the Maryland Institute. Baltimore, 1854.
2. Minutes of the Philadelphia Society for the Promotion of Agriculture, from 1785 to 1810. Philadelphia, 1854.
3. Séléna, on Famille Samanéenne. By J. A. Gleïsès. Paris, 1838.
4. Navigation de l'Amazon. By M. De Angelis. Montevideo, 1854.

www.ingramcontent.com/pod-product-compliance
Lightning Source LLC
LaVergne TN
LVHW010157110826
845151LV00002B/543

* 9 7 8 1 4 2 5 5 3 6 7 3 2 *